T0355793

BORGATA

Also by Louis Ferrante

Tough Guy: A Memoir

Mob Rules: What the Mafia Can Teach the Legitimate Businessman

The Three Pound Crystal Ball: The Theory of Sleep A.I.D. and the Unconscious Mind's Exclusive Access into the Corridors of Time

BORGATA

RISE OF EMPIRE: A HISTORY OF THE AMERICAN MAFIA

VOLUME 1

OF THE BORGATA TRILOGY

LOUIS FERRANTE

PEGASUS BOOKS
NEW YORK LONDON

BORGATA

Pegasus Books, Ltd.
148 West 37th Street, 13th Floor
New York, NY 10018

First Pegasus Books cloth edition January 2024

ISBN: 978-1-63936-601-9

10 9 8 7 6 5 4 3 2

Printed in the United States of America
Distributed by Simon & Schuster
www.pegasusbooks.com

For
Bruce and Madeline Ramer,
Lady Annabelle Weidenfeld,
and in memory of Lord George Weidenfeld,
who asked me to write this history.

CONTENTS

Author's Note

I write this history, rather regrettably, with the single-mindedness of a prosecutor, forced by the purpose of my task to ignore the Italian people's long historical record of glorious achievements and contributions to humanity so that I can focus solely on their crimes.

Italy has been called 'Mother of the Arts', 'Mother of the Opera', 'Mother of High Culture', 'Mother of the Renaissance' and 'Mother of the Church'. Her achievements are known the world over and she has borne us the most brilliant children: Dante, Petrarch, Boccaccio, Galileo, da Vinci, Verdi, Vivaldi, Rossini, Puccini, Michelangelo, Raphael, Titian, Ghiberti, Verrocchio, Donatello, Bernini, Volta, Beccaria, Bocelli, Pavarotti, Marconi, Fermi, and the list goes on and on. But any mother is capable of turning out a bad son. For this, Italy may be called 'Mother of the Mafia'. We should be careful to judge any fruitful mother by the character of her many children, as noted above, not her errant child. Nevertheless, even a wayward son is worthy of a proper evaluation, perhaps more so. Let us not, however, confuse the good with the bad.

Preface

When the historian William Shirer began writing his masterpiece, *The Rise and Fall of the Third Reich*, he was criticized by some for beginning to write a history of Nazi Germany only a few years after the Reich had fallen. Many scholars believed then, as they do now, that it takes decades for facts to surface and debates to settle. But Shirer deflected the criticism that his work was premature by citing that 'almost all of the documentary material became available at [the Reich's] fall'. Since the Nazis had kept meticulous records, many of which had been recovered by the Allies after the war, there was a paper mountain of irrefutable evidence upon which Shirer could rely. The mafia, in contrast, has never kept records – doing so is punishable by death – and this lack of documentary material, especially with regard to the early days of the mafia, has created a void for mafia historians who have attempted to fill in the blanks with imaginative writing more commonly seen in the field of historical fiction. And because the mind and experiences of an academically trained historian are very different from those of a mobster, the blanks have always been filled in from an alien perspective. This is why, when mobsters read mafia books in prison, you hear a lot of: 'Not true!' 'Bullshit!' 'Gimme a break!' and 'Who wrote this crap?'

Historians start off with facts and events and must bridge the gaps, which vary in size. To do so accurately, the English philosopher and historian R.G. Collingwood believed that history is interpreted best by people who understand the experiences of the figures responsible for pivotal events. Publishing houses regularly pay homage to Collingwood when they seek out experts to write histories relevant to their expertise. A publisher would not contract me to write a history involving people I know nothing about. Why then do publishers repeatedly commission writers who have never stolen so much as a candy bar, or have never felt the cold steel of a stiletto, a handgun or a handcuff, to write histories of the mafia? Because they have never encountered an actual historian who has lived in the mafia's world, spoken their tongue, committed their crimes, drawn their blood, fled justice with them, and served prison time alongside them; I am them, and I am also a historian. Even the seemingly endless shelves of mafia memoirs are written by mob snitches who recite a very biased account of their crimes into the ears of co-authors and ghostwriters who, in turn, add an additional degree of distance between the mobster's mind and the printed page. The snitches, moreover, by evading punishment for the many offenses they have committed and displacing that punishment onto others, have ceded the precious time needed for honest reflection which ordinarily results in a humility and clarity that none of them seem to possess. The ancient Greeks believed that wisdom is gained through suffering, which speaks to a phrase we often said in prison: 'Those who *inform* never *reform*.' I once faced the remainder of my life in prison but refused to snitch. I spent many years in a dark, dank prison cell where I fell in love with books and began reading eighteen hours a day while teaching myself the writer's craft. If today I am possessed of any wisdom, it was born during that unspeakable suffering and isolation.

This trilogy is the very first mafia history written by someone who has lived The Life and knows intuitively which stories make sense and which do not, what might have taken place and what could never have happened. While engaged in research for this history, I often encountered stories that were obviously untrue but have been repeated for decades by mafia historians and documentary television commentators. Mafia historians, like all modern historians, rely on, among other sources, previous histories as a foundation for their research, as I have also done. But without an extra sense to alert them when something is off, errors are repeated and reinforced with each new account, and stories, however false, receive what can be classified as a time-honored certification. The problem often lies in one author accepting information from another without critical examination. Before you know it, a series of books have reinforced a falsehood. You may wonder, could a dozen historians all be wrong? They can, indeed, if eleven successive authors copied false information from the first. And this, at times, I found to be the case. In such instances, I have relied heavily upon my own insight to disentangle fact from fiction and correct the record, explaining, whenever possible, how the story likely came about, and why. By debunking some myths and setting the record straight, I hope this history becomes as much a resource for future historians as it is a source of entertainment for the casual reader. To be sure, I sometimes concurred with a standing interpretation of events, in which cases I could only tell the stories from a more insightful perspective. In either event, I am immensely indebted to the many journalists and historians I have read and quoted.

Aside from the discrepancies noted above, I encountered another issue with regard to source material. As mafia prosecutions have increased over the last few decades and mafia turncoats have tirelessly yapped away, revealing countless 'secrets', researchers have come to rely on indictments, trial transcripts and newspaper articles in an attempt to connect the dots and form a cohesive history. But although police, prosecutors and informants have been helpful to historians, these sources are highly inadequate and often misleading. We typically assume that defendants in criminal proceedings are wont to lie since we do not expect people who are charged with crimes to be truthful. But a problem we seldom wish to confront as a society is that prosecutors also lie in order to secure convictions, and informants tell tactical lies to save their own skin, grind personal axes, spare friends and lovers, or hide their ill-gotten wealth from the government – they have been telling lies their entire lives; it is difficult to suddenly embrace the truth without altering it, even slightly. With criminal defendants, defense attorneys, prosecutors and snitches all depreciating the truth, the courtroom is, at best, a chamber of inaccuracies that cannot be relied upon without some degree of skepticism.

Another issue prevalent in mafia cases is something similar to the defense used during the Nuremberg trials. This is when a mafia turncoat attributes all of his evil deeds to his boss, claiming he was only following orders. Gambino crime family underboss, Salvatore Gravano, when testifying against his boss, John Gotti, was not about to tell the jury that he was murdering men for personal gain, then stealing their assets. Instead, he served up a tale of how he was just following the don's orders – while omitting his own depraved motives. Prosecutors are always willing to meet such deceit halfway in lieu of placing a witness on the stand who may appear more savage to a jury than the defendant they wish to convict. Here, again, we are confronted with a false narrative that enters the historical record as hard truth because it was supposedly forged in a court of law.

While writing the latter part of this sweeping history, in volume three, I relied heavily on personal experiences; I was privy to a number of the events that I have recounted and was close with many of the men who were directly involved. I sometimes inquired of them as to specific deeds they had participated in or had first-hand knowledge of. The men, none of whom had ever snitched, spoke with me because they trusted me. They knew I had never snitched either, and this carries a lot of weight in our world. Although they trusted me, they still spoke to me in code, using an evasive mafia jargon sprinkled with a variety of hand gestures, facial expressions, hints, incomplete thoughts, half-sentences and suggestions. Their motive was not to confuse me: they knew I would understand them perfectly; it is just that they are accustomed to speaking in riddles and find it impossible to depart from this manner of communication under any circumstance. While inquiring about certain events that took place later on in this history, I once walked the beach with a dear friend of mine who is still a high-ranking member of a crime family. With the loud surf and the sound of seagulls drowning out our voices, we talked in code. I finally said to him, 'The stuff we're talking about is from twenty years ago. No cop or agent would even give a shit about it today.' We laughed and went back to code.

Throughout this history, I sometimes refer to the United States as *America*; know that I am well aware of the Earth's geography, but as this history does not include any major references to South or Central America, I am referring to the United States. I use *mafia* and *mob* interchangeably, as well as *mafioso*, *mobster*, *gangster*, *racketeer* and other similar terms; you should have no problem following me. *Borgata*, which is the title of this book, is how we refer to a mafia family; it is sometimes spelled *bourghata*, and sometimes written and pronounced *brugad*.

At the American mafia's height, from the 1930s to the 1960s, there were twenty-six borgatas operating in almost as many metropolitan areas across the country. Since some of them were rather small and insignificant, or disappeared after a short time, I have chosen to use the approach of a screenwriter who introduces only the characters and scenes that move the plot forward, dispensing with peripheral events that contribute little or nothing to the mafia's historical progress or overall decline. Just as a Roman historian will confine him- or herself to events in Rome while at times following Scipio to Carthage, Crassus to Persia, or Caesar to Gaul, our Rome is New York, while our history will also take us to New Orleans, Las Vegas, Cuba and other so-called 'provinces' of the mob's large empire that played a pivotal role in its colorful history.

Following the mafia's earliest origins in Sicily, which cover a few short chapters and may sound a bit academic, I settle into a conversational tone which will hopefully make you feel as though we are sitting across from one another in a pub, casually chatting about the mafia. Before I strike that tone, I have done my best to trace exactly how and why, over the course of centuries, the mafia formed inside the Sicilian womb. I believe my exhaustive research in this area, resulting in the conclusions I have drawn, will stand as the seminal work on the mafia's earliest beginnings.

Marc Bloch wrote in *The Historian's Craft* that behind all historical events, 'There are men, and it is men that history seeks to grasp. Failing that, it will be at best but an exercise in erudition.' Once we have covered the mafia's origins, we will transcend erudition as men begin to emerge from the haze and faces come to the fore. As you will see, few men offer a better character study than those you are about to encounter in this history. The ancient historian Plutarch, aside from casting individuals as the makers of history, highlighted the vices and virtues of great men. I will, at times, mimic the style of Plutarch by pointing out how certain mobsters did something wrong or right, according to mafia rules, and either lived or died because of it. I will let you know when someone should not have been killed and also when someone deserved to die, according to those rules. Note that I no longer condone violence, but I am writing from the perspective of a mobster who understands the laws of La Cosa Nostra and would like you, dear reader, to understand them as well.

Having referenced the ancient world, let us turn to Edward Gibbon, who, in 1764, 'sat musing amidst the ruins' of Rome when the idea of writing *The History of the Decline and Fall of the Roman Empire* took shape in his mind. More than a millennium separated Gibbon from the era he decided to write about on that fateful day. How much more insightful would Gibbon's account have been if he had actually lived alongside the caesars and stepped out of those very ruins, a position I find myself in as I begin *Borgata: Rise of Empire*.

Introduction: 'Where'd Daddy Go?'

In 1979, a Jordanian immigrant to the United States, Khaled Fahd Darwish Daoud, spotted the demand for American cars in the small but wealthy Arabian country of Kuwait. The ambitious Daoud began to purchase used cars from automobile auctions in New York and New Jersey and ship them to Kuwait at a large profit. In Kuwait, where petrol was practically free, the full-sized Chevy Caprice, Buick Electra and Oldsmobile Regency were especially in demand, but at some point, the supply of these models had dried up at the auctions. While hobnobbing with fellow car dealers, Daoud heard some chatter as to why and decided to play detective. He poked around a waterfront loading dock in New Jersey where the cars were regularly lined up before being shipped out to sea. After jotting down the sequence of vehicle identification numbers found on the dashboards, Daoud ran a check and learned that many of the cars were stolen; this explained why he was no longer seeing them at the auctions. He contacted the New York Police Department and told them what he had discovered. I am sure Daoud was informing for personal reasons; he was pursuing the American dream and felt it was being shattered by a group of car thieves. But he must have hung up the telephone feeling a sense of justice, having tipped off the authorities to a major auto crime ring. Who knows, maybe after the culprits were busted and sent to jail, Daoud could read about it in the newspaper and tell his family back home how he had become a sort of Sherlock Holmes in America.

Daoud awaited these headlines, unaware of the wire he had tripped when making that telephone call to the police. Detective Peter Calabro of the NYPD's Auto Crime Unit contacted Gambino family soldier Roy DeMeo of the auto crime ring, and told him that his profitable business endeavor was about to end abruptly because of a trouble-maker named Khaled Daoud who had just reported evidence of stolen cars at the docks. DeMeo, who may have killed over a hundred men in the course of his talented career as a hitman, politely thanked Detective Calabro for the tip. DeMeo then hatched a plan. He reached out to a man who knew Daoud; that man, in turn, told Daoud about two Chevy Caprices that were up for sale at an auto collision shop in Brooklyn. Daoud bit the bait and asked to inspect the cars. But the night before the inspection was scheduled to take place, Daoud phoned DeMeo's intermediary to tell him he would be arriving at the auto shop the next day with a partner of his who was also interested in purchasing the cars. Perhaps these men were pooling their resources, or this other gentleman was putting up the money for Daoud. Or maybe Daoud intended to do a quick flip on the spot and profit without doing much work. Whatever the case may have been, here is where the plot thickens. Daoud's colleague was Ronald Falcaro, husband to a loving wife and devoted father of three young children. Falcaro was not a criminal, nor did he snitch on DeMeo. He had absolutely nothing to do with stolen cars or the mafia. He was a wholesale car dealer hoping to make a day's pay.

Let us pause for a moment and take a look at the new landscape with Falcaro painted onto the canvas. Having lived The Life, I understand the rules: Daoud butted his nose where it did not belong and jeopardized the income and freedom of men who do not take kindly to whistleblowers. To these men, Daoud was a problem that had to disappear. But what about Falcaro? DeMeo was a seasoned mobster who knew the mob's rules, one of which is that the murder of an innocent person must be avoided at all costs. Not because the mob cares about the sanctity of human life, but because it is bad for business. According to mob rules, Daoud was guilty but Falcaro was innocent. What, then, should DeMeo do? The only option for DeMeo was to postpone the phony car sale and call off the hit until Daoud could be ambushed alone. But instead of rescheduling Daoud's funeral, DeMeo simply said to his cohorts, 'We just shoot them both, and make 'em disappear.'

As Donna Falcaro kissed her husband, Ronald, and asked him to be home in time for their youngest child's birthday party, Roy DeMeo laid out a vinyl pool liner to catch the blood of two unsuspecting men. While Falcaro met up with Daoud and they drove to the auto body shop together, DeMeo and his crew were sharpening butcher knives and screwing silencers onto handguns. Not one of them had the slightest reservation about killing an innocent man.

The shooters were in position and the overhead lights were turned down as Daoud and Falcaro entered the shop. As the two men squinted in the dark, most likely trying to glimpse the cars they were hoping to purchase, Falcaro asked the man who greeted them at the door, 'Your electricity get cut off?' This thought, this question, might have given Falcaro the slightest sense that something was wrong. Nothing as dark as murder but perhaps one of two thoughts crossed Falcaro's mind: 'Do I wanna deal with guys who can't pay their electric bill?' or 'Can I get the cars cheaper if they're in such dire straits?'

We will never know what crossed Daoud's mind since whatever thought he had at that same moment was interrupted by a bullet that tore through his brain. For Daoud, the American dream was a nightmare he would not awaken from.

Falcaro was darting for the door before Daoud even hit the floor. But these hitmen were not amateurs; Falcaro's exit was sealed off. He absorbed rapid gunfire, collapsed to the floor, and his crumpled body was dragged onto the pool liner alongside Daoud.

Many people who work full-time prefer to get the bulk of their workload out of the way before lunchtime. DeMeo was no different. With this double homicide now out of the way and two lifeless bodies lying at his feet, DeMeo could finally enjoy some lunch. 'Go get some hot dogs and pizza,' he told a crew member. Ironically, DeMeo craved a meal most kids would eat at a birthday party, like the one Donna Falcaro was preparing for in the Falcaro home.

Before lunch arrived, DeMeo began cutting up the bodies with boning knives. When his crew returned with lunch, DeMeo ate a slice of pizza with blood-covered hands. He was already an expert at dismembering bodies and took some time to teach one of his crew members the best way to sever an arm from a shoulder as if he were a chief medical examiner showing an intern how to perform a proper autopsy.

Let us pause to look at the landscape, once again. This time, I will ask you to pretend you're a mobster. You therefore understand that Daoud had to die. And whether or not Falcaro had to die makes no difference at this point since he is now dead. But what happens next will almost make what happened already seem normal in comparison. DeMeo and his crew obviously stripped Falcaro of his clothing in order to dismember his body; okay, we get that, easiest way to get the job done. But after cutting Falcaro's limbs and head off, the crew sliced off Falcaro's penis and stuffed it into the mouth of his decapitated head. We already know that this innocent man did not deserve to die.

That being the case, why was his corpse subjected to such a vulgar act that reeks of sexual deviance? Or did these killers have the mentality of children who, when playing the game of Circles and Squares, get excited when circular objects fit into matching holes?

Donna Falcaro hid her worries while watching over a houseful of real children, some of whom would grow up without a father. And for years to come, they would never know what happened to their dad. Donna reported her husband missing and grappled with her own emotions while struggling to answer the simple question, 'Where'd Daddy go?'

On the surface of this despicable affair lies a group of psychotic mafia killers. But the root of this horror story involves the history of nations, peoples, ideas and cultures. And it all begins on one of the most beautiful islands on Earth.

Let us leave this macabre scene behind, along with Roy DeMeo who we'll meet again in Volume Two, and depart for the island of Sicily.

Part One

Sicilia

Chapter 1
The Conquered Conquerors

When I was in junior high school, a fellow student once told me that conquerors from Africa invaded Sicily and raped all the women, which explained my darker complexion and curly hair. At the time, I had no idea what he was talking about and I don't think he did either, though he had probably heard this from an adult. Nonetheless, it is true that conquerors from both Europe and Africa had arrived on the 10,000-square-mile Mediterranean island of Sicily at different times throughout the centuries, and of course rape did occur, but the historical record suggests that it did not happen on any grand scale, unlike, for instance, during the barbarian invasions of Rome or the Soviet race for Berlin. And although many of Sicily's long list of occupiers took the island by force, some came to relieve an old empire that had grown weak and tired and unable to defend its island possession; the transition was more like a Monopoly deal in which a player lands on Boardwalk or Park Place and claims it. There are even instances in which one royal personage bequeathed the island to another, just as a contemporary billionaire might leave a private island to a son or daughter. One foreign ruler offered to exchange Sicily for Tuscany or Sardinia, as if he were at the exchange counter of a retail store, returning an item he was unhappy with.

Likely because of Sicily's many foreign occupiers, Sicilian men were especially protective of their women. Any foreigner who cast covetous eyes on daughters and wives was looking for trouble, as was the case on Easter Monday, 1282, when Sicilians in Palermo had gathered in a square to listen to vespers sung from inside the church of Santo Spirito. At the time, the French were occupying the island. When a French soldier made an untoward remark to a young Sicilian newlywed, her husband became enraged and sliced him up like a cheese pizza. The groom's buddies – who all happened to carry knives to vespers – diced up the rest of the French soldiers in the square. The spark grew into a wildfire as 'Death to the French' went up as a rallying cry across the island. Some 2,000 Frenchmen were killed overnight, many of whose peckers were cut off and stuffed into their mouths; the French occupation ended abruptly. Historians have tried without success to pin the origin of this massacre on the conspiratorial plotting of France's enemies, but after thorough debate it continues to rest on the spontaneous actions of a jealous husband who reflected the male population's anger toward foreign soldiers who had become overly interested in their women. Like the fall of Troy, this bloodletting was jazzed up into a spectacular oral tale and repeated for centuries as a warning to occupiers that it may be okay to take the Sicilians' agriculture – for fair market value, of course – but never their women.

In Sicily, family ties were often thicker than in other areas of Europe, in part because wives were often more than just wives; they were blood relatives. I was imprisoned with a mafioso from Palermo, Sicily, who told me he had married his cousin. I thought he meant his second or third cousin until I learned that his wife, who looked just like him, was his first cousin. I spoke with other Sicilians I was locked up with and found that several of them had also married first, second and third cousins, and came from identically constructed families. This was strange to me since we do not typically marry our cousins in America. Not because they would not make good wives, but because it is largely unacceptable in our culture. I am certainly not claiming that all Sicilians wed their cousins, but for centuries the local marriage pools in some of the relatively isolated towns and villages were more like puddles; everyone knew each other and somewhere along the ancestral lines they were connected by blood. A large family was also a source of power and protection, offering a patriarch absolute control over a village. Clans that were not connected were often at odds, resulting in long blood feuds, which constituted a strategic reason to intermarry: survival. Sicilian-American mobster Salvatore 'Bill' Bonanno would confirm the continuation of this practice when he wrote in 1999: 'In the world I come from, it is impossible to understand events – whether they are marriages, political alliances, or killings – unless there is some understanding – literally – of just who was actually related to whom.'

When mafia families were eventually formed, these marital practices continued as we will see, and each mafia family became an extension of a blood family that picked up where genes left off. This is not to suggest that Sicilians are a purebred people; drops of foreign blood spread across centuries have trickled into their bloodline, making them a potent DNA cocktail of Greek, Phoenician, Carthaginian, Roman, Vandal, Hun, Byzantine, Arab, Norman, Spanish and all other occupiers who came and went. Sociologist Gaspare Nicotri spoke to the visceral result of this intermixture when he noted: 'The Sicilian thinks and feels like an Arab, acts like a Greek, and views life like a Spaniard.' But despite this long and measured blood transfusion, Sicilian culture never reflected any cataclysmic shifts. To be sure, there are many visible traces of variant cultures in the Sicilian make-up, as Nicotri pointed out, but they can be likened to the absorption of cultures collected by diaspora Jews along their march through the centuries. Wandering Jews survived exile intact by absorbing new cultures in small, digestible doses while never surrendering their identity; Sicilians have accomplished a similar feat while standing still. The reason for their impermeability is that cultural identity is bound by Darwinian law; the stronger culture conquers the weaker.

The English present us with an excellent example to drive home this point. Besides the Roman invasion of Britain in AD 43, the only other successful invasion of the island was when William the Conqueror crossed the English Channel in 1066. Some historians have argued that the English, although they had lost to the Normans on the battlefield, were victorious in the long run since they possessed the dominant culture which survived. As the Norman invaders assimilated, the English slowly absorbed their conquerors, reversing the crown of victory onto the English head. A similar curiosity seems to have occurred in Sicily during successive invasions over the course of centuries, including a Norman invasion around the same time period – 1060 as opposed to 1066 – which, for the very same reason, left an even fainter mark on Sicily than it had on England.

Lastly, when we view Sicily as a centuries-long hub for foreign invaders and occupiers, we tend to sympathize with such a beleaguered people who have had the miserable luck of residing at the crossroads of empires. But let us not be fooled; the contemporary populace, through centuries of even slow and limited mixing, are as much the offspring of the invader as they are of the besieged. Sicilians are not a spineless, timid people; they are fearless and aggressive, tough, smart, industrious, hard-working and purpose-driven, not the kind of people you might imagine cowering behind their curtains each time a strange ship sailed into port. They are as much the conqueror as they are the conquered. And they may have become so in the same way that we are what we eat – they swallowed their conquerors.

But can we draw a connection between the make-up of the Sicilians of yesteryear and the Sicilians of today, some of whom are the subjects of our story? George Orwell, for one, would allow us to construct this ancestral bridge. Orwell once asked: 'What can the England of 1940 have in common with the England of 1840? But then,' he continued, 'what have you in common with the child of five whose photograph your mother keeps on the mantelpiece? Nothing, except that you happen to be the same person.' Likewise, the Sicilian men I knew in the late twentieth century would have sliced your balls off if you looked at their wives the wrong way or spoke to their sisters without permission; I can easily imagine them in the square, AD 1282, dicing up the French.

Although we are currently discussing the Sicilian people, which is very different from a criminal organization, the mafia possesses one of the strongest, most enduring subcultures in the world, and it sprang directly from Sicilian culture which survived the centuries with little alteration and revolved around family, which we will turn to presently.

Quite a number of historians have theorized that the successive foreign occupations of Sicily throughout the ages created a prolonged state of political instability which forced the Sicilian people to govern themselves through unwritten laws. There is ample evidence to contradict this theory. To start with, some occupations lasted hundreds of years, longer than the entire existence of the United States. In that long period of time, Sicilians had ample opportunity to work with the government or rebel against it, yet they did very little of either. The answer to why can be found within the family unit, which eighteenth-century French philosopher Jean-Jacques Rousseau said is 'the most ancient of all societies, and the only one that is natural'. As long as the Sicilian family felt free and independent, it mattered little whose royal finger was resting on the map of Sicily. This confused many outsiders who looked in at Sicily from a variety of alien perspectives that did not place similar emphasis on family, and left many to wonder how Sicilians could all but ignore changing governments and care so little about national sovereignty. Another French philosopher, Voltaire, fell into this category of confused outsiders when he wrote that Sicily 'has always been subject to foreign nations, the slaves in turn of the

Romans, Vandals, Arabs, and Normans, and the vassals of the Pope, the French, the Germans, and the Spaniards – nearly always hating their masters and rebelling against them, but not making any real efforts worthy of freedom, and continually stirring up sedition with the only result of changing their masters'.

With only a passing glance at Sicily's long historical record, Voltaire's assessment seems fairly reasonable. But a closer look reveals the statement's inaccuracies. National sovereignty and individual liberty are very different; plenty of sovereign states enslave their people. Sicilians seldom rebelled in search of national freedom as long as they possessed individual freedom, which is the freedom to live as one pleases, without interference from one's government. When Sicilians did rebel, it was often in search of food, coinciding with a drought or a bad crop. Spontaneous bread riots spurred by hunger are not the same as political uprisings born of abstract revolutionary ideas fostered in talkative French salons, à la Voltaire. As the American philosopher Eric Hoffer duly noted, revolutions form at the bottom and the top, above and below the heads of the middle class. In Sicily, there was no vibrant intellectual class at the top pushing a revolutionary agenda toward the bottom, inciting them to action. Sicilians have always placed the greatest importance on familial independence, entirely disinterested in chasing Voltaire's skewed idea of state sovereignty in which he and his countrymen swore allegiance to one oppressive king after another; they finally beheaded one, then empowered a little Corsican tyrant who they lost to an English gaoler, before they returned to a fat and lazy overindulged monarch.

For more than two millennia, government after government did not care much about governing Sicily, which is the way Sicilians liked it. The target of each occupier was the island's rich resources, never the Sicilian people, and any attempts at implementing social or political change failed miserably. Conquerors who fared best and endured longest knew that the most efficient way to milk the island dry was to leave the people to themselves. As long as goods made it to port on time – i.e., wheat, wine, wood, citrus, sulfur, etc. – rulers exhibited, at best, a dilettante effort at effecting good government. And because empires powerful enough to lay claim to Sicily were also strong enough to control the trade routes and dominate European commerce, Sicilians enjoyed the wealthiest market for their goods.

Voltaire's famous satirical tale, *Candide*, is also the name of the book's hero. Candide's restless wanderings at last bring him to a small patch of earth where he is content to live out his life as a simpleton. 'We must cultivate our own garden' are Candide's closing words. Though it escaped Voltaire, Sicilians had been cultivating their own garden, literally and figuratively, for centuries, while those around them fought over the deed to their property.

I have lived in some of America's toughest prisons where upon the arrival of a new warden, the inmates would approach *him* and tell *him*, 'This is how we do things around here.' As long as our way of life did not conflict with the administration's overall mission, the warden did not care to make any changes. Nor did the inmates, who truly control a prison, give a rat's ass about who was 'in charge'. The same can be said of the Sicilian people and the relationship they maintained with their many 'rulers'.

We have poured the cement for the mafia's foundation, a concrete mix that took centuries to dry and included strong cultural roots, indestructible family bonds and a long succession of weak central governments, happily displaced by local rule which we will discuss more thoroughly in the next chapter. These are the building blocks of the mafia, a far stretch from a criminal empire, but just as the first building blocks are a far stretch from a skyscraper, the structure cannot rise without them.

Chapter 2
Blood and Soil

The few historians who have delved into the mafia's pre-recorded history in an attempt to discover its origins are in unison in stating that the organization is rooted in feudalism. But after a word or two on the subject, they quickly move on to the mobsters we are familiar with, leaving a historical gap that raises more questions than it answers. In search of evidence to support or deny the claim, I read a stack of books about feudalism and found plenty of connections to support the theory. But before we construct a bridge between the medieval world and the modern mafia, let us take a brief look at how feudalism evolved in Sicily, as it lends further insight into the mafia's origins.

After Rome defeated Carthage in a series of wars that ended in 146 BC, the Romans became masters of the ancient world, and laid claim to the fertile island of Sicily, making it a Roman province. To bring agricultural order to Sicily, considered the 'Republic's granary', Romans divided the land into large estates, called *latifundia*. Each estate was governed by a Roman aristocrat, usually an absentee owner who left a manager in charge while peasant families worked the land. (Curiously, during several hundred years of Roman rule, Sicilians showed little to no interest in becoming Romans; as I pointed out earlier, though ruled from above, Sicilians have always been independently minded.) By the fourth century AD, barbarian tribes from the north swooped down on Rome as the empire was hobbling along on a cane. One such tribe, the Vandals, claimed Sicily and the island spent some time in Vandal hands until the Byzantine Empire snatched away this prized possession. Sicily remained in Byzantine hands from AD 535 to AD 827 when it was claimed by an Islamic army that crossed the Mediterranean Sea from present-day Tunisia. Contrary to their savage military campaigns, Islamic rulers were rather enlightened and typically allowed communities to keep their own laws and institutions. Confronted with no major changes from above, the Sicilians, who had welcomed the Byzantines, now welcomed these Arabs who introduced agricultural innovations and planted new crops, such as pistachios, melons, mulberries, oranges and lemons (the lemon grove industry would, in time, become the mafia's first entrée into industrial racketeering). Commerce thrived, construction flourished, and Palermo, which would one day become the Sicilian mafia capital of the world, was transformed into one of the most cosmopolitan cities of Europe, with Arabs, Jews, Greeks, Slavs, Spaniards and Africans walking the streets and doing business together.

Life was good until the Arabs of Sicily began to bicker among themselves in the eleventh century. One faction called out to the European mainland for help and a Christian army responded by kicking the Arab rulers off the island altogether, and exchanging the Roman-rooted *latifundia* for European feudalism (though the two were very similar). On this page of Sicily's long history, we begin to see striking examples that connect the feudal world with the modern mafia, some of which I will now describe.

In early feudal times, the law was an unwritten set of mutually accepted customs that were enforced by a lord, which perfectly defines mafia law, which is enforced by a don. As the need for written legislation increased across Europe, the orally transmitted village laws of Sicily retained their importance in many parts of the island as Sicilians wondered why they should abide by dictates of unknown authorship as opposed to the trusted word of their ancestors; legalese seemed like a new trick to dilute the power of the patriarchy. To this day, the mafia has its own set of oral laws that are privately enforced and based on traditions that are oblivious to, or even contemptuous of, written law, which harkens back to this early period in Sicilian history.

Moving along, the structural bond between lord and vassal was nearly identical to the modern relationship between mafia don and soldier. During feudal times, lord and vassal entered into an eternal relationship, known as commendation; to this day, a mafia don and his newly recruited soldier seal their eternal relationship in a strikingly similar initiation ceremony. In what was known in feudal times as an 'act of fealty', the vassal placed his hand on a Bible or the relic of a saint, while swearing an oath and vowing to 'sacrifice my life against all whom he pleases . . . without any exception whatsoever . . . thy friends shall be my friends, thy enemies shall be my enemies'. Likewise, a mafia initiate burns a picture of a saint in his hands while swearing to kill or die for his don and his new family. 'If I betray my friends and my family,' recalled an Italian-American mobster, Anthony Accetturo, while divulging his secret past during the 1990s, 'may my soul burn in hell like this saint.'

No weapons were allowed at a commendation ceremony, just as no weapons are permitted at a mafia initiation ceremony, besides the ceremonial dagger. In feudal times, there was no 'written agreement corresponding to the oath of a vassal', just as there is no written agreement outlining the oath or relationship between don and soldier. After the commendation ceremony was completed, a lord had total power over his vassal and that vassal no longer had any right to a family life unless such was granted to him by his lord. This is not unlike a mafia initiation ceremony where a new member is told that if his family at home is in desperate need of his help but his mafia family calls, he must answer the call of his mafia family first. In the 1990s, Italian-American mobster Alphonse 'Little Al' D'Arco revealed that he was told at his initiation ceremony, 'This family comes first . . . If you do not abide by these rules, you will be killed.' During the same decade, mafia princess Rosalie Bonanno (formerly Profaci) wrote that her mobster husband 'had told me early on in our engagement that he was already wedded to something else, a particular philosophy of life, and that if during our marriage he had to choose between keeping the commitment and vow of that life-style and the commitment and vows of this marriage, he was serving notice now he would have to choose the first'.

The feudal ceremony was sealed with a kiss, just as a mafia initiation ceremony is sealed with a kiss.

In my research, I was also able to find etymological connections between feudalism and the modern mafia. Another word for vassal was friend, and official members of a mafia family today refer to themselves as 'friends'. Taking this a step further, in the French feudal system, eternal relations were expressed in the phrase *amis charnels*, meaning 'friends by blood'. While writing about this blood bond, historian Marc Bloch stated: 'The general assumption seems to have been that there was no real friendship save between persons united by blood.' Bloch further pointed out, as the feudal fraternity expanded to include non-blood relations, that 'the act of association was likely to take the form of a fictitious "fraternity" – as if the only real solid social contract was one which, if not based on actual blood-relationship, at least imitated its ties'. This description is identical to the bonds that tie together a mafia family, which begins as a large family clan that, over time, expands to include non-blood relations by welcoming men who are considered 'bound by blood'. (At a mafia initiation ceremony, blood is actually drawn from an initiate's trigger-finger to symbolize this 'fictitious fraternity', and the patriarch of an extended family clan is referred to as 'godfather', which accurately defines his role as the representative father of a large family made up of both blood and non-blood relations.)

Very much like *amis charnels*, mafia members still use the term *amico nostro*, meaning 'friend of ours'. When one mobster is introducing a second mobster to a third, an automatic friendship is expected of the newly acquainted men as in the feudal oath 'thy friends shall be my friends'. If, by chance, a 'friend' is killed, the mafia family does not rest until the murder is avenged, which also dates back to feudal times when the 'whole kindred . . . took up arms to punish the murder of one of its members or merely a wrong that he had suffered'.

Following the commendation ceremony, lord and vassal had certain obligations to one another, as do don and soldier after the latter has been inducted into the family. A lord was obligated to provide protection for his vassal, just as a don must protect his soldier. If a vassal got into a beef with a member of the aristocracy, his lord was obligated to defend him. In the same way, if a soldier gets into a beef with a high-ranking member of another mafia family, his don will defend him. If two vassals under the same lord got into a beef, the lord would preside over the dispute and his ruling was final. Today, this conflict resolution is known in the mafia as a 'sit-down'.

A vassal's failure to appear when summoned to a lord's court constituted a grave offense with consequences that could include death. If a soldier does not 'come in' when called by his don, his failure to appear may also result in death. 'No matter what time of day or night,' recalled mobster Little Al D'Arco, 'you must respond immediately.'

In feudal times, a 'notorious association [was] formed for executing criminal justice . . . a private tribunal', just as mafia justice is usually decided by a tribunal: the boss, his underboss and their *consigliere* (counselor). And just as the primary job of a consigliere is to advise his don, a vassal was expected to 'give the lord advice if the latter asked for it'. Eventually, vassals decided the cases of other vassals, just as mafia captains, or *capos*, preside over disputes between soldiers.

A vassal had the right to share in any plunder and was sometimes granted a fief or the right to collect a tax on fish, beasts, crops, etc. In return, the vassal kicked up a piece of the action to his lord. This is identical to at least one aspect of how the mafia economy works.

If, for a moment, you had imagined that feudalism was a legitimate form of government whereas the mafia is not, German philosopher Georg Friedrich Hegel reminds us that feudalism was a 'bond established on unjust principles . . . a private one . . . subject to the sway of chance, caprice, and violence'. Is this not identical to the mafia?

The early Sicilian mafia was referred to as an Honored Society, or *Onorato Società*, and mafiosos were considered men of honor. Even the mafia's code of honor seems to have been taken directly from chivalry, which was feudalism's code of honor. Not only was Sicily exposed to chivalry by the countries of Western Europe, but the Moors of Spain and the Arabs also had a rich chivalric history, and both occupied Sicily for extended periods of time. Their chivalrous code included loyalty, strict obedience to one's superior, avenging the death of a friend or loved one, and keeping one's word, all found in the mafia's unwritten *code of honor.*

The seventeenth century marked the decline of feudalism in England and, by 1789, it was abolished in revolutionary France. It lingered in Sicily until 1812 when the British, who had established a military presence on the island to prevent it from falling into the hands of Napoleon Bonaparte, disassembled the island's feudal system. According to German criminologist Henner Hess, 'physical violence until 1812 was the legal instrument of the ruling caste by which it maintained its status' through private armies. After this violence was monopolized by the state, certain regions of Sicily fiercely resisted the end of feudalism and it does not appear that these private armies were completely disbanded but assumed a new role of organized resistance, while some men seem to have fallen in with newly emerging mafia families. For a contemporary analogy of what this might have looked like, following the 2003 US-led invasion of Iraq, Saddam Hussein's private army, or Republican Guard, was hastily disbanded with no plan or effort to reassign its many soldiers or assimilate them into a new economy. As a result, a well-trained army of angry and aimless able-bodied men joined the most violent insurgent groups, presenting the US military and its allies with a catastrophic problem that could have been avoided early on. The abrupt end of feudalism seems to have created a similar problem in Sicily among private armies whose role in society had vastly diminished, if not evaporated altogether. The men who controlled these private armies were known as *gabellotti*.

From the Middle Ages until the nineteenth century, Sicilian land barons enjoyed the pride and privilege of owning large estates without having to physically work them. They left overseers in charge of their land, or, more often, leased the estates to *gabellotti*. The barons expected the *gabellotti* to drain every last drop of sweat from the peasants and harvest every last seed from the land – and they did, while robbing the barons blind. They skimmed the cream of the crop and sold it on the black market. They chopped down and sold the most valuable trees, controlled the land rights and water supply, charged road taxes and tolls, and collected high rents from the peasants by way of threats and violence.

Some historians believe that the private armies controlled by the *gabellotti* evolved into the mafia, while others contend that the *gabellotto*, who was also a moneylender and the sole authority over the local labor force, usurped the baronial lands and morphed into the modern mafia don. The evidence, however, is sketchy, and further confusion is added to the debate by eminent sociologists who have formed contradictory conclusions. British historian Eric Hobsbawm, for example, wrote: 'All the heads of the local *mafias* were men of wealth . . . overwhelmingly men of the middle class, capitalist farmers and contractors, lawyers and the like.' Henner Hess, meanwhile, wrote, much to the contrary, that many mob bosses were 'not from the middle, but from the lower stratum' of society. I lean toward Hess's view, contending that, even if the original dons were 'men of wealth', they were soon displaced by men of 'the lower stratum', who were far more relatable to the people around them. In my own experience, mafia dons have always been liked and respected by the working people whom they live among. They typically defend underdogs, get people jobs, and dish out favors to the poor and needy. I am not suggesting that any mafia don is Mr Nice Guy, as an element of fear surrounds even the most benevolent don, but I can assure you that hard-working citizens in the neighborhoods I frequented were seldom afraid of the local mafia don. They knew the rules and knew how to benefit from his favors without placing themselves in jeopardy. My own mafia don's Fourth of July parties in South Ozone Park, Queens, were far from unattended. They were crowded with average citizens: men, women and children alike, from all ethnic backgrounds. None of these people were afraid of any of us. It is therefore hard for me to imagine that rent collectors, or the men who pushed people around and squeezed every last drop of sweat from their pores, were able to become well-liked and respected mafia dons.

'Mafia godfathers are like godfathers to everyone,' said General Angiolo Pellegrini of the Sicilian Anti-Mafia Investigation Department, 'the person who dispenses justice and rights wrongdoings.' General Pellegrini is correct; mafia dons have always been appreciated for their administration of justice in places where, on account of isolation or ignorance of the law, there was none. Since a don's authority is exercised by proxy through his soldiers and associates, I can personally speak to countless beefs I settled on the street. Often, hard-working people, who were aware of my power, approached me for help. The problems were usually spats between neighbors that were beyond the reach or concern of the law, or minor disputes that could be settled in small claims court – if only they had the money or wherewithal to employ such remedies, or could afford to take the days off from work needed to drag their poor souls into a courtroom. And yet, while standing on a sidewalk or seated at a table in a café, I could dispense with the whole affair in the space of a few minutes, often leaving both parties relatively satisfied. Let us not delude ourselves; even within the most advanced nations on earth, the law is remote and incomprehensible to the better part of humanity, especially the lower classes. Yet these same people are expected to live under its rule. I assure you, from personal experience, that in theory the law is within their reach, but in fact, it is as inaccessible and unintelligible to them as the *Code of Hammurabi*.

Returning to the notion that the *gabellotti* had morphed into mafia dons, I find it hard to believe that men who represented every form of injustice and oppression, and were known as local tyrants, were able to assume the role of mafia dons, who granted favors and enforced local law to the overall benefit of the community, after the land barons were pushed out of the picture. Certainly not without revitalizing their image and drastically altering their relationship with the people around them. This is, however, highly unlikely since people seldom forgive an iron fist, and an iron fist, even more infrequently, relaxes. It is more likely that a don would emerge from the figure of him who stepped up and displaced the *gabellotto*, maybe even killed him, and in turn won the hearts of the people by removing their taskmaster. Perhaps, in some cases, lesser-known men rose up from the private armies the *gabellotti* controlled.

What remains undeniable is that, during a roughly fifty-year period, between the fall of feudalism in 1812 and the unification of Italy – which included Sicily – in 1861, local strongmen who emerged from the peasantry began to assume roles previously reserved for feudal lords and land barons. Charismatic leaders, often patriarchs of large families, began to call themselves *don*, a title once reserved for nobility and adopted from the island's one-time Spanish occupiers.

As we have seen, the mafia's strongest fertilizing agent was planted in Sicily during the Roman Empire and was known as *latifundia*, which was remodeled as feudalism during the High Middle Ages and remained a socio-political system Sicilians were comfortable with, even after its demise. When feudalism was abolished, strongmen replaced feudal lords and kept feudalism alive when it should have been tossed onto the trash heap of history. Instead, its collapsed and heavily molded walls were salvaged and used to support the mafia's emergent structure. A modern-day mafia family, untethered to land, is a living, breathing, walking, killing, mobile feudal system that has not been informed of its extinction, and continues to exist in the twenty-first century as though inside a perforated time capsule.

Chapter 3
Secret Societies

The next stage in the development of this feudal subculture which endured after it was officially demolished in 1812 was the previously mentioned unification of Italy in 1861, which would ironically result in the unification of a burgeoning mafia.

Until the second half of the nineteenth century, there was no nation of Italy. As the Roman Empire receded into history's rear-view mirror, a patchwork of independent city-states emerged up and down the Italian peninsula over the course of centuries, each with its own government, laws, coinage and culture. Some city-states spoke their own languages and dialects. By the mid-1800s, only one 'Italian' in forty spoke what we now regard as Italy's national language. Just imagine, if the many city-states of Italy were this distinct from one another when all that separated them was an imaginary border, how much more distant was an island separated by a sea, as is Sicily, where a unique blend of Latin, Greek, Spanish and Arabic was spoken.*

By the mid-1800s, a movement to unify Italy, known as the *Risorgimento*, swept across the Italian peninsula as soldiers fought to eject the Austrians, who ruled in the north, and the French, who ruled in the south. 'To suppose that Italy, divided for centuries,' wrote one Italian critic of the movement, 'can peacefully be brought under the power of a single state is madness.' When southern Italians heard the

---

* My father's parents were from Bari, my mother's father was from Naples, and her mother was from Sicily. My family communicated in English and any attempts to speak in 'Italian' were short-lived since my mother's father, who spoke a dialect of Neapolitan, could not have a smooth conversation with my mother's mother, who spoke a dialect of Sicilian, and they both rolled their eyes when listening to my father, who spoke Barese, which many other Italians consider to be one of the hardest dialects to follow.

As with language differences, Italy's regional mentality carried over to America. When I was young, fellow Italian-Americans often asked me where I was from, meaning what part of Italy was my family from. Being able to say three places – Bari, Naples and Sicily – increased my chances of being acceptable to some, while rendering me a mutt to others. Italy is only Italy to the tourist.

slogan 'Long Live Italia!' they wondered what it meant. Some Sicilians thought 'Italia' was the name of their new queen. (Over a hundred years later, in the 1960s, sociologist Danilo Dolci still encountered Sicilians who had no idea what Italy was.)

As Sicilians became exposed to the idea of unification, they eventually fought for it, but did so in order to rid themselves of their latest rulers, while further motivated by the promise of land redistribution. In return for their help, Italian politicians promised Sicily independence once the foreigners were kicked out, but after the French and Austrians were ejected, and Victor Emmanuel II was proclaimed the first king of a unified Italy, the new nation denied Sicily its independence and ousted the peasants from any land they had occupied. (It is widely believed that the Sicilian plebiscite held in October 1860 to include the island in Italy's unification was fixed.) Most Sicilians felt duped, and viewed Italy as the latest of their long list of foreign overlords. As a result, Sicilians did not then, and many do not even today, consider themselves to be Italian; they are Sicilians! In fact, all of the diverse Italian city-states continued to identify more with their own particular region. One Italian sociologist referred to Italy as 'a shimmering canvas on which a mad painter had mixed the most diverse and strident colors'. Even the military hero who fought to unify Italy, Giuseppe Garibaldi, was pessimistic about the future when he said, 'It has taken 100 years to unify Italy. It will take another 100 years to unify the Italian people.' As for Sicily, Garibaldi undershot the mark since it has now been over 150 years and Sicilians are still Sicilians, as my own grandmother made clear to me anytime I referred to her as an Italian.

After unification, Italy's cadre of fledgling statesmen proved their inexperience by instituting high taxes across Sicily, implementing compulsory elementary education guided by a rapidly evolving bureaucracy, and conscripting the island's young sons into the Italian military. The Sicilians' well-known hatred for conscription dates back to Roman times. When the Roman general Scipio Africanus was warring with Hannibal, a Sicilian cavalry corps was assembled, but the men grumbled so much about leaving their families behind that Scipio became aggravated and told them to just stay home. And they happily did. As for the French Bourbons, of all the European territories they ruled, Sicily alone was exempt from conscription; the French did not trust Sicilians to fight for French causes. To put this in perspective, in my own country, African-Americans did not attain their full civil rights until the late 1960s, yet they fought valiantly in every US conflict dating back to the revolutionary war. The British Empire trusted its Indian, Canadian and Australian regiments, whose extraordinary valor largely contributed to the Allied victories in both world wars. The answer to why Sicilians were traditionally exempt from serving in the armies of their masters was, as referenced earlier, because Sicilians would not lay down their lives for foreign causes, patriotic ideals, or international diplomacy gone awry; they fought only for their families. When young Sicilian men were called to service, many retreated into the mountains and lived as bandits while sending money home to their families.

Promised but denied independence, overtaxed and conscripted, for Sicily this whole Italian experiment was off to a very bad start. The island's natural reflex was to push back and cut off any inroads attempted by Italy's central government. But the Italian government would not be put off so easily; it was striving to conform with the new attitudes of Western Europe and demanded that Sicily, along with all of southern Italy, transform into a liberal democracy. Overnight, Sicilians were expected to crawl out from under the dead weight of centuries and fall in step with the marching band. Those of us who study history would have seen this as preposterous. 'Centuries are required to form a political system and centuries needed to change it,' wrote French sociologist Gustave Le Bon, who did not believe in forcing one's own utopian dreams – or schemes – on another nation. People do not exchange long-held ideas so easily and feel more secure with a tyranny they know than a 'freedom' to which they are unaccustomed. The better part of the island made it abundantly clear that they preferred local rule over an insensitive, distant constitutional monarchy with a parliament based in faraway Rome (originally Turin).

Raising the stakes in this stand-off were the newspapers of Western Europe which criticized Italy for not bringing its southern regions in line, which included Sicily. What to do? Instead of the Italian government closely examining the island's political chains that had been rusting for centuries; instead of realizing how low the literacy rate was, and how high the poverty rate was; instead of running a delicate hand along the social fabric to see where it was torn, the new Italian government began to judge, castigate and tyrannize Sicily as if it were an uncivilized island of inferior brutes. Italy's northern elites discussed the problems of southern Italy, first and foremost Sicily, at salons, dinner parties and in parliamentary debates, ultimately labeling this national headache the 'Southern Question'. Thus, it happened that intellectuals from northern Italy, believing themselves to be highly evolved Europeans as they were closer to the major continental centers of progress, took on the Southern Question. It is important to note that Western European elites who resided north of the Alps were originally wondering how everyone south of the Alps had fallen behind the rest of Europe. Suddenly, northern Italians were trying to move the Alps and say that they were just fine and that all the riff-raff were to be found south of them (even though no one truly knew where this imaginary line between north and south lay). Nevertheless, northern Italians attempted to duck further scrutiny by redirecting the finger-pointing to the lower regions of Italy.

The study of issues surrounding the Southern Question became known as *meridionalismo*. Traveling *meridionalisti* visited Sicily on fact-finding missions, and some of their descriptions of the islanders read like Darwin's recording of the peculiar animals he sighted on the Galápagos. Northerners wrote books and articles that denigrated their new southern country folk, sometimes referring to them as barbarians, while others heartily revived the idea originated by Montesquieu that the world's idiots tend to live in warmer climates. Two investigations into the Southern Question are worthy of note for their diametrically opposed views, one of which painted Sicily as something we would imagine from the island of Doctor Moreau, where people ran around with abnormal heads and acted with the angry and amoral behavior of tortured animals. The other view was highly enlightened, but considered by some as defeatist since it instructed the Italian government to leave the incorrigible island to itself. I will begin with the former.

Italian criminologist Cesare Lombroso, known as the 'father of modern criminology', wondered why criminals act the way they do. While tackling the Southern Question, Lombroso touched on Sicily's social problems but largely attributed its – and the rest of southern Italy's – rampant criminal behavior to the atavistic tendencies of its barbaric population. Lombroso's book *L'uomo delinquente* (The Criminal Man), published in 1876, posited that the born criminal (*delinquente nato*) was someone whom evolution has left behind. (Author Bram Stoker's description of the blood-sucking vampire Dracula is taken, almost verbatim, from Lombroso's *Criminal Man*.)

According to Lombroso, born criminals commit abhorrent acts due to a catalog of inherent psychological and physical abnormalities that include peculiar-shaped and oversized skulls – which Lombroso was fond of measuring. As northern Italians sunbathed in the warm glow of Lombroso's reassuring conclusions which served to boost their already condescending attitude toward the south, we will turn to the bleak but enlightened view of Sicily which was in stark contrast to Lombroso's idea of born losers with overgrown heads.

In a quest to answer the Southern Question, two Tuscan journalists, Leopoldo Franchetti and Sidney Sonnino, traveled to Sicily the same year Lombroso published his *Criminal Man*. They found peasants living in a state of squalor with widespread illiteracy, hardly any public works, and no universal system of social justice. At one point, the travelers came upon a priest who had been shot by his cousin. They inquired as to why, wondering how cruel the cousin must be to shoot a man of the cloth, and learned from the locals that the priest was the more violent criminal who got what he deserved. The traveling duo also found that the Sicilian police, instead of arresting criminals, would typically broker a deal on the spot between the criminal and the aggrieved party, having the criminal return part of the theft before taking a cut for themselves in return for their mediation. Franchetti and Sonnino further found that 'violence can be freely employed by whomever has the means to do so'.

Sicily's uniquely corrupt system included every rung of the social ladder from policemen to politicians, rich and poor, men and women alike; even the clergy were in on the charade, as noted above. The strongest family in every village controlled the local government, and the patriarch held unconditional authority over every aspect of daily life. The duo concluded that the patriarch's presence was so indispensable to the community's welfare, and the government so helpless to displace him, that it made little sense to try to do so. They did not believe that Sicilians could fix their own problems since this wretched state of affairs was totally normal to them; it would be like trusting a lunatic to evaluate himself and prescribe his own therapy. Of course, there were some Sicilians who saw their age-old system as flawed, but there was no public mechanism for civic reform; if there was, it would have been as thoroughly infiltrated and corrupted as every other institution.

Franchetti and Sonnino's bleak report, presented to the Italian government, sounded very much like the unwritten conclusion successive foreign governments had reached for centuries, as evidenced by their propensity to quickly forsake any undertakings directed toward social and economic reform. If Sicily had a tumor and our travelers were doctors, they had opened her up and closed her just as fast, after noticing how far the cancer had spread. With no foreseeable solution, they urged Italy to leave this strange island to itself. Let Sicily proclaim independence while Italy waves goodbye from the nearby shores of Calabria.

Franchetti and Sonnino's recommendation to the Italian government may have been correct for the following reason: by abandoning the island to itself, Sicily would have been deprived of an external enemy at which to hurl the slings and arrows of blame. Forced to look inward, Sicilians might have faced an enlightening moment of self-reflection. They instead united around a corroded social contract they felt was under attack from mainland Italy, now considered a foreign enemy. The obvious counterargument to this opinion is that petty tyrants would have been permitted to flourish, unchecked. It so happened that they did exactly that anyway, and because of Sicily's new connection to the mainland, those same tyrants, who would become known as mafiosos, would corrupt the whole of Italy. Politicians of the new democratic system needed votes which mafia dons could deliver on election day. Because the mafia employed so many locals, could offer favors, extend loans, and issue threats to secure an election, the mafia's backing of any political candidate was crucial to attaining elected office in many regions of Sicily.

Beginning shortly after Italy's unification and continuing into the modern day, a contradiction arose in which many crooked politicians loudly condemned the mafia out of one side of their mouths, while quietly asking for their assistance out of the other. And since any political party often needed to carry the electorate in Sicily in order to rule in Rome, this political plague spread to the mainland. Thus, through control of Sicily's ballot boxes, obscure dons, who passed their days sipping espresso in an aged and crumbling piazza, would manipulate the power structure in Rome and influence the whole of Italy. The Italian government should have accepted the scalpel Franchetti and Sonnino had handed them. But the northern elites were not about to liberate such a rich part of their new nation. Moreover, how embarrassed they would be before the eyes of Europe as a thousand newspaper editors peered down from the Alps, eager to see how they answered their

Southern Question. Lastly, what if Sicily one day fell into the hands of an enemy?

The Italian government refused to be persuaded by the facts outlined in Franchetti and Sonnino's report and brushed it aside. Instead of heeding theirs and other reports from northern visitors who saw in Sicily a 'world of semi-feudalism, based on archaic notions of honour, in which blood feuds abounded, and liberalism was scarcely understood', the Italian government began a vicious campaign of suppression believing it was 'not possible to govern except through terror'. Their attempt to have Sicily conform to European standards resulted in a textbook cultural clash. When any age-old culture collides with modernity, it seems as if centuries of combustion have been released in an explosive struggle for supremacy (the West's present struggle with parts of the Islamic East present us with a contemporary example). But two thousand years of culture cannot be stamped out by a police raid; Italy's brute tactics only strengthened Sicily's defiant resolve by forcing its 'criminals' underground and violating what French sociologist Emile Durkheim might have referred to as the island's shared moral sense, which drove common Sicilians on every level of society straight into the arms of the very men Italy wished to destroy – the local rulers who were morphing into . . . the mafia.

Franchetti and Sonnino's report concluded that widespread corruption was an open part of Sicily's socio-economic system and by no means a secret society. This made sense; if the majority of Sicilians had no problem with the system, and nor did the police, there was no reason to drag it underground. How, then, did an open mode of behavior, primarily perpetrated by men who were living according to age-old principles of feudalism, suddenly become a secret society, and why?

The answer to *why* is that certain *men of honor*, around which all of the elements of society were entwined, were suddenly labeled criminals by a far-off government in Rome.*

* According to a twentieth-century school of thought called Labeling Theory, the local leaders of Sicily were not heads of criminal organizations until Italy proper labeled them as such. Another twentieth-century school of thought believed that when any particular deviance becomes widespread, society tends to normalize it, until it is no longer considered criminal. For example, I have known men who have served twenty years in prison for selling marijuana, a plant that is now sold legally in the same states that had once punished them so severely. The point being, what much of Italy considered criminal was seen by many Sicilians as normal behavior.

As to *how* they became a secret society, they grasped onto a recently proven model for survival. In eighteenth- and nineteenth-century Europe, a number of politically inspired secret societies that mimicked Freemasonry popped up across the continent with intent to overthrow the old European order; the Tugendbund in Germany, the Hetairia in Greece and the Jacobins in France were just a few. In Italy, there were the Adelphi, the Guelphs, the Italian Federati, the Brother Protectors and the Carbonari, a society that directed most of its political agitation toward the ruling Austrians, who responded by increasing police pressure on the group, even punishing people who knew members but failed to report them to the authorities. With the Austrian government on the hunt for anyone connected with the Carbonari, the group developed secret rituals such as 'special handshakes, secret codes, and invisible ink'. The Carbonari also had 'an initiation ceremony, complex symbols, and a hierarchical organization' in which members swore to 'keep the secrets of this Society, and neither to write, print, or engrave anything concerning it'. Their initiation ceremony included words such as 'I consent, if I perjure myself, to have my body cut in pieces, and then burned'. To do the cutting and burning, the Carbonari recruited a 'well-organised body of men, ready to obey the commands of invisible superiors, and enter, at a word, upon any enterprise'. These men formed ties with groups of brigands while engaging in 'protection rackets, smuggling, and contract assassinations'. Does all this not sound exactly like the mafia? Whatever the mafia did not inherit directly from feudalism, they appropriated from the secret societies of Italy which were all around them in the nineteenth century.

The Carbonari were broken down into camps of ten to a hundred men with a *capo di carbonari* in charge of each group. This the mafia has adopted to a tee, with *caporegimes* – capos – in charge of crews that exist within a mafia family. The Carbonari's ranks swelled into the thousands and the network became so popular that it attracted notable figures such as the English poet Lord Byron, who was appointed a capo; he hid weapons and helped fugitives escape justice. At one time, the Carbonari's *capo di tutti capi* was Filipe Michele Buonarotti, a direct descendant of the great Michelangelo. Another prized recruit was Giuseppe Mazzini, known today as the 'father of modern Italy'. The energetic Mazzini, who drank enough coffee to keep a Starbucks afloat, has left us a vivid account of his initiation ceremony:

> I was conducted one evening to a house . . . where, after ascending to the topmost storey, I found the person by whom I was to be initiated . . . he questioned me as to my readiness to act . . . and to sacrificing myself, if necessary, for the good of the *order*. Then, after desiring me to kneel, he unsheathed a dagger, and recited the formula of oath . . . causing me to repeat it after him.

Mazzini could have been explaining an initiation ceremony into a mafia family which includes the same oath, same dagger, and a sworn sacrifice for the good of the *family*, as opposed to the *order*. Here is a strikingly similar mafia oath as recalled by a soldier in the Italian-American mafia, Joseph Valachi, during the 1960s:

> They called us in one at a time . . . there was a gun and a knife on the table . . . I repeated some words they told me . . . He [Valachi's don] went on to explain that they lived by the gun and by the knife and you die by the gun and by the knife . . . Then he gave me a piece of paper, and I was to burn it . . . This is the way I burn if I expose this organization.

In time, Mazzini grew disenchanted with the Carbonari and broke away to form his own secret society called Giovane Italia, or Young Italy. Members were organized into squads and *noms de guerre* were given to avoid police detection just as nicknames are given to mobsters, in part for the same reason. Members were also forbidden to go to the authorities for any reason just as the mafia forbids members from going to the police. Even the mafia's idea of a 'social club', where members gather to play cards and drink espresso while discussing criminal activities, seems to have stemmed from this period of secret societies; one of Italy's founding fathers, Camillo Benso, Count of Cavour – who proudly proclaimed, 'I devoted all my strength to being a conspirator . . . searching for fellow-conspirators' – had a whist club in Turin which acted as a façade for secret political discussions.

The members of Young Italy 'were enrolled with utmost care, and only after minute inquiries concerning their character and antecedents so as to avoid the admission of spies or persons who might be readily seduced into treachery'. Whether by coincidence or mimicry, the mafia is just as concerned with pedigree, believing that a man from good stock is less likely to betray his friends and family because he is imbued with a sense of duty taught to him at a young age. Allow me to momentarily zoom in on the word *duty*, a word responsible, in Italy, for more deaths than cholera.

In 1851, Giuseppe Mazzini wrote a patriotic book titled *The Duties of Man*, the inspiration for which likely came from the American revolutionary work by Thomas Paine titled *Rights of Man*, except that the slight change in title speaks to the prevailing Italian attitude that man's *duties*, as opposed to his *inalienable rights*, are of primary importance. Italians have charted the heavens, can break glass with their voices, paint the Sistine Chapel, sculpt the Trevi Fountain, scribe the *Divine Comedy* – and stab you in the heart for insulting their manhood or cut your balls off and shove them down your throat for violating their women. Because it is their duty! Even some of Italy's greatest artists have been mixed up in violence, largely due to an Italian culture that, at least on a provincial level, condoned bloodshed when personal duty called. Benvenuto Cellini sculpted magnificent statues, including the well-known *Perseus with the Head of Medusa*, yet in his riveting autobiography he proudly speaks of beating and stabbing men who, he felt, asked for it by challenging his manhood.

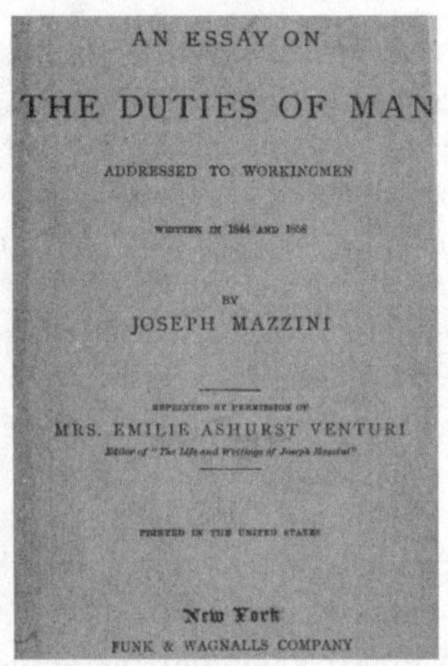

AN ESSAY ON

THE DUTIES OF MAN

ADDRESSED TO WORKINGMEN

WRITTEN IN 1844 AND 1858

BY

JOSEPH MAZZINI

MRS. EMILIE ASHURST VENTURI

New York

FUNK & WAGNALLS COMPANY

CONTENTS.

	PAGES.
CHAPTER I.	
Introduction—1844	5–20
CHAPTER II.	
God	21–32
CHAPTER III.	
The Law	33–43
CHAPTER IV.	
Duties Towards Humanity	44–56
CHAPTER V.	
Duties Towards your Country—1858	57–63
CHAPTER VI.	
Duties Towards the Family	64–71
CHAPTER VII.	
Duties Towards Yourselves	72–83
CHAPTER VIII.	
Liberty	84–92

The Duties of Man *by Mazzini; note Chapter VI, Duties Towards the Family.*

Another violent artist bound to duty was Michelangelo Merisi, better known as Caravaggio. Caravaggio's criminal record is as long as his list of famous paintings, and on one occasion he killed part-time pimp Ranuccio Tomassoni. Caravaggio was trying to cut Tomassoni's pecker off when he nipped an artery near the groin causing Tomassoni to bleed out. Caravaggio then went on the lam, continued his violent lifestyle, and eventually disappeared. Though a number of Caravaggio's enemies were looking to square up with him, most historians are convinced that Tomassoni's four brothers, also duty-bound to avenge the death of their sibling, disposed of Caravaggio.

I can reference other Italian writers and artists but we need not look any further than myself. I am a self-taught, international best-selling author who has been accused in open court of numerous acts of violence, including beating and shooting men with the same hand that holds this pen. Though I do not contend to be an artistic genius in the category of Cellini or Caravaggio, I do believe my problem was quite similar to theirs in that I belonged to a subculture that placed great importance on, as Mazzini said, *the duties of man*. And one of those duties was to defend myself, my honor, my family and my friends from real or perceived slights and threats. Each time I had committed an act of violence, I had thoroughly convinced myself that this was what I was doing. In my subculture, the duty a man has to his own wife is just as significant as it is convoluted. I had played cards amidst a poker table full of killers, loansharks and hijackers, and we never once questioned the moral integrity of our lifestyles, yet one of the men among us was regularly badgered for not going home to his wife each night. To be clear, it was okay that he had a *gumare*, or girlfriend, on the side, but it was his duty to provide for his wife and return home to her each evening. When he did not do so, we called him a *disgrazia*, which likely stems from the idea that he was disgracing his family name. During the infamous Maxi mafia trials in Italy, held from 1986 to 1992, *pentito* Tommaso Buscetta accused Don Luciano Leggio of a string of brutal murders. Leggio responded in his own defense by saying that Buscetta had no right to talk because he did not care for his own wife. Leggio truly believed that he was impugning the witness; to Leggio, committing murder was being dutiful while failing in marital duties was worthy of severe condemnation. Had Leggio been judged by a jury from Corleone, the Sicilian town where he was from, he may have been acquitted. (We can be fairly certain how Cellini and Caravaggio would have polled had they been part of his jury.)

A similar devotion to duty was inherent in Mazzini's secret society which was largely responsible for the unification of Italy. After that unification was achieved, all of Italy's secret societies became obsolete and naturally disbanded, but their most successful tactics – secret rituals, sworn oaths, violent retribution for traitors, a structured army with soldiers, capos and a boss, unwavering opposition to state authority, social clubs used to gather and discuss strategy, an emphasis on duty – were picked up by Sicily's newly labeled 'criminals' who needed a vehicle to carry them into the underworld where they would function as an invisible government. Thus, the mafia, the most fearsome and brutal secret society the world has ever known, was born.

The house is complete; we need only name it.

The Italian Enlightenment philosopher Giambattista Vico believed that by studying the history of words in any given language, we can glean clues as to that same people's cultural development. I am sure, if Vico were alive today, he would be interested to know where the word *mafia* came from.

Historians agree that the word is of Arab origin. When the Arabs lost Sicily to the Normans, a strong Arab-Berber resistance movement, which included former rulers and bandit gangs, was forcibly driven into the western region of Sicily. They settled in and around Palermo and Agrigento, exactly where the mafia was born and continues, to some extent, today. The Arab contribution to the architectural landscape, language and mores of this region cannot be overstated. Thus, it is not surprising that etymologists have traced the word *mafia* to various Arabic words such as *mahfaz*, which means protection; *mahjas*, which means boasting; *mahfil*, which means a gathering; *mahias*, meaning a man who is bold; and *mahie* or *mafie*, which could mean either the private armies hired to protect large estates or the caves where bandits hid. Others contend that the word *mafia* is rooted in the Arabic *muafah*: *mu* meaning strength and *afah* meaning to protect. All of these possibilities seem credible given the long and strong Arab influence on the island.

Another word I have not seen referenced anywhere but interests me greatly is *mahdi*, a term most of us in the West are familiar with

A church in Palermo that resembles a mosque, highlighting the Arab influence on the island.

through the famous Siege of Khartoum, where British General Gordon Pasha lost his life to an army commanded by the self-proclaimed *mahdi*, Muhammad Ahmad. From the *Encyclopaedia Britannica*: 'Belief in the *mahdi* has tended to receive new emphasis in every time of crisis . . . seen as a restorer of the political power . . . the title has tended to be claimed by social revolutionaries . . . who desired thus to acquire power against an existing government.' Post-Italian unification Sicily was clearly thought of as a 'time of crisis' for the Sicilian people, both socially and politically. And the local mafia could have easily been considered a 'restorer of the political power' that was being threatened by the 'existing government'. Could mafiosos be considered social revolutionaries? Certainly not today, but back then they could have been seen as such by the people of western Sicily. No group showed more of a hatred and contempt for institutionalized power than the Arab-Berbers of western Sicily, who could have been viewed as a sort of collective version of the *mahdi* or, more accurately, the *mahdist* regime, known as the *mahdiya*, which is a single letter away from the word *mahfiya*, or *mafia*. I will submit this theory to future historians for debate as we move on.

In *The Arab Mind*, author Raphael Patai recorded a number of brilliant observations about the Arab people that connect honor with family while emphasizing the importance of extended family relations as a means of protection in a tribal world where no authority, power structure or means of conflict resolution existed beyond the patriarch who can easily be likened to a mafia don ruling over a family. In fact, entire passages of Patai's book can be used verbatim to define a mafia family, and ancient Arab poets regularly extolled *hamasa* (bravery), *muruwwa* (manliness) and *sharaf* (honor), which happen to be the three most desirable traits of a true mafioso. Even the Arab system of male guardianship of wives, daughters and sisters, which continues today in some Arabian countries, was prevalent in parts of Sicily. British historian John Julius Norwich, a frequent traveler to Sicily, wrote a book about the island in which he pointed out 'the curious absence of women' in villages, which he considered to be the result of 'Sicily's Islamic past'. 'They are seldom seen in the cafés,' wrote Norwich while reflecting on his travels to the island during the late 1960s, 'these are entirely dominated by men.' In 1990, mafia princess Rosalie Bonanno reflected on her Sicilian-American upbringing during the 1950s. 'I was not allowed to leave the house unless I had a destination,' wrote Bonanno, 'and then I could go only if I was accompanied by one of my brothers or a cousin.' Rosalie's husband, Salvatore 'Bill' Bonanno, said that while he was courting her, 'Ro and I couldn't go to a movie together unless I bought tickets for a whole row of cousins and other relatives.'

The mafia also engages in certain violent actions that can be traced to Arab origin. To this day, mobsters will sometimes strangle victims with a garrote, just as the Ottomans used a silk bowstring. The mafia is also known to castrate some of its victims; where does this come from? British historian Hugh Thomas tells us that during the Spanish Civil War, General Francisco Franco tried to 'restrain the Moors from castrating the corpses of their victims – an established Moorish battle-rite'. We must wonder if this macabre rite, so often committed by the mafia, was practiced in Sicily by the Arabs, perhaps the Arabs of Spanish descent. It has always been thought that mafia victims who were castrated had violated women, but plenty of mafia victims who did not violate women have suffered the same mutilation, so it seems possible that it was done to emasculate enemies, the same reason the Moors castrated corpses in Spain (and why the ancient Greeks told us that the king of the Titans, Kronos, cut off his father's nuts and flung them into the sea).

As for the word *mafioso*, which is used today to refer to a mobster, we can trace its origin more easily. A similar word, *mafiusi*, enters the lexicon for the first time in 1863 during the performance of a play in Palermo. The play, which is set in 1850, is about life in a Palermo prison and is titled *I Mafiusi la Vicaria* (The Mafiusi of Vicaria Prison). This is our first encounter with the word in modern times though we may never know if the staged play publicized a common street slang or gave mobsters their name. Perhaps both. The written word *mafia* officially appears in a police report for the first time in 1865, which can serve as the mafia's official birthdate and perfectly coincides with our timeline of events.

Poster advertising the play I Mafiusi la Vicaria.

Today, *omertà* is used to express the mafia's *code of silence*, but its origin has a deeper meaning. *Omertà* stems from the Sicilian *omu*, or Latin *homo*, meaning 'man'. *Omertà* was originally a one-word catch-all to define manliness and all that it entailed, much of it having to do with a man's *duty*, the importance of which was discussed earlier. Benito Mussolini's Prefect of Palermo, Cesare Mori, who attempted to crush the mafia in Sicily during the 1920s, defined *omertà* in a way that further attests to the word *mahdi*, or *mahdiya*, being the root of the word *mafia*. 'Omerta would tend to flourish in a country like Sicily,' wrote Mori, 'where justice and social protection were most seriously deficient, and where the chief source of injustice and tyranny was the government itself. It would tend to be looked on as a noble quality in acts of reprisal and work against the government.' Mori's definition of *omertà* is too close to the *Encyclopaedia Britannica*'s definition of *mahdi* for us to overlook the obvious connection between the two words, which reinforces the trail that leads us back to the Arab-Berbers of Sicily as the mafia's founding fathers.

Now that we have constructed the house and given it a name, it is time to meet the family who will occupy it. They will, at times, prove smart, industrious, intuitive, and be guided by a strict set of principles. But as author Dorothy Sayers once wrote: 'The first thing a principle does – if it really is a principle – is to kill somebody.' And so, the house will sometimes appear extremely dysfunctional, and will eventually devolve into a house of horrors with blood and guts splattered all over the walls.

At last, it is time to enter this house and see what the family is up to. As this is a history of the American mafia, I have carefully selected events in Sicily that include mafiosos who will travel to America, allowing us to trace the mafia's migration and follow the criminal plague as it spread to the New World.

Part Two

The Story Begins

Chapter 4

A Rose without a Nose and a Marquis with Bloody Clothes

James Rose was a British businessman who lived in Palermo, Sicily, where he partnered with an American entrepreneur, Benjamin Gardner, to form a sulfur-mining company in Lercara Friddi, a town approximately forty miles outside of Palermo. In 1876, Rose's sons, George and John, boarded a train from Palermo to Lercara Friddi where they planned to inspect the company mines. They arrived at the train station below the town just after 10 a.m., where the brothers split up; George traveled the rest of the way in a horse-drawn passenger coach while John, accompanied by two of his employees, rode uphill on horseback. Along the ride, John and his traveling companions encountered two Sicilian men, dressed like 'country gentlemen'. When the men asked John Rose to identify himself, one of Rose's employees sensed trouble and interjected, giving Rose a fake name. Rose quickly corrected his employee, an error that would cost him two ears and a nose. The Sicilians seized the bridle of Rose's horse and ordered him to dismount as two more Sicilians rode up behind the group. When all four Sicilians pointed their rifles at Rose, he made a dash for it, clumsily tumbling down the hillside as the Sicilians fired several shots above his head. One of the Sicilians caught up with Rose and asked him why he had so rudely run off without bidding adieu. The jokester's name was Antonino Leone, one of the most renowned bandit leaders in all of Sicily.

Rose was brought to a cave where the bandits attempted to draft a ransom note, but after fiddling with a pen, they found themselves staring at a blank page and admitted their weak grasp of the English language. They could have asked Rose for help but probably did not trust him, so they raided the estate of an Italian nobleman and kidnapped his American house guest, ordering him to write their ransom note. Since poor people seldom traveled farther than their feet could carry them, the bandits assumed the American, being in Sicily and staying with a nobleman, was wealthy. But the American insisted he was a struggling artist. One of the bandits, Giuseppe Esposito, put him to the test by ordering him to draw a portrait of him. The artist did such a good job on the portrait that Esposito fell in love with it, and even more in love with himself. Convinced the American was a genuine artist, the bandits put him to work on the ransom note, which Esposito ordered him to draft on the back of his portrait so the world could see what a handsome fellow he was; it did not occur to Esposito that the portrait could be used by police to identify him.

The ransom note was sent to the mother of John Rose. Because love sometimes has a spending limit, like a credit card, Mrs Rose did not pay the ransom. A second note was sent, but she still didn't pay. A third note contained one ear belonging to her son, but still no money was sent to secure his release. The fourth note contained John Rose's remaining ear and, according to some reports, the tip of his nose. At this point, Mrs Rose could either wait for enough parts to put her son back together at home, or pay the ransom. She finally coughed it up and John Rose was set free, as was the artist.

Following Rose's release, the Italian government gave in to British pressure and mobilized a strike force to hunt down the bandit gang responsible for his kidnapping. During a shootout, Italian soldiers killed nine members of the gang, including their leader, Leone. Esposito was wounded and arrested but escaped from prison shortly thereafter. With a steep reward on his head, he fled to America where we will be catching up with him shortly.*

The Rose ransom was said to have been paid through a mafia intermediary and it is quite possible that Rose's abductors, Leone and Esposito, were put up to the crime by the local mafia don who wished

---

* There are two accounts of Rose's treatment during his captivity. London newspapers claimed that Rose was well treated, while American newspapers had the bandits snipping off his ears; some journalists added his nose. Though it is difficult to find evidence one way or the other, the American press may have embellished the facts to sell newspapers, while the British press had just as much reason to hide certain facts, to avoid a public demand for a military invasion of the island and avert an international crisis. The perseverance with which the Italian government hunted down the gang, and the reward put on Esposito's head after he escaped from prison, even chasing him to America, seems more in line with injuries sustained as opposed to a happy farewell where Rose was granted one last look at Esposito's handsome face. Since not much changes in the world of primitive banditry, we may glean a clue as to what happened to Rose when John Paul Getty III was kidnapped in Italy ninety-seven years later. Getty was also held in a cave and his ear was cut off and sent to his family, with a promise that the other ear would follow if the ransom was not paid.

to muscle the mine owners, or force a desirous outcome over one problem or another. There is evidence that certain bandit gangs developed a working relationship with mafia families that sprung up across western Sicily, mostly in the rich mining and agricultural regions of Palermo, Trapani and Agrigento, and that kidnapping victims were often targeted for more than just money. Whether or not Leone and Esposito were put up to the deed by the local don, their actions would nonetheless drive the mine owners into the market for protection, which mafia bosses happily provided for a price. Besides mining camps, the endless rows of orange and lemon groves in and around Palermo needed the same security. Like mine owners, landowners were targeted by the mafia, which mastered what can be called a 'schizophrenic protection racket' in which the aggressor and the savior were one and the same; a mafia don would typically cause a problem for a landowner then offer to fix it for a price. In time, the local dons from each region controlled the entire infrastructure surrounding the mining industry and citrus market and 'advised' the landowners who to hire and who to use from their own vast network of haulers, buyers and agents. If a landowner did not comply with a polite request from their local don, buildings were vandalized, horses and cattle were rustled, and relatives were kidnapped, as was the case with John Rose. In one particular incident, the landowner insisted on hiring his own manager, as opposed to the man recommended by the local don; his chosen manager was quickly shot and killed but the mafia steered clear of killing the actual land baron. Why is obvious; bending a baron into shape was profitable, whereas deadly force would bury the wallet they were slyly

Picking lemons in a grove located near Palermo, Sicily.

picking. Would the mafia cross that line? We'll soon see as we encounter Emanuele Notarbartolo, who fearlessly challenged the mafia in Palermo.

The house of Notarbartolo dated back to the Holy Roman Empire. By the nineteenth century, members of the Notarbartolo family had been awarded fiefdoms and titles for over a thousand years, and at times resided in castles.

The Marquis Emanuele Notarbartolo was a brave man who fought for Italian unification alongside Garibaldi. After unification, Notarbartolo was elected mayor of Palermo, leaving office in 1876, the same year John Rose was abducted. After his term as mayor, he became director-general of the Bank of Sicily while dedicating most of his personal time to raising his children and farming his 125-hectare estate, named Mendolilla.

Early on the morning of 1 February 1893, the robust 59-year-old traveled to the Sciara railway station in Palermo where he boarded a train and entered a first-class compartment. He hung up his hat and coat, then sat down and leaned back for a nap. When the train stopped at the Termini Imerese station, new passengers boarded the cars and the stationmaster, while making his rounds, noticed that Notarbartolo was still sleeping. The train left the station. Before the next stop, Notarbartolo was awakened by two men wearing dark coats and fedoras pulled low to their eyes. Minutes later, Notarbartolo's dead body was thrown from the train like a sack of potatoes with twenty-seven stab wounds. Like a scene from Agatha Christie's *Murder on the Orient Express*, Notarbartolo's killers had waited for the darkness of a tunnel between the Termini and Trabia stations to strike at their target, and tossed his body out while the train was moving. His killers got off at the next stop as casually as travelers who are running ahead of schedule.

Emanuele Notarbartolo murdered by assassins in his train compartment.

Notarbartolo's body was recovered near the tracks and identified. Besides multiple stab wounds in his flesh, there were slash marks across his hands, evidence that he had desperately fought for his life. An examination of his private compartment confirmed the same; seats were slashed and the dead man's bloody palm prints were pressed against the window.

Notarbartolo was a war hero, a marquis, a mayor and a man known for his public service and integrity. Who killed him, and why? A train is not a big place and death by double daggers is not a quiet affair, but no one could identify his killers, who must have rubbed against other passengers as they squeezed through aisles, said a passing word or two to someone or another, had their tickets punched by the conductor, and had blood on their clothing when they exited the train. The lack of witnesses willing to come forward pointed in one direction – the mafia.

Police investigators ran into a brick wall. Where they did not run into a wall, they built one. One police inspector, who had submitted a personal request to lead the investigation, disposed of evidence at every chance he got. He also misled honest investigators, sending them in any direction except where the evidence led.

Emanuele Notarbartolo's loving son, Leopoldo, was an Italian naval officer who would one day attain the rank of admiral. Upset over the law's delay, he launched his own investigation in a daring attempt to bring his father's killers to justice. The young man tenaciously pored over his father's old files, banged on doors, followed up on countless leads, and even traveled to a Sicilian expatriate community in Tunisia, in search of clues. Over the next several years, Leopoldo pieced together what he believed to be the circumstances behind his father's death. The conspiracy he uncovered revealed a network of criminal connections that stretched from a bank's board of directors to a mob boss to a member of parliament.

Leery of the police, Leopoldo gathered up his evidence and visited his father's old friend Antonio Starabba, after Starabba became the prime minister of Italy. Like Emanuele Notarbartolo, Starabba was also a Sicilian nobleman and former mayor of Palermo whose official title was Marquis di Rudini. Leopoldo told Starabba what he had learned, knowing that Starabba, who sat in the nation's highest office, had the power to command a proper inquiry. When Leopoldo finally revealed to Starabba whom he believed to be the main culprit behind his father's murder, Starabba replied, 'Why don't you just hire some good mafioso to kill him for you?' The problems of Sicily, and how an outdated Sicilian mindset was already infecting the whole of Italy, cannot be summed up any better than by the prime minister's reply. Leopoldo did not heed Starabba's advice. Due to the young man's tenacity, the case came to trial under Starabba's successor, Prime Minister Pelloux. Pelloux had also been a friend of Emanuele Notarbartolo and it is likely that Leopoldo had visited Pelloux, as he had done Starabba, when Pelloux assumed office. Pelloux had the wherewithal to move the venue from Palermo to Milan where trial proceedings began on 11 November 1899, nearly seven years after Emanuele Notarbartolo had been thrown from a speeding train.

At trial, the evidence was revealed to be weak. The prosecutor dragged two men into court who worked on the train and accused both of conspiracy, insisting they must have at least seen the murder take place. The first to take the stand was Pancrazio Garufi, the train's brakeman. The prosecution contended that Garufi, who sat at the back of the last carriage, must have seen Notarbartolo's lifeless body fly through the air. Without Garufi's involvement, the prosecution claimed, the killers would not have had the confidence to toss the body from the train. Poor Garufi could have been looking in the opposite direction, reading, eating, picking his nose or sleeping, given the boring nature of his job between stops. He could have even seen Notarbartolo's body fly past him, then spent the rest of the ride convincing himself that he did not see what he had just seen, terrified for his own life. If Garufi knew something but kept it to himself, can we blame him? How much can the average railway worker assist with justice when a police investigator was caught hiding evidence and the prime minister of Italy recommended hiring a hitman?

The next man to take the stand was the conductor, Giuseppe Carollo. Surely, insisted the prosecution, since Carollo had to collect the assassins' tickets, he must have had a good look at them. But Carollo was of no help. His repeated denials made him look guilty to some; to others, he appeared plain terrified. Although Garufi and Carollo worked on the same train together and lived a stone's throw from one another, they denied even knowing each other, which likely meant that both men knew the drill.

After watching terrified men who wished they had never been called into a courtroom, the jury viewed a courageous young man approach the witness stand in naval uniform with the disciplined stride of an officer. Trained to be cool under fire, Leopoldo Notarbartolo held his chin high as he took a seat and waited to begin. He was only twenty-three years young when his father had been killed. He was now approaching thirty, and had dedicated much of his adult life to bringing his father's killers to justice. The Notarbartolo family crest was a lion and Leo the Lion was about to roar. In a deep voice, Leopoldo fired his first salvo at his father's killers: 'I believe that the murder was a vendetta and that the only man who hated my father is Commendatore Don Raffaele Palizzolo, the member of parliament. I accuse him of being the instigator of the crime.'

The courtroom gasped. Palizzolo was a long-standing member of the Italian parliament, known for campaigning while surrounded by mafiosos. He was also the man who Prime Minister Starabba had advised Leopoldo to whack. Like a medieval pope, Palizzolo sat up in bed each morning while receiving supplicants who bore him gifts in return for his generous favors; he was now being accused of murder.

After accusing Palizzolo, Leopoldo captivated the Milanese courtroom with a long story of how his father, Emanuele, had never been a team player in the Sicilian sense of the term. To start with, his father's estate, Mendolilla, had an abundance of water wells which were as valuable in Sicily then as oil wells are in Arabia today, but Emanuele refused to cede control of them to the mafia. And although Emanuele physically worked his own estate, unlike so many other nobles, he still needed to hire laborers but refused to employ anyone who was pushed on him by the local mafia don. After being elected mayor of Palermo in 1873, Emanuele took office with high hopes of weeding out corruption. He attempted a major clean-up of the Customs Bureau, which did not sit well with the mafia since tight customs meant less smuggling. He also struck a hard blow at MP Palizzolo after discovering that Palizzolo had siphoned money from a fund for the poor. Emanuele forced Palizzolo to repay the money. On top of the forced refund, the mere accusation of defrauding the poor smeared Palizzolo's reputation as a caring community leader.

Leopoldo believed that his father's actions against Palizzolo led to reprisals that predated his murder in 1893. In 1882, eleven years prior to his death, Emanuele Notarbartolo was abducted and held in a cave, and set free only after a fifty-thousand-lira ransom was paid. His kidnappers were later captured by the authorities, not far from Palizzolo's estate. This proximity was not legal evidence of Palizzolo's involvement in the conspiracy but everyone in Sicily understood the island's uncharted criminal jurisdictions; the kidnappers would not have acted unless their crime had been sanctioned by the local mafia don, who happened to have a very close relationship with Palizzolo. Though this and other circumstantial evidence pointed toward Palizzolo's involvement in the kidnapping, he was never officially charged with the crime.

After Emanuele Notarbartolo's release from captivity, the nobleman brushed himself off and went on with his life, though he must have known that the mafia's world is mired in messages; aside from reaping a ransom, his kidnappers were likely issuing a stern warning to leave Palizzolo alone. He did not heed the warning. In 1888, Palizzolo was voted onto the Bank of Sicily's board of directors and found himself elbow-to-elbow at a conference table with Notarbartolo, who was the bank's director-general. Once again, Notarbartolo sought to weed out corruption, this time inside the bank, and discovered widespread fraud that involved Palizzolo. Notarbartolo fired off a report to the government in Rome, demanding that they stand behind his efforts to clean up the bank. Instead, the government asked Notarbartolo to resign his position.

Once Notarbartolo was gone, it was like the teacher had left the classroom; the unruly kids, or board members, went berserk. Among a host of other crimes, the bank became involved in a scam to pump money into a firm, Navigazione Generale Italiana (NGI). By artificially inflating the stock price of NGI, Palizzolo and his cohorts helped the firm to secure government contracts, and received kickbacks in return for their help. At the same time, Palizzolo pushed through bank approvals for whatever NGI wanted, while he regularly loaned the bank's money to mafia associates who applied for credit in the names of fake people, dead people, and little children. By 1892, the government was finally preparing to crack down on the bank's nefarious practices by reappointing Notarbartolo to the director-general's chair. It was apparent to everyone, including Palizzolo, that Notarbartolo was being sent back to clean house. Something had to be done to stop him.

This dark tale was told by Leopoldo Notarbartolo as he seized upon this long-awaited public platform to present the findings of his independent investigation. But we all know how hard it is to bring a member of parliament to justice in any country, even today; imagine nineteenth-century Italy. Adding to the obvious difficulties, the allegations came from a grieving son rather than an official police investigator. Luckily for Leopoldo, he still had the backing of Prime Minister Pelloux, who surprised at least half of Italy when he responded to Leopoldo's testimony by rushing a vote through the Chamber of Deputies, removing Palizzolo's parliamentary immunity. Pelloux even cut off the telegraph wire between Rome and Palermo, preventing Palizzolo from getting wind of the vote and setting sail in that same wind. Unaware of the storm making its way from the mainland, Palizzolo was arrested that evening, bringing a halt to his forty-year political career.

While Palizzolo is left to prepare for his murder trial from a prison cell, let us explore the possibility that the conspiracy to murder Notarbartolo reached even higher than Palizzolo. Meet Ignazio Florio, the largest shareholder of NGI and one of the wealthiest men in all of Italy. So powerful that he had a mafia boss for a gardener, which is like having the Pope for a chauffeur.

Chapter 5
Illustrious Corpses

Johann Wolfgang von Goethe once said if he had to choose between order and justice, he would choose order. Sicily's land barons evidently concurred with Goethe and engaged in a Faustian relationship with mafia dons who measured out a formula of favors, threats and violence to ensure labor peace and optimum production while guaranteeing order and stability. Ignazio Florio, the richest man in all of Sicily, hired a gardener to plant vegetables, trim bushes and prune roses on his estate. This gardener, Francesco Noto, was also the local godfather.

The foundation of Ignazio Florio's fortune dates back to an earthquake that struck Calabria in 1783, forcing two brothers, Ignazio and Paolo Florio, to leave the mainland for Palermo, Sicily, where they opened a small spice shop. From this meager storefront they earned enough money to buy vineyards and produce Marsala wine. In time, they began mining sulfur, an essential ingredient for the production of paper, and started a tuna-processing plant, revolutionizing the fish-packing industry by preserving tuna in olive oil for the first time in the commercial market. They established a reputable steamship line, started an insurance firm, and bought or built a number of other profitable businesses. And it all began with an earthquake.

It took the family about a hundred years to build this empire – and one generation to destroy it. Just as it had begun with an earthquake, it ended with a tornado by the name of Ignazio Florio Jr, who made bad business decisions, took on too much debt, failed to diversify into emerging markets, squandered the family fortune and wiped out everything in his path, including, I am convinced, Emanuele Notarbartolo.

Born in 1869, Ignazio was just twenty-five years old when Notarbartolo was murdered. Two years earlier, he had inherited the largest fortune in Italy. Given the mafia's inseparable connection to the land in Sicily, it is likely that, along with the family fortune, Ignazio inherited some form of working relationship with the mafia. If he did not, then he established one with his 'gardener', Francesco Noto. Given

Ignazio Florio and family.

Noto's role as a gardener, we shall refer to the war that transpired under his leadership as Sicily's War of the Roses, which was fought between the House of Florio and the House of Whitaker, the latter being of English descent. (Both families attended Queen Victoria's funeral by royal invite.)

The Whitaker family arrived in Sicily around the same time as the Florio brothers who had traveled from Calabria. The Brits had a taste for Marsala wine and the Whitakers practically pioneered its production and export. The Florios entered the wine industry sometime later and became the Whitaker family's chief competition. Since the social arena can be just as competitive as the business world, Ignazio Florio's wife, Franca Florio, was in competition with Joshua Whitaker's wife, Euphrosyne 'Effie' Whitaker. The Whitakers had introduced British-style lawn parties to Palermo's high society and Effie was the reigning social queen. Her three private tennis courts were each named after a canto in Dante's *Divine Comedy*. But if you got stuck playing on *Campo Inferno*, it meant that Effie was unhappy with you, and you were essentially being told to go to hell. If the *Divine Comedy* courts were not pretentious enough, Effie also rode around in an open carriage with a parrot on her shoulder – a parrot, I might add, that pooped on a silver towel. Given the tennis courts and the parrot's poo-poo pad, we can imagine Franca Florio whispering behind Effie's back.

Franca Florio had an aristocratic title and a few lire when she married Ignazio, but nothing compared to the Florio fortune which allowed her to throw lavish parties and become a patron of the arts. While Franca and Effie were engaged in a tug of war over the tiara of high society, a far more dangerous undercurrent of hostility was brewing beneath the din of party laughter. One afternoon, the laughter abruptly stopped as Effie Whitaker watched her prized parrot plop to the ground, dead. It had been shot out of a tree during one of her lawn parties. The party pooper who had picked off the pampered parrot was Vincenzo Florio, privileged punk and younger brother to

Ignazio. Anyone who loves pets can easily imagine how incensed the Whitakers must have been over the parrot's senseless death, but what followed the parroticide was not revenge against Vincenzo. Instead, Effie Whitaker's ten-year-old daughter, Audrey, was kidnapped. I am fairly certain that something unrecorded happened between the parrot's death and Audrey's kidnapping; either the Whitakers struck back at the Florios and Audrey was a counterblow, or the Whitakers failed to strike back, revealing weakness, and emboldening the Florios to up the stakes, bringing the generations-old rivalry to a head. Whichever the case may be, we do know that Noto the gardener had arranged Audrey's kidnapping, and he would not have done so without Florio knowing about it, the same way we suspect that Raffaele Palizzolo was privy to the kidnapping of Emanuele Notarbartolo.

Though we do not know if little Audrey was also accustomed to pooping on silver towels, we can be sure that her captivity was not the indulged life she was used to. Luckily, her parents quickly forked over the ransom of 100,000 lire, and the little girl was freed. The Whitakers may have been doubly disgusted over the parrot and the kidnapping, but when questioned by the authorities, they denied the abduction had even taken place. The Brits were not managing the world's largest empire by accident; they knew how to survive in other people's backyards. Since the Whitakers did not squeal, it is here they will exit our story as we move over to the Florio estate.

Sometime after the Audrey matter had been put to rest, the Florio family awoke one morning to find that a number of valuables had been robbed from their house during the night. Florio did not report the crime to the police but went straight to his gardener, Noto, and asked what he planned to do about it. We can be sure Noto was embarrassed, and we might imagine that his first suspects were the Whitakers, but in Sicily, stealing from an estate had nothing to do with the estate owners and everything to do with their private protectors. Robbing or vandalizing a large estate that was already under a don's protection was considered an insult, known as a *sverge*, toward the don. Someone wanted Noto to lose face in the eyes of the wealthy family who buttered his bread. To maintain his role as the Florios' watchdog, Noto would have to avenge the *sverge*.

First, Noto figured out who had committed the crime. Although it had nothing to do with the Whitakers, it had something to do with his own mafia crew in relation to little Audrey's kidnapping. Two of the kidnappers, Giuseppe Caruso and Vincenzo Lo Porto, were disgruntled over their meager share of the ransom and robbed Florio's house to even up, and embarrass Noto in the process. Once Noto figured out who the house burglars were, he dished out more of the ransom money to Caruso and Lo Porto, which, Noto would have known, is a sure sign of weakness; a mafia don does not give money to men who steal from him: he kills them! But Noto needed to quickly recover Florio's possessions so he could regain his credibility within the Florio household. The valuables were returned to their proper places but face is much harder to recoup, and that takes violence. Noto was not done. Caruso and Lo Porto were asked by fellow thieves to take part in a heist. They agreed, and on the night of the heist, they showed up at the rendezvous and were riddled with bullets then dumped in a pit. For Noto to complete the act of saving face, Florio would have needed to know the fate of the men who had robbed his house. Any doubt that Florio knew what had happened to them evaporated when Lo Porto's hapless widow sought out Ignazio Florio's elderly mother, Baroness Giovanna d'Ondes, and asked her for financial help to raise her fatherless son. The Florio matriarch spat back, 'Don't waste my time, your husband was a thief.' If the baroness knew that Lo Porto had died for his thievery, so did her son, Ignazio.

Just as I am convinced that Ignazio Florio had knowledge of Lo Porto and Caruso's murders, I contend the same for Notarbartolo's murder. Florio was the biggest fish behind the Bank of Sicily scam which pumped up the stock value of his company, NGI. But although his name repeatedly popped up during the investigations into the bank fraud *and* the Notarbartolo murder, his immense wealth and power placed him beyond the reach of the law.

The eighteenth-century Danish-Norwegian poet Johan Herman Wessel may have unwittingly explained for us why Raffaele Palizzolo was in prison but Florio was not when he wrote the tale of 'The Blacksmith and the Baker'. The blacksmith murdered a man and everyone in his small town knew he was guilty. The judge demanded that justice be done, but since there was only one blacksmith in the town and his skills were needed, the townsfolk told the judge they had two bakers and could part with one. One of the bakers was charged with murder, the judge was content and the people went on with their lives. In our story, Ignazio Florio was the blacksmith; although he was in the process of losing his fortune, he was still the single wealthiest man in Sicily, employing over sixteen thousand people in and around Palermo, which the press referred to as Floriopolis. Raffaele Palizzolo was one of the bakers, or just another corrupt politician who could be sacrificed.

Ignazio Florio once took a trip abroad. When he returned home, his wife Franca found a pair of ladies' underwear in his luggage. He bought her a pearl necklace and she forgave him. It seems that as long as Ignazio allowed Franca to run around town with the checkbook, she did not care if he ran around the world with ladies' underwear on his head. The means by which Ignazio solved this domestic incident is a perfect example of how he escaped Sicilian justice; blood on his hands or underwear in his luggage, Ignazio's money had the power to blind. That is why Raffaele Palizzolo, and not Ignazio Florio, was the reputed kingfish of the Notarbartolo murder trial that was moved to a Bologna courtroom in September 1901.

Leading up to the trial, Florio tried to help Palizzolo from afar by funding a campaign to get him re-elected to parliament so the jailbird could wave his parliamentary immunity in the air with one hand and wave goodbye to the courtroom with the other. Even Florio's mother, Baroness d'Ondes, threw her weight behind the campaign, calling on her network of wealthy friends to donate. Florio money underwriting Palizzolo's campaign while Palizzolo was sitting in jail on a murder rap should increase our suspicion that Florio was an unindicted co-conspirator. Despite the vigorous effort to get Palizzolo re-elected, voters opted for his opponent and Palizzolo remained in custody. But he would not suffer alone; one of the hitmen who murdered Notarbartolo on the train was scheduled to join him.

Leopoldo's investigation uncovered one of his father's actual killers, a reputed member of the mafia and part-time 'lemon trader', Giuseppe Fontana. After learning Fontana's identity from Leopoldo, the police issued an arrest warrant for Fontana who went on the lam. He was not, as you might imagine, roughing it in a cave; he hid out on the estate of a nobleman who was also a member of parliament. After the nobleman dictated Fontana's terms of surrender to the police, Fontana was driven to prison in a fancy carriage, the era's equivalent of being dropped off in a limousine.

As part of their defense, Fontana and Palizzolo denied knowing one another despite the fact that Fontana was linked to Palizzolo's home turf, and also to the Notarbartolo kidnapping in 1882, which happened in the same area.

Palizzolo's trial defense was that he was the victim of a nasty frame-up by his political opponents. However false his claim, there is an underlying truth to his assertion in the sense that political backstabbing was the only means by which corrupt politicians were ever brought to justice, and sheer politics was the reason why Florio was not seated in the dock between Palizzolo and Fontana.

At trial, Fontana claimed to be away from the island when the murder took place. He was also able to turn the prosecution's words against them. The prosecutor had labeled Fontana a mafia don, but indicted him as a hitman. Fontana spotted this apparent discrepancy and argued that if he was a don, what was he doing on the train bludgeoning someone with a dagger? Surely, he would have dispatched his loyal henchmen to take care of it. Fontana's argument was valid, yet a Bolognese jury returned a guilty verdict for both Palizzolo and Fontana, who each received a thirty-two-year sentence. Done deal.

Not quite. The Italian judicial system had given the public justice; now it was left for things to quiet down before they could overturn the verdict. (This exact script would play out in major mafia trials for the next hundred years; the courts would give the public convictions then reverse the cases on appeal after the media coverage died down.) After six months, the appellate court in Rome threw out the guilty verdicts on a technicality. Palizzolo and Fontana were again presumed innocent, though left in jail to await a retrial. Some believed, in this particular case, that the guilty verdicts were vacated by the appellate court with national peace in mind after the politically minded Palizzolo ordered his Sicilian followers to condemn 'Bolognese justice'. With the help of Florio money and a Florio-owned newspaper, *L'Ora*, Palizzolo beat the regional drum and argued that the mafia was an invention by northern Italians, used to demean *all* Sicilians.*

* *L'Ora* was founded by the Florio family but the official owner of the newspaper was Carlo di Rudini, son of former prime minister Antonio Starabba, aka Marquis di Rudini, the man who had told Leopoldo Notarbartolo to hire a hitman. Given this business relationship, there is no wonder why Starabba was disinclined to pursue an official inquiry into a banking scam or a murder case which somehow involved the Florios, the largest shareholders of his son's newspaper. Time and again, we see that Franchetti and Sonnino's synopsis of widespread corruption was spot on.

When the upcoming retrial became a heated dispute between Sicily and Bologna, the trial venue was moved to Florence. As trial preparations were being made, Matteo Filippello, who was suspected of being Fontana's co-assassin, suddenly surfaced. It is unclear if Filippello would have been sitting at the defense table with Palizzolo and Fontana, or appearing as a witness for the prosecution. Nor did it matter. Shortly before the trial began, Filippello was found in a rented apartment hanging from a banister. His death was ruled a suicide but, in those days, forensic science was too immature to spot foul play. Filippello's passing was certainly timely for Palizzolo and Fontana, who did not need another witness *or* co-defendant. They were acquitted on 23 July 1904, eleven years, five months and twenty-two days since Notarbartolo had been brutally murdered in his train compartment. London's *Daily Express* summed up the prevailing sentiment with an article headline that read: 'Victory for the Mafia'.

It was nothing short of that.

The mafia was initially reluctant to kill noblemen, likely why Notarbartolo was at first kidnapped and let off with a warning. Only after his warning went unheeded did the mafia decide to eliminate him. Because the public's response was inadequate, Palizzolo and Fontana got away with murder, and the mafia would go on to kill or threaten nobles at will. As a result, Palermo's two hundred dukes, barons and princes would all bow before the authority of the mafia. Decades later, the many murders of prominent men would come to be known in Italy as *Cadaveri Eccelenti* – Illustrious Corpses; Notarbartolo was the first of many to come.

As for Leopoldo Notarbartolo, who valiantly challenged the mafia, his long investigation had bankrupted him and he was forced to sell his father's estate, Mendolilla. Raffaele Palizzolo wrote a book about his ordeal and made his way to the United States for a book tour. As for Fontana, he continued to kill for the mafia, racking up more hits than The Beatles until, like Giuseppe Esposito of the Leone gang who abducted John Rose, he became part of a larger trend of Italian criminals who fled to America where they were welcomed by newly established mafia families. Fontana ended up in New York while Esposito landed in New Orleans, the two cities where our history of the American mafia will begin.

Part Three

L'America

Chapter 6
The Mafia's Plymouth Rock

The mafia's arrival in America is deeply entwined with the Italian-American experience. In the 1860s, the same decade that Italy was unified and southern Italians felt increasingly estranged from their new nation's political process, the United States abolished slavery and suddenly needed low-wage workers to replace slave labor. The rapid industrial growth of the United States further increased the need for hard-working Italian immigrants. Between 1880 and 1930, over five million Italians crowded onto ships in search of a new life in America. Over 80 percent were from southern Italy, while 1.5 million of that southern exodus were from the island of Sicily. Most traveled across the ocean in third class, and many in steerage, the name for storage places near the steering mechanism of the ship, devoid of toilets, heat and ventilation. Besides the stink of body odor and human waste, diseases were rampant among passengers, some of whom died along the way.

Italian family lands on Ellis Island.

The rough Atlantic crossing was only the start of their journey. After arriving in New York Harbor, passengers were quarantined on an anchored ship for hours or days before being brought over to Ellis Island on a barge. (Before 1 January 1892, immigrants disembarked at Castle Garden, originally built as a fort on the southern tip of Manhattan.) Immigrants were led to the Registry Room where medical examiners performed a visual inspection and used a nub of chalk to draw a letter on their shirts and blouses; an L was for lameness, S for senility, CT for trachoma, and an X if the person was suspected of being a 'moron' – many received this mark simply because they could not speak English. Appalled by the looks of the people arriving at America's front door, psychologist Henry Herbert Goddard stationed two women beside the long queue, instructing them to count the number of immigrants who appeared dumb. Based on their tally, Goddard concluded that 79 percent of Italians were idiots who should be returned home. The dream that inspired them with the strength and courage to cross a dangerous ocean and take a faithful leap into the unknown had devolved into a nightmare as the rejects were sent back to sea with the shadow of Lady Liberty darkening their already somber faces; some jumped overboard and drowned.

Those who were admitted into the country had to find a job and a place to live. While speaking little to no English, and experiencing an overload of environmental and cultural changes, they gravitated toward their own kind for comfort, crowding New York's squalid tenements where they heard the language they knew, smelled the food they had always eaten, and commiserated with old friends and relatives who had arrived before them. Outside the tenements, their new world was a savage jungle where they were taken advantage of and referred to as wops, greaseballs, ginzos, geeps, goombahs, guidos, dagos, pizza-niggers, niggers-turned-inside-out and guineas (a name originally given to Blacks from what is now the Republic of Guinea, a country in West Africa; it was applied to Italian-Americans on account of their darker-than-white complexions. Although the disgraceful term 'pizza-nigger' was applied exclusively to Italian-Americans, it served as a side blow to African-Americans; as if the heavy burden of their long-endured direct discrimination was not enough to carry, African-Americans were now being denigrated by way of comparison to another group of undesirables. The same can be said of the term 'niggers-turned-inside-out'.) One day, mafia don Joe Bonanno would look back on his own migration, writing, 'The country needed our cheap labor, but other than that we didn't feel especially welcomed here. People tended to make fun of us, or to revile our customs, even the food we ate. We had only each other.' Mobster Vincent 'Jimmy Blue Eyes' Alo later recalled his youth in Manhattan, saying, 'Italians were considered dirt in those days . . . the scum of the earth.'

Immigrants who were unable to find work in New York spread out across the country. Some, in search of an honest day's pay, responded to faraway messages from relatives, trekking over mountains and crossing rivers to get there. Sometimes, the journey paid off, while other times they were duped by false rumors. One group of newly arrived immigrants was lured to Alabama after being told about a beautiful residential community that awaited them. Upon their arrival, they were told to clear a tract of land and build the community that supposedly awaited them.

Italians lynched in the South.

Searching for work was the way in which Italians blanketed the United States and built so many of the prosperous communities we know of today. In the southern United States, they were hired on old farms once fueled by slave labor, and they were prohibited, along with African-Americans, from occupying public spaces like beaches and parks. In fact, next to Blacks, Italians were the most frequently lynched ethnic group across the South and were hated by the Ku Klux Klan only second to Blacks. Discrimination against Italians became so bad that a cartoon in New Orleans showed a group of Italian immigrants packed into a cage as it was being lowered into a river. The cartoon's chilling caption read: 'The Way to Dispose of Them.'

Cartoon of Italian immigrants packed into a cage and drowned in a river.

Despite these hardships, law-abiding Italians gave their blood and sweat to build a young nation. But there was a breed of Sicilian who carried a disease endemic to his tiny island. The disease went undetected on Ellis Island and would fester in heavily populated cities, which are breeding grounds for all diseases. Carriers of this plague were men like Giuseppe Fontana and Giuseppe Esposito, who would spread it across the United States as they moved with groups of honest Italian job seekers. The author of the cruel cartoon noted above would argue that men afflicted with this criminal strain in their blood belonged in a cage. And for a brief time, the bandit Esposito was confined to one. But he escaped his prison cell and fled to America. His fellow criminals smuggled him aboard a ship and helped him around all the American checkpoints lawful Sicilians had to pass through. He then made his way from New York to New Orleans, Louisiana, where he changed his name and purchased a small fishing boat. Esposito did not choose New Orleans because he fancied Cajun cuisine, was into voodoo or wished to hide his handsome face with a mask at Mardi Gras; he was greeted by a network of Sicilian mafiosos who awaited his arrival.

New Orleans had been a magnet for pirates, smugglers and other criminals since before the American Revolution. The Spanish and French

Empires had, in turn, occupied Louisiana just as they had Sicily, and their long-distance rule left the doors open for corruption that reached pandemic levels, just as it did in Sicily.

After the United States acquired New Orleans from a cash-strapped Napoleon Bonaparte as part of the Louisiana Purchase in 1803, every form of criminal from around the country flocked there because of its widespread reputation for lawlessness. Drinking, gambling and murder were rampant, and crooked police and politicians were so derelict in their duties that the 'body of a murdered man . . . had lain in the street for three days, while the police took no notice'. The crime rate was so high that even criminals could not stand the anarchy. Attempts at organizing the underworld were made by gang leaders such as John Murrell, who was said to have four hundred murderers under his leadership, and Jean Lafitte, who commanded over a thousand criminals. But any effort to impose order over smuggling, gambling and bordellos never lasted long. That is, until the Sicilian mafia arrived.

The Mediterranean-like climate in Louisiana and its sugar and cotton plantations made it a preferable destination for southern Italians in search of work, while mafiosos considered it their Plymouth Rock, a ready-made criminal empire that need only be tamed. By all accounts, New Orleans was the first city to host a mafia family in the New World and even predated the mafia's appearance in New York. As early as March 1869, one newspaper wrote that New Orleans was infested with 'notorious Sicilian murderers, counterfeiters and burglars'.

When Giuseppe Esposito arrived in the city sometime in the late 1870s, he was greeted by a thriving underworld community. The fugitive who had kidnapped John Rose, survived a fierce gunfight with the Italian army, escaped prison like Papillon and sailed into the United States illegally was an instant legend among Sicilian criminals, making him a desirable recruit for the nascent New Orleans mafia.

Esposito was doing rather well for himself until the spring of 1881, when he got into a shouting match on the street with a hot-blooded Sicilian woman who finished up her rant by throwing a bottle at his head. A local reporter witnessed the commotion. Aside from getting a glimpse of what can be considered a typical Sicilian courting ritual that often ends with a passionate kiss, the reporter heard the woman call the man *bandito*. Although the reporter did not understand their language, he knew the meaning of this word and told Detective Dave Hennessy about the *bandito* he had seen arguing with a woman on a public street.

New Orleans Police Chief David Hennessy.

Born in 1857, Dave Hennessy was a tall, mustachioed 23-year-old detective who lived with his mother. His father was a thrice-wounded Civil War hero who became a policeman after the war. The only problem with Hennessy Sr's valiant war record was that he was a Union hero in a proud southern city. As such, he was never accepted by the people he served. In 1869, he was murdered during an argument in a coffee house. A murdered father who was disdained by his own community left a chip on young Dave Hennessy's shoulder. Eager to make a name for himself, Hennessy asked the reporter to point out the *bandito* he had seen arguing with a woman. The two men walked around town together until they spotted Esposito sitting in Raphael's Italian restaurant. Hennessy pulled aside the owner, Raphael, and asked him to nonchalantly listen in on Esposito's conversation. Raphael told Hennessy that he could not do that since Esposito spoke a different Italian dialect than him. This may have been true, but I am sure Raphael would have given Hennessy the same answer, or excuse, if it was not.

Next, Hennessy showed his ambition when he hired a professional artist to surveil Esposito and draw a sketch of him. (Given Esposito's vanity, he may have sat for the portrait, if asked.) Meanwhile, Hennessy figured out who he was tailing, and learned that there was a $5,000 reward being offered by the Italian government in return for Esposito's capture. The sketch of Esposito proved accurate enough for Hennessy to run it over to the Italian consulate, and receive, a few weeks later, confirmation that it was Esposito. The Italian government, however, did not trust a cop in his mid-twenties to make the arrest so they hired their own private detectives to take Esposito into custody. Hennessy wanted the collar and persuaded his superiors to push back. A deal was struck and a joint task force of four detectives that included Hennessy ambushed Esposito on the street and hustled him into a waiting carriage. By July, the bandit was transferred to

New York and extradited. Back in Italy, the recaptured fugitive was indicted for eighteen murders, convicted and sentenced to death, later reduced to life in prison. As for the young detective at the center of the arrest, a star was born.

Newspapers all over the United States and Europe painted Dave Hennessy as a fearless detective and a unique expert on the mafia, a secret society that was believed to exist but hardly anyone knew anything about. He was hailed as a 'model of American manhood', as citizens cheered him on as a future senator, maybe even a president. Unfortunately for Hennessy, his fifteen minutes of fame ended in shame.

New Orleans police chief Thomas Boylan was about to retire from his post. The young Hennessy felt he deserved the old veteran's job, especially after all the fanfare that surrounded him following Esposito's capture. But a politically connected man by the name of Thomas Devereaux also wanted the chief's job. The fact that Devereaux could even be considered for the position speaks volumes about the corruption inside the New Orleans Police Department. Five years earlier, Devereaux was vying for the same spot with Richard Harris. Both men knew the chief's job was a ticket to wealth since a built-in system of graft was inherited with the desk; the city's numerous casinos and bordellos all bribed the police department to permit them to operate, and the envelopes trickled upward.

Devereaux and Harris's rivalry took a dangerous turn when someone fired a bullet at Devereaux. The bullet missed and although Devereaux did not see who shot at him, he suspected Harris and felt strongly enough about his hunch to put a bullet in the back of Harris's head. Devereaux was apprehended near the crime scene. He beat the case, but lost his job with the police department. Not because he had been arrested for murder, but because the politicians who empowered him were swept from office; the flotsam went out with the tide.

That was 1876. By 1881, Devereaux's tide was rising again, just as Police Chief Boylan was planning to retire. This time, Hennessy stood in Devereaux's way. The stage was set for another showdown. Hennessy knew that Devereaux had murdered Richard Harris over the same job, so he assumed his own life was now in jeopardy and decided to strike first. To help him out, Dave Hennessy recruited his cousin, Mike Hennessy, a former cab driver who also became a detective. Early one morning, the cousins wandered the streets in search of Devereaux. When they spotted him standing inside the front window of an office, Mike drew his gun and opened fire, shattering the glass. As witnesses ducked and dove for cover, the cool Devereaux returned fire, dropping Mike who fell to the ground with a bullet lodged in his neck. As Devereaux took aim to finish Mike off, Dave slipped into the office through a side door and fired a bullet into the back of Devereaux's head. He then helped Mike into a passing cab and they fled the scene.

Despite the fact that most of the public agreed with the *Daily States*, which reported that it was a 'deliberate and bloody assassination', the Hennessys beat the rap, but were booted from the police force. Mike migrated to Houston, Texas, where he was shot to death in a fight, while Dave went to work for a private detective agency. Some years passed until, in a peculiar turn of events, John Shakspeare (sometimes spelled Shakespeare) was re-elected mayor of New Orleans in May 1888 and appointed Devereaux's killer, Dave Hennessy, as the new police chief. New Orleans was starting to make Sicily look like Tibet during prayer time.

As the new police chief, envelopes from payoffs across the city landed on Hennessy's desk and he dutifully greased the politicians, like Shakspeare, who kept him in office. His only problem was the New Orleans mafia, who had their own laws. By the time Hennessy became chief, over a hundred murders in and around the city had been attributed to Sicilian vendettas. Sometimes only the heads and torsos of victims were found. But as gruesome as the homicides were, the Sicilians only killed each other; surely, they would never kill a cop? Unless, that is, the cop crossed the line and became too involved in their affairs.

Back in the spring of 1869, a handful of criminals were driven from Palermo and found their way to New Orleans amidst a flood of Sicilian immigrants. They assembled a borgata called the Stoppagherra (sometimes spelled Stuppagghieri or Stoppaglieri), commonly referred to as the Stoppers. In the autumn of that same year, the Stoppers found themselves involved in a power struggle with a borgata named the Giardinieri, commonly known as the Gardeners, which was headed by Charles Matranga. Matranga built up an army of several hundred soldiers, presenting the Stoppers, headed by Joseph Provenzano, with a serious problem. (After Giuseppe Esposito was arrested, some members of the New Orleans Italian community tried to help him fight extradition. Esposito's most fervent supporter was Provenzano, who falsely claimed that Esposito was living in New Orleans during the time his alleged crimes had been committed in Sicily. This false alibi placed Esposito and Provenzano in cahoots. It seems that Provenzano wanted the tough and fearless Esposito in his borgata to help him battle Matranga.)

With an army of sworn killers behind him, Matranga swallowed up most of the city's illegal rackets before setting his eyes on the docks, which belonged to Provenzano. Joseph Provenzano and his brothers, Vincent, George and Peter, owned a stevedore company and maintained a monopoly on the waterfront, unloading fruit and vegetable shipments from South and Central America destined for New Orleans's French Market (which was taken over by Sicilians) and other produce markets across the country. Matranga knew that whoever controlled the stevedores controlled the entire industry, since a delay at the docks could suffocate the market by allowing quickly perishable fruit and vegetables to rot. But Provenzano was not so easy to push aside. He employed hundreds of Italian laborers, and was revered by the Italian community which constituted a large voting bloc, giving Provenzano political power and access to New Orleans's ruling class.*

---

* Because the citrus groves in Sicily had been a favorite mark for the mafia, mafiosos arrived in New Orleans already masters at dominating the fruit market from every imaginable angle. Maintaining control of New Orleans's fruit and vegetable market along with its loading docks was no different from controlling a citrus grove, sulfur mine or vineyard in Sicily. And because New Orleans also received shiploads of citrus from Sicily, we can reasonably conclude that fugitive mafiosos sometimes rode in with the bushels. There is another reason the mafia was able to organize the docks so well, and it is a tragic irony of the Italian-American experience. Italians were hired for their tireless work ethic; and because management preferred to hire Italians above anyone else, many ports across the country were dominated by them. This, in turn, paved the way for Italian organizers to unite the labor force, and exert total control over shipping and commodities. One New York official said of the Italian immigrant worker, 'We can't get along without the Italians', while a diplomat noted that 'the Italian immigrant ... is a human production machine'. Not surprisingly, the largest labor racketeering opportunities for the mafia stemmed from the indispensability of this Italian machine. As for the smooth relationship between labor racketeer and laborer, we can attribute that to the Sicilian peasants' centuries-long acquaintance with the *gabellotto*. Just as adolescent America was in desperate need of Italian immigrant workers, the country also benefitted from the mafiosos who organized and controlled them. It may never be said that the mafia played a positive role in America's formative years, but it can be argued that it was perhaps, at times, a necessary one, just as Georg Friedrich Hegel speaks of selfish men who unwittingly serve history's purpose.

Matranga's men launched attacks on Provenzano's stevedores, who were beaten, stabbed and shot, while Matranga sent word to the shipping companies that the Provenzanos were out and the Matrangas were in. At some point, Provenzano realized he was outnumbered and conceded defeat; he left the docks and opened a grocery business. But Matranga wanted that, too, leaving Provenzano no means of survival and forcing him to go to war. When word of an impending mob war reached Police Chief Hennessy sometime in the spring of 1890, Hennessy offered to mediate a sit-down between Matranga and Provenzano. At the sit, the men aired out their grievances before Hennessy insisted they shake hands and make peace. This peculiar effort from a police chief would have been extremely odd, except in New Orleans where even the top cop once beat a murder rap. The men shook hands and Hennessy may have applauded his own agility after crossing into the underworld and averting a mafia war, but his applause was short-lived.

On the evening of 6 May, a horse-drawn carriage carrying Matranga's stevedores was ambushed while the men were on their way home from the docks. Of the six men in the carriage, three were wounded by gunfire, including Charles Matranga's brother, Anthony, whose leg was blown off. Hennessy showed up at the crime scene, enraged. He felt duped by Matranga and Provenzano's phony handshake and ordered the arrests of a dozen Provenzano mafiosos suspected of ambushing the Matranga crew. While the Provenzano crew awaited trial, seven defendants were let off for lack of evidence. The other five went to trial, including Joseph Provenzano. By the time closing arguments were heard, it was apparent to just about everyone in the courtroom that the police had thrown the case. Rumors circulated that Hennessy had ordered his underlings to 'get them off'. Many accused Hennessy and Provenzano of being business partners in a bordello, the Red Lantern, which catered to the wealthy. This crooked relationship would, in part, explain why Hennessy had called the sit; he had a personal investment in Provenzano's safety. But if Hennessy wanted to save Provenzano and his crew at trial, why had he arrested them in the first place? It seems Hennessy was truly angered with his business partner's duplicity, while also under public and political pressure to make an arrest. Despite the police officers' poor performances on the witness stand, the jury returned guilty verdicts for all the defendants.

Though prosecutors were satisfied with the convictions, rumors that the men in blue had tried to help the men in black persisted until the court was forced to convene a special grand jury. Not surprisingly, the investigation went nowhere, and although the public may have been placated, Don Charles Matranga was not. Provenzano and Hennessy's alliance, exposed at both the sit-down and the trial, presented Matranga with a far more formidable foe than the Provenzano–Esposito alliance that ended when the latter was extradited. Matranga did, however, receive unwitting assistance from a judge who sentenced Provenzano and his crew to life in prison.

Matranga was now the undisputed mafia don of New Orleans, with complete control over the waterfront, the French Market and any other rackets he wanted to nurture or usurp. But his victory celebration did not last long. A month after the Provenzano crew were convicted, the same trial judge, the Honorable Joshua Baker, vacated the life sentences and granted all of the defendants a new trial. Fresh rumors began to circulate, this time that the judge had been bribed. Newspapers speculated as to the possibility of a hidden hand working to free the Provenzanos.

Matranga may not have read the newspapers but he could read the writing on the wall; the fix was in and everyone seemed to be in on it, except him. If he sat back and did nothing, the Provenzanos would likely return to the streets and reclaim the docks with the help of the city's police chief who was cozy with the mayor. Matranga needed to put a stop to this all-powerful alliance before it destroyed him. He could have ordered a hit on the Provenzano crew or at least clipped Joseph Provenzano after his release from prison. With over a hundred murders attributed to the mafia, it was clear the city was not overly concerned with Italians killing each other. Instead, Matranga, whose greed and ambition started this whole affair, doubled down with a dose of stupidity and marked the wrong man for death – Police Chief Dave Hennessy.

Chapter 7
Dagos Did It

Chief Dave Hennessy had remained in the background during the first Provenzano trial while directing his officers to muddy up the case. Now, rumor had it that he would assume center stage at the scheduled retrial and offer direct testimony on behalf of Joseph Provenzano. When reporters questioned Hennessy about these rumors, he did not confirm or deny them. By choosing Provenzano over Matranga, Hennessy was sending a clear message to the mafia that he was the highest authority in New Orleans, and, as such, he would hand-pick the head of the Italian underworld, which one report estimated at over a thousand men.

Hennessy began to receive death threats but the tough cop, who had blown Devereaux's brains out, told people, 'The mafia doesn't scare me!' The threats did, however, concern Mayor Shakspeare, who reached out to the Boylan Private Detective Agency for help.* The agency assigned Captain William 'Billy' O'Connor to shadow the young police chief. One dark, rainy evening, O'Connor and Hennessy left police headquarters and stopped for a dozen oysters before continuing on to the chief's house. Partway there, O'Connor said goodnight, allowing the chief to walk the final two blocks to his house, alone. It is unclear why O'Connor, who was paid to protect the chief, would abandon him for the final stretch, which is the most dangerous part of the route since ambushes are usually set up where people are known to come and go.

Holding an umbrella against the rain, Hennessy walked toward his house where he still lived with his widowed mother. He was approximately fifty feet away from his front door when someone whistled and the light rain was turned into a heavy hail of gunfire as five assassins

---

* Former police chief Thomas Boylan owned a private detective agency with Mike Farrell. The agency employed some 250 officers. When Farrell died an 'untimely death', Boylan had the agency to himself, and renamed it the Boylan Private Detective Agency.

with sawed-off shotguns appeared out of the darkness and fired at Hennessy. Slugs tore into his flesh, breaking bones. The tough Hennessy somehow managed to return fire with his Colt revolver, scattering the hitmen into the night, before he collapsed on a doorstep and yelled, 'Oh Billy, Billy!' Billy O'Connor, who was close enough to hear the shotgun blasts and see flashes in the darkness, ran to the scene and found Hennessy a bloody mess. 'They have given it to me,' said Hennessy. 'And I gave them back the best I could.'

Chief Hennessy returns fire.

'Who gave it to you, Dave?' asked O'Connor.

Hennessy whispered a one-word reply that would cripple the New Orleans mafia in its infancy and result in the largest mass lynching in US history: 'Dagos.'

Chief Hennessy was rushed to Charity Hospital in a horse-drawn ambulance. A staff of interns cut away his coat and vest which had over a dozen bullet holes, then washed the blood off his body so surgeon J.D. Bloom could examine him. Hennessy's skin looked like a paper target at a shooting range with 'four ugly, gaping wounds . . . on the upper and lower chest regions'. One slug had settled near his heart while another had torn through his lungs. Dr Bloom could not do much but bandage Hennessy up and send for a priest.

Cops and reporters descended on the hospital where Dr Bloom confronted them with the harrowing news of Hennessy's life-threatening injuries. Officer Billy O'Connor told everyone present, including reporters, that Hennessy had blamed the shooting on the 'dagos'. Police Sergeant Richard Walsh arrived at the hospital, and, against Dr Bloom's advice, he entered Hennessy's room and asked him what had happened. Hennessy repeated to Walsh that, 'The dagos shot me', but failed to identify anyone or explain how he had reached this conclusion. 'Dago' was the derogatory name attributed to the entire Italian-American community of thirty thousand people in New Orleans. Was Hennessy shot by thirty thousand people? As Hennessy lay dying, surrounded by cops, city officials and the mayor, no one seems to have asked him if he had seen anyone he could identify as Italian or heard anyone speak or yell in Italian. Or did officials ask but choose to ignore his answers or omit them from the public record? When the official police recorder, David Hollander, asked the chief if he could make a statement for the record, Hennessy declined. When another cop, William Beanham, showed up at the hospital, he also asked Hennessy if he knew who had shot him. Yet again, there is no record of Hennessy answering Beanham's question with any specificity besides 'dagos'. Curiously, Hennessy told Beanham to 'take care of' money he had in his pants pocket; Beanham removed a 'neat roll of bills'.

A crowd gathered outside the hospital where they held an overnight vigil as police officers were ordered to 'prevent any Italians from leaving [New Orleans], and arrest all suspicious looking characters'. Countless innocent Italians were subjected to mass arrests, police brutality and unlawful home invasions. Any Italian who could not prove his whereabouts for the past twenty-four hours was punched, kicked, slapped and sent to the clink, including pre-teen boys. A number of Italians were beaten and arrested for the simple reason that they could not answer questions in English. When mothers and wives arrived at the station house to visit their jailed sons and husbands, they were assaulted by an angry crowd who forbade them passage into the building.

Chief Hennessy's grief-stricken mother arrived at her son's bedside. 'God be merciful,' she said, sobbing. 'I lose in you, Davey, a good boy . . . they have taken you from me.'

On Thursday morning, 16 October 1890, approximately nine hours after Chief Hennessy had been shot, his face twitched and he gurgled out his last breath. After he was pronounced dead, the angry crowd in front of the hospital turned raucous and swelled by the minute. With no evidence to support his claim, and before allowing the law to run its course, Mayor Shakspeare – who resembled the Bard only in name while endowed with a wretched mix of his most notorious characters – ordered his clerk to read a public statement, declaring Chief Hennessy the 'victim of Sicilian vengeance . . . Heretofore, those scoundrels have confined their murdering among themselves. None of them have ever been convicted because of the secrecy with which the crimes have been committed and the impossibility of getting evidence from people of their own race.'

A mayor's job is to quell a riot; Shakspeare was trying to start one when he said, 'We must teach these people a lesson they will not forget for all time.' He ordered his police to further 'scour the whole neighborhood [and] arrest every Italian you come across'.

Newspapers condemned 'the Dagos', a damning accusation that spared no man or woman of Italian descent, including many who were born in the United States. As telegrams expressing sympathy for the chief arrived from across the country and around the world, the press retold stories of the John Rose kidnapping while neglecting to mention Hennessy's assassination of Thomas Devereaux, his alleged obstruction of justice in the Provenzano trial, and accusations that he was partners with Provenzano in a high-end bordello while collecting a steady stream of graft from countless others. With the exception of a few publications, every newspaper joined in condemning the entire Italian-American community for executing a hero cop. The Sicilians were referred to in the *Times-Picayune* as 'oath-bound assassins', and echoes of Cesare Lombroso, who had once measured the skulls of Italian criminals, could be heard when the *New Orleans Times-Democrat* wrote: 'The little jail was crowded with Sicilians whose low, receding foreheads, repulsive countenances and slovenly attire, proclaimed their brutal natures.' Accusatory articles were not confined to America's southern publications. The *Baltimore News* wrote: 'The disposition to assassinate in revenge for a fancied wrong is a marked trait in the character of this impulsive and inexorable race.' *Harper's Weekly* described the suspects as belonging to a 'murderous society'. Everywhere Italian-Americans went, they were accosted in the street, often with the derisive taunt, 'Who killa de chief?'

Several Italian men were arrested with concealed handguns, and a sawed-off shotgun was found near the crime scene. Known as a *lupara*, the weapon had a retractable stock so it could be folded like a pocketknife and hidden under an overcoat; it was said to be a favorite weapon of the New Orleans mafia. Initially, five suspects were charged with murder and held without bail at the local jail. For their own safety, they were loaded into a mule-drawn paddy wagon and transported to Parish Prison, where thicker walls and stronger bars provided a better fortress against a riotous assault from a rowdy crowd that was calling for street justice. Parish Prison's warden, Lemuel Davis, armed his guards and told them to prepare for a siege.

Mayor Shakspeare appointed a Committee of Fifty to investigate Chief Hennessy's death, a sham investigative body more akin to an instrument of terror, like Robespierre's Committee of Public Safety. The group was a who's who of New Orleans high society without a single Italian, and, of course, no Blacks, who were known to be sympathetic to Italians. Since wealthy men think in terms of money and it pains them to spend their own, the committee voted themselves a hefty budget to be drawn from the city's coffers and used for expenses. They rented offices in the cotton-exchange building where they decided to keep their work secret. At least one newspaper wondered why the mayor chose a 'hothead' like Edgar Farrar to chair the group, but it soon became apparent that a hothead was exactly what the mayor wanted. While Farrar claimed the committee was formed to repress violence, he began his new task by sending a harsh open letter to the entire Italian-American community, demanding they help with the investigation of 'Stiletto societies in this city . . . We want you to come forward and give us all the assistance and all the information in your power. Send us the names and history . . . of every bad man, every criminal and every suspected person of your race in this city . . . vendettas must cease and assassinations must stop. To these things we intend to put an end, peaceably and lawfully if we can, violently and summarily if we must.' The message was clear: help us solve this crime or your entire community should brace itself for indiscriminate violence. As a result of this open threat, Italians were afraid to walk the streets. Most stayed inside their homes, and with no Italians working, New Orleans came to a standstill.

Chief Hennessy was given an elaborate funeral with full honors. His body lay in state at City Hall, where the body of Confederate president Jefferson Davis had lain in repose a year earlier. Thousands of mourners lined the streets to watch his casket pass, preceded by a riderless horse. I do not know why but Italians love wakes and funerals, so they must have regretted having to miss this one, except, that is, certain members of the Provenzano clan who were not in jail; they rode in the eighth carriage of the long procession.

The jailed Joseph Provenzano played the Hennessy hit like a flute, yelling to reporters from the barred window of his cell that Charles Matranga had ordered the hit. He called the crime cowardly and deserving of a lynch mob. 'We were shocked to hear of the chief's death Thursday morning,' said Provenzano, 'we knew him well, were friends and he was one of our witnesses.' He went on to say that Matranga was head of the Stoppers, not him, and that the 'Mafia Society', which murdered two of his other witnesses, existed in major cities all over the country.

The Committee of Fifty continued to investigate Hennessy's death as the police pounded the pavement. Fourteen more suspects were added to the original five, and all were indicted by a grand jury, nine for murder and ten as accessories to the crime. The indictment included a fourteen-year-old boy who was said to have signaled the hitmen with a 'peculiar whistle'.

The prosecution's case centered around a shanty located directly across the street from Hennessy's house. Since the hitmen seemed to have appeared out of nowhere, police surmised that they were hiding inside this shanty, lying in wait for the unsuspecting police chief to make his way home. A poor Italian cobbler, Pietro Monasterio, lived in the shanty and the police assumed the hitmen would have needed Monasterio's permission to use his one-room home. But the law required more than a hunch to charge Monasterio as an accessory to murder, so the cops claimed that the soles of his muddy boots fit perfectly into boot prints left in the dried mud on the street outside his shanty. Let us assume the prints were a perfect match. Is it not appropriate for a man's

Pietro Monasterio's shanty (ramshackle structure with awning) where hitmen were suspected of hiding.

boot prints to be outside of his home? Or did the police think that Monasterio flew, like Peter Pan, into his house every night? This allegation against Monasterio was further debunked by a witness who saw Monasterio standing on the street in his underwear, only minutes after the shooting, yelling for someone to help the chief. Unlike movies and television, hitmen do not dress up to the nines for a hit, but they certainly do not go in their undies either, then decide to help the man they had just tried to knock off. The police were apparently grasping at straws as they tried to answer the public's cry for justice.

As for some of the other men who were charged, Antonio Marchese and his fourteen-year-old son Osperi (the alleged whistler) were friends with Monasterio and visited his shanty every now and then. They were said to be seen in the area on the night of the murder. Bastian Incardona 'looked suspicious' and had a criminal record; he also lived in an apartment above Charles Matranga. This connection to a mob boss made him appear guilty of something, but a closer look at Incardona revealed that he was a 25-year-old gofer for Matranga who had no other place to live; he cleaned Matranga's house and took care of his horse in return for room and board. Manuel Polizzi was identified by a cop who claimed he had seen him fleeing the crime scene. Antonio Bagnetto was picked up with a gun and told the cop who had stopped him that he could keep the weapon if he let him go. This would make Bagnetto a fool, perhaps a frightened fool, and also guilty of bribery, but not necessarily guilty of murder; he was on the indictment. Antonio Scaffidi, who was an associate of Charles Matranga, fit the description of a man seen by neighbors. Scaffidi also fit the description of ten thousand Italian males in New Orleans.

Another co-defendant was Joseph Macheca, who lived in a mansion on Bourbon Street. Macheca was one of the wealthiest businessmen in New Orleans, which set him apart from the poorer ragamuffins on the indictment. Macheca's fleet of steamships transported fruit from Latin America to New Orleans and his business was dependent on stevedores, which placed him at the center of the waterfront feud between Matranga and Provenzano. Macheca had originally used Provenzano's stevedores to unload his ships, but after Matranga took over the docks, Macheca had no choice but to shift his business over to Matranga. Being a business associate of Matranga was not enough to slap Macheca with a murder charge, but his alibi sounded shady. On the night of Hennessy's murder, Macheca and Matranga had attended the theatre together accompanied by a small entourage of hangers-on. Several witnesses saw the men in attendance and believed they had gone out of their way to make themselves seen and heard. Following the performance, Macheca went to an after-hours party at a swanky bordello where the madam, Fanny Decker, told Macheca about the attempt on Chief Hennessy's life. Macheca is said to have replied, 'I'm glad he's shot.' This cold comment does not prove complicity but Macheca had gone a step further, badmouthing Hennessy all over town in the days and weeks leading up to the murder. One policeman, Officer Cenance, claimed that Macheca was so incensed about Chief Hennessy's open endorsement of Provenzano that Macheca blatantly told Cenance that he had the power to put Hennessy in a box. Macheca later claimed to have meant he had the power to corner Hennessy with damning information, which is consistent with the expression, but some thought it was street slang for a coffin. The police also linked Macheca to Monasterio's shanty where the hitmen had supposedly hidden; Macheca was said to have paid the rent on behalf of Monasterio. When Macheca was arrested, reporters asked him if he had been planning to leave town. He replied that he had 'no intention of escaping, for if he wanted to, he could have left on one of his steamers'. He should have.

Don Charles Matranga was also arrested. Although there was no evidence against him, you cannot prosecute a mafia trial without a genuine mobster in the dock, and a don is great for headlines, which District Attorney Charles Luzenberg needed to compensate for a weak case. Luzenberg eventually narrowed the roster to nine defendants, severing the others from the indictment before trial.*

The nine defendants were as follows: Charles Matranga, Joseph Macheca, Pietro Monasterio, both Marcheses (father and son), Antonio Scaffidi, Antonio Bagnetto, Bastian Incardona and Manuel Polizzi. Pretrial accommodations inside Parish Prison are revealing with regard to the defendants' financial status. Matranga, Macheca and a couple of others had a sort of *Goodfellas* prison arrangement in which they paid extra money for better living conditions and enjoyed feasts ordered from local restaurants. Given my own experience inside

* In an interesting twist, Luzenberg had been the judge who presided over the murder trial of Dave Hennessy for the killing of Thomas Devereaux. Joshua Baker, who was on the prosecution team that attempted to convict Hennessy at that same trial, was now Judge Baker, presiding over this trial, in which Luzenberg was the prosecutor. Musical chairs.

prison, I would lean toward these privileged individuals being the official mobsters of the lot, Macheca being the possible exception but wealthy enough to join the clique and enjoy their protection in return for footing the bill. Some of the other co-defendants, all of whom were subjected to inhumane prison conditions, complained of being harassed and assaulted by other inmates. Their cowardly complaints and inability to defend themselves heightens my strong doubts that they were mobsters or capable of murder. Bitching to prison authorities is, by prison rules, equal to squealing, and not fighting back is spineless; both would fly in the face of *omertà*. Based on the above, the real mobsters were the guys feasting upstairs, as opposed to the schleps eating shit, from people and off plates, downstairs.

As if being regularly assaulted inside the prison was not enough cruelty for the poorer defendants to endure, one day a man by the name of Thomas Duffy showed up at the prison. Duffy told the guards that he may be able to identify Antonio Scaffidi as one of the gunmen who had shot the chief, and would like to have a better look at him. Duffy was a 29-year-old newsboy which offers us a glimpse into his mentality, only to be outdone by a thirty-year-old with a lemonade stand. When the guards returned to the visiting room with Scaffidi, Duffy drew a handgun and shot him in the neck (he was likely aiming for the head or the heart). Incredibly, Scaffidi was wounded but lived. Duffy was arrested on the spot but the judge treated him lightly, sentencing him to a mere six months in jail. Had Duffy's act of vigilantism been severely punished, the city might have avoided the carnage that was about to happen.

After Chief Hennessy had been killed, Detective William Pinkerton, founder of the famous Pinkerton Detective Agency, shot off a letter to Mayor Shakspeare which read, in part, 'I will do everything in my power to bring this murderer to justice, placing my whole agency at your call.' While the prisoners awaited trial, the Committee of Fifty took Pinkerton up on his offer. Pinkerton hatched a plan to get one of his undercover agents, Frank DiMaio, locked up inside Parish Prison under the false name of Antonio Ruggiero, an identity taken from a bandit serving time in an Italian prison. DiMaio's plan was to gain the prisoners' trust before attempting to glean incriminating evidence. But DiMaio's cover was quickly blown; on the very first night of his incarceration, DiMaio was lying on a bunk in a dark cell when he heard one prisoner tell another to beware of an informant who had just arrived at the prison. Instead of abandoning his mission, DiMaio homed in on Manuel Polizzi, who suffered from a mental disorder that predated his arrest and had rapidly deteriorated under his present circumstances. Knowing Polizzi's mind was fragile, DiMaio taunted him, telling Polizzi that he had overheard his co-defendants planning to poison him. Pretending to spare him from this plot, DiMaio would smack food out of Polizzi's hands and spill his drinks on the floor, telling him they were mixed with arsenic and cyanide. He even detailed the slow and painful death Polizzi could expect from poison. Though the imbalanced Polizzi did not, or could not, offer up any useful information, he barely ate anymore and withered down to flesh and bone.

On the morning of 16 February 1891, the trial began. Charles Matranga and Joseph Macheca, the mafia don and the big businessman, both dressed the part. Antonio Scaffidi, who had recovered from his neck wound, dressed like a male fashion model posing for a retro cover of *Gentlemen's Quarterly*, with chest hairs sweeping over his open shirt collar. The rest looked like they were shot through a Salvation Army clothing box. The worst of the lot was Manuel Polizzi who, thanks to Frank DiMaio, had snapped altogether; he wore loud, loose-fitting striped pants, like a circus clown.

The courtroom was packed, with standing room only until a no-standing rule was enforced to alleviate some of the congestion. A disorderly crowd loitered outside. During the trial, Prosecutor Luzenberg brought in Hennessy's bloody clothes as evidence and spoke with great conviction in his voice but it was all a bluff to disguise his weak case. It soon surfaced that the prosecution witnesses, who had supposedly identified the defendants, did not do so by facial recognition but by their clothing. One evening, at the prompting of the defense attorneys, a sheriff brought the jurors to the crime scene. After walking around like amateur sleuths, the jurors found it impossible to identify their police escort who was standing only forty feet away. The nearest street lamp was 185 feet away from where Chief Hennessy had fallen. And rain on the night Hennessy was killed would have made the scene even murkier.

Back in the courtroom, the jury did not like that Billy O'Connor, the last man to speak with Hennessy before he was shot, and the first to speak with him afterward, was never called to the stand by the prosecution. Would O'Connor's story stand up under cross-examination?

Did he have any personal reasons to avoid the scrutiny of defense attorneys? Was O'Connor too dirty to wash up for a court appearance? O'Connor's early departure from Hennessy on the night he was killed was inexplicable and raised a few eyebrows. Instead of getting O'Connor, the jury was treated to a round of theatre when world-renowned prizefighter John L. Sullivan showed up at the trial as a celebrity spectator. The great bare-knuckle boxer was obviously not there to support the dagos accused of killing his fellow Irishman. To magnify his presence, Luzenberg seated Sullivan next to the jury box. The defense did, however, have its own entertainer in attendance; throughout the trial, Polizzi randomly stood up and screamed in Sicilian, and even tried to jump out of a window.

The defense attorneys, whom the newspapers claimed were paid for with mob money, were successful in repeatedly tripping up the state's witnesses; many retracted their earlier testimonies when faced with mounting contradictions. After Luzenberg wound up his case, Judge Baker ordered a not guilty verdict for Charles Matranga and the state forsook its case against Bastian Incardona, the young man who lived and worked on Matranga's property. Although Matranga was likely guilty of ordering the hit, no evidence whatsoever had been presented against either of these two defendants and it became abundantly clear that they were only there to bolster the public and prosecutorial claim that the murder was committed by the mafia. The state also failed to prove the existence of any 'vendetta society' or 'mafia society' which the newspapers continuously promised its readers. Still, Judge Baker's decision to release the high-profile Matranga was strange, especially given the heated climate, and leaves us to wonder if Matranga had found a back channel to the judge's quarters.

The case went to the jury on 12 March, and they reached a decision on the 13th. When Judge Baker was handed the verdict, he stared down at the paper for several minutes; the jury was unable to reach a verdict for Scaffidi, Monasterio and Polizzi, while the others were acquitted. When the verdict was read aloud, the courtroom spectators were frozen in a state of 'mute amazement', while even the defendants stared at each other in disbelief. The Italian community felt vindicated but their joy would not last long. We have no good reason to believe the jury had acted immorally, yet District Attorney Luzenberg proved to be a sore loser when he blurted out that the jurors had been bribed. Luzenberg's accusation rested on a brief sideshow in which

Don Matranga was indeed accused of hiring a dirty detective to bribe certain jurors, but the plot had fallen apart after it was exposed in open court, and the trial had resumed. Now, unhappy with the verdict and terrified of becoming the target of public condemnation, the cowardly Luzenberg screamed foul play, which shifted the public's anger away from himself.

Instead of freeing the acquitted defendants on the spot, Judge Baker ordered them all returned to Parish Prison, including Bastian Incardona and Charles Matranga. Baker claimed the need to hold them all on a related charge but the law did not support his claim. When Baker had declared a mistrial for Matranga, he must have thought that the public would have other chum to chew on, which would explain why he had stared down at the verdict, stunned, for several minutes. Now, he was faced with everyone going free and he feared the public's fury.

As word of the verdict spread, more and more citizens gathered outside the courthouse. Soon, the mob became more unruly than the first mob that swelled in front of the precinct when the Italian suspects were initially rounded up. At that point, the mob had demanded justice, which is a form of vengeance. Now, feeling that justice had eluded them, they wanted pure vengeance.

Chapter 8

Vengeance with the Swiftness of a Hawk

The morning after the verdict, the *Times-Democrat* ran the following advertisement signed by sixty-one of the city's elites:

ALL GOOD CITIZENS ARE INVITED TO ATTEND A MASS MEETING ON SATURDAY, MARCH 14, AT 10 O'CLOCK A.M., AT CLAY STATUE, TO TAKE STEPS TO REMEDY THE FAILURE OF JUSTICE IN THE HENNESSY CASE.

COME PREPARED FOR ACTION.

The Clay statue, located at the intersection of Canal and Royal Streets, was a public meeting place since 1859 when the statue was erected to honor the late US senator Henry Clay, known as the 'Great Compromiser', but any chance of compromise was as dead as Clay. On Saturday morning, some seven thousand citizens responded to the advertisement and crowded around the statue. Businesses throughout the city were closed so everyone could attend the rally, which was the brainchild of William Parkerson, a short, fat, balding, 35-year-old evil genius who was Mayor Shakspeare's political fixer and chief liaison between the mayor's office and the Committee of Fifty. Appointed head of 'a movement to correct the failure of justice', the politically minded Parkerson knew that popular support had the power to excuse murder, which he was bent on committing when he mounted the statue's pedestal and condemned the city's 'Mafia Society', telling the good citizens of New Orleans, 'When courts fail the people must act!' At the close of his speech, he asked them, 'Are you strong enough to do your duty?' The crowd screamed and hollered that they were.

Other speakers included Walter Denegre, who asked the crowd, 'I want to know whether or not you will assert your manhood.' In his speech, he accused some of the jurors of being bribed, to which

Lynch mob meets at the Clay Statue.

the crowd responded, 'They were bought with Dago money.' J.C. Wickliffe, an attorney and editor for the *New Orleans Delta*, also mounted the pedestal and told the crowd that good citizens were 'at the mercy of organized assassins and midnight murderers'. He asked, 'Shall the execrable Mafia be allowed to flourish in this city?' Wickliffe, who had been expelled from West Point Military Academy for 'lack of discipline', was well suited to lead an undisciplined mob that shouted, 'To the Parish Prison. Hang the Dago murderers.'

One perceptive journalist, who was present as an observer, later noted, 'There are always excitable speakers and hot-headed, noisy listeners in such assemblies, but there were hundreds who made no noise, and standing there grim and silent constituted the element in which the real danger lay.'

The mob headed for Parish Prison. Not since the South had declared secession had so many southern men marched through the streets with smiles on their faces and blood on their minds. Women waved handkerchiefs, excitedly cheering the men as they passed; this loud public approval from the opposite sex turned sheer madness into machoism. At Royal and Bienville Streets, a hand-picked 'execution squad', made up of about forty men dressed in frock coats and derby hats with double-barreled shotguns resting on their shoulders, took up in front of the mob. Two level-headed detectives, appalled by the scene, raced ahead of the crowd to warn Warden Lemuel Davis what was approaching. Davis heroically armed his men and ordered them to defend the prison from an imminent attack, while Sheriff Gabriel Villere pled for help from the military, to no avail. With each block, the mob swelled until some fifteen thousand people converged on the prison. Women leaned from windows with opera glasses while children cheered from rooftops. According to one report, 'Telephone poles, lamp posts, and every available tree held a bundle of human forms.'

William Parkerson approached a locked door and insisted that Warden Davis open the gates and throw his prisoners to the wolves. Speaking through an iron grate, Davis implored Parkerson to disperse the mob. An agitated Parkerson told Davis to open the damn door or he would dynamite it. Davis adamantly refused then ran off to unlock the cell doors of the Sicilian prisoners, telling them to hide as best they could. The prisoners asked Davis for guns to defend themselves but Davis denied their request. His high morals cut both ways; just as he refused to hand men over to their unlawful executioners, he would not arm prisoners against citizens. Warden Davis again urged the prisoners to hide while he and his men did their best to stave off an attack.

Beyond the prison walls, the mob cut down a telegraph pole and used it as a battering ram. Once the door was breached, Davis's guards lowered their guns and some handed them over to the invaders, one of whom told Davis, 'We want the dagos', and threatened to hang him, too, if he stood in their way. Davis's courage never wavered in the face of damning odds but his frightened guards told Parkerson that some of the wanted inmates were hiding in the women's section of the prison. Parkerson stationed a sentry at the door to keep out the angry crowd, ordered several men to surround the prison's perimeter so no Italians could escape, then sent his armed executioners inside to sniff out their prey. Knowing all was lost, Warden Davis pleaded with the executioners 'not to shoot indiscriminately'.

Rather curiously, the lynch mob's leader, William Parkerson, issued explicit orders not to harm Charles Matranga and Bastian Incardona, the two men whose cases had been dismissed by Judge Baker before the jury had returned a verdict. Why would Judge Baker and now William Parkerson let off Matranga, a bona fide mafia don and perhaps the only man of the entire lot who had the means and motive to murder Chief Hennessy? If the lynch mob's true goal was to right the verdict and stamp out the mafia in New Orleans, why tip-toe around the big boss?

The execution squad split up into groups. One hunting party ran off toward the women's section while two other parties scoured the men's section. Outside, the mob eagerly awaited the sound of gunfire. It took only a few minutes before several Sicilians were cornered in the women's yard; they were lined up against a wall and shot from a few yards away. Whoever did not immediately die had his brains blown out at point-blank range. More Sicilians were trapped in a corridor in the men's section; their heads were blown off by buckshot. Whether crammed under a staircase, squeezed into a barrel or packed into a dog house, Sicilian prisoners – some of whom did not even stand trial for the murder of Chief Hennessy – were forced from their inadequate hiding places, shot in their heads, and left to soak in pools of blood that oozed from their icily still or quivering bodies. Following each fusillade, cheers went up outside the prison walls as men doffed their hats, yelling, 'Death to the dagos.' When the mob was no longer satiated by sound effects, Parkerson threw some red meat to the dogs in the form of Antonio Bagnetto. Six white men and three Black men kicked and dragged the injured Bagnetto over to a tree where they strung him up. The mentally unfit Manuel Polizzi was the next appetizer on the menu. As the crowd passed Polizzi's body over their

Battering down the door of Parish Prison.

Sicilian prisoners dead in the yard.

heads, they tore off his clothes. A young boy scaled a lamppost and tied a cord around the top as the other end was tightened around Polizzi's neck. After Polizzi's naked body was raised like a flag, the mob pelted him with stones while men took target practice with shotguns, revolvers and old muskets, the bullets spinning his body around like a barber pole.

After the last Sicilian prisoner was murdered, Tom Duffy, the overgrown newsboy, helped several deputy sheriffs arrange the mutilated bodies for a public viewing. For five hours, thousands of people, including women and children, filed through a large room to view the glazed eyes and distorted faces of their victims, the exceptions being Bagnetto and Polizzi, who were left suspended like crucified Roman enemies left to hang along the Appian Way as a warning to others.

When done for the day, William Parkerson climbed atop an overturned streetcar as the crowd cheered and yelled, 'God bless you!' Parkerson replied, 'God bless you and the community.' Now that everyone was blessed, the blessed mob was told by their blessed instigator, 'You have acted like men: now, go home like men.'

Newspapers condemned not the murderous mob, but the evil dagos. The *New York Times* ran a headline: 'Chief Hennessy Avenged; Eleven of His Italian Assassins Lynched by Mob'. The *Washington Post* expressed similar sentiments. *Leslie's Weekly* recognized the possibility of the victims not being true members of the mafia but still excused the lynch mob, writing, 'No reasonable, intelligent, and honest person in the United States regrets the death of the eleven Sicilian prisoners in the New Orleans jail.' Even future US president Theodore Roosevelt weighed in when he wrote in a letter to his sister, Anna Roosevelt Cowles, 'Personally I think [the lynchings] rather a good thing.'

When Mayor Shakspeare was asked by the *St. Louis Post-Dispatch* if he regretted the lynchings, he boldly replied, 'No, sir, I am an American citizen, and I am not afraid of the devil. These men deserved hanging . . . They were punished by lawful means. The men who did it were all peaceable and law abiding. The Italians had taken the law into their own hands and we had to do the same.' When William Parkerson was cornered by a reporter who asked him uncomfortable questions, Parkerson blamed everything on the mob, describing them as if they were incognitive sharks who could not be stopped from biting. 'After the first taste of blood,' he said, 'it was impossible to keep them back.' He made no mention of the chum he threw from the Clay statue. When asked about the cowardice of shooting outnumbered, unarmed men, Parkerson responded that his executioners saw the Italians not as men, but as 'reptiles'.

The international community was not as cold; the Italian press was outraged as were journalists from other European nations, summed up best by a dispatch from London that captured the American spirit rather precisely: 'Italy's indignation is shared by the whole civilized world. In nearly all such cases in America the disease, corruption, is at the root of the evil. The Americans are at once the most patient and the most impatient people in the world, and when they have grown tired of any grievance they move to their vengeance with the swiftness of a hawk.'

Some of the murdered Sicilians were paupers who were buried in Potter's Field, an unlikely burial site for authentic mobsters, confirming my earlier suspicion that at least the poorer defendants were not sworn members of organized crime. Note that Charles Matranga was never touched, just as William Parkerson had ordered. Public opinion would never again offer the city this ideal opportunity to rid itself of a mafia don, yet the leaders of the lynch mob failed to seize it, despite the crowd's demand for Matranga's head. When Parkerson had announced the names of those who had been killed, a hundred voices yelled back, 'Where is Charles Matranga?'

'I did not want him touched,' said Parkerson. 'The judge ordered him acquitted, and it was proper that he should not be hurt.'

It seems Matranga, who was first let off in the courtroom, then spared from execution, was aligned with men in high places who had more to gain by saving his hide. Were these men also involved in Chief Hennessy's death? Hennessy had one of the most desirable jobs in New Orleans, and just as Hennessy had been closely aligned with Joseph Provenzano, whoever coveted Hennessy's job may have spotted an accomplice in Matranga. Recall that Thomas Devereaux killed Richard Harris, and Dave Hennessy killed Thomas Devereaux; murder was clearly the career path to the top of the New Orleans Police Department, just as it is in the mafia, creating natural alliances between the two worlds. Although we may never know who Matranga's secret partners were, we can be sure that it took powerful people to help him step around the bodies of his dead co-defendants and return home to his family, unscathed. Once again, it seems that justice was served with the innocent lives of more bakers while the blacksmith continued to ply his trade.

Just as Matranga got on rather well, living into his eighties, so did Provenzano, leading some historians to wonder if the whole ordeal was really about the mafia. According to one theory, the mafia was used as a pretext to correct a citywide economic imbalance. Within a short time of their arrival in New Orleans, many Italian-Americans went from rags to riches, dominating every industry they stepped foot in. The lightning speed with which they achieved upward mobility upset the status quo. Since the end of slavery, white elites had worked hard to keep Blacks at the bottom of the social and economic structure, and Italian-Americans, according to the *New York Times*, 'were often marked as black because they accepted "black" jobs in the Louisiana sugar fields or because they chose to live among African-Americans' who they labored alongside, fraternized with and voted with at the ballot box. The city elites, who thoroughly enjoyed oppressing – and lynching – Blacks, thought it high time to let these new 'pizza-niggers' know where they stood in the social order.*

With fruit and veggie kingpin Joseph Macheca dead, and Matranga and Provenzano temporarily sidelined, the city council passed Ordinance 5256, authorizing the newly formed Louisiana Construction and Improvement Company to ban Italian-owned businesses from the waterfront. With one stroke of the pen, control of the docks was shifted away from Italian-Americans and placed in the hands of the very men who had signed the original newspaper advertisement,

* Although a small number of African-Americans did take part in the lynchings, the vast majority sympathized with, and stood firmly behind, the Italian-American community in its time of need, even risking their personal safety while attending burial services for the victims.

calling on citizens to take justice into their own hands. In a show of solidarity, the stock exchange, cotton exchange, sugar exchange and the board of trade endorsed the lynchings and commended the citizens for their integrous actions. The city's business elites, who gained so much from the lynchings, also controlled most of the city's newspapers; this may explain, in part, the whitewashing of Chief Hennessy's reputation which persists in books and publications today. If Hennessy was seen as dirty, then the businessmen who wanted to displace Italian labor and leadership from the waterfront might not have gotten the result they wanted.

When Mayor Shakspeare was asked about the current state of the mafia, he said, 'The reign of the mafia in New Orleans has ceased.' Shakspeare was dead wrong but the New Orleans mafia did temporarily recede into the shadows while, at the same time, their cousins in New York stepped into the light.

Chapter 9
Man Is a Wolf to Man

At the crack of dawn on 14 April 1903, a cleaning woman was walking along the sidewalk on 11th Street in New York City when she came upon an upright barrel with a wool coat draped across the top. She curiously reached out a hand to lift the coat and saw a shoe – with a foot in it. She screamed her lungs out until pedestrians ran to her aid, followed by a police officer who quickly notified detectives. A short while later, Detective Arthur Carey pulled the body from the barrel and laid it on the sidewalk as beat cops linked arms to keep back a growing crowd of onlookers. Since the corpse was still warm, Carey concluded that the male victim, who had been shoved into the barrel after being folded in half like a cheap cot, was dead less than two hours. A scarf around the victim's neck hid multiple stab wounds to the throat. Carey did not find a wallet or any identification cards on the victim, just a small crucifix and a silver chain used for a pocket watch; the watch was missing. Based on the victim's darker skin tone, Carey believed he was Greek, Armenian or Italian, with Sicilian as his first choice given the brutality of the crime. Though Carey had a reputation for solving homicides, he was admittedly stumped when it came to Sicilian murders due to the Sicilian community's pin-drop silence. He sent for 'the Dago', who everyone on the force knew to be Detective Joseph Petrosino, considered the police department's 'Italian expert'.

Joseph Petrosino was born in Padula, Italy, in 1860. His father, Prospero, was a tailor; his mother, Maria, died when he was a boy. In 1873, Prospero and his children left for New York, where Joseph worked long days as a shoeshine boy in front of police headquarters on Manhattan's Mulberry Street. At night, he played violin and listened to Verdi. At seventeen, Joseph began working for the sanitation department as a street cleaner, sweeping trash and shoveling horse manure. The beat cops who regularly encountered Joseph on the streets took a liking to him, and he may have provided them with

A young Joseph Petrosino.

information about things he saw and heard around the city. By October 1883, the 23-year-old Petrosino had become a policeman, one of the first Italian-Americans on a predominately Irish-American police force.

One consul general in New York said that the Italian ghettos 'were virtually without police supervision with the exception of the regular Irish policeman at the corner of the street, who did not care a rap what Italians did among themselves so long as they did not interfere with other people'. Believing the Italian community would be safer if policed by their own, Theodore Roosevelt, after being appointed police commissioner, raised Petrosino to detective sergeant, the first ever Italian-American to hold this rank in the nation's history. It was a proud achievement for Petrosino, who was still 'the Dago' to his fellow officers, though most referred to him this way with no intended malice – unlike the treatment he received from his own community, many of whom considered him a traitor. Southern Italians viewed men in uniform as tax collectors or military recruitment officers and could not disconnect Petrosino's police uniform from that of any other oppressor. He was especially hated by the mafia who thought of him as the bottom of the barrel, which returns us to the barrel abandoned on 11th Street.

Petrosino raced to the crime scene. After Detective Carey brought him up to date, Petrosino looked over the body and deduced from the victim's better cut of clothing and soft hands that he was not a manual laborer. He examined the barrel and noticed white granules in its joints. He opened his pocketknife and collected some on the edge of its blade, then touched the blade to his tongue, confirming that it was sugar. A layer of sawdust lay at the bottom of the barrel. Sawdust was commonly strewn across the floors of saloons and restaurants in Manhattan so that patrons could spit tobacco and toss cigarettes to the floor. Petrosino swept his hand through the sawdust, finding bloodstains, onion peels and cigar butts. The cigars were Toscanos, a strong, cheap brand often smoked in Italian ghettos (and by Clint Eastwood in spaghetti westerns). From the sugar, and the sawdust speckled with onion peels and Toscanos, Petrosino concluded that it was a sugar barrel from an Italian eatery. Given the victim's features, the savagery of his wounds, and the gruesome manner in which he was disposed of, Petrosino confirmed Carey's hunch and concluded that the victim was Sicilian, and the murder was the work of the Sicilian mafia.

Petrosino tipped over the barrel and saw the letters 'W & T' stenciled into its base, a clue that might lead him to its owner. The barrel was submitted as evidence while the corpse was transported to the city coroner, where Dr Albert Weston performed an autopsy. Dr Weston recorded eighteen stab wounds to the neck and two that severed the jugular vein. He deduced from the meal in the victim's stomach that he was Italian. Assuming the victim had not swallowed a gondola, we can assume that Weston found some form of pasta. Once the autopsy was concluded, the coroner's office put the body on ice and several police officers led their informants past the corpse to see if anyone could identify it. During this procession, a sneaky reporter from William Randolph Hearst's *New York Journal* snapped a photo of the corpse. Hearst ran the gory photo in the *Journal*'s morning edition, selling out his newspapers while ramping up public pressure to solve the crime.

Detectives Petrosino and Carey, who complemented each other like macaroni and potato salads, learned that the 'W & T' on the base of the barrel stood for Wallace & Thompson, a sugar distributor that supplied New York's restaurants and bakeries. They visited Wallace & Thompson's headquarters where they questioned a clerk, asking him if he had any Italian customers on his client list. The clerk knew of only one Italian customer who had recently purchased two barrels of sugar; his name was Pietro Inzerillo, and he owned an Italian café. The detectives dropped in on

SMOKING TO CLOSE.

MAN WHO WAS FOUND MURDERED IN A BARREL, HIS CLOTHING AND SOME OTHER ARTICLES THAT MAY HELP TO IDENTIFY HIM.

BIG STRIKE ON "L" ROAD IS NARROWLY AVERTED.

Dissatisfied Committee and Men Were Actually Voting Last Night on the

Barrel murder; front page of the New York Evening World.

Inzerillo, who did not seem nervous about a visit from two detectives, whereas law-abiding citizens typically do get anxious when cops rap at the door. Nor did Inzerillo seem concerned when the detectives asked him if they could see the sugar barrels he had recently purchased from Wallace & Thompson. Inzerillo showed the detectives to the basement where one of the barrels was standing in plain sight. The detectives saw this as a clue until Inzerillo explained to them that after the other barrel was emptied, he had left it in the alleyway behind his café and had no idea who might have taken it away. The detectives grinned, knowing Inzerillo was lying but they were unable to prove it.

Meanwhile, the chief of the New York division of the Secret Service, William Flynn, was reading Hearst's newspaper when he saw the photo of the corpse and recognized the dead man's mug. Flynn called on Police Inspector George McCluskey, informing McCluskey that he and his Secret Service agents had been surveilling an Italian-American counterfeit ring, and on the night of the murder they had noticed a new face among the crowd. Flynn was fairly sure that this new face belonged to the victim, who, in Flynn's estimation, was not a Manhattanite since the others seemed to be chaperoning him around town. Flynn identified each of the gang members for McCluskey, including the café owner, Pietro Inzerillo. In return for providing this valuable information, Flynn asked McCluskey to delay any arrests, since his Secret Service agents were still surveilling the group, and removing them from the street would derail their undercover operation. With a terrified city on his hands and public pressure mounting by the minute, McCluskey ignored Flynn's request and rounded up the counterfeiters. Within a single day, a dozen known members of the Lupo borgata were in police custody. The arrests provide us with a snapshot of an emerging New York mafia family at the beginning of the twentieth century. All twelve men were Sicilian-born criminals who had either lawfully migrated to the United States or fled Sicily as fugitives. Ignazio Lupo, known as 'Lupo the Wolf', was the don. (*Lupo* means 'wolf' in Italian. He sometimes used his mother's maiden name, Saietta, when arrested. In time, Agent Flynn would trace sixty murders to Lupo the Wolf, giving credence to the Roman playwright Titus Maccius Plautus, who wrote that 'man is a wolf to man'.)

Lupo was originally from Palermo where he owned, of all things, a bookstore. (Mao Zedong and Giacomo Casanova were once librarians, arguably, and respectively, the world's most prolific killer and the

NEW YORK, THURSDAY, APRIL 16, 1903.

PHOTOGRAPHS TAKEN AT POLICE HEADQUARTERS TO-DAY OF THE TWELVE MEN ARRESTED ON SUSPICION OF BEING INVOLVED IN BARREL TRAGEDY.

Mug shots of the barrel murder suspects, offering us a glimpse of New York's first borgata.

world's greatest lover; Lupo was a mediocre combination of the two.) In 1898, Lupo fled a murder rap in Sicily, was convicted *in absentia*, and landed in New York City in 1900, where other mafiosos welcomed him with open arms. One of his first rackets was horse theft, a primitive crime that started in Sicily and continued in New York, a city that had over 200,000 horses before the production of automobiles. Lupo's crew transported the stolen horses to the farmlands outside of Manhattan or sold them in other cities across the country. Many were cut up and sold for meat, making the crime as impossible to solve as the Alfred Hitchcock murder in which a woman kills her husband with a frozen leg of lamb then feeds it to the policemen who arrive to question her. Lupo eventually moved on to dozens of other rackets like counterfeiting and extortion, and established himself as leader of one of the first known borgatas in the United States, which was likely on account of his reputation in Sicily given the lightning speed with which he rose to the top of the heap. (Before his ultimate downfall, Giuseppe Esposito experienced a similar meteoric rise in New Orleans, largely on account of his legendary reputation in Sicily, leading us to conclude that a man's reputation was his unwritten résumé, a custom that continues in the mafia today.)

Like most mafiosos at the time, Lupo maintained strong connections to Sicily, welcoming fellow immigrants and fugitives, including Giuseppe Fontana who had been acquitted of the Notarbartolo murder. I suspect that Lupo was also linked to Ignazio Florio, partly

Ignazio 'Lupo the Wolf' Saietta.

on account of his connection to Fontana, but there seems to be an additional reason. Lupo opened a grocery store on Elizabeth Street in New York City that supplied Italian-Americans with imported olive oil, artichokes and aged cheeses from Italy. With success, he opened more stores across the city, and maintained a seven-story building on Mott Street as his main location, which the *New York Times* called the 'most pretentious mercantile establishment . . . with a stock of goods over which the neighborhood marveled'. As a ceaseless flood of Italian immigrants poured into the city, Lupo recognized the need for housing and started a company called the Ignatz Florio Co-operative Association. The cooperative purchased plots of land across New York and built six-story tenements, helping to establish an early mafia foothold in New York's construction industry which continues unabated today. Given the above, we are left to wonder if Lupo offered Florio, a man whose fortune was sinking in southern Italy, a chance to break into a healthier economy. Although I could not find a single historian who connected the two men, I am confident enough to at least raise the possibility of their relationship, given the name of Lupo's cooperative, and the continuing connections Lupo had to the mafia in Sicily which guarded Florio's estate.

The other interesting character hauled in by Police Inspector McCluskey was Lupo's underboss, Giuseppe Morello. Morello was from Corleone, a Sicilian village south of Palermo, made famous by *The Godfather*'s Don Corleone, a fictional character created by author Mario Puzo. Morello's stepfather, Bernardo Terranova, was a Corleonisi mafioso who groomed his young stepson in The Life. Morello was a fast learner and quickly earned himself a name in Sicily. By early adulthood, he was suspected of killing a man and fled to the United States, arriving in 1892. Surprisingly, Morello did not immediately turn to crime but braved the sweat of legitimate labor. Together with his wife and children, Morello traveled to Louisiana, where the graves of the lynched Italians were still grassless. From here, the family wandered around the country in search of agricultural work, like Steinbeck's Joad family. They planted sugar and picked cotton until Morello decided he would rather break other people's backs than his own; they returned to New York and settled in East Harlem, which one writer described as being 'as thoroughly Italian as Rome, Naples, Palermo, or Messina'. In Harlem, Morello fell in with Lupo, who married into the Terranova family, making them relatives.

Morello – born with a deformed hand that was attached to a short arm, resulting in nicknames such as 'Little Finger', 'The Clutch' and 'The Claw' – was seized by the long arm of the law, when McCluskey hauled him in on the barrel-murder rap, along with Lupo and the rest of their crew.

As a consolation for ignoring Agent Flynn's request to delay the arrests, Inspector McCluskey threw Flynn a bone, allowing him to search the suspects' houses. Flynn hoped to find evidence to support his counterfeiting case but instead stumbled upon handwritten letters in Morello's attic that pointed to a network of Sicilian mafiosos who were spreading across the United States like locusts. Most were letters of introduction to fellow mobsters, preceding a fugitive's arrival in a city and asking that they welcome and support the newcomer. Flynn confiscated these letters and filed them away for future use. He was patient and methodic, unlike McCluskey, who had jumped the gun and now had problems building a case against the men he had rounded up prematurely. Everyone refused to talk.

Giuseppe Morello.

Inspector McCluskey, also known around police headquarters as 'Chesty George', was faced with the prospect of sucking in his chest for a change and releasing the Sicilian suspects back onto the street, when a mysterious letter arrived on his desk:

> I know the man who was found in the barrel. He comes from Buffalo . . . The police have made the proper arrests, bring the condemned Giuseppe Di Priemo from Sing Sing, promise him his liberty and he will tell you many and many things.

Since DiPrimo (spelled Di Priemo in the letter) was an Italian name, McCluskey, like Detective Carey before him, yelled out, 'Send for the Dago!' Detective Petrosino arrived at police headquarters, read the anonymous letter and left for Sing Sing maximum security prison, where he requested to see inmate DiPrimo, who had been convicted of passing counterfeit bills by Agent Flynn. DiPrimo was brought to the visiting room where Petrosino showed him the photo of the corpse. 'That is . . . my brother-in-law,' said DiPrimo. 'What has happened?' DiPrimo thought he looked ill in the photo. Petrosino cleared up his confusion, telling him that his brother-in-law was dead, and that he had been murdered. DiPrimo fainted then awoke and began to talk, but his chattiness was driven by the initial shock; within moments, he clammed up. Given Petrosino's understanding of the mafia, he did not believe that fear was the factor behind DiPrimo's silence, but *omertà*; DiPrimo wanted to exact vengeance himself. DiPrimo eventually gave Petrosino the address of his sister's home in Buffalo, not to assist in the investigation but as a duty to his sister who needed to learn the fate of her husband.

DiPrimo was returned to his prison cell and Petrosino headed back to New York City, where he told Inspector McCluskey that DiPrimo had positively identified the victim as Benedetto Madonia. Petrosino then left for Buffalo to inform the widow of her loss, and to question her and her family. After arriving in Buffalo, Petrosino spoke with the victim's 21-year-old stepson, Salvatore, who told him, 'My father was killed by the mafia because he threatened to reveal secrets.' When Salvatore refused to elaborate, Petrosino spoke with the victim's widow, Lucia Madonia, who told him that her brother, the jailed DiPrimo, had asked her husband, Benedetto Madonia, for money. She surmised that DiPrimo needed the cash for legal fees or possibly to bribe a judge in order to get a lighter sentence.

Upon Petrosino's return from Buffalo, he went straight to police headquarters, where he examined the personal possessions that were taken from the suspects after they were rounded up. What piqued Petrosino's interest most had been found on Tomasso 'Il Bove' Petto (Petto the Ox). Petto was the only man who put up a fight when arrested. Tucked into one of his pockets were a few cheap Toscano cigars, matching those that were found in the barrel, and a pawn ticket issued for a pocket watch, redeemable at Fry's Capital Loan Company in the Bowery section of Manhattan. Petrosino hooked up with Detective Carey and the two visited the pawn shop, where they handed the clerk the ticket. The clerk gave them a pocket watch that was pawned by Petto in exchange for a dollar. Petrosino returned to Buffalo and showed the pocket watch to the Madonia family, who confirmed that it belonged to the silver chain found in Madonia's pocket. As Petto was scheduled to be sprung from jail on a $500 bond, the pocket watch was presented as evidence, just in time to keep him in the clink. The rest of the crew was released on bail.

Petto the Ox, second from left.

Assistant District Attorney Francis Garvin empaneled a jury and began an inquest. He summoned the Madonias to Manhattan, while Petrosino arranged for DiPrimo to be brought down from Sing Sing. With so much publicity surrounding the barrel murder, the courtroom was packed, but the case fell apart when Lucia and Salvatore denied that they had recognized the pocket watch. Salvatore really poured it on, adding that there must be a million watches just like it. As for DiPrimo, his trip downstate amounted to a mini-vacation from Sing Sing; he gave Garvin nothing, even claiming that Petto, whom he despised, was his pal. Many thought that DiPrimo had been frightened into silence but Petrosino still believed that DiPrimo was planning his own vengeance. And he would have plenty of time to think about it back in Sing Sing, where he was promptly returned.

The café owner, Pietro Inzerillo, was called to testify about his missing barrel. That went nowhere, as anyone could have guessed. At the end of the inquest, Petto the Ox was released, a free man – and the New York mafia had gotten away with its first highly publicized murder.

In the years that followed, the circumstances behind Madonia's death slowly came to light. Since Madonia was a relative of DiPrimo, DiPrimo's boss, Giuseppe Morello, had asked Madonia to come up with money to help the jailed DiPrimo get a lighter sentence after he was arrested for passing counterfeit bills. It is unclear if the money was supposed to pay for a well-connected lawyer, or to bribe a judge, perhaps both since a crooked lawyer was often the conduit to a dirty judge. Madonia obliged, but Morello kept the cash for himself. After DiPrimo received no mercy from the court, Madonia felt swindled and wrote Morello a letter, demanding his money back while chastising Morello for not looking after his crew. The letter infuriated Morello, who lured Madonia in for the kill. Madonia was eating his last supper at Morello's restaurant, located in Little Italy, when Morello entered with Petto the Ox, who repeatedly stabbed Madonia in the throat. After being knifed to death, Madonia's body was dragged over to the slop sink where his blood was drained. His killers then knotted a scarf around his neck and folded his corpse into the barrel which Inzerillo brought over from his café. The barrel was then thrown into the back of a horse-drawn wagon (yesteryear's equivalent of getting trunked in a Cadillac), and Madonia was left on the street so others could see what happens to anyone who questions Morello.

Lupo was unhappy with Petto's petty theft which led to the discovery of his pawn ticket. And since the mafia does not use Wite-Out to correct mistakes, but Rub-Out, Petto was in trouble. Knowing his life was in danger, he took it on the hop. Agent Flynn tracked him to Wilkes-Barre, Pennsylvania, over a hundred miles northwest of New York City. If Flynn knew where Petto was hiding, so did Lupo and DiPrimo, who both wanted him dead. On 21 October 1905, Petto was crossing a street when five rifle shots rang out and found their mark, leaving holes in Petto the size of a 'teacup'. His cold-blooded reputation was likely the reason why his killer walked up to his fallen body and plunged a dagger straight into his heart, making sure he was dead, Dracula-style.

If this bloody episode were the mafia's edition of Orwell's *Animal Farm*, we could conclude that the Wolf killed the Ox. But Detective Petrosino revealed his own hunch when he commented, 'DiPrimo was smarter than we were.'

Not being able to convict anyone for the barrel murder was a blow to Detective Petrosino's pride. When he encountered Lupo on the street, he took out his frustration the old-fashioned way; according to the *New York Times*, Petrosino 'gave Lupo a severe beating'. Lupo licked his wounds but the mafia never forgets or forgives an insult. Unlike average citizens who do forget and forgive, the reason why Raffaele Palizzolo, the Italian MP acquitted of killing Emanuele Notarbartolo, was cheered by a crowd of Sicilian-Americans as he disembarked from the SS *Martha Washington* in New York.

After Raffaele Palizzolo beat a murder rap in Italy, he made a bid for his old parliamentary seat. To raise funds for his campaign, and to promote his new book, *Le Mie Prigioni* (My Prisons), which spun his ordeal into a martyrdom, he traveled to America. In a show of solidarity – or naiveté – thousands of Sicilian-Americans greeted him at the pier in June 1908; many in the crowd sported campaign buttons with Palizzolo's mug. But Italian-Americans who despised the mafia were embarrassed by Palizzolo's visit, and Detective Petrosino was chief among them. What especially galled Petrosino was Palizzolo's claim to be a staunch enemy of the mafia, and his offer to help the NYPD combat organized crime by assisting them as a consultant. Aware that Palizzolo was directly connected to the Sicilian mafia, and that several witnesses who had testified against him in Italy had fled to New York where they turned up dead, including one man who was cut in half like a hero sandwich, Petrosino made every effort to disrupt his rallies and bring his tour to an early end. It worked; Palizzolo cut his trip short and the two men stared at each other for a few awkward moments as Palizzolo's ship weighed anchor. (Some accounts say that Petrosino was assigned to Palizzolo's police guard. If so, we can imagine him disgruntled over the assignment and being the same nuisance.)

Although it was satisfying for Petrosino to see Palizzolo off to sea, Gotham's Italian-American community still had other problems that were summed up by the *New York Journal* when it published an article that read, in part, 'The Italians pay their taxes, and pay their rent, and do a great deal of hard work. They are entitled to police protection

AND THEY HAVE NOT HAD IT.' In light of such sentiments, Petrosino asked Police Commissioner William McAdoo to create an Italian squad to police the Italian-American ghettos. For the better part of 1904, McAdoo put Petrosino off. Finally, on 14 September, he granted Petrosino's request. Petrosino asked for twenty men but was only given five, along with a shoestring budget. McAdoo's approval seemed more an act of appeasement since the new squad had no office or telephone line, and was forced to use Petrosino's private apartment as its headquarters until he was able to wrangle more funding out of McAdoo. Using an array of costumes for undercover work, Petrosino and his 'little band of zealots' locked up and deported dozens of mafiosos, including Don Vito Cascia Ferro.

Born in Palermo on 22 January 1862, Ferro was the son of peasants. As a youth, he had some vandalism charges on his police record, crimes that were probably committed on behalf of the mafia (as you will recall, deliberate damage to an estate was called a *sverge*, which involved robbery or vandalism). In 1898, Ferro graduated to kidnapping when he snatched the teenage Baroness Clorinda Peritelli di Valpetroso. After being arrested for the abduction, Ferro claimed he had done it for love, transforming an Amber Alert into *La Bohème*. He was given a suspended sentence and set free. In time, Ferro taught himself how to read and write, and married a schoolteacher. He dabbled in politics and preached anti-property propaganda to the poor, while, at the same time, he became a powerful mafia don and was suspected of just about every crime under the sun. He eventually traveled to New York but was returned home by Petrosino, who knew of his reputation in Sicily. Like lovers who cross oceans with the face of a paramour in a locket, Ferro left America with a photograph of Petrosino tucked away in his pocket; love and hate can evoke an equal degree of fixation. Upon his return to Sicily, Ferro was hired as an estate manager by a nobleman

Vito Cascia Ferro.

and sitting member of parliament, the Honorable Michele di Ferrantelli. (There is no doubt that Ferrantelli's relationship with Ferro was identical to that of Ignazio Florio and Noto the gardener.)

Police Commissioner McAdoo was credited with the stunning success of the Italian squad and allowed Petrosino to beef up his ranks to forty men. Since other officers were not happy with more dagos entrusted with more power, police photographers refused to photograph arrestees brought in by the squad. Tension inside the department was at its height when Mayor George McClellan replaced Commissioner McAdoo with Theodore Bingham, who was aware of Petrosino's outstanding police work, talk of which had reached Italy. In appreciation for the 'brilliant work performed in the . . . arrest of criminals in flight from Italian justice' the Italian government presented Petrosino with a solid-gold timepiece. The generous gift flattered Petrosino but may not have been bestowed upon him with the utmost sincerity. The US government did not believe that the Italian government was using its best efforts to stop the flow of criminals into the United States. Italian authorities were suspected of turning a blind eye or making it easy for criminals to forge travel documents. Italy was suffering from high poverty and unemployment; anyone willing to leave was one less mouth to feed, and who better to go than a criminal? Considering Italy's suspected duplicity, Bingham decided to send Petrosino on a secret mission to Sicily to uncover the names of Sicilian fugitives who were hiding in New York. Petrosino had been so successful at establishing a vast network of criminal informants in Manhattan that Bingham was sure he could do the same in Palermo.

'Joe, you may be safe and all right up in the north,' said one of Petrosino's colleagues from the Italian squad, 'but look out for yourself . . . when you get down in the south.' Even Petrosino's priest told him, 'Don't go to Italy . . . I am afraid that you will not return alive.'

'Probably not,' Petrosino answered. 'But it is my duty to go and I am going.'

Almost incredibly, Bingham was sending Petrosino to the same island he had been filling up with deported criminals for years. The same island where Palizzolo, who was kicked out of the States by Petrosino, held political power. The same island where Lupo, who Petrosino had beaten senseless on a Manhattan street, maintained excellent mafia connections. The same island where Vito Cascia Ferro, who still carried a photograph of the detective, was a revered mafia don. And the same island where blood vengeance was not just culturally acceptable, but demanded. Upon hearing Bingham's assignment, Petrosino told everyone he was not afraid, but his elephant balls must have shriveled up into raisins.

Chapter 10
An Evening in Sicily

Detective Petrosino once said, 'The police department is the only wife I have a right to have.' But after reaching the top of his profession, the lifelong bachelor finally courted a woman and asked her father for her hand in marriage. The father refused, concerned that Petrosino's job placed him in 'constant danger of assassination'. Only after the father died did Petrosino marry his beloved Adelina. On 30 November 1908, Adelina gave birth to a baby daughter, also named Adelina. Petrosino did not like being away from his Adelinas and, at forty-eight, he was looking forward to the pastures when he was sent to the slaughterhouse. Aware of the dangers involved with his trip to Sicily, Petrosino visited a lawyer and signed power of attorney to Adelina.

An older Detective Joseph Petrosino.

Commissioner Bingham instructed Petrosino to first travel to Rome and inform the Italian government that he was en route to Sicily on police work but to withhold the specifics of his secret mission, which included intelligence gathering, identifying fugitives who were now living in the United States, and building a network of informants in Sicily.

On 9 February 1909, Petrosino placed a .38 caliber Smith and Wesson revolver in his suitcase and said goodbye to his wife and daughter, then boarded the 475-foot steamship *Duca di Genova*. The NYPD was essentially sending an overaged stubby man with a standard-issue stubby gun to take on the entire Sicilian mafia, in Sicily! The Rambo movies are easier to believe.

After boarding the ship, Petrosino checked into a first-class cabin under the guise of a Jewish businessman, Simone Velletri, who was traveling to Italy 'in search of a cure for a digestive complaint'. The ship steamed out to sea at 4 p.m. Later that evening, Petrosino became seasick. When he got over his seasickness, he left his cabin and mingled with other passengers, who recognized the world-famous detective from his regular appearances in New York newspapers that circulated the globe (we are left to wonder how he could claim he was a Jewish businessman with a case of the farts). The ship's purser, Carlo Longobardi, was especially enamored with Petrosino who was, in turn, flattered by his attention. Petrosino told Longobardi old cop stories and confided to him that he was on a secret mission to Sicily. When other passengers noticed Petrosino, including a twelve-year-old boy who was traveling with his mother, Petrosino continued to speak about his police work and often alluded to the purpose of his trip. Given the long list of passengers to whom Petrosino entrusted his secret, he may as well have walked the deck wearing a sandwich board that read '**I am an undercover detective**' on one side, and '**Don't tell anyone**' on the other.

The ship's first-class section was cordoned off from lower-class passengers such as Paolo Gratucci, who ignored the partitions and became a nuisance to passengers who were afraid to confront him. One passenger finally told the captain. Since the captain had, of course, heard that Detective Petrosino was on board, he sought him out, asking for help. Instead of avoiding a confrontation, Petrosino went looking for Gratucci and must have put him in his place since Gratucci lay low for the remainder of the voyage. The ship also had on board several passengers whom Petrosino had personally deported; they, of course, recognized him, leaving us to wonder how he made it across the Atlantic without being thrown overboard.

On the evening of 21 February, Petrosino stepped off the gangplank in Genoa, Italy, the birthplace of Christopher Columbus whose first ocean voyage garnered less attention. A shipload of passengers, who knew Simone Velletri's true identity and exactly where he was going, dispersed across Europe. As hard as it is to believe, Petrosino was not his own worst enemy. Back in New York, Police Commissioner Bingham proved just as irresponsible. On 20 February, one day before

Petrosino disembarked in Genoa, the *New York Herald* published the following:

> Lieutenant Joseph Petrosino has gone to Italy, specifically to Sicily, in order to obtain important information bearing on Italian criminals residing in the United States and in particular in New York, where the police, who would like to initiate the deportation of many criminals, lack the necessary evidence of their records in Italy.

Bingham's leak amounted to an obituary for Petrosino as other New York newspapers picked up the story, as did the *Herald*'s European desk. As Petrosino boarded a train for Rome where he planned to submit his official letters of introduction, the entire western hemisphere could have read where he was going and why.

Once in Rome, Petrosino visited the US ambassador to Italy, Lloyd Griscom, then dropped in on the Italian police chief, Francesco Leonardi, giving him a watered-down version of his mission. Leonardi thought that Petrosino was quite full of himself but their meeting was cordial. After concluding his business in Rome, Petrosino decided to visit his brother, Vincenzo, who lived in Padula. Vincenzo greeted Petrosino at the train station, where Petrosino said, 'My trip is secret. Nobody's supposed to know.' Vincenzo took a newspaper clipping from his pocket and said, 'That's exactly what I wanted to talk to you about.' Petrosino read the article while cursing up a storm. At this very moment, Petrosino had every right to return home on the next ocean liner, and slam the article on Bingham's desk along with his badge. Instead, the obedient detective boarded a train for Naples, where he caught a mail boat to Palermo.

Meanwhile, back in New York, mafiosos had written to friends and relatives in Sicily, alerting them to Petrosino's imminent arrival. More ominous than missives were actual mobsters; Carlo Costantino and Antonio Passananti, two of Lupo's loyal henchmen, were aboard another vessel en route to Sicily. They were instructed by Lupo to cross the ocean and call on Don Vito Cascia Ferro, the boss of Palermo, where Petrosino arrived on 28 February 1909, a week after his secret mission was reported by the press.

In Palermo, Petrosino walked the streets disgusted by the sight of campaign billboards promoting Raffaele Palizzolo's re-election to parliament. He checked into the Hotel de France under a new name, Simone

Valenti di Giudea, and began a habit of dining at Café Oreto, a small eatery located a stone's throw from his hotel. Getting down to business, Petrosino rented a typewriter under yet another alias, Salvatore Basilico, then visited the American consul in Palermo, William Bishop, to explain his secret mission. Petrosino initially avoided the Sicilian police as they were known to be heavily infiltrated by the mafia. He instead reached out to several informants he had once traded favors with in Manhattan, believing he could pick up with them in Palermo, but he had no power in Sicily to offer rewards and was seen by them as a liability.

For reasons unknown, Petrosino abandoned his initial caution with the Palermo police department and dropped in on Commissioner Baldassare Ceola. Judging from Ceola's record of their conversation, he also felt that Petrosino was full of himself. Ceola, who had airs of his own, locked horns with Petrosino after the latter accused the Palermo police chief of fraudulently clearing criminals for passage to the United States. Ceola insisted that any ex-criminals were 'rehabilitated'. Petrosino knew this to be untrue, easily proven by their rampant criminal conduct in New York. Despite Ceola's disagreements with Petrosino, he felt obligated to offer him police protection due to the many known and unknown enemies Petrosino had all over the island. Ceola also wanted to avoid the international headache that

Cartoon of Italy happily sending its criminals and mafiosos to America.

a dead American detective would cause the Palermo police department. Petrosino declined Ceola's offer, telling him he had just as many friends in Palermo as he did enemies, meaning his informants whom he mistook for friends. Ceola attempted to talk sense into Petrosino, but after his counsel was rebuffed, he left the meeting in a huff, claiming he needed to return to work; he could not stomach another minute of Petrosino and pushed him off onto Lieutenant Poli, head of Palermo's Mobile Brigade. In the likely event Petrosino encountered trouble in Sicily, Ceola covered his ass by writing a report in which he noted that Petrosino was talking too much all over town, and telling everyone his 'secret' business. Either Petrosino had lost control of his tongue, or the poor man knew he was doomed and decided to make a complete spectacle of himself in the hope that a bright spotlight would ward off the mafia, which typically shuns publicity.

Petrosino walked the streets unattended, bumping into disgruntled criminals he had deported. Ernesto Militano and Paolo Palazzotto were two such men, who spotted Petrosino outside the US consulate where they were applying for travel visas. 'There goes Petrosino, the enemy of the Sicilians,' yelled one. 'He's come to Palermo to get himself killed.' Note that this man was not clairvoyant.

At Café Oreto, where all the waiters knew Petrosino's identity and business agenda, known criminals began showing up to stare at him from across the restaurant as he ate. At least two of these criminals had been deported by Petrosino, one of whom he had dealt a bloody beating as a bon voyage. Their presence should have prompted Petrosino to at least find another restaurant, but his vanity would not allow him to budge before the glaring eyes of scoundrels.

On the evening of 12 March, Petrosino was dining in Café Oreto when two of the informants he was working with entered and found him at a back table, eating pasta. They whispered something to Petrosino before he haughtily dismissed them with a wave of the hand. The men left as fast as they had come. After Petrosino finished dinner, he paid his tab then put on his overcoat and left the café. Instead of returning to his hotel, as was his custom each night, he headed for the Garibaldi Gardens, located across the street from the café. With an umbrella in hand, Petrosino walked along the exterior of the gardens, stepping around muddy puddles left by a wintry rain. It was 8:50 p.m. when three gunshots rang out in the night. There was a brief pause before a fourth shot was fired on the heels of the last echoes.

Bullets entered Petrosino's shoulder, cheek and throat; another was stopped by his clothing. He expired at the foot of a sign advertising a theatre performance being held that evening. Oddly enough, Police Commissioner Ceola was attending that same performance in a private box. Given Ceola's earlier report on Petrosino, it is unlikely that he was surprised when the news reached him, via a police aide who whispered in his ear.

Just as Ceola had feared, Palermo was thrust under an international spotlight. Forced to investigate a murder that could have been avoided, Ceola searched Petrosino's hotel room and found a notebook with a final entry that read, 'Vito Cascia Ferro . . . dreaded criminal.' Based on this entry, Ceola questioned Ferro who provided him with a solid alibi; he was with the Honorable Domenico De Michele Ferrantelli, a member of the Italian parliament. Ferrantelli confirmed that Ferro was in the town of Burgio, over a hundred miles south of Palermo, assisting him with a political campaign.

A witness at the scene, Luigi Schillaci, told police he had seen Petrosino's killers but Schillaci soon came down with a severe case of amnesia. Another witness was more recollective, saying he had noticed Carlo Costantino and Antonio Passananti – the men sent by Lupo – sitting on a bench in the park, just a few hours before the hit. The police believed that the informants who had interrupted Petrosino's dinner had laid the trap by offering to introduce Petrosino to yet another informant who he was to meet inside the Garibaldi Gardens. The men then left Café Oreto and told Costantino and Passananti that Petrosino was on his way.

Not long after Petrosino was murdered, Lupo the Wolf arrived at a hideaway cabin in upstate New York where his crew was printing sheets of counterfeit Canadian currency. After entering the cabin, Lupo told Giuseppe 'Uncle Vincent' Palermo, 'It was successful.'

'Then it was surely well done,' said Uncle Vincent.

'It never could have missed in Palermo,' replied Lupo. 'He was fool enough to go there.'

Police Commissioner Bingham learned of Detective Petrosino's death through a telegram sent from Consul William Bishop that read:

> PETROSINO SHOT, INSTANTLY KILLED . . . ASSASSINS UNKNOWN. DIES MARTYR.

Could Bingham have been surprised by the tragic news after sending Petrosino to Sicily without backup then leaking news of his secret mission to the press? Bingham swore to avenge Petrosino's death but to do so, many believed he would have had to commit suicide.

Mayor McClellan declared Petrosino's funeral a public holiday and a quarter of a million people filled the streets to witness the procession. Of the many mourners who paid tribute to the fallen detective was an

Petrosino's funeral wagon arrives at the home of his widow.

elderly African-American man, William Farraday. When Farraday asked his employer if he could have the day off to attend Petrosino's church service, he was asked why. 'Well, boss,' said Farraday, 'Officer Petrosino saved my life one night many years ago when I was attacked . . . and I'se never forgot it.' As a young officer, Petrosino was walking the beat when he witnessed a group of white men attack Farraday on Canal Street in Lower Manhattan. Petrosino fearlessly dodged into the melee, swinging his billy club at the heads of Farraday's attackers until they dispersed. Farraday was certain he would have been killed that day had Petrosino not intervened on his behalf.

Taps were played at the cemetery but the solemn honor was eclipsed by an article in the *Washington Post*, which called for an end to immigration from the south of Italy, blaming all southern Italians for the death of New York's hero cop. Once again, as in New Orleans, the real mafiosos suffered no consequences whatsoever as innocent Italians were stigmatized and paid a heavy price for the mafia's evil deeds.

Detective Petrosino's death was demonstrative of the futile efforts to stem the tide of Sicilian criminals flowing into the United States, which continued, unabated, as the mafia's ranks swelled in the New World. It was not long before fugitives like Esposito, Fontana, Lupo, Morello and Matranga were joined by young Sicilian men who were raised in The Life and either had arrived in America as children or were natural-born citizens. As the mafia expanded into metropolitan areas across the country, one might have guessed that tight-knit Sicilians, who had relied on each other for centuries, would have encountered extreme difficulties while navigating America's diverse landscape which included ethnic gangs from just about every part of Europe. But the Sicilians, who were part Greek, Arab and Spanish, understood how to form new alliances with anyone from anywhere; one such alliance would propel them to the very top of organized crime in America, a position they would hold for over a hundred years.

Chapter 11

The Mafia's Aristotle

Since Roman times, Palermo's Jewish community lived in harmony with everyone around them. That came to a sudden end in the fifteenth century when the Spanish Inquisition reached Sicily, a possession of Spain at the time. Some Jews were tried and killed while others packed up their belongings and fled the island, many arriving in the New World, recently opened to Europeans by Christopher Columbus. For the next four hundred years, Jews trickled into America until nineteenth-century pogroms in Eastern Europe created a mass exodus that coincided with the southern-Italian immigrant wave into the United States. In big cities like New York and Chicago, Jews were crammed into ghettos alongside Italians. Like their new neighbors, most Jews were honest, hard-working immigrants; also like their neighbors, there were a few ruffians in their midst. In a single generation, these renegade Jews, many of whom were reared in religious homes, exchanged their kippahs for stilettos and contributed to the rise of the American mafia nearly as much as the Sicilians who created it.

Manhattan Island. Early twentieth century. Under the rusty fire escapes of New York's Hester Street, beneath plumes of chimney smoke, a mile from the paper-littered floor of the New York Stock Exchange, a half-mile from filthy skids of dead fish on South Street, among a tumultuous horde of chattering immigrants spewing a dozen languages, engulfed in a foul stench of body odor, chicken shit and horse manure piling up under peddlers' pushcarts, there on a narrow street where brick tenements blocked out the light of Lady Liberty's torch in the distance, a young Sicilian whose family had recently left Lercara Friddi, Sicily, in search of a better life, bumped into a young Jew whose family fled pogroms sweeping across Poland. On that cold winter's day, Salvatore Lucania (later known as Charles Luciano) met Maier Suchowljansky (later known as Meyer Lansky). Together, they

Mulberry Street, a block from Hester Street where Lansky and Luciano first met.

would usher the American mafia into an age of prosperity. But before we acquaint ourselves with these future titans of organized crime, let us meet the tutor responsible for their criminal upbringing.

Arnold Rothstein did not grow up in a dingy overcrowded tenement like Luciano and Lansky. His father, Abraham Elijah Rothstein, nicknamed 'Abe the Just', was a reputable Manhattan businessman, once honored by the renowned Supreme Court Justice Louis Brandeis. Abe lived according to the Jewish Orthodox tradition of his ancestors; he studied Torah daily, wore a yarmulke, regularly attended synagogue, and kept the Sabbath. His marriage to Esther was arranged, and, in 1882, she gave birth to Arnold, the second of the Rothsteins' five children.

Arnold's brother Harry followed in his father's footsteps and excelled in school. Arnold was the exact opposite; he hated school, and thought that religion was antiquated. He once told his father, during an argument, 'Who cares about that stuff? This is America, not Jerusalem. I'm an American. Let Harry be a Jew.' At sixteen, Arnold dropped out of high school and began to hang out in pool halls which doubled as gambling dens. While still in his teens, he kept meticulous records of his wins and losses and realized that the house played at a steep advantage. After Rothstein got married, he rented two brownstones on West 46th Street. He and his wife lived in one, the other was turned into a casino where Rothstein held high-stakes gambling tournaments that were covered by an admiring press, who dubbed him the 'King of Gamblers'. Most of the city's top newsmen were intrigued by Rothstein, including Damon Runyon, who modeled his character Nathan Detroit on Rothstein in his famous book and musical, *Guys and Dolls*. F. Scott Fitzgerald also modeled his character Meyer Wolfsheim on Rothstein in his classic novel, *The Great Gatsby*. Likely because of the favorable press he received, Rothstein was the first mobster to rub shoulders with tycoons, Broadway stars and starlets, sports champions, heirs and heiresses; it seemed everyone with fame or money wanted to be around Rothstein, and he invited them all to his casino.

Arnold Rothstein.

In order to operate a casino in Manhattan, Rothstein needed the backing of New York's Tammany Hall, the true command post for the state's political power as opposed to its capital in Albany. Located in Manhattan's Union Square, the Hall was founded shortly after the American Revolution, and hosted its first meeting in 1786 by members who referred to themselves as Braves and Sachems (Tammany was the name of a deceased Indian chief). The Hall was dominated by WASPs – White Anglo-Saxon Protestants – until the 1840s, when a potato famine in Ireland killed off about a million men, women and children; another million fled to New York, where the Irish, already acquainted with centuries of oppression, stuck together and established themselves as the largest voting bloc, enabling them to seize control of Tammany, the most corrupt, longest-running political machine in American history.

Arnold Rothstein relied on the protection of Tammany's political powerhouse, Timothy 'Big Tim' Sullivan, who unofficially controlled the city's illegal casinos and, according to a *New York Times* informant, 'was heavily interested in the race track business, and . . . stood at the head of a chain of pool rooms'. Sullivan partnered Rothstein with Willie Shea, a crooked ward leader and openly corrupt building inspector. 'Rothstein's a good boy, and smart,' Sullivan told Shea. 'You'll stick with him and you'll make a lot of money.' Shea did, and soon wanted to throw Rothstein out of his own casino, telling Sullivan that Rothstein was 'different from us', meaning he was Jewish. Sullivan would not hear it and insisted that Shea show Rothstein the respect he was earning.

To draw the city's highest rollers to their casino, Rothstein paid sexy showgirls and cunning men to steer 'marks' through his front door. The 'steerers' were paid a percentage of their mark's losses. One steerer, Vernie Barton, brought in Charles Gates, son of steel and barbed-wire tycoon John 'Bet a Million' Gates. Charles took a bath at the roulette wheel and wrote a check for $40,000 to cover his losses. Willie Shea cashed the check and took off with the money. Rothstein told Barton to track down Shea, who, when confronted, told Barton, 'Tell the Jew I've got the money and I'm going to keep it.'

Instead of personally confronting Shea, Rothstein went straight to Big Tim Sullivan, who sided with Rothstein and asked him how he wanted to handle it. Rothstein wanted to let Shea keep the $40,000 since it was the cheapest way out of their partnership. Word of Rothstein's cool-headed reaction spread across the city and showed him off as a valuable Tammany asset where smart Irish political leaders counted money, not freckles. It was not long before Rothstein opened more casinos and became Tammany's bridge to the underworld. If anyone needed a license to operate a bar or a casino, they visited Rothstein. If they needed to buy a judge or a police captain, they went to Rothstein. Rothstein also helped the politicians on election day.

Long before Rothstein arrived on the scene, Tammany politicians used street gangs to help them win office. Using fake names and disguises, gang members across the city were recruited on election day to walk in and out of polling booths. These 'repeaters', who voted multiple times, would first vote with a beard (if they were old enough to grow facial hair), then return to the same polling station an hour later with a mustache, and once more bare-faced, before heading off to another polling station. In the event a repeater was detained by a poll-watcher, gangsters with phony police badges would show up to assume custody of the repeater then send him off to the next polling station. Given the value of these repeaters on election day, Tammany protected gang leaders from prosecution all year round. The only problems gangsters ever had were with each other. Fights between rival gangs could last for days. Like the barricades in revolutionary France, they would overturn carts and pile up paving stones for a protracted battle that was fought with fists, knives, bats, wooden planks and pistols, anything they could get hold of. Just as Tammany was becoming fed up with these bloody antics which drew bad press, Rothstein presented the politicians with an alternative; he recruited and trained smart young hoodlums who stuck to business and helped win elections without acting like barbarians the rest of the year.

Rothstein held court at Lindy's Delicatessen in Midtown Manhattan. On any given day, men would steadily stream in, sit close to him and whisper, then leave; he might confer with a union organizer who needed help with a labor strike, a cop who wanted a promotion inside the force, a gangster who needed a gun permit, a hijacker who needed a fence, a horse trainer with a tip on a race, or everyday people looking to borrow cash. Lindy's was also the underworld equivalent of Aristotle's Lyceum, where Rothstein schooled young men like Charles Luciano, Dutch Schultz, Joe Adonis, Al Capone, Albert Anastasia, Lepke Buchalter and Frank Costello, who would one day hold Tammany Hall in his pocket. Rothstein's introduction to many of these men came through Meyer Lansky, who Rothstein met in Brooklyn while the two were attending a bar mitzvah. Rothstein saw promise in Lansky and invited him to dinner so they could discuss business. By then, Lansky was best friends with Luciano, who would later say that Rothstein showed him how to dress and taught him the proper etiquette required in higher circles where bigger money circulated. Rothstein encouraged his pupils to think big, he stressed the importance of a handshake, and financed their endeavors. He also told them that ethnic rivalries were foolish, that if they wanted to get anywhere in America they would have to forge broad underworld alliances.

Since the second half of the nineteenth century, Saratoga Raceway in upstate New York had been a relaxing getaway for the rich and famous. Business titans like Cornelius Vanderbilt and August Belmont vacationed there, as did Civil War generals Ulysses S. Grant, William Tecumseh Sherman and Philip Sheridan. Arnold Rothstein ended up in Saratoga in 1919 when a gambler, Henry Tobin, asked him to bankroll his casino. What started as a loan resulted in a partnership. To get things underway, Rothstein greased the palm of Saratoga's Democratic boss, Dr Arthur J. Leonard. He then bribed the Republicans to keep everyone happy. When Saratoga district attorney Charles Andrus swore he would never let 'that Jew' open a casino, Rothstein did not take it personally; he correctly suspected that Andrus felt left out, so he fattened up a cash envelope and shut him up, too. After taking over an estate named Bonny Brook Farm, which Rothstein shortened to The Brook, he sent for his favorite protégés so they could work the floor and get some experience in the world of high-stakes gambling and horse racing. Meyer Lansky and his pal Charles Luciano were literally and figuratively off to the races. They made a few bucks and learned a few lessons, preparing them for Rothstein's next big move that would make Lansky and Luciano multimillionaires and position Luciano for a takeover of the New York mafia.

Chapter 12

Give the People What They Want

Alcohol is as American as apple pie. The pilgrims stocked the *Mayflower* with a liquor bar, the colonists liked to drink, and General George Washington gave his soldiers a daily ration of rum or whisky. According to documentary producer Ken Burns, by 1830, 'Americans spent more money on alcohol each year than the total expenditures of the federal government'. By the 1840s, a national debate centered around prohibiting its sale. By 1855, New York State, appalled by all the hard-drinking Irish and German immigrants pouring onto Manhattan Island, cited a litany of mental and physical ailments attributed to alcoholism, and passed a temperance law that banned the sale of hard liquor. Although the law was ruled unconstitutional, New York was not alone in its crusade; a total of thirteen states went 'dry' before the outbreak of the American Civil War. A growing debate to end slavery overshadowed the Prohibition movement, and during the war, alcohol was needed to sedate wounded soldiers and lift their spirits. Following the war, the debate resumed with renewed vigor and, by 1917, Congress pushed through the Eighteenth Amendment to prohibit the sale of alcohol with a two-thirds vote in the House and a majority in the Senate.

Even before the amendment went into effect, a national crime wave began when a half-million dollars in alcohol was stolen from government warehouses. Americans went into a 'wild scramble' to buy up the last available liquor, while some raided public libraries in search of books that explained how to make alcohol. Liquor dealers hit the streets, selling swigs from a flask hidden inside their boots, hence the name 'bootleggers'. As for the mafia, had they funded a lobby in Washington, they could not have achieved anything near to what was just handed to them by Congress. With an army of criminals that swelled far beyond the original Lupo borgata, mafiosos spotted an opportunity in the organized sale of illegal alcohol. Knowing that public sentiment would be favorable to anyone who supplied the people's widespread demand for liquor, the mob, until now known only for murder and extortion, tidied up their sordid image. German immigrants hated the government for depriving them of beer; Italian immigrants despised the government for taking away their wine; as for the Irish, compared to this, the potato famine was like getting shorted a few French fries at McDonald's. Everyone viewed mobsters, who provided them with alcohol, as their saviors. In New York alone, the mob opened thousands of speakeasies (the state was estimated to have over thirty-two thousand at its peak). Some required a secret knock or password for entry, increasing the mystique for average citizens who felt they were part of a harmless rebellion. Women, who, for centuries, felt chained to traditional domestic roles, were liberated in these clubs where they danced, drank, smoked, gambled, and swore like men.

In 1919, the same year the Eighteenth Amendment was ratified and became part of the US Constitution and the same year Rothstein took over The Brook in Saratoga, the Chicago White Sox made it to baseball's World Series. Several embittered players, who had tried but failed to get their salaries increased, put themselves up for sale. Some accuse outfielder 'Shoeless Joe' Jackson of being the instigator, while others say it was pitcher Eddie 'Knuckles' Cicotte along with first baseman Arnold 'Chick' Gandil. Whoever thought up the scam, it is clear that most of the starting line-up were willing to throw the Series for a hundred grand. Joe Sullivan, a Boston gambler, told Cicotte and Gandil he would ask Rothstein – widely known as 'The Bankroll' for his regular funding of 'larcenous schemes' – to pay off the players. Ex-featherweight champion Abe Attell wired Rothstein, telling him, 'The Series could be fixed. The White Sox were for sale.' Rothstein did not think they could get away with it. 'I don't want any part of it,' said Rothstein. 'You might be able to fix a game, but not the Series. You'd get lynched if it ever came out.' It seems Rothstein passed but made a heavy bet with the insider knowledge he now had. He won a few hundred grand on the Series and the press, aware of his winnings, claimed he had bankrolled the bribe. Whether Rothstein was directly involved or not, the underworld also knew he won big on the Series, as did Irving Wexler, aka Waxey Gordon, when he introduced Rothstein to Big Maxie Greenberg, who was looking for an investor to fund a large smuggling operation across the Great Lakes which connected Michigan with Canada, where the production and sale of alcohol was still legal. Waxey was a low-level street thief who started out as a pickpocket, became a drug dealer, and eventually borrowed money from Rothstein to open a chain of Chinese opium dens around the city. Big Maxie was a Detroit hoodlum who was once pardoned for a bank job by President Woodrow Wilson, who was lobbied by Maxie's pals in the St Louis political machine which was just as corrupt as Tammany Hall.

In the fall of 1920, Waxey and Maxie met with Rothstein on a bench in Central Park where Maxie explained that he and his gang were perfectly located on the banks of the Great Lakes to receive smuggled liquor shipments from Canada. To put the operation in motion, Maxie needed $175,000 to buy a flotilla of boats and a convoy of trucks. Rothstein quizzed Maxie and was satisfied with his answers but would not commit without having time to think it over. When they met again the next day, Rothstein told Maxie he would bankroll the operation, with conditions. In return for his investment, Rothstein wanted Maxie to sign over ownership of any real estate he owned. As for Waxey, Rothstein told him to take out a life insurance policy on himself with Rothstein's own insurance agency, listing Rothstein as the sole beneficiary. Although Rothstein was typically non-violent, it could be taken as a veiled threat; Waxey's death would cover some of the loss if the deal went south.

As always, Rothstein brought more than just his investment to the table. After hearing that the Canadians were taking advantage of Americans by constantly increasing liquor prices, Rothstein suggested they expand the operation across the Atlantic Ocean and buy whisky straight from a distillery in the United Kingdom, where Rothstein had a connection. Samuel Bloom was one of Rothstein's favorite gambling marks who happened to own shares in a distillery across the pond. The next time Bloom gambled over his head, Rothstein told Bloom he would forgive his debt in exchange for exclusive US rights to his overseas Scotch. Bloom agreed and Rothstein set up a pipeline between Glasgow, Scotland, and Atlantic City, New Jersey, where one of Rothstein's trusted confidants, Nucky Johnson, controlled the coastline.

Enoch 'Nucky' Johnson did not invent Atlantic City or the corrupt political machine that ran it. The city itself was the idea of Dr Jonathan Pitney, who believed that salt water and ocean breezes were the Earth's natural cures. Pitney was sure that Atlantic City would make a great health resort for the wealthy. That his dream of building a paradise to promote good health through a unity of earth, mind and body would become the capital of debauchery is one of history's little ironies.

Nucky Johnson inherited control of the city from Louis 'The Commodore' Kuehnle, who owned the Kuehnle Hotel, a meeting place for businessmen and politicians in need of a conference center with benefits, like drinks on Sunday (illegal in New Jersey, even before Prohibition) and prostitutes every day, which Kuehnle felt should never be illegal. By offering his hotel as a meeting place for the powerful, Kuehnle accumulated his own power and became the hub through which all favors and public appointments passed. He ruled the city for twenty years with a slot machine mentality which pays out a fair percentage of what it takes in. While Kuehnle shook down everyone in town, he dished out large sums of money to modernize the city and maintain it as the Mecca of northeastern hedonism. With total control of prosecutors, judges, the treasurer and the sheriff, all of whom he appointed, Kuehnle needed only to avoid spats with politicians from outside his city who wielded more power than him. This he failed to do, and was taken down after he angered President Woodrow Wilson with a blatant act of voter fraud. One year, Kuehnle's squads of repeaters performed a bit too well; through a slight miscalculation, Atlantic City gave Wilson's opponent more votes than the city had voters. Wilson ruined Kuehnle, who was sent to prison in December 1913. His absence created a vacuum filled by 25-year-old Nucky Johnson, who was the son of Kuehnle's trusted sheriff, Smith Johnson.

Nucky Johnson would run Atlantic City for the next thirty years. The economy relied on visitors who wanted to have fun, and since no fun meant no visitors, Nucky and his pals thought of Prohibition as a joke, worthy of a toast. When Rothstein needed a coastline to receive liquor shipments from Europe, he reached out to Nucky. Rothstein's plan was to have ocean vessels anchor just outside the three-mile limit, beyond which were international waters. Speedboats would then relieve the ships of their cargo and race the liquor to shore. It was an odds game; some made it past the US Coast Guard cutters while others were nabbed. Rothstein's attitude was like that of the British government during the Battle of the Atlantic's 'tonnage war', fought at sea during the Second World War; all that mattered was how much merchandise – in this case liquor – made it through to supply the nation. Rothstein eventually increased his odds by bribing Coast Guard officers, something Winston Churchill could not do with German wolfpacks.

Besides the Atlantic City coastline and the Great Lakes, Rothstein also received liquor shipments through Boston Harbor and the tip of Long Island. From these points of entry, Rothstein's liquor fanned out across the country. To manage the distribution arm of his operation, Rothstein brought in a team of middle managers, beginning with Meyer Lansky and Charles Luciano, both of whom had proven themselves trustworthy and capable at The Brook in Saratoga. Lansky would later say, 'He picked me because I was ambitious and hungry.' It was an understatement.

Overnight, the young Luciano, who was eager to climb the mafia ladder, found himself in a premier place among his fellow mobsters who were producing 'bathtub gin', 'rot gut' and other homemade crap *du jour* that could not compete with Rothstein's aged whisky. When Luciano became the mob's primary source for fine spirits, he suddenly found himself not only wealthy, but extremely popular in the underworld. Since he would use his new status to seize control of Lupo the Wolf's borgata, with Lansky beside him, the two men are worthy of a more formal introduction.

Chapter 13

They Were More than Brothers

Meyer Lansky was born in Grodno, Poland, in 1902, to Max and Yetta Suchowljansky. Fleeing pogroms, the family arrived on Ellis Island in April 1911 after traveling steerage in the SS *Kursk*. Meyer quickly learned English and shortened his name to Lansky because his Polish surname was difficult for Americans to pronounce. Lansky's grade-school teachers were impressed by the boy's natural intelligence and he would one day say, 'I loved school' – three words seldom, if ever, heard from a mobster. He graduated from junior high school in 1917.

Meyer Lansky.

One day, Lansky's mother gave him money to purchase food for the family before the Sabbath. On his way to the butcher, he passed a crap game on the street, tried his luck, and lost his family's Sabbath dinner. He felt miserable about it since the family was poor, but he went back the following week and kept losing until he learned that the 'winners are those who control the game'. He found out the winners were Italian mobsters, and to control the game he needed to partner with an Italian.

Charles Luciano was born Salvatore Lucania in 1897, to Antonio and Rosalie Lucania in the sulfur-mining village of Lercara Friddi, where John Rose had once shared a cave with the Leone gang. For the rest of Luciano's life, the smell of sulfur reminded him of poverty and hunger. Emigrating to America was Antonio Lucania's dream. In Lercara Friddi, he slaved away as a laborer and dropped coins into a bottle each month until he had enough money to purchase the fare for the family's ocean voyage. In April 1906, the family traveled in steerage and settled on the Lower East Side of Manhattan where Jews and Italians lived on top of each other. Antonio found work but struggled to make ends meet. Like Lansky's parents, the Lucanias stressed the importance of honest toil and the couple's other children, two of whom were boys, never became involved in crime.

Charles Luciano.

Luciano attended school in America but his poor grasp of the English language, and the ridicule he received because of it, contributed to him becoming a truant. He did odd jobs, even carrying groceries home for adults, approaching them as they left the market. The more money he earned, the less he went to school until he finally dropped out. Revealing an early knack for leadership, Luciano assembled a gang of young Italian toughs who sold Jewish boys protection and 'promised that nobody would beat them up or tear up their schoolbooks'. When Luciano encountered Lansky sloshing through the snow on a wintry day, he asked him for five cents a week, and was told, 'Go fuck yourself.'

Luciano retold the story as an adult, saying, 'I patted him on the shoulder and said, "Okay, you got protection for free." [Lansky] just pulled away and yelled, "Shove your protection up your ass, I don't need it."' Luciano went on to say, 'For some reason I took a liking to this kid. He was very gutsy standing there and telling me to go fuck myself.'

The next time the two boys saw each other, Lansky and his Jewish pals were swimming naked in the East River, being harassed by Irish boys who would sometimes toss their clothes into the water or jump in and push their heads beneath the surface. Luciano's gang jumped in, too, and the water around them 'became stained with red'. One of the Italian swimmers had stabbed the leader of the Irish gang, whose body later 'washed up on the bank downriver'. Lansky was impressed by the *aquacide* and viewed Luciano's gang as a model of strength and solidarity; he began to assemble his own crew of Jewish toughs. When Luciano saw that Lansky had his own gang, they formed a nonaggression pact and, according to Lansky, 'agreed to combine forces when there was conflict with the Irish'.

As both Luciano and Lansky came from hard-working families, they were under parental pressure to pursue an honest living. Lansky's father got him a job in a tool and die shop, hoping he would become a mechanical engineer, while Luciano went to work delivering women's hats for a company on West 24th Street in Manhattan. At the time, the going rate for a seventeen-year-old delivery boy was five dollars a week, but the owner, Max Goodman, started Luciano off at six. 'That extra buck made me important,' Luciano would later say. 'A dollar was a fortune.' Goodman took a shine to Luciano and invited him into his home on Friday nights, where Luciano shared Sabbath dinners with Goodman and his family. Goodman's mentoring and hospitality were a tug in the right direction, but the devil was yanking on Luciano's other shoulder.

One day, while delivering hats, Luciano spotted a local drug dealer, George Scanlon, and told him he wouldn't mind delivering drugs, too. Scanlon knew the hat deliveries would make for an excellent cover and Luciano began working two jobs at once. Each morning, Luciano tucked small packets of heroin into the hatbands then replaced the hats neatly into their boxes and delivered heroin and hats all day long, alternating Goodman's stops with Scanlon's. This street hustle earned Luciano upwards of a hundred bucks a week. While the overlapping jobs showed off Luciano's ambition, it also revealed his nature as a double-crosser; Luciano was betraying Goodman, the man who paid him more than the going rate and invited him into his own home to share sacred meals with his family.

In June 1916, after making a dope delivery to a pool hall, the nineteen-year-old Luciano was ambushed by police who found heroin in one of his hats. Luciano pled out to unlawful possession and was given a year in Hampton Farms Penitentiary. Antonio Lucania was ashamed of his son's wayward behavior and refused to show up in court or visit him in jail.

When Luciano was first arrested, Max Goodman was harassed by police, suspected of operating a heroin ring with young boys as his runners. Goodman was able to prove his innocence and, instead of writing Luciano off, he mercifully visited him in prison while attempting to guilt him into giving up crime. 'Why did you do this to me?' Goodman asked Luciano, while on a prison visit. 'If you needed money, you should have come to me.' Luciano wept and Goodman vowed to help him get out of prison early if he promised to go straight. Luciano agreed to the deal and Goodman wrote letters to the parole board on Luciano's behalf, promising them that he would assume the role of Luciano's surrogate father and rehire him at his hat company, if the boy was granted an early release. With Goodman's help, Luciano was sprung in six months. But Luciano had no intention of holding up his end of the bargain. The young ex-convict told his pal Lansky, as he exited prison, 'My only mistake was that I got caught.' Luciano justified his betrayal of Goodman by saying, 'What I'd promised Goodman would make me nothin' but a crumb, workin' and slavin' for a few bucks, like all the other crumbs.'

Returning home, the ex-crumb told his family never to call him Salvatore or Sal again because everyone in jail called him Sally, and Sally was a girl's name. 'I changed my name to Charlie,' he said, causing his father to spit on the floor and walk out of the house, disgusted. Antonio still allowed Luciano to live at home until he discovered a gold belt buckle in Luciano's belongings. Antonio walked around the neighborhood with the buckle in hand and learned that a local jewelry store had been knocked off; one of the stolen items was the gold belt buckle. Antonio ran home and beat the daylights out of Luciano. 'You are not my son!' he yelled. 'You are only a thief and cannot live in my house anymore! Get out!' Luciano's mother cried her eyes out as Luciano left, never to return. He began a full-time career in crime with his lifelong partner, Meyer Lansky. A friend of theirs would later say of the two, 'They were more than brothers . . . They would just look at each other and you would know that a few minutes later one would say what the other was thinking. I never heard them argue . . . They were always in agreement with each other.'

As we return to the start of Prohibition, when Arnold Rothstein tapped Lansky and Luciano as his main distributors, Lansky used his tool and die background to outfit Model T Ford automobiles with secret compartments to smuggle liquor, while Luciano used his growing mafia connections to expand their sales across the country. Lansky brought along his close friend, Benjamin 'Bugsy' Siegel, while Luciano recruited his pal, Frank Costello, who Rothstein became especially fond of.

Francesco Castiglia, who would later change his name to Frank

Costello, was born in Calabria, Italy, in January 1891, to Luigi and Maria Castiglia. In 1896, the family traveled to America and settled in East Harlem, where Blacks, Jews and Italians lived together in poverty. Luigi, a proud man who had fought in Garibaldi's army, never seemed to find his way in America. He tried his hand at a grocery store but it went under. He went to work as a laborer, but after busting his hump all week with a pickaxe, he got beaten up and his pay was stolen by a gang of Irish thugs who called him a guinea. Young Frank Costello never forgot the image of his father walking through the door that day, beaten and broke. His father's experiences seemed to prove the futility of hard work and likely contributed to Costello's trajectory in life.

As a teenager, Costello was a Sabbath goy for Orthodox Jews. They must have treated him well since he not only married a Jew, but also partnered with Jews in business for the rest of his life, which returns us to Rothstein's bootlegging operation. Costello was tasked with bringing liquor to shore inside the three-mile limit. Rothstein was so impressed with Costello's success in New York and New Jersey that he gave him money to turn two islands off the Canadian coast into transfer stations. Costello used the money to rent a small squadron of seaplanes and install a chain of coastal radio stations so he could monitor and direct the shipments. In Manhattan, Costello opened speakeasies. In one of his main clubs, he built a bar that operated like those revolving bookcases we typically see in mystery movies; whenever the law rapped at the door, Costello's bartender pressed a button and the bar disappeared behind a wall.

Frank Costello.

Rothstein monopolized the bootlegging industry until a number of small but violent gangs sprang up, resulting in murderous disputes and robberies. Uncomfortable with all the violence, Rothstein left the operation to his protégés who, perhaps on account of their slum-jungle upbringing, did not shy away from gunfire. After Rothstein bowed out of the business, the young toughs revealed their animal instincts. Samuel Bloom, who was part owner of the distillery in Europe that supplied their alcohol, found himself, once again, in debt to Rothstein to the tune of $100,000. When one of Lansky and Luciano's loads of Scotch was hijacked, the duo suspected Bloom of tipping off the hijackers. When they heard that Bloom had squared up with Rothstein one week after the hijacking, Luciano took it as circumstantial evidence of his guilt and sentenced Bloom to death. He was last seen leaving his apartment on West 57th Street, and is said to have been encased in cement and dumped into the Hudson River. Since Bloom's guilt was uncertain and the actual hijackers were given a pass, the murder may have boiled down to the fact that Bloom was no longer in bloom. Some wondered if Luciano and Lansky hijacked the load themselves, then blamed it on Bloom to cut out the pesky middleman who was still receiving a percentage of each shipment.

Rothstein's protégés were clearly making their way to the top by perfecting a combination of Rothstein's brainy business acumen – and Giuseppe Morello's barrel diplomacy.

Chapter 14

Luciano Ups the Stakes While Rothstein Craps Out

Back in January 1910, a member of Ignazio Lupo's counterfeiting ring was arrested and quickly cracked under police pressure. His information led to the arrests of Lupo and his underboss, Giuseppe Morello. Lupo and Morello blew trial. At sentencing, Morello asked for sympathy, trying to use his short arm to get a shorter sentence, but the judge was not hearing it; he hit Morello with twenty-five years, and sentenced Lupo to thirty. With Lupo and Morello behind bars, Ciro Terranova, who was related to both men, took over the borgata. He was soon challenged by Giuseppe Masseria, who was also related to Lupo. Like Lupo and Morello, Masseria had fled a murder rap in Sicily and landed in the United States, where he fell in with Lupo's borgata. He was an obedient soldier until Lupo and Morello were gone, and Terranova, known as the 'Artichoke King', seemed more interested in cornering the market in imported artichokes than running a borgata. Masseria easily pushed him aside and became 'Joe the Boss'.

Giuseppe Masseria.

Lupo was paroled in 1920 after serving ten years of his thirty-year sentence. Although he returned to crime, he made no attempt to reclaim his borgata. Morello followed Lupo out the door, but, unlike Lupo, Morello wanted his old position back. Knowing Morello could fill a barrel as good as Jack Daniel's, Masseria made him his new underboss.

Masseria's borgata was made up of soldiers from Palermo and Corleone (Masseria was from Agrigento but was considered part of the Palermo–Corleone alliance on account of his blood ties). Just over sixty miles southwest of Palermo is the picturesque coastal town of Castellammare del Golfo, which produced mafiosos like Silicon Valley turns out computer geeks. When enough fugitives and immigrants from Castellammare del Golfo landed in the United States, they formed their own borgata and were not about to obey men from Palermo. Their leader in New York was Salvatore Maranzano, who arrived in the United States in 1918. Maranzano was well educated and spoke fluent English, Italian, Sicilian and Latin, which he may have picked up during a semester in seminary school. Though he was a killer, a bootlegger, and a drug and human trafficker, he liked to read Roman classics and spent a lot of time in the opulent library of his Brooklyn home. He dressed conservatively and wore no jewelry except for an expensive wristwatch and a gold wedding band. Like Lupo and Terranova, Maranzano also owned an import business and invested in real estate.

Even before the start of Prohibition, Maranzano's borgata had bumped heads with Masseria's borgata. After Prohibition began, the rivalry deepened as each borgata did its best to mobilize the Italian ghettos 'into an army of alky cookers and booze-runners'. Their home-grown distilleries grew out of the Italian-American tradition of families who made their own wine at home. The Sicilian bosses pushed the homemade-wine makers to increase their output from a few cases meant for family and friends to kegs that could be sold on the black market. But their homemade booze was no match for Luciano's quality liquor fermented in the Scottish Highlands. 'The old mafia leaders', said Meyer Lansky, 'didn't have the sophistication or the contacts' to rival their pipeline, originally set up by Waxey, Maxie and Rothstein and still maintained by a variety of other Jewish and Italian gangsters in major cities around the country who enjoyed dealing with Luciano. As Luciano and Lansky's hybrid crew of Italians and Jews conducted business across the country, Maranzano and Masseria sank into bitter territorial disputes that devolved into talk of warfare.

Luciano was making a small fortune in the liquor business, and for reasons that can only be attributed to greed, he continued to sell heroin, a profitable side business he had never given up since his days as a delivery boy. On 5 June 1923, Luciano was dropping off a package when his customer flashed a badge and said, 'I'm a federal agent. You're under arrest.' Agents Lyons and Coyle booked Luciano, who later said, 'I must've been crazy . . . I could've sent any one of fifty guys.' It was Luciano's second drug bust and the repeat offender no longer had Max Goodman to pen letters to the parole board. The agents threatened Luciano with hard time unless he agreed to talk. According to Luciano, after realizing he was doomed, he offered to give up the drug spot but not the dealers. Instead of using his one telephone call to dial a lawyer, Luciano called his brother and told him to move a box of heroin from one apartment to another. He then gave the agents the new address. The agents raided the empty apartment on Mulberry Street and found $75,000 worth of heroin (over a million dollars in today's currency). Because of Luciano's assistance, the charges were dropped and Luciano walked.

When word spread that Luciano had snitched, the criminal empire he was building with Lansky was in jeopardy of crumbling. Lansky invited Luciano to a kosher delicatessen on the Lower East Side to explain how he planned to stop him from being branded Lippy Luciano. Over a bowl of matzah ball soup, Lansky said they would launch a public relations campaign to impress people and counteract the negative talk. A heavyweight fight between Jack Dempsey and Luis Angel Firpo was coming up at the Polo Grounds on 14 September 1923. Lansky told Luciano to buy up all the front-, second- and third-row tickets available and gift them to anyone who meant anything in their world. Following Lansky's advice, Luciano purchased two hundred ringside seats at a cost of $25,000, a staggering sum in his day, though I do not know a rat alive who would not dish out the same amount or more to un-rat themselves. It amounted to a grand a year for the twenty-five years Luciano could have spent behind bars.

Once Luciano purchased the tickets, he and Lansky told Frank Costello and Ben Siegel to spread word that Luciano owned all the best seats in the house. Luciano then handed the tickets out to everyone who mattered, including a few Tammany Hall*igans*. To help Luciano prepare for the big night, Arnold Rothstein took him to a men's store and fitted him for 'something conservative and elegant', according to Luciano. Rothstein picked out a gray double-breasted suit, dark blue silk tie and a gray cashmere topcoat (to hide his tail). 'Within twenty-four hours,' said Luciano, 'I was the most popular guy in the United States.' The amazing recovery of Luciano's reputation was due to Lansky's genius, and lends startling insight into human nature; so what if you're a no-good, yellow-bellied, low-down, dope-dealing snitch, as long as you're handing out gifts and are popular, everyone will love you.

Salvatore Maranzano, who also received tickets from Luciano, was envious of his popularity. He approached Luciano, ringside, at the end of the evening and said, 'I have a business proposition for you.' Maranzano invited Luciano to a meeting at a social club in Manhattan's Little Italy where he intended to explain his proposition.

Luciano went to the club, accompanied by Frank Costello. Maranzano greeted them at the door and threw his arms around Luciano, saying, 'I understand you now like to be called Charlie. Somehow, I find it difficult to think of you as anything but Salvatore. Tell me, my name was not good enough for you to keep? There is something about it which shames you?' Attacking someone's name choice is not the best conversation starter. Maranzano followed this error up by quoting Julius Caesar in Latin, leaving Luciano to wonder, 'Why the hell couldn't he have said it in English?' As this one-way conversation continued, Maranzano seemed so enthralled by his own voice that he either could not see or did not care that Luciano was visibly 'disgusted'. Maranzano finally got around to his proposition. 'Come into my organization and I promise you that you will prosper along with it. I will make an important place for you, my son.' Calling Luciano 'my son' was another blunder, especially given Luciano's estrangement from his own father.

Maranzano then told Luciano that he did not care for the men Luciano hung around with, meaning Jews. Luciano took this as a personal insult since he considered Lansky his brother; as for Costello, he had recently married a Jewish wife. Maranzano finally said that if Luciano accepted his offer, he would fold up his own bootlegging operation (which was dying anyway on account of inferior booze), and appoint Luciano a capo in his borgata. Luciano must not have looked too impressed since Maranzano increased his offer to include a piece of every racket his borgata was involved in, including gambling, loansharking and hijacking.

Luciano and Costello left the meeting without giving Maranzano an answer. They soon met with Lansky, Ben Siegel, Joe Adonis and

Vito Genovese, all of whom distrusted Maranzano's intentions and advised Luciano to decline his offer. Luciano sent word back to Maranzano that he would pass; to soften the rebuff – or rub it in his ass – Luciano sent Maranzano a case of his finest twelve-year-old Scotch.

When Joe Masseria heard that Luciano had spurned Maranzano's offer, he asked to meet with Luciano. Luciano hated Masseria, who he described as 'short, fat [and] first cousin to a pig', but they found common ground in their mutual dislike of Maranzano. Masseria made Luciano a similar offer to Maranzano's, while he too took issue with Luciano's many Jewish friends, asking him if he was planning to join a synagogue anytime soon. After listening to their identical pitches – and biases – Luciano realized the two men were exactly the same; though one was short, fat and sloppy, and the other tall, lean and polished, they were both sly and condescending. Luciano told Masseria he would think it over as he made his way to the door. Masseria took Luciano's non-committal as a 'no' and began to plot against him, fearing that if Luciano somehow fell in with his enemy, Maranzano, Luciano's thriving liquor business would bolster his rival's war chest. To weaken Luciano, Masseria began to attack his fleet of liquor trucks. Within days of their meeting, Luciano's loads were being hijacked all over the tri-state area, and Prohibition agents on Masseria's payroll were raiding Luciano's warehouses.

Luciano's young crew of Italians and Jews were tough, but they did not have the strength to challenge either borgata, leaving Luciano two choices: he could either kiss Masseria's ring, or accept Maranzano's proposal. After discussing both options with his crew, Luciano decided to accept Masseria's offer with one condition. Luciano and Joe Adonis went to see Masseria, who greeted them at the door then directed them to a table filled with Italian cuisine. After they ate, Luciano said he would accept Masseria's offer on condition that he replace Giuseppe Morello as Masseria's underboss. Masseria complained but gave in to this masterstroke on Luciano's part; as he left the meeting, Luciano was next in line for the throne and had slid himself into position for a palace coup. (We have no record of Luciano's initiation ceremony into Masseria's borgata. We must assume, at the time he was being courted by Masseria and Maranzano, that he was still a free agent. Once he accepted Masseria's offer, he must have taken an oath before he was fast-tracked for promotion.)

Over the next few months, Luciano enriched Masseria's borgata by replacing his homemade alcohol with shipments of Scotch. Maranzano, who felt bested by Masseria and rejected by Luciano, saw their alliance as an overt act of aggression. As Maranzano prepares for war, let us return to Arnold Rothstein, who was preparing for death.

In the autumn of 1928, members of Arnold Rothstein's immediate family noticed a drastic change in his demeanor. Lansky said that his gambling was out of control, and reporters who regularly covered the King of Gamblers were getting tips from sources that Rothstein's days were numbered. Some writers, like Damon Runyon, did not believe the rumors; he brushed them off as frivolous street talk, meant to get Rothstein to bow before one threat or another. When the rumors got back to Rothstein, he handled them the same way he handled everything else in his life – with a bet. Rothstein weighed the odds on his own death, which he must have thought were better than fair when he took out an additional $50,000 life insurance policy on himself. Like any true gambler, he wanted to go out with a win.

Around the same time, Rothstein placed another big bet. Democratic governor Al Smith of New York was running for president against Republican Secretary of Commerce Herbert Hoover. Early on, when people who liked Smith thought he had a chance, Rothstein was not deluded and bet heavily against him. A Jew who understood bigotry did not believe the country was ready for a Catholic president. When voters at last figured out what the great oddsmaker had known all along, the spread widened to 20–1, about equal to betting on a Shetland pony at the Kentucky Derby. Rothstein, who had also laid heavy money on Franklin Delano Roosevelt as Smith's replacement for New York governor, was poised to collect $600,000 – if he could make it to election day.

On the evening of 4 November 1928, Rothstein was holding court at Lindy's Delicatessen when the cashier, Abe Scher, told Rothstein he had a phone call. Rothstein took the phone from Scher and listened in silence for a few moments. He then hung up and said, 'I'm going over to see McManus. I'll be back in a half-hour.'

Rothstein and George 'Hump' McManus had recently been involved in a high-stakes card game together in which Rothstein lost $300,000 but refused to pay off his markers, claiming the 'game was rigged'. McManus, who hosted the game, had vouched for all the players, and was therefore stuck with the debt. Rothstein put on his hat and coat then walked over to the Park Central Hotel where he went up to Room 349 and knocked. A drunk and agitated McManus opened the door and Rothstein entered the room. McManus waved a handgun around while insisting that Rothstein square up. Whether it was a willful or accidental discharge, or McManus had fired in a drunken rage, Rothstein ended up with a bullet in his abdomen. Just before 11 p.m., the elevator operator heard footsteps on the stairway; it was Rothstein, who barely made it to the lobby, hunched over, grasping a railing with one hand and holding his stomach with the other. 'Call me a taxi. I've been shot,' he said to the elevator man as he somehow managed to hand him a tip. (Well done!) The doorman ran off to find help as another hotel employee flagged down Patrolman William Davis, who asked Rothstein, 'Who shot you?'

'Don't ask questions,' snapped Rothstein. 'Get me a cab.'

With a bullet lodged in his gut, Rothstein wanted the cab to take him home, where he could summon a doctor and keep the incident relatively quiet. But the patrolman insisted that Rothstein go directly to the nearest hospital. Rothstein then dictated which hospital and demanded that his own personal doctor treat his wound. After Rothstein was taken away, other cops arrived at the scene. They were confronted by cab driver Abe Bender, who was holding a Colt .38 Special which the cabbie had seen sliding across the street after it was thrown from a third-story window. When the cabbie handed the gun to a police officer, he was scolded for destroying fingerprint evidence. 'I'm a hackie,' he said, 'not Sherlock Holmes.' The intoxicated McManus had tossed his heated revolver out the window like a hot potato, nearly hitting pedestrians with it. When the cops arrived in Room 349, no one was there; curtains were blowing in the open window and a table was littered with empty whisky bottles and cigarette butts, probably from an earlier card game. There was an overcoat in the closet with the name George McManus stitched in the lining.

Rothstein arrived at the Polyclinic Hospital where Detective Patrick Flood, a veteran cop who knew Rothstein, asked, 'What happened to you, Arnold?'

'I've been shot,' said Rothstein, stating the obvious.

'Who shot you?'

'I won't tell you.'

'Were you shot in the hotel?'

'Please don't ask me any more questions,' answered Rothstein, who is reported to have ended the inquiry by placing a finger to his lips and saying, 'I'm not talking. You stick to your trade and I'll stick to mine.'

Rothstein was rushed into the operating room where a single bullet was removed from his abdomen; it had passed through his bladder and intestines. Reporters descended on the hospital, wondering, along with the police, if Rothstein would identify his shooter but he slipped into a coma and died on 6 November, forty-eight hours away from what would have been his massive election-day payoff. Detectives searched for George McManus, who came from a family of cops. As McManus hid out in the Bronx, his brothers spread rumors that Rothstein died for welshing, the worst thing you can say about a professional gambler. Luciano was one of three suspects picked up for questioning. Since he was not a viable suspect, my best guess is that, following his snitching debut, the law had brought him in to see if he had heard anything on the street. McManus was eventually captured and acquitted at trial.

The *New York Times* estimated Rothstein's net worth at over twenty million dollars (over 350 million in today's currency). The 46-year-old rebel, whose Orthodox family had considered him dead years earlier, was buried with a kippah and prayer shawl. If there is such a thing as mitzvahs in the underworld, Rothstein may have earned his ancient burial garb. After the cotton market collapsed in 1922, Rothstein's father, Abe the Just, went bust. Instead of filing for bankruptcy, Abe began to sell off his assets in order to pay his debts. When Rothstein's brother Jack told Rothstein that their father was going broke, Rothstein wanted to help but knew his father would never accept assistance from a criminal. Rothstein told Jack to take their father to a particular bank for a loan. Rothstein then went to the bank's president and gave him Liberty Bonds as security for his father's anticipated loan application, then swore the bank president to secrecy. Abe got the loan and climbed out of debt, never knowing his wayward son had saved him. He showed up at his son's services to perform the Mourner's Kaddish.

In May 1929, Luciano and Lansky paid the Maker of Mobsters a posthumous honor by holding the first national conference on organized crime in Atlantic City, New Jersey, which Rothstein had opened up for them through Nucky Johnson. The underworld's Aristotle was dead but the students who sat at his feet were just getting started.

Chapter 15
The Atlantic City Conference

In May 1929, mobsters from around the country gathered in Atlantic City, New Jersey, to discuss the murderous bootlegging wars plaguing Chicago, and to plan for the expected repeal of Prohibition now that a countermovement to legalize alcohol was in full swing. The attendance list, with names such as Torrio, Moretti, Mangano and Corolla, Stromberg, Schwartz, Bernstein and Berkowitz, sounded like a group of Italians in search of a construction seminar had accidentally wandered into a dental convention.

The emperor of Atlantic City, Nucky Johnson, booked his guests into the exclusive Breakers Hotel on the boardwalk. Since the hotel refused to accommodate Italians and Jews, Nucky booked their rooms under WASPy names, hoping to quietly slide them past the front desk. When the hotel manager saw Al Capone and Harry 'Nig' Rosen loitering in his lobby, he tried to throw them out, nearly getting himself killed. Nucky showed up just in time to save the manager's life then escorted Capone and Rosen to the Ritz, where he helped them forget the insult with wine, women and food.

Nucky secured a conference room at the President Hotel where Meyer Lansky suggested to the attendees that upon Prohibition's repeal, they replace their national bootlegging operation with a gambling syndicate to include state-of-the-art casinos. Lansky, who had once blown his family's cholent on a roll of the dice, knew the lure of gambling and anticipated hundreds of millions in revenue. Unlike other rackets, like drug trafficking which gave mobsters a bad name, gambling would allow them to give the public what they wanted, as they did with alcohol. They talked about spheres of influence across the country, mutual ownership in casinos, the distribution of slot machines owned by Frank Costello, and access to a national race wire controlled by Moses Annenberg.

When Moses Annenberg was a boy, newspaper circulation wars in big cities were fought block by block, like trench warfare. Newspaper distributors would assemble a band of young thugs to terrorize the competition; skulls were cracked, newsstands were burned, delivery wagons were overturned, and readers of the 'wrong' newspaper were sometimes assaulted on the street. It was not uncommon to see these thugs drop their drawers and piss on a pile of newspapers that belonged to their competitor. A closer look at their water pistols would show that many did not yet have hair on their nuts, and quite a few, like Moses and Max Annenberg, were missing their foreskins.

When publishing tycoon William Randolph Hearst decided to extend his newspaper empire into Chicago, his manager, Solomon Carvalho, told him, 'It's a tough town, we'll have to shoot our way in.' Carvalho hired the Annenbergs and paid them according to results. They beat and vandalized the competition, helping Hearst plant his flag in the Windy City. As for the daily delivery of Hearst's own newspapers, the Union Stock Yard route was as dangerous as the narrow pass at Thermopylae. Moses drove through it every night in darkness when no one else would dare. Stunts like this, and the results he and his fellow thugs were able to deliver, earned him a solid name on the street. As he matured, he relaxed his fists and hid his fearless grin behind a businessman's smile. He opened one, two, three and eventually thirty news distribution agencies across the country. In 1922, he received a telephone call from Frank Brunell, a tired businessman nearing age seventy who was caring for a sick wife. Brunell, who had built the *Daily Racing Form*, wished to sell his business and retire before he died. He wanted cash and knew that Annenberg had plenty of it. Annenberg gave Brunell $400,000 wrapped in a newspaper. He then added the race wire to the *Racing Form* and became one of the wealthiest men in America, and one of the most sought-after partners in the American mafia since whoever controlled the wire had a monopoly on racing information being delivered to bookmakers across the country in real time. The wire, sent over a vast telegraph network, provided a stream of up-to-the-minute information on the health of horses, their past performances, the condition of the track, weather, late scratches and other important data that means more to a professional gambler than a horse's name and the number on its saddle towel, the stuff that sways casual bettors who don't gamble for a living. Bookies paid a monthly fee for the service.

After Arnold Rothstein died, Frank Costello, who was also present in Atlantic City, claimed two of Rothstein's prized protégés, Phillip

'Dandy Phil' Kastel and Frank Erickson. Kastel, another Lower East Side Jew like Lansky and Siegel, became Costello's most trusted casino partner, and Erickson, a New York mobster of Scandinavian descent, partnered with Costello in his nationwide bookmaking operation. To service their bookies, Costello and Erickson struck a deal with Annenberg at the conference.

Of the many conferees, there were two men who were conspicuously absent, Salvatore Maranzano and Joe Masseria. They had not been invited for a number of reasons, one of which was their attitude toward Jews, while another was their antagonism toward each other, both of which would have put a damper on the festivities. How well the conference progressed without them confirmed how little they were needed. In their absence, Luciano seized an opportunity to tell his fellow Italians that both bosses were too clannish for the young visionaries, while Lansky sent the same message to his Jewish pals.

The conference broke up and the New York delegation returned home, eager to get back to business. But their plans were interrupted when hostilities broke out.

Chapter 16

War and Its Opportunities

On 14 February 1930, Detroit's don, Salvatore 'Sam Sings in the Night' Catalanotte, died of pneumonia without appointing a successor. His underboss, Gaspar Milazzo, moved up. Salvatore Maranzano was childhood pals with Milazzo and naturally backed his elevation in Detroit, as did Stefano Magaddino, the boss of Buffalo, New York. All three dons – Maranzano, Magaddino and Milazzo – were *paisanos* from Castellammare del Golfo, which concerned Joe Masseria, who feared the Castellammareses were growing too powerful. Masseria told Detroit capo Chester La Mare he would back him if he made a move to displace Milazzo. On 31 May, Milazzo was gunned down while having lunch at a fish market in Detroit.

Back in New York, Maranzano correctly blamed his nemesis, Masseria, for Milazzo's death in Detroit and considered it a declaration of war against the entire Castellammarese clan. Maranzano assembled a war council and gave spirited speeches about the danger of Castellammarese extinction if they allowed Masseria's aggression in Detroit to go unpunished. He then visited Magaddino in Buffalo who pledged his support in the event of war.

When war finally broke out, Luciano seized an opportunity to deride tribal thinking, warning his fellow mobsters that it would destroy the American mafia in its infancy. At the same time, Luciano secretly welcomed the conflict as a means to weaken both borgatas, which could allow him a path to power. Another mobster who viewed the war as an opportunity to advance his own interests was Tommy 'Three-Finger Brown' Lucchese, a Sicilian-born member of Tom Reina's Bronx-based borgata, and a close friend of Luciano.

Tommy Lucchese was born in Palermo in 1899, and traveled to the United States at age eleven, settling with his family in East Harlem's overcrowded tenements. A juvenile delinquent, he was thrown out of his house by his law-abiding father who felt ashamed of his son's delinquency (bearing a striking resemblance to Luciano's home life, and not very different from Costello's early life, lending some credence to behavioral psychology which would suggest that America's inner-city criminal environment had more to do with their decisions than their hard-working, upright parents). As a young man, Lucchese lost his right index finger while working in a machine shop. Sometime afterward, as he was being fingerprinted for an arrest, a cop jokingly called him 'Three-Finger Brown' after the Chicago Cubs pitcher, Mordecai 'Three-Finger' Brown, who threw a mean curve ball, turning his handicap into a unique advantage that won him entry into baseball's Hall of Fame.

Lucchese would eventually be worthy of the mafia's hall of fame and his exceptional career began here, when he reported to Masseria that his boss, Tom Reina, was planning to side with Maranzano during the war. Masseria blew his top and sent for Luciano, who, unbeknownst to Masseria, was secretly working with Lucchese. Masseria told Luciano to dispose of Reina, immediately. 'Reina was a man of his word . . . and he was a very honorable Italian,' said Luciano, '[but he] hadda be eliminated so I could keep on . . . movin' up.' Luciano dispatched his pit bull, Vito Genovese. When Reina saw Genovese on the street, he smiled and waved. 'When he done that,' said Luciano, 'Vito blew his head off with a shotgun.' The smile that was wiped off Reina's face appeared on Lucchese's face as he expected to be rewarded with the vacant throne. But Masseria backed the elevation of Joe Pinzolo, who was, according to Luciano, 'fatter, uglier, and dirtier than Masseria'.

As Lucchese now planned to do away with Pinzolo, Albert Anastasia, born Umberto Anastasio, told Luciano that if he ever planned to replace Masseria, he first needed to declaw 'The Claw'. Luciano appreciated Anastasia's concern. If anything were to happen to Masseria, Giuseppe 'The Claw' Morello, who had served ten years in prison, viewed himself as the rightful heir to the borgata that was originally started by him and Lupo.

Albert Anastasia.

On the afternoon of 15 August 1930, Morello and two of his men were counting money in their Harlem office when Anastasia and Frank 'Cheech' Scalise busted through the door and shot to death the fifty-year-old Morello along with his two associates. Anastasia and Scalise made off with $30,000 while removing Luciano's main obstacle to the throne.

After the shotgun death of Tom Reina, Maranzano correctly assumed that Masseria had issued the order to kill Reina, not knowing that Masseria was maneuvered into it by Luciano and Lucchese. Masseria now assumed that Maranzano was behind the hit on Morello, issued as a retaliatory strike. As the two men accused each other of two murders that were secretly orchestrated by the young Turks, Luciano added yet another layer of intrigue by falsely reporting to Masseria that Maranzano had farmed out the hit on Morello to Maranzano's ally in Chicago, Joe Aiello. In response, Masseria sent word to the boss of Chicago, Al Capone, to kill Aiello, who was riddled with machine-gun fire on 23 October 1930. Almost incredibly, Luciano's crew was knocking off their future opponents while walking around preaching the senselessness of war.

Meanwhile, Tommy Lucchese figured out how to get rid of Joe Pinzolo. On 5 September, Lucchese invited Pinzolo to go over some books at the California Dry Fruit Importers, located in the Brokaw Building on Broadway. As Pinzolo looked over invoices, Dominic 'The Gap' Petrilli walked up behind him and fired two bullets into his head. Since the space was leased to Lucchese, he was questioned by police but quickly released for lack of evidence. After Pinzolo was dead, Lucchese and his pal Tom Gagliano reached out to Maranzano to explore the possibility of aligning with him. Wasn't this exactly what Lucchese had told Masseria that Reina was planning to do, which led to Genovese blowing Reina's head off? Numerous witnesses attest to Masseria's voracious eating habits. If he was what we would refer to today as a 'stress eater', he must have been eating himself into oblivion while trying to figure out what these young sneaks were up to next.

The war resulted in a recruitment drive, forcing the Sicilians to open La Cosa Nostra (Our Thing) to men from other regions of Italy. One war recruit of Neapolitan descent, Joe Valachi, said the Sicilians all knew each other, and since many were related through blood or marriage, they needed unknown faces to achieve the element of surprise when ambushing one another on the streets.

As Maranzano beefed up his ranks with new recruits, he armored his Cadillac with steel plates and bullet-proof windows. According to Maranzano's favorite soldier, Joe Bonanno, the don would sit in the back seat 'with a machine gun mounted on a swivel between his legs'. If true, it could not have been more than a ludicrous display of theatrics since it is difficult to imagine who or what he could destroy with a burst of machine-gun fire from this tight spot besides his own driver and the car's luxurious interior. Maranzano also packed two pistols, which he tucked into his belt like an outlaw in a spaghetti western. The don's flair for the dramatic extended to his strategies. Like the Allied generals who planned the Somme offensive, Maranzano wanted to pull off a masterstroke that could bring the war to a sudden end. When he received a tip from Lucchese that Masseria's men were known to frequent an apartment inside of a building complex in the Bronx, Maranzano ordered Joe Valachi to rent two apartments with views of the courtyard, setting up a crossfire the next time the enemy walked in or out of the complex. One day, Valachi's hit teams watched twenty or so men go inside the apartment for 'some kind of big meeting'. When the meeting broke up, the men left in pairs. The hit teams believed Masseria had entered so they waited for him to emerge, but they grew impatient when he did not come out and feared losing an opportunity to claim a trophy; when Steve Ferrigno and Manfredi 'Al' Mineo walked across the courtyard, they were cut down by machine-gun fire. After this double homicide, which exhibited Maranzano's skillful planning, Masseria's men defected in droves.

Maranzano celebrated the double hit and subsequent defections by inviting his men to a lawn party near Hyde Park, New York, where Franklin Roosevelt was born and raised as a boy, and would, as president of the United States, entertain Britain's King George VI. To the haughty Hyde Park community's everlasting embarrassment, Roosevelt served the king hot dogs at a picnic table; we can only imagine what they thought of this spectacle.

Back in Manhattan, Masseria, who was hemorrhaging men and money, became increasingly unhinged. In a fit of madness, he demanded that Luciano hand over his entire liquor business at once. If he did not, Masseria threatened to have Luciano's 'eyes gouged out [and] his tongue ripped from his mouth'. Masseria went on to say, 'They'll find you with your prick in your mouth, which is all you deserve.' Luciano took the threat in silence, but once out of Masseria's presence, he called an emergency meeting with Costello, Genovese, Lansky, Siegel and Adonis. Siegel wanted to immediately load up and hunt down Masseria but cooler minds prevailed. After Luciano listened to everyone's point of view, he decided to take Maranzano up on an open offer he had made to the underworld. Before we move on to what that offer entailed, it is necessary to take a brief trip back in time to see how Luciano got his famous nickname since he fabricated a story around it to disguise the real reason for his upcoming deal with Maranzano, and the double-cross that followed.

Shortly after the war had started, Luciano was nearly beaten to death on Staten Island. His flesh was burned with cigarettes and his right cheek slashed with a knife. While stumbling along Hylan Boulevard, half-dead, he was spotted by a beat cop who rushed him to a nearby hospital. While Luciano's face was being sewn up with fifty-five stitches, detectives arrived to question him. Luciano claimed he had been abducted in Manhattan by three gunmen, shoved into the back seat of a car, beaten unconscious, and dumped on Huguenot Beach on Staten Island. The detectives knew Luciano's story was, at best, incomplete but could not get any more out of him.

After being bandaged up, Luciano returned to Manhattan where he told his cronies a never-ending variety of stories about the scar that changed according to his audience; he once claimed he was beaten over a woman, then a gambling debt, a ransom and so on, using the incident to his advantage so many times that he stretched about six hundred miles out of a six-inch scar. The tale that is relevant to our story has to do with Maranzano. According to Luciano, after Masseria had threatened his life, Luciano reached out to Maranzano and offered to betray Masseria. Maranzano supposedly accepted Luciano's offer on condition that Luciano kill Masseria with his own hands. Luciano said that he refused and was knocked unconscious for his refusal. When he came to, he said he was hanging by his thumbs from a rafter with a half-dozen masked men around him. Maranzano again asked him to kill Masseria, and again Luciano refused; this time, he was beaten and burned with cigarette butts. Each time Luciano was knocked unconscious, the men threw buckets of dirty water in his face to wake him. Luciano then claimed to have kicked Maranzano in the groin, sending him to the floor in agony, before Maranzano sliced his cheek with a stiletto. It is inferred that Luciano finally agreed to Maranzano's terms in exchange for his life and was released from captivity.

Two decades later, as if Luciano had forgotten his earlier lies, he casually admitted the truth to authors Sid Feder and Joachim Joesten, who asked him how he got his infamous scar. With no hesitancy, Luciano said, 'The cops. They were just trying to find out things.' Feder and Joesten believed this answer, as did Frank Costello, who would one day confide to his attorney that cops had beaten and scarred Luciano. We may never know exactly why the cops did it but we do know that Luciano's PR man, Meyer Lansky, who once saved Luciano's reputation by telling him to hand out tickets to the Polo Grounds, now transformed his humiliating scar into his legendary nickname. Lansky told everyone that only luck could have saved his pal on that fateful night, and named him 'Lucky Luciano', giving him a sexy nickname to conceal what must have been an embarrassing ordeal. How 'lucky' we would all be with a Lansky cleaning up our messes and steering our destinies. Now, let us return to the present moment in which Luciano has decided to reach out to Maranzano.

In early 1931, Maranzano made an underworld announcement that he had no beef with Masseria's men, only Masseria. He let Masseria's soldiers know they could end the war by killing their boss. When Luciano decided to take Maranzano up on his offer, he used the scar that Maranzano had supposedly given him as proof that he was forced into it when, in fact, he was hiding his own ambition. One of Luciano's soldiers, Anthony 'Tony Bender' Strollo, arranged a walk-talk between Luciano and Maranzano at the Bronx Zoo. It is curiously appropriate that men who lived their lives like wild animals inside of a domestic setting should meet at the city zoo. As innocent children pointed at cages with awed smiles, they were unaware that the most dangerous beast among them was on their side of the fence. This public place was chosen because neither man trusted the other, the same reason why they brought along henchmen: Tommy Lucchese, Joe Adonis and Ben Siegel followed a few steps behind Luciano; Joe Bonanno and Joe Profaci followed behind Maranzano. By the end of the walk, Luciano had agreed to kill Masseria. He then went back to Masseria to do what he did best – lie.

Luciano told Masseria that he had worked out an intricate plan to knock off all of Maranzano's top capos in one fell swoop. A mediocre liar would have left it at that, but given Luciano's rare talent for assertive mendacity, he poured it on, getting into details. Masseria, while relishing the thought of victory, met deceit halfway. After Luciano talked his tongue dry, he invited Masseria to a celebratory lunch. Any of us who have experienced downfalls in life have learned never to tempt the gods by celebrating too early. But Masseria was too excited to wait and accepted the invitation to Nuova Villa Tammaro restaurant on Coney Island. Luciano told Masseria, 'Scarpato fixes the sauce like the old country.' This should have been Masseria's clue that he was being had; Luciano left the old country while barely off his mother's tit.

Vito Genovese, Ben Siegel, Albert Anastasia and Joe Adonis were chosen as the shooters while Ciro Terranova – the Artichoke King who was displaced by Masseria – would drive the getaway car.

On 15 April 1931, Luciano and Masseria drove to Coney Island together. Around noontime, they entered the restaurant and were greeted by owner and host Gerardo Scarpato. Masseria ate like an American senior citizen at a Chinese buffet as Luciano slowly sipped wine and barely picked at the food. After having pastries and coffee, Masseria was ready to leave but Luciano kept him around by suggesting they digest their meal while playing a few hands of cards. Masseria agreed to play 'for an hour or so'. Scarpato fetched the house deck and handed it to Luciano then excused himself to unwind on the boardwalk. Scarpato may not have known exactly what was about to happen but he knew when to take a powder. We do not know what Luciano was thinking as he stared at Masseria from across the table but there is a story from Luciano's youth that may lend insight into the gist of his thoughts at this moment.

As we will recall, Luciano's dad, Antonio, saved every penny to bring his family to America. When they first arrived, they could not afford beds so they slept on the floor. At some point, Antonio borrowed a few bucks from a local loanshark named Moliari so he could buy a bed for Luciano's sisters. While struggling to feed his family, Antonio fell behind on his weekly payments. During this time, a relative in Sicily shipped the family a dried ham. When Moliari showed up at Antonio's home with intent to take the bed as collateral for the unpaid debt, he spotted the ham hanging in the kitchen and took it, leaving Luciano's family hungry and humiliated. From that moment on, I am convinced that Luciano despised the old-time mafiosos. Given this traumatic childhood experience, we can easily entertain the idea that Luciano saw Masseria's sweaty fat face as a juicy round ham sitting atop his shoulders.

Luciano glanced at his wristwatch then excused himself, telling

Masseria he needed to use the toilet. After Luciano disappeared, four gunmen burst through the door and fired twenty bullets at Masseria who slid off his chair, pulling the tablecloth down with him; it was draped around him like a toga as he lay dead on the floor with the ace of spades stuck between his fingers (some say it was later placed there by a policeman or a news photographer).

Masseria dead in a pool of blood.

After the gunmen left, Luciano pulled the toilet chain then strolled out of the men's room. When the cops arrived, Luciano told them he had heard the gunfire. 'As soon as I finished drying my hands,' he said, 'I hurried out and walked back to see what it was about.' Since no one would abandon a safe place to see what twenty gunshots were about, the cops knew he was lying but could not prove it. With a touch of dark humor, Vito Genovese later commented that Masseria himself would have been proud of the hit. Lucky Luciano was one step closer to power.

Chapter 17

Sic Semper Tyrannis!

When Joe Masseria and Salvatore Maranzano were vying for Lucky Luciano's liquor business and had made him similar offers to join their borgatas, Meyer Lansky cautioned Luciano, saying, 'Once you accept such an offer, you'll find yourself under their total control. Neither will hesitate to kill you . . . You're the pawn in their game. Only it isn't a game. Our lives are at stake.' Based on this advice, Luciano decided to kill both men. Even before Masseria's body was loaded onto a meat wagon, the young Turks were already planning to whack Maranzano. Since the war was officially over and Maranzano was its undisputed victor with a seemingly unbreakable alliance of Castellammareses behind him, the job would require a lot more finesse than the lunchtime hit on Masseria. Luciano needed to arrange the politics in his favor or risk a counterstrike that could wipe out him and his crew. To this end, Luciano was helped by Maranzano's detestable vanity, displayed without restraint once he reigned supreme.

After winning the war, Maranzano invited several hundred mobsters around the country to a large banquet hall in the Bronx. Like Napoleon Bonaparte, who crowned himself emperor in Notre Dame Cathedral, Maranzano had arranged his self-coronation, attending to even the smallest details. As hundreds of attendees filtered into the hall, they saw Maranzano at the front of the room, seated on a 'throne-like chair'. By decorating the walls with religious icons and hanging a giant crucifix over his chair, Maranzano seemed to be tying his reign to the will of God. His pomposity may have been enamoring in feudal Sicily, but Americanized mobsters found it odious. Once the seats in the hall were filled, Maranzano began walking around, telling certain men to get up and sit somewhere else. When done with his seating arrangements, he returned to his high chair and declared that the men to his right were honest while those to his left were dishonest. The men heckled Maranzano as one man on the dishonest side got up from his seat and sat on the honest side. The noise continued until Maranzano scrapped whatever was on his mind and said, 'All right . . . Sit down, all of you, it doesn't matter where.' He now assured them, 'What's past is past', then moved on to his prepared speech.

Even Maranzano's detractors could not find fault in his dramatic and inspiring oratory, which held most of the room spellbound as he called upon history and tradition to form a new American mafia based on the Sicilian model (which, as noted in earlier chapters, evolved over the course of centuries, and was drawn from feudalism and nineteenth-century secret societies). Some of the younger men, like Luciano, knew very little about mafia history, while others who were recruited during the war were not from Sicily; the speech was designed to make everyone feel part of something much larger than themselves, and it worked.

When done with his speech which doubled as a historical lecture, Maranzano called on Luciano, who later said he had the 'nerve to pat me on the head when he asked me to come and sit next to him'. Maranzano appointed Luciano, who was now the leader of Masseria's borgata, as his second-in-command. (To be sure, Luciano was not part of Maranzano's borgata, so the appointment must have been nothing more than an official recognition that Luciano was the second most powerful man in the room.) Maranzano then named his new *capo-regimes* and allowed soldiers to fall in with capos they were comfortable with. At last, according to Luciano, 'He told us he was the supreme ruler. He would give everybody their orders and in the future they would all have to accept his rule and share their profits with him.' This was the blunder Luciano was looking for; he needed more than a gaudy chair and a large crucifix to make his case against Maranzano, and now he had it. As a student of Roman history, Maranzano should have known that any talk of a supreme ruler could be met with the shout, *Sic semper tyrannis!*

Maranzano sat in his chair fanning himself like a prima donna as everyone queued up to pay homage and hand him envelopes filled with cash; some reports say he was given over a million dollars, while more conservative estimates range from $100,000 to $150,000. Al Capone, who was originally aligned with Masseria, sent $6,000 and invited Maranzano to Chicago for a second celebration, with an open invitation to any New Yorkers who wished to attend. Before leaving for Chicago, Luciano asked Maranzano if Lansky could accompany them. Maranzano said it was okay for Lansky to tag along, but a

Jew was forbidden to attend meetings. Luciano accepted these terms but used them to smear Maranzano as a bigot, telling his powerful Jewish associates across the country that they would never enjoy equal opportunities under Maranzano.

Having collected a small fortune in the Bronx and Chicago, Maranzano threw himself another GoFundMe banquet, this time in Brooklyn. By the third banquet, some mobsters began to wonder if Maranzano was a racketeer or a *banqueteer*. Younger men, who were enamored by Maranzano's first speech, were tiring of his encores. When Luciano spotted their discontent, he spun Maranzano's brilliant but exhausting rhetoric about tradition into a misguided plight to drag the rackets into the Dark Ages. As Luciano was winning more and more men over to his cause, he received a visit that would bring his plot to a head.

Barnett and Rose Buchalter migrated from Russia and settled on the Lower East Side, where Barnett opened a hardware store and Rose raised their many children, one of whom was Louis, born on 6 February 1897. His mother affectionately called him 'Lepkeleh', a Yiddish term of endearment, which was shortened to Lepke. When the 'soft-voiced, soft-eyed, rather shy' thirteen-year-old boy's father died, Lepke's personality underwent a drastic change. His widowed mother accepted an invitation to live with one of her older sons in Colorado, and left Lepke with his older sister in Williamsburg, Brooklyn. With no parental guidance, Lepke spent a lot of time on the streets until he was introduced to a courtroom in 1915. More arrests ensued, resulting in a trip to a boys' reformatory followed by a five-year stint in Sing Sing. When Lepke came home from prison in his mid-twenties, he hooked up with his childhood pal Jacob 'Gurrah' Shapiro. As boys, Lepke and Gurrah had robbed pushcarts together on the Lower East Side; as adults, they became involved in labor racketeering, another racket perfected by the late Arnold Rothstein.

Shortly before the First World War, Marxist ideas spread across the globe and new labor unions popped up in New York's garment industry, resulting in tension between workforce and management, both of whom turned to gangsters for help. Bosses hired thugs to break up picket lines, and union leaders hired more thugs to beat up scabs. With both sides relying on hired muscle, Rothstein spotted an opportunity. His involvement began when union leaders, while locked in a struggle with management, turned to Rothstein's highly respected dad, Abe the Just, for mediation. Abe was clearly out of his league and referred them to another businessman who told them they had knocked on the wrong door when visiting Abe; Arnold was the man to see. The union leaders sought out Arnold Rothstein, who looked into the problem and found out that mobster Jacob 'Little Augie' Orgen was defending the union, and Jack 'Legs Diamond' Noland was standing behind management. Since Rothstein had mentored both men, he easily persuaded them to halt the violence while he brought the two sides together to work out their differences. With police and politicians on speed dial, and command over the paid thugs, Rothstein continued to offer his services to labor and management, while dictating the rules of the game. Despite the immense profits he earned in his role as an unofficial labor mediator, Rothstein bowed out of the business when it became too violent, the same reason he had abandoned bootlegging.

Following a deadly war between rival gangs that all wanted a piece of the labor pie, Lepke, who led one of the gangs, killed off his competition and rose to the top of the heap. Lepke and Gurrah built an army of over two hundred *shtarkers* (Yiddish for tough guys), and acted as a security and mediation firm for both sides of the industry. Not content with being a paid muscleman and arbitrator, Lepke began to infiltrate the unions he was working with. Each craft in the garment industry had its own union that fell under the umbrella of the Amalgamated Clothing Workers of America, headed by Sidney Hillman. Since Amalgamated was too big and strong to confront head-on, Lepke decided to compromise them by attacking the Cutters Union and their truckers. The Cutters, who cut fabric into patterns that were used to make clothing, and their truckers who transported the materials, constituted a comparatively small union with just under two thousand workers. But Lepke's strategy was clever, and quite similar to that of the US Eighth Air Force in 1943, when it targeted ball-bearing factories in Schweinfurt, Germany; without the tiny balls, the massive German war industry would grind to a halt. Likewise, if Lepke could shut down the tiny Cutters Union along with their trucks, the entire garment industry would grind to a screeching halt and drag Sidney Hillman to Lepke's doorstep. As one might expect, Hillman did not appreciate a hoodlum like Lepke interloping in his fabric fiefdom, so he paid to have Lepke killed, but the plot failed. When Hillman realized he could not get rid of Lepke, he begrudgingly began to work with him – until Hillman's hatchet man, Bruno Belea, turned to Salvatore Maranzano for help. At this point, Lepke would have been in serious trouble had he not had his own Italian rabbi to call on.

As Lepke was on his way up and tightening his grip across the garment industry, he became a natural target of the mafia. Although Lepke controlled an army of *shtarkers*, he did not have the strength to take on an army of sworn assassins, but the mafia works in such a way that if you partner with one mobster, he, in turn, keeps the rest at bay. Lepke partnered with Lucky Luciano, who he met through Meyer Lansky, while he also maintained close ties to Albert Anastasia.

As for Sidney Hillman, his relationship to Bruno Belea was like Henry Ford's relationship to Harry Bennett, who was tasked with handling Ford's dirty work (Bennett regularly dealt with Detroit mobster Pete Licavoli, and Lucky Luciano's pal Joe Adonis, when it came to problems with the United Auto Workers Union). Bruno Belea visited Maranzano, who agreed to help and announced his entry into the affair by dispatching a gang to bust up a clothing shop protected by Lepke. The shop owners, Guido and John Ferrari, gathered up their workers and drove off the vandals. Maranzano felt bested by the Ferrari brothers so he had Guido murdered. Instead of retaliating, body for body, and getting drawn into a war he could not win, Lepke aimed straight for the jugular and pressured Luciano to knock off Maranzano. Once Maranzano was gone and Sidney Hillman was neutered, Luciano would reap a larger share of Lepke's expanded rackets. But Luciano did not need this added incentive to convince him that Maranzano had to go; Lepke's contest with Hillman did, however, speed up the hands of Time.

Chapter 18

Luciano's Superb Statesmanship

Before Lucky Luciano launched his coup against Salvatore Maranzano, he conjured up a trick to win over more supporters and create a plausible defense for his actions. He claimed to have solid information from a source, as usual Tommy Lucchese, that Maranzano had drawn up an actual hit list with the names of Luciano and his supporters. Although this hit list has received absolutely no scrutiny from historians, I am convinced that it was thoughtfully drawn up not by Maranzano, but by Luciano, since it contained only the names of men Luciano still needed to win over, while also serving as an excuse for his coup. For starters, Meyer Lansky and Ben Siegel did *not* make the list, nor did Albert Anastasia. This is strange since these were some of the most dangerous men around Luciano. If Maranzano were to whack Luciano, Anastasia and Siegel would certainly retaliate, and who would want to leave Lansky's brain around, even functioning in a jar? I submit that these men were not on the list because Luciano did not need to win them over to his cause through fear-mongering.

Al Capone *was* on the list. Capone had just established a strong alliance with Maranzano in return for Maranzano recognizing Capone's leadership in Chicago; Luciano needed to break that alliance. Dutch Schultz also made the list. Schultz, a born killer who cornered the beer market during Prohibition, headed a murderous gang that Luciano wanted on his side. Further evidence that points to Luciano as the author of this list can be found in the single hitman supposedly tasked with extinguishing every target on behalf of Maranzano. Maranzano, who only trusted Sicilians, specifically those from his hometown of Castellammare del Golfo, supposedly put his hit list, which grew longer by the day, in the hands of an Irish-American, Vincent 'Mad Dog' Coll. How Coll was expected to drive around Manhattan and Chicago killing so many people was never explained by Luciano, who must have known this was impossible when he attempted to answer this problem by claiming that everyone on the list would be invited to Maranzano's office – if they could fit – where Coll would be waiting for them in a back room; he would suddenly pop out and mow everyone down. Maranzano's office was in the newly built New York Central Building on Park Avenue (today's Helmsley Building), where he was known as the president of the Eagle Building Corporation. Maranzano took great pride in his office and it is ridiculous to think he would choose it as the scene of a massacre. Then what? Return to work the next day like nothing happened?

New York Central Building; located at 230 Park Avenue.

Luciano's choice of Mad Dog Coll as Maranzano's alleged hitman was calculating, and had to do with Dutch Schultz, who was, at the time, engaged in a bloody feud with Coll. Choosing Coll as the hitman made it personal for Schultz who swallowed the bait and came over to Luciano's side.

With Meyer Lansky working as his chief strategist, Luciano and his crew began meeting at Ratner's kosher restaurant on the Lower East Side. Over pickles and pastrami, they discussed the first part of their plan, which was to analyze Maranzano's daily habits and movements and record the addresses he frequented. While closely examining Maranzano, the plotters discovered his Achilles heel, later explained by Joe Bonanno, who said, 'Maranzano loved perfection. He took great pride in his ledgers, his account books, his records and files.' When Lansky found out that Maranzano was known to fuss over his books, he told his brother, Jake Lansky, to inform the Internal Revenue Service that Maranzano was a tax cheat. On several occasions, IRS agents visited Maranzano's office and combed through his books but found no discrepancies, as Lansky had suspected. But Lansky was playing the long game; he was getting Maranzano used to unannounced visits from federal agents, which played into the next part of his plan: to have hitmen visit Maranzano posing as IRS agents. Since, at the time, Jews could pass for government accountants quicker than southern Italians, who Maranzano might sniff out, Lansky supplied the hit team. Three Jewish gunmen were brought in from Chicago and would work with Samuel 'Red' Levine, another of Luciano's favorite assassins who killed as readily as Genovese, Siegel and Anastasia. Lansky lodged the hitmen in a safe house where he showed them photographs of Maranzano, and trained them to walk and talk like stiff federal agents.

On 10 September 1931, just five months since Masseria was whacked in Coney Island, Tommy Lucchese visited Maranzano's ninth-floor offices in the New York Central Building, telling him he needed to discuss an urgent matter. After greeting Maranzano in the reception area, Lucchese hooked his arm under Maranzano's arm and began to lead him toward Maranzano's private office. Like any other wild predator that isolates its prey from the pack before killing it, Lucchese was separating Maranzano from his bodyguards. As this was happening, there was a loud rap at the door. The door swung open and four men identified themselves as federal agents; they were short-spoken and authoritative, just like Lansky had taught them. They demanded to speak with Maranzano then ordered everyone else to stand against the wall, including Lucchese and Maranzano's secretary, Grace Samuels, who was about to lose her last paycheck and would never work for another Italian again. While two agents held everyone at gunpoint, the other two directed Maranzano into his private office, completing what Lucchese had started a moment earlier. Once Maranzano was in his office, the men closed the door behind them and drew switchblades. Flick. Flick. Maranzano flew into a desperate rage and was beating off his attackers until they drew guns and shot him. After Maranzano crashed to the floor with six knife wounds and four bullet wounds, the hitmen fled, leaving two hats behind that were traced to hat stores in Chicago. Lucchese poked his head into the inner office to make sure Maranzano was dead, then 'calmly rode the elevator to the ground floor and faded into the crowd on Park

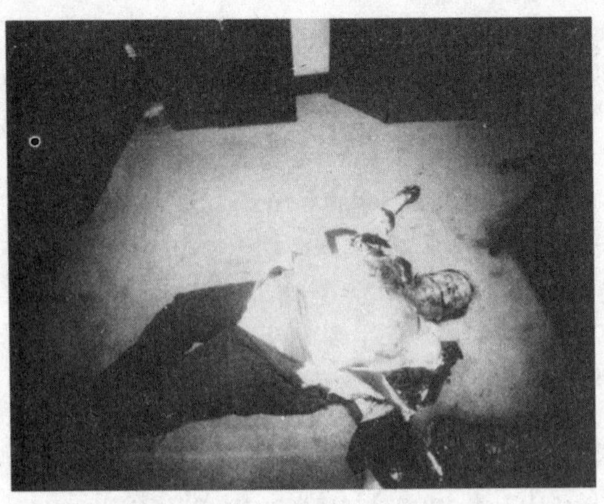

Maranzano dead in his office.

Avenue'. To avoid police questioning, Maranzano's useless bodyguards took off.

Now that the deed was done, the 33-year-old Luciano assumed the role of Brutus, the tyrant slayer. He sent word around the underworld that he was indeed responsible for the hit on Maranzano, but insisted that he had acted in self-defense, citing the phony hit list as the pretext for his actions. He even claimed that his hit team, as they were exiting the building, had bumped into Mad Dog Coll, who was on his way up to speak with Maranzano about the hit list; this last lie was to suggest that Luciano had acted in the nick of time. As Luciano moved quickly to consolidate power, his only obstacle appeared to be the Castellammareses, who would want to avenge their fallen leader. How Luciano dealt with this problem speaks to his political savvy.

Before Maranzano took over the Castellammarese clan, their elder statesman was Stefano Magaddino, the don of his own borgata in Buffalo, who, according to an agent for the immigration service, 'runs everything in Niagara Falls but the cascades'. Magaddino's exalted stature waned as Maranzano's power increased, and although Magaddino had no intention of removing Maranzano – that we know of – we can only imagine how happy he was to see him go. Understanding these internal Castellammarese politics, Luciano asked Joe Bonanno, who was the recently deceased Maranzano's chief aide and protégé, and also Stefano Magaddino's younger cousin, to take over Maranzano's borgata and become head of lower New York's Castellammarese clan (as opposed to Magaddino's Buffalo branch, which was the clan's upstate borgata). This offer won over Bonanno as well as his cousin, Magaddino, since Bonanno routinely relied on Magaddino's wise advice. Since Bonanno was only twenty-six years old at the time, Magaddino reclaimed the clout he once had as the clan's elder statesman, and mobsters were, once again, inclined to visit Buffalo's nearby resort town of Niagara Falls where they could pay homage to Magaddino. (No one has ever suggested that Magaddino knew of the Maranzano hit beforehand but it is quite possible that Luciano had passed him a wink or whisper since it is certainly consistent with Luciano's nature to resolve problems ahead of time.)

After the crown that fell off Maranzano's head rolled onto Joe Bonanno's lap, Bonanno, who once considered Maranzano his 'hero', a man he felt 'honored and privileged just to be near', now called him a 'misfit' who 'didn't live in Sicily anymore'. Bonanno said, 'Luciano had given me a credible explanation for his actions', resulting in Bonanno telling Luciano, 'I have no quarrel with you.' What quarrel might he have had? That Luciano had not done it sooner?

Following Maranzano's death, newspaper reporters wrote that Luciano had ordered dozens, if not hundreds, of men killed across the country; articles called to mind the Palermo massacre of 1282 when referring to his purge as the Night of the Sicilian Vespers. There is no evidence to support any of this and Luciano, himself, debunked the myth later in life – but he did not bother to refute it at the time since it gave him an air of omnipotence, prompting men to fall in line faster, fearing they may be added to his long, albeit spurious, casualty list. Luciano did, however, perform a light house-cleaning which involved the murders of three men, about the average count for these takeovers, give or take a body.

In contrast to Salvatore Maranzano's pompous coronation, Lucky Luciano assumed the helm with no fanfare. He silenced any talk of him becoming the *capo di tutti capi* when he made it clear that he was only taking over Masseria's borgata, and appointed Vito Genovese as his underboss. Tom Gagliano got his own borgata, with Tommy Lucchese as his underboss (Lucchese was and would continue to be the real power but he preferred to stay in the shadows). Joe Profaci, who was suspected of secretly siding with Luciano, got his own borgata with his brother-in-law, Joe Magliocco, as his underboss. Vincent Mangano got his own borgata, with Albert Anastasia as his underboss. And Joe Bonanno, as noted, took over Maranzano's borgata. This marks the advent of lower New York's five mafia families which still co-exist today.

Just as any new government won by coup seeks recognition from abroad, Luciano made it a point to visit other mafia leaders around the country. Al Capone invited everyone to Chicago for a national conference so he could honor Luciano, as Capone had once done for Maranzano. At that gathering, as you may recall, Luciano had asked Maranzano if Lansky could accompany him, and was told that Lansky could come along but could not attend meetings. Now, Lansky, Siegel, Dutch Schultz, Morris 'Moe' Dalitz and Harry 'Nig' Rosen were all invited to attend the meetings along with Capone's Jewish pal, Jake

'Greasy Thumb' Guzik. From this conference forward, every mafia summit would have enough Jews for a minyan.*

Capone put everyone up at the Congress Hotel, where his bribed Chicago police force acted as security. Unlike Maranzano's loathsome fundraising events, the Chicago conference was used to resolve national problems, strike new deals and toast to a prosperous future. Some men tried to pay homage to Luciano, handing him cash-filled envelopes, but he prudently turned them away.

Before the conference began, Luciano explained to a limited audience of Sicilian mafiosos how he planned to undo the overly traditional aspects of the mafia that did not apply in America. He pointed out the absurdity of men fighting over what area of Sicily they came from. Luciano wanted everyone to know that more than killing Masseria and Maranzano, he had killed their antiquated ideas. Luckily for Luciano, Lansky was present to gauge the audience's expressions. During a break, Lansky pulled Luciano aside and told him to tone it down, assuring Luciano that if he tried to reinvent the wheel, they would run him over with it. He warned Luciano not to insult their deep-rooted Sicilian culture which was, after all, the glue that made them superior to other ethnic gangs. When, at one point, Luciano expressed the foolishness of oaths sealed in blood, Lansky advised him to honor this ritual since most men respect oaths and feel duty-bound to adhere to them until death. Luciano heeded Lansky's sound advice and kept the old traditions in place, which saved the day. Later, in front of a larger audience, Luciano recited the rules he had learned from Maranzano, most of which he had, until now, ignored or disparaged.

To keep peace among the borgatas, Luciano created the Commission, a ruling body to debate policy and arbitrate interfamily disputes. Each boss would have a seat at a round table that came with a vote, and their rulings had the force of law. (It is telling that the Commission was an American idea, with no Sicilian origin; democracy, albeit with tyrannical features, was rubbing off on the mafia. In later years, Sicilians did adopt their own version of this ruling body, calling theirs the Cupola.) Luciano placed quotas on borgata memberships to keep them roughly equal in strength and prevent any one man from building an army that dominated the rest. Lastly, the old-world title of don,

* When hijacker Joe Howard beat up Jake Guzik and bragged that he had made 'the little Jew whine', Capone tracked down Howard and emptied a revolver into his face.

which I will continue to use now and then, was scrapped in favor of boss, a clear sign of America's corporate culture.

Back in New York, Luciano moved into the Waldorf Towers, Suite 39C, under the assumed name of Mr Ross; his rent was almost $8,000 annually (close to $150,000 in today's currency). Everything about Luciano's personal life was a complete break with Sicilian tradition, beginning with his residence in a luxury hotel where he slept with a harem of prostitutes. Luciano made no attempt to marry a virtuous wife (while keeping a *gumare* on the side), nor did he raise a large Italian family while hoping for boys to carry on his name. But despite his personal departure from domestic custom, he somehow kept his borgata steeped in tradition, including honoring the dead, even when he made them that way; no one was prohibited from attending Maranzano's funeral. He was laid to rest with all the pomp that befitted his melodramatic personality.

Joe Masseria and Salvatore Maranzano had terribly underestimated Lucky Luciano, who had once said to Meyer Lansky, 'I may have to do a lot of killing before I get control, but I'm willing.' As it turned out, others did all the killing for him, men like Vito Genovese, Ben Siegel, Albert Anastasia and Red Levine. Luciano admitted this later in life when he said:

> Did I ever kill anybody myself? That depends on how you look at it. If it means, did I ever pull the trigger and actually knock somebody off myself, then the answer is no . . . On the other hand, if you look at it from the strict letter of the law, where an accessory or a guy who gives the orders to make a hit is just as guilty as the guy who pulls the trigger, then I guess I done my share.

Because Luciano had never personally killed anyone, Sicilian mafiosos raised on *omertà* would not have considered him a real man. Masseria had taunted Luciano about this perceived shortcoming, as did Maranzano, who mocked Luciano after the hit on Masseria, telling him, 'You should have arranged for me to have pictures of you pulling the trigger.' It seems that Masseria and Maranzano had overlooked the threat posed by Luciano, never imagining that a man who had never killed anyone with his own hands – could kill them both!

The mafia's civil war was over and Manhattan's Pompey and Caesar were dead and buried. Luciano would usher in the Golden Age of Augustus.

Part Four

The Building of Empire

Chapter 19

Expanding the Realm – and Attracting Unwanted Attention

With the war and the old dons out of the way, the newly crowned bosses were ready to respond to new opportunities. Just as fate had given them Prohibition, it had also presented them with another gift in October 1929 when the stock market crashed. As fortunes evaporated in minutes and hopeless men jumped from buildings, the mafia was smiling from ear to ear; flush with cash from years of bootlegging, they were perfectly positioned for their second windfall in a decade. As a result of the crash, from 1929 to 1931, a string of bank failures decimated the economy. Credit became tight and many distressed businessmen, who had been turned away by the surviving banks, visited mobsters who gave on-the-spot loans in return for collateral, or shares in their businesses. These loans paved the way for the mafia's entry into a variety of American industries, many of which they remain ensconced in today.

A few mobsters spread their cash around the dirty little world of politics. Frank Costello, who Luciano appointed as his consigliere, replaced Arnold Rothstein as Tammany Hall's chief underworld liaison. Politicians knew, with Costello as their de facto campaign manager, election victories were guaranteed. Costello's power over the Hall gave him and Luciano a say at the 1932 Democratic National Convention, held in the mafia-controlled city of Chicago. The front-runners for the nomination were former New York governor Al Smith and current New York governor Franklin Roosevelt. Luciano and Costello hedged their bets by backing both men. Roosevelt won the nomination but crossed them by refusing to make good on favors he had promised them. Oddly, Luciano held no grudge against Roosevelt, saying, 'We was both shitass double-crossers. He done exactly what I would've done in the same position.'

Nevertheless, the convention turned out to be a networking event for Frank Costello who wanted to distribute his slot machines throughout the country. By 1932, Costello had placed over twenty-five thousand slot machines across New York, distributed by the Triangle Mint Company, which Costello owned with his gambling partner, Dandy Phil Kastel. Most were placed in social clubs, back rooms of cafés, candy stores and restaurants. To circumvent the state's anti-gambling laws, Costello rigged the machines to pay out mints which acted as tokens that could be exchanged for cash or merchandise when presented to the store owner. Store owners were provided with a telephone number to call in the unlikely event their machines were confiscated or the owner was arrested. 'When the detectives arrested me,' said one store owner, 'I called the number. I said, "They are taking the machine out and me with it." By the time we got to the station house a bondsman was there, and I was out in five minutes.'

On the floor of the convention, Costello targeted Louisiana senator Huey 'Kingfish' Long, who welcomed gambling across his state. 'The people seem to want gambling,' said Long. 'So let 'em gamble.' After Costello struck a deal with Long, Dandy Phil Kastel shipped a thousand new slot machines to New Orleans. Luciano later said that Long pocketed approximately three million dollars from Costello's machines which 'raked in more than $37 million'. Meyer Lansky added that he had personally deposited Long's money into a Swiss bank account. To distribute his machines, Costello partnered with the New Orleans mafia, which was alive and well, contrary to Mayor Shakspeare's post-lynchings claim that, 'The reign of the mafia in New Orleans has ceased.' Senator Long, however, would soon be deceased; on 8 September 1935, he was assassinated by a disgruntled family member of a political opponent. Long's bodyguards were rather assertive when disarming the assassin; he had fifty-nine bullet holes in his body. Long's last words were, 'God, don't let me die. I have so much to do.' Dandy Phil Kastel had even more to do now that Long was dead and Kastel and Costello had lost their most ardent political supporter in Louisiana. The politics briefly turned against them until Kastel was able to make new connections by spreading around the graft.

After Franklin Roosevelt won the presidency, he repealed the Eighteenth Amendment in December 1933, bringing the syndicate's fourteen-year bootlegging run to a screeching halt. Former secretary of state Elihu Root wrote: 'It will take a long time for our country to recover from the injury done by that great and stupid error in government.' It was an understatement as the ramifications of bootlegging, which included police, political and judicial corruption, persisted long after repeal. Countless public officials who were corrupted by Prohibition kept their hands out for the next bribe, and their sordid relationships with the mafia continued unabated as they became elected representatives or rose to new heights in the public sector.

The Italian–Jewish relationship Luciano had nurtured paid off in spades as Meyer Lansky opened casinos along the eastern seaboard and Lepke Buchalter steamrolled over numerous labor unions, now that Maranzano was gone and no one else had the power to stand in his way. After conquering the garment industry, Lepke went after the baking unions by again targeting the industry's weak flank, its truckers. With the help of William 'Wolfie' Goldis, Lepke created the Flour Truckmen's Association, and vandalized the trucks of any companies that refused to fall in line. When union leader William Snyder voiced grievances over Lepke's intrusion, Wolfie Goldis invited Snyder to Garfein's restaurant so he could discuss his complaints over dinner. Around 10 p.m., as Snyder sat at a table talking with Goldis and several associates, Goldis's brother, Morris, entered the restaurant and put a bullet in the back of Snyder's head. The tablecloth was a bloody mess but the negotiations had been wrapped up pretty tidily as Lepke slid the baking industry into his pocket. Next, Lepke targeted the printers, cobblers, leather workers, umbrella makers, dyers, milliners, butchers and other unions, which were all brought to heel with the help of mafia muscle.

Lepke moved into a Central Park West penthouse, not far from Luciano who still lived in the Waldorf Towers. In the opening line of *Pride and Prejudice*, Jane Austen wrote: 'It is a truth universally acknowledged, that a single man in possession of a good fortune, must be in want of a wife.' Lepke fit Austen's bill and married a British-born widow, Betty Wasserman. The ex-convict who once robbed pushcarts with his sidekick, Gurrah, was enjoying life as a happily married multimillionaire when his tranquility was upset by a one-time choirboy who, due to life's mysterious twists and turns, would become Lepke and Luciano's fiercest adversary.

Thomas Dewey was born in Owosso, Michigan, on 24 March 1902. As a boy and while attending high school, he sang in the church choir and dreamed of becoming an opera singer, an impossible goal in a small town of eight thousand people where whistling 'Old MacDonald

Had a Farm' was considered the bar for musical excellence. After high school, Dewey entered the University of Michigan and completed his undergraduate degree, then traveled to New York where he studied law at Columbia Law School while pursuing his dream of becoming a tenor, an increasingly unattainable aspiration about which his parents said, 'Let Tom get it out of his system.' On his twenty-second birthday, Dewey's parents drove from Michigan to Manhattan to hear him perform at a studio concert. Unfortunately, Dewey lost his voice halfway through 'Der Doppelgänger'. He blamed it on laryngitis, but the embarrassment, to his parents' relief, got it out of his system; he regretfully concluded, 'the glamor of a singing career had faded completely'. After graduating from Columbia Law, Dewey went to work as an attorney for a Wall Street firm where he met George Medalie, the son of a rabbi who would become, in essence, Dewey's rabbi.

George Medalie was born and raised on the Lower East Side, where many of the nation's top criminals had grown up, but he carved a different path out of the jungle. He graduated Phi Beta Kappa from City College of New York and entered Columbia Law School on a Pulitzer scholarship. After graduating, he went to work at the district attorney's office, and eventually settled into private practice where he met Dewey. When Medalie was asked by President Hoover's attorney general, William Mitchell, to head up the US Attorney's Office in the Southern District of New York, he accepted the job and tapped the 28-year-old Dewey as his new chief of the Criminal Division. Dewey admitted that he was 'young and inexperienced in criminal matters', but felt the job offer was 'irresistible'. In March 1931, Dewey began his new job and was suddenly a very powerful man, supervising a staff of sixty attorneys. 'This is the most fascinating job I've ever had,' Dewey told a friend, 'and I'm trying to learn something about it.' Dewey was a quick learner. By August, he had prosecuted and convicted his first real gangster, Legs Diamond, along with two of his henchmen, John Scaccio and Paul Quatrochi.

Thomas Dewey.

On 1 November 1933, Medalie resigned his prestigious position, and returned to private practice where the big bucks were waiting. Thirty-one-year-old Dewey was appointed acting US attorney until the 25th of the month, when President Roosevelt appointed Martin Conboy to take his place. Unwilling to play second fiddle to Conboy, Dewey also planned to resign, but before leaving, he prosecuted Waxey Gordon, the low-level hoodlum who, on the eve of Prohibition, had introduced Arnold Rothstein to Big Maxie Greenberg in Central Park. Since then, Waxey had become a multimillionaire from bootlegging and invested his money wisely, buying hotels, cargo ships and semi-legitimate breweries that manufactured 'near beer', which was dealcoholized beer. The breweries, which operated during Prohibition, were federally licensed and would have turned a decent profit, but Waxey could not resist the temptation to turn out the real stuff. Since real beer could not be trucked out the front door, Waxey set up an underground pipeline that calls to mind Victor Hugo's elaborate description of the Parisian sewer system in *Les Misérables*. From large vats inside his two manufacturing plants, the real beer was pumped underground to adjoining houses where powerful machinery, in turn, pumped the beer into a long hose that meandered through New Jersey's public sewer system. The hose ran for several blocks until the beer was pumped up into garages where barrels were filled and loaded onto a fleet of trucks for transport. According to Waxey's brewmaster, the operation turned out an average of five thousand barrels a week.

Notwithstanding this intricate underground operation, Dewey thought the easiest case to bring against Waxey was for federal income tax evasion. He questioned hundreds of witnesses and plodded through telephone toll records which led to the discovery of two hundred bank accounts that belonged to Waxey, none of which were in his name. When Waxey heard about his impending indictment, he took off. A tip led Dewey's lawmen to the Catskill Mountains, where Waxey was hiding in a cottage in the hamlet of White Lake with a gun under his pillow and his bodyguard, Joey the Fleabag, watching the front door. Fleabag was sandbagged by police and Waxey was brought downstate to stand trial. Dewey showed the jury how Waxey had earned an estimated $1,338,000 in 1930 alone, but claimed only $8,100, and paid ten bucks in taxes. All told, Dewey proved that the former pickpocket had netted close to five million dollars from his breweries, hotels and nightclubs while pickpocketing the IRS and spending lavishly on tailors, fancy cars, antiques and interior decorators. Dewey made sure the jurors, all of whom were likely buckling under the weight of the Depression, heard about Waxey's expensive ten-room flat on Manhattan's ritzy West End Avenue where he built a library of expensive leather-bound first-edition books, which, Dewey commented to the jury, were never opened. The jury was out less than an hour before returning a guilty verdict. Waxey was sentenced to ten years.

After his courtroom triumph, Dewey returned to private practice and may never have been seen or heard from again, but the wheel of fate was not done turning. On 15 May 1935, New York's Tammany-controlled district attorney's office was accused for the umpteenth time of protecting the mob. DA William Copeland Dodge overlooked nearly every organized racket in the city, focusing instead on communism and prostitution. When a grand jury was launched into racketeering and political corruption, Dodge dragged his feet until the grand jury, led by Lee Thompson Smith, began to subpoena witnesses on their own, leading the press to dub them the 'runaway' jury. Backed by a number of civic groups, Smith asked Governor Herbert Lehman for a special prosecutor, saying, 'We have labored under the most difficult handicaps. Every conceivable obstacle has been put in our path.' Governor Lehman instructed Dodge to appoint a prosecutor from a list of four attorneys he recommended. All four turned down the offer while jointly proposing Thomas Dewey for the job. Lehman balked at their recommendation but eventually yielded to pressure and Dewey eagerly assumed the role of special prosecutor in July 1935.

Getting right down to business, Dewey dug into the 750 pages of minutes provided by the runaway grand jury then searched for a headquarters from where he would launch the very first concentrated attack on organized crime. Dewey rented three-quarters of the fourteenth floor of the Woolworth Building, a skyscraper located across the street from the United States Attorney's Office. Secrecy was paramount. With seven entrances to the lobby, and one leading directly to the subway, aspiring informants could creep in and out of the building, which was constantly surveilled by Dewey's uniformed police and undercover detectives who were tasked with spotting members of organized crime who might feel inclined to monitor the building and take note of Dewey's visitors. Special witnesses would be escorted to Dewey's private office on freight elevators located at the rear of the building. Thirty-five cubicles were spread across ten thousand square feet of office space where witnesses could speak behind Venetian blinds that were drawn before they entered so, according to Dewey, 'spies in adjacent buildings' could not use a 'telescope and

Woolworth Building, where Thomas Dewey launched his attack on organized crime.

see who's in here talking with us'. An 'untappable telephone cable' was installed and strict instructions were given to telephone operators to prohibit outgoing calls unless they were pre-approved by Dewey. The standard locks on filing cabinets were replaced with tamper-resistant versions and each day's accumulation of wastepaper was burned in the basement furnace. Dewey's seventy-six-member staff included twenty deputy assistant district attorneys, ten investigators, ten accountants, and twenty stenographers who were confined to 'one large room under constant supervision against leaks'.

To announce his crusade, Dewey used a radio broadcast to speak directly to the people of New York, imploring them to visit him at the Woolworth Building where they could provide confidential information about organized crime. 'Any man who brings testimony to my office can be certain that his name, his testimony and his person will receive absolute protection,' Dewey said over the air. 'A prosecutor's strongest weapon is complete secrecy and the protection of his witnesses . . . If you have evidence of organized crime, of whatever kind, and however large or small, bring it to us. The rest is our job. We will do our best.' Dewey's speech resonated; the phone lines and front doors were flooded as thousands of citizens responded with tips. In fact, so many showed up that Dewey stationed a man in his reception area who 'could tell with a real degree of certainty whether someone was genuinely distressed about something for which there was a legal remedy or whether he or she belonged in the observation ward at Bellevue Hospital'. It so happened that Dewey's first big case was against a gangster who should have been condemned to the mental ward at Bellevue, Dutch Schultz.

Chapter 20
The Dutchman

Arthur Flegenheimer was born on 6 August 1902, to parents of Austrian-Jewish descent. He was raised in the South Bronx among a lower-income blend of Blacks, Italians, Irish and Jews. His father, Herman, was a saloon keeper who walked out on the family when Arthur was a boy. Later in life, Arthur would tell reporters that his father had died and not deserted; he was either repeating what his mother had told him or what he preferred to believe. At fourteen, he quit school to help his mom get by. He sold newspapers, ran odd errands, and was a roofer for a short time before he turned to crime. Aged seventeen, he took a pinch for burglary and was sent to a reformatory on Blackwell's Island (later known as Roosevelt Island). For being a disobedient inmate, he was moved to a work farm in Westhampton, New York, where he escaped, was recaptured, and served a total of fifteen months before returning to the Bronx with a new name, Dutch Schultz (which he took from an old-time thug who had achieved some local fame).

During Prohibition, Schultz was hired to protect convoys of beer trucks from getting hijacked. By 1928, he and his pal Joe Noe had purchased a few old trucks and quickly monopolized the beer industry in the Bronx while seizing some territory in Harlem. Their beer blitz made them more than a few enemies and Noe was gunned down while parking his car on West 54th Street and 6th Avenue. Schultz was in an office above the street when Noe was ambushed below. Schultz supposedly stepped out onto the balcony and shot down at the gunmen who were firing at Noe. I am surprised that no one has ever wondered if Schultz's bullets were aimed at the hitmen, or at Noe; it is worth considering since Schultz had the most to gain from Noe's death and would eventually reveal himself as a homicidal maniac with an incurable penchant for disposing of partners, once commenting to an associate, 'I don't take in nobody as partners with me.' The beer business now belonged to Schultz alone and he curiously resumed operations within an hour of Noe's death, as if it never happened, adding to my suspicions.

Vincent 'Mad Dog' Coll was an Irish immigrant whose childhood makes the hardships depicted in *Angela's Ashes* look like a pampered life. His sister died at seven months old. His mother died of pneumonia when he was only seven. One brother died at seventeen, another at twenty-three, both from tuberculosis. And his father died at what can be considered, given the above, the ripe old age of forty-nine. Young Vincent and a surviving brother, Peter, were placed in a Catholic missionary home on Staten Island. They lived there for three years until they began a spate of petty but violent crimes that landed them in prison. Vincent was paroled in 1927 and joined the Schultz gang in 1928. By 1930, he had put together a splinter group of Schultz crew members who were unhappy with their meager piece of the pie. They launched a rebellion against Schultz, who took them to war. Over the next year, there were casualties on both sides.

Finally, on 28 July 1931, Coll and his gang made a major mistake when they targeted Joey Rao, a Schultz ally. They sprayed the street but missed Rao, accidentally injuring five children who were playing nearby; one was killed. The public was furious and wanted justice for the deceased five-year-old, Michael Vengalli, who was laid to rest in a tiny coffin. After Coll was labeled a 'baby killer' by the press, he assumed a fake identity, altered his appearance, and hid out. A few months later, Coll was nabbed and took the case to trial. His high-priced attorney beat up the star witness on the stand and the baby killer walked. But street justice awaited Coll now that Schultz had the support of the entire underworld, who did not need the same evidence as a jury to convict and sentence Coll to death. (If we take a moment to reflect on Lucky Luciano's coup against Maranzano, it becomes perfectly clear why Mad Dog Coll was the ideal gangster for Luciano to weave into his tall tale about a hit list. Are we to believe that Maranzano would have hired a baby killer, hated by the public, the police, the press and the underworld, to knock off his enemies? It is hard to imagine that Maranzano would even invite Coll to his upscale office while everyone was gunning for him. Luciano knew that Coll was despised and would not be around long enough to refute his lie. And even if he was, who would believe a baby killer?)

Unable to find Mad Dog Coll, Schultz picked off Peter Coll instead; he was gunned down on a Harlem sidewalk. Schultz then ambushed and killed two more of Coll's crew before he put a $50,000 bounty on Coll's head. He even walked into a police precinct and told the cops

Vincent 'Mad Dog' Coll exiting the court house.

on duty, some of whom were on his payroll, 'I'll pay good to any cop who kills the mick.' One dumbfounded policeman asked Schultz if he knew where he was. Schultz snapped back that he did.

On 8 February 1932, Schultz was tipped that Coll was staying at the Cornish Arms Hotel, and was regularly using the telephone booth across the street, located in the back of the London Chemists Drugstore. Schultz assembled a crack squad of assassins, who watched the block. When Coll was about two minutes into his next telephone call, a car rolled to the curb outside. Death was less than a hundred feet away as Coll rambled on inside the booth. Two men waited in the car as lookouts while a third entered the drugstore, walked straight to the back, and told the employees and customers, 'Keep cool now and you won't get hurt.' He threw aside the flap of his overcoat, raised a Tommy gun, and sprayed the phone booth. Coll was trapped inside of a glass coffin while at least fifteen slugs hit his brain, heart and body. The hit team's getaway was seamless, apart from a beat cop who briefly contemplated the glory of heroism but realized he would not be around to enjoy the accolades and allowed them to escape. After Coll was buried, Schultz was the undisputed beer baron of New York. His next target was Harlem's policy racket.

*

Even before the Great Depression, more than half of American households were living below the poverty line. In congested areas like Harlem, the policy ticket offered working people a brief escape from their hopelessness. Any poor soul could bet a nickel or a dime and win six hundred bucks if the three numbers they chose to play that day hit that evening. The policy bankers were wealthy men who flew under the radar until one banker, Caspar Holstein, was kidnapped. The *New York Times* connected Holstein's disappearance to his vast ill-gotten wealth, which commanded the attention of Dutch Schultz.

When Holstein's $50,000 ransom was paid and he fled town with the remainder of his money, it confirmed, in Schultz's eyes, that the policy racket was worth a fortune. Schultz did his homework and found out that Wilfred Brunder and Jose Miro were two more wealthy policy bankers. When Brunder and Miro were targeted by the law – also as a result of Holstein's abduction which drew attention to the racket – they fled town and Big Joe Ison took over their policy banks. Schultz dispatched Abraham 'Abe' Landau and Abraham 'Bo' Weinberg to kidnap Big Joe. Schultz did not demand a ransom like the small-minded hoods who kidnapped Holstein, but focused on the big picture and had his men tell Big Joe he would either accept Schultz as his new partner or die. Big Joe was no match for a small bullet; he folded and Schultz had a foot in the door, which he swung open by sending his men around Harlem, offering policy bankers protection from kidnappers – primarily himself – while promising to blindfold the police through his corrupt relationship with Tammany Hall. When the bankers did not immediately cave, storefronts were sprayed with bullets, runners were roughed up and robbed, and Schultz's crooked cops arrested bankers on gambling charges.

The go-to lawyer for policy bankers in trouble with the law was Richard 'Dixie' Davis. Schultz recruited Davis to work a flimflam; each time one of Davis's clients was arrested, Davis told them he might be able to help, then sent them to see Schultz, directing them straight into the lion's den. Once the Harlem bankers were under Schultz's control, Dixie Davis continued on as Schultz's liaison with assembly leader and future New York City mayor Jimmy Hines, who made sure the cops looked the other way, and the courts were rigged to dismiss any accidental arrests.

Things were looking up for Schultz, until policy banker Jose Miro, who had fled to San Juan, Puerto Rico, got tired of the tropics and returned to Harlem. He paid his back taxes, served a skid-bid, then demanded his racket back from Big Joe Ison who ran to Schultz for help. Schultz told Miro, 'You do what I say, or I will kill you', putting an end to Miro's triumphant return. When policy banker Wilfred Brunder returned to reclaim his racket, he was given the same *fait accompli* and kicked to the curb.

The next man to be flattened under Schultz's steamroller was Alexander Pompez, a wealthy Cuban-American who owned a popular cigar store where he sold Cuban stinkers and pushed policy tickets on the side. Unhappy about giving up his racket or partnering with Schultz, Pompez told Jose Miro that if they all stuck together, they could resist Schultz. Miro squealed on Pompez who was called to a meeting where Schultz laid a .45 automatic on the table then asked him to repeat the remark. Pompez shit a double corona and denied he had ever said such a thing. Even though it was three o'clock in the morning, Schultz dispatched his thugs to wake up Jose Miro and drag him to the meeting. Miro, who arrived in his pajamas under an overcoat, confirmed the comment. Pompez pleaded for his life and agreed to Schultz's terms before Schultz scolded both men, Pompez for passing the comment and Miro for ratting him out.

Although Schultz terrorized the bankers, the bettors benefitted from his total control of the racket. Before Schultz took over, if two or more bettors hit the same winning numbers at once, the banker would declare bankruptcy and close shop, then reopen two weeks later. Schultz made sure the bankers no longer stiffed the poor bettors. From then on, if a banker got hit hard and claimed he did not have enough money in reserve to pay out, Schultz fronted the money (with interest, of course) and made sure the winners were paid. Schultz was not doing this because he cared about the poor; he knew when bettors lost faith in the game, they stopped playing. In time, Schultz reduced the possibility of multiple winners at once by bringing in his criminal genius, Otto 'Abbadabba' Berman (born Biederman), who was paid $10,000 a week for his skills. Each evening, the three winning policy numbers were determined by the last three digits of the final income amassed each day by the legal horse-racing tracks in New York. This tally was published in the daily newspapers' horse-racing section which every bettor could access at a newsstand. Throughout the day, Berman's bookkeepers would collect all the policy slips across Harlem and isolate the numbers that were bet most frequently. Berman would then go to one of the state's horse-racing tracks where he had access to the computation rooms, and place enough bets on the last race to manipulate the total and decrease the odds of it resulting in a multi-payout.

As for the runners who collected the slips for the bankers, after Schultz took over, their arrests dropped by 80 percent. To achieve this steep decline, any honest cops were quietly transferred out of Harlem following a telephone call from Jimmy Hines to the police commissioner. With Schultz in charge, the illegal racket became so open in Harlem that signs in store windows read: 'Play the Daily Number Here'. It seemed everyone was happy and no man alive had what it took to challenge Schultz – but a woman did!

Stephanie St Clair was known as Madame Queenie, or the Tiger from Marseilles because she told people she was from France and not the French Caribbean island where she was born. Queenie moved to Harlem as a young woman. By 1932, she had built up a medium-sized policy operation that made her fairly wealthy. She shot and stabbed men, and took a stab at getting everyone to unite against Schultz. When they wouldn't listen, she tried the race card, telling people that Schultz had no business collecting money from 'the racket he stole from my colored friends'. Queenie even tried to 'frame colored policemen' who were on Schultz's payroll, considering them traitors. But African-Americans who did not see black and white, but green, were happy with Schultz, who tried to kill Queenie; she escaped his assassins by hiding in the basement of her apartment building as they searched for her upstairs. Unwilling to quit, Queenie launched a letter-writing campaign, revealing details about Schultz's racket to Harlem newspapers and the police commissioner. She even barged into the mayor's office but was subdued by aides. She apparently had a poor understanding of what she could say to the law in defense of her own unlawfulness, and was finally arrested. At trial, she took the stand in her own defense and squealed on judges, district attorneys, and the crooked cops who had switched their allegiance from her to Schultz. Not surprisingly, she was sent to jail. With Madame Queenie out of the way, the policy racket was, according to Irving Ben Cooper who compiled a report for the Commissioner of Accounts, grossing $100 million a year (two billion dollars in today's currency).

After Schultz's crew pushed through Harlem like a colony of army ants on the march, Schultz organized his own union, the Metropolitan Restaurant and Cafeteria Association. He bullied waiters, workers and restaurateurs into joining; one victim was told, 'You'd better do as we say. You wouldn't look very good without your ears.' Another victim had a stink bomb dropped down the chimney of his restaurant. The racket made Schultz millions while it angered Lepke Buchalter, who considered anyone else's union activity as an encroachment on his personal domain. This made Schultz instant enemies with Lepke's partner, Luciano, who was already eyeing Schultz's Harlem policy racket for himself. As Lepke and Luciano wondered how they would handle Schultz, Thomas Dewey had assembled a grand jury to go after him for tax evasion (the jury was assembled before Dewey left the US Attorney's Office; the case was taken up by his replacement, Martin Conboy). It was a tougher case to prove than that of Waxey Gordon, whose luxurious spending habits contributed to the evidence against him. Schultz, in contrast, lived like Silas Marner. According to Luciano, he 'dressed like a pig' and would not pay more than two dollars for a shirt. Prosecutors were still able to find evidence that Schultz sold more beer than an Oktoberfest and did not pay taxes on any of it. Before a grand jury handed down the indictment for failing to pay $92,103 to Uncle Sam, Schultz was in the wind. Or, shall we say, a light breeze since it did not carry him far; he hid out in Manhattan, bouncing from one safe house to another while continuing to run his operations.

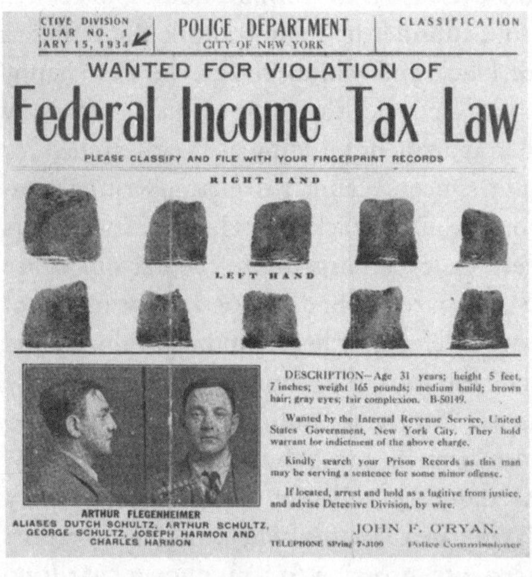

CTIVE DIVISION
ULAR NO. 1
ARY 15, 1934

POLICE DEPARTMENT
CITY OF NEW YORK

CLASSIFICATION

WANTED FOR VIOLATION OF

Federal Income Tax Law

PLEASE CLASSIFY AND FILE WITH YOUR FINGERPRINT RECORDS

RIGHT HAND

LEFT HAND

DESCRIPTION—Age 31 years; height 5 feet, 7 inches; weight 165 pounds; medium build; brown hair; gray eyes; fair complexion. B-50149.

Wanted by the Internal Revenue Service, United States Government, New York City. They hold warrant for indictment of the above charge.

Kindly search your Prison Records as this man may be serving a sentence for some minor offense.

If located, arrest and hold as a fugitive from justice, and advise Detective Division, by wire.

ARTHUR FLEGENHEIMER
ALIASES DUTCH SCHULTZ, ARTHUR SCHULTZ, GEORGE SCHULTZ, JOSEPH HARMON AND CHARLES HARMON

JOHN F. O'RYAN.
TELEPHONE SPring 7-3100 Police Commissioner

Dutch Schultz wanted poster.

Wanted posters were hung in every police station, post office and federal building as detectives looked for Schultz, but the fugitive had enough cops on his payroll to keep them driving around with blinders on. Finally, President Roosevelt's treasury secretary, Henry Morgenthau, wondered where the tax cheat was hiding and put pressure on New York mayor Fiorello LaGuardia and FBI director J. Edgar Hoover to find him. With

Hoover's agents searching for Schultz – the same trigger-happy agents who cut down John Dillinger, Pretty Boy Floyd, and Baby Face Nelson – Schultz feared becoming another FBI trophy and surrendered. He was granted bail with a condition that he not leave the state of New York.

While pending trial, Schultz's attorneys argued that he was too famous from recent media attention to receive a fair hearing in Manhattan; they asked that the proceedings be moved away from the city. The motion was granted and the case was moved to Syracuse, New York. Meanwhile, Schultz tried to square up with Uncle Sam. He sent a team of accountants and lawyers to Washington where they offered to pay Schultz's back taxes, but they were turned away. 'I am a rich man, but I tried to pay and the government would not accept,' Schultz lamented to reporters after a court appearance, 'therefore I am not guilty of willful failure to file.' He went on to say, 'I offered $100,000 when the government was broke and people were talking revolution, and they turned me down cold.' Schultz offered the same hundred grand to the New York Democratic Committee, hoping they could help him, but they also turned him down. After everyone ran away from his money, Schultz turned to God; before trial, he walked into a church and converted to Catholicism.

In the spring of 1935, Schultz got a hung jury in Syracuse. For the retrial, his case was transferred to the small Adirondack town of Malone, New York. Schultz may have been cheap but he knew when to dip into his wallet; he bounced from bar to bar buying everyone drinks, handed out twenty-dollar bills on the street, donated to all the local charities, and hired a public relations firm to spit-shine his image. The town was mesmerized by this odd newcomer who also enjoyed a little downtime, reading biographies on Genghis Khan and Napoleon Bonaparte.

Between Schultz's steep attorney fees and his spending spree in Malone, he began to complain about money and ordered Abbadabba Berman to create new mathematical schemes to increase the output from his policy racket. He also tightened his squeeze on his Harlem managers, which finally roused them into an open rebellion. Schultz withdrew his demands, which quelled the uprising but also emboldened them. The next time Schultz told Jules Martin, who managed his restaurant union, to run twenty grand up to him, Martin balked. He complained to a crony that Schultz was demanding too much of their racket, which was already strained by direct extension of all the same screws being put to Schultz. Martin was not being completely honest; he forgot to mention that he had already begun to skim in order to set himself up for a post-Schultz world. Schultz found out about Martin's deceit and again ordered Martin to bring him the money, without delay. Schultz's attorney Dixie Davis accompanied Martin to the hotel where Schultz was staying. Inside the room, Schultz accused Martin of skimming $70,000 from the union. Martin initially denied the charge, but after Schultz socked him with a right cross, he fessed up to skimming $20,000. The figure no longer mattered once Martin admitted to stealing; a man who will steal twenty bucks will just as readily steal twenty million, the only boundary being opportunity. Schultz, who was currently demanding a fair trial in his own case, passed judgment, rendered a verdict, and sentenced Martin to death in the time it took him to remove a .45 caliber handgun from his waistband. Schultz jammed the gun barrel into Martin's mouth and blew his brains all over the room. Schultz then turned to Dixie Davis – who later said that Schultz murdered Martin 'as casually as if he were picking his teeth' – and politely apologized for the mess. Schultz summoned Bernard 'Lulu' Rosenkrantz, who removed Martin's body from the room and dumped it in a snowy ditch.

As luck would have it, Schultz got another hung jury in Malone, where many residents felt he was being persecuted by a hypocritical government that spent over a million dollars in taxpayer money to try a man who owed one-tenth of that in back taxes, and had tried to pay the bill. The angry judge chastised the jury, and an even angrier Mayor LaGuardia, after hearing the verdict, publicly declared, '[Dutch Schultz] won't be a resident of New York City.' After LaGuardia banned him from the lower boroughs, Schultz found himself lost in upstate New York.

The *Flying Dutchman* is a mythical ghost ship forbidden to cast anchor in any port, forever doomed to wander the world's oceans. According to the poet John Leyden, the crew of this vessel were 'guilty of some dreadful crime'. Sir Walter Scott wrote that the ship was 'loaded with great wealth, on board of which some horrid act of murder and piracy had been committed'. Was not the fate of the *Flying Dutchman* strikingly similar to that of Dutch Schultz, a man 'guilty of some dreadful crime . . . loaded with great wealth' who thought nothing of the 'horrid act of murder'? Like the ship, Schultz was forbidden to drop anchor in his native port of New York where his wife and newborn son resided. In light of the fate he shared with this ship, we will henceforth refer to Dutch Schultz as the Dutchman.

The Dutchman set up shop in a hotel suite in Bridgeport, Connecticut. From here, he reasserted command over his operations while mixing with socialites; he even took up riding, with crop and boots. Before long, Thomas Dewey, who was building a new case against the Dutchman, was up his ass. Dewey questioned people around him, including the Dutchman's riding master, who told Dewey about several shady-looking characters who visited the Dutchman at the stables. When the Dutchman realized Dewey would never quit, he decided to face the music; he had already walked out of two courtrooms and was confident he could do it again. He surrendered himself in Perth Amboy, New Jersey, made bail, and planted a flag in Newark where he could oversee his empire, just across the Hudson River.

While the Dutchman had been fighting his trials in upstate New York, he appointed Bo Weinberg as his acting street boss. When Weinberg became convinced that the Dutchman would be convicted at trial, he met with Lucky Luciano and agreed to turn over the Dutchman's policy empire in return for a 15 percent managerial role. When the Dutchman found out about this betrayal, Weinberg disappeared without a trace. According to Dewey, who consulted with a slew of informants, 'Weinberg was taken out in a boat on the Harlem River and was made to watch while concrete dried around his feet and ankles. Then, in his concrete shoes, he was dumped overboard.'

What supposedly happened after Weinberg went missing has been repeated by historians for the past eighty-five years and is untrue. We are told that the Dutchman slipped into Manhattan to ask the Commission if he could kill Dewey, who was the root cause of his latest problems. The Commission meeting was supposedly headed by Luciano and Lepke, with Costello, Adonis and Lansky present. To start with, Luciano was the only one of these men who even had a seat on the Commission, which he shared with four other bosses, none of whom were mentioned. We are further told that this faux Commission told the Dutchman to stand down. 'Dewey's gotta go!' the Dutchman is reported to have shouted in response. 'I'm hitting him myself in forty-eight hours.' Are we to believe that the Dutchman, who had never asked anyone for permission to kill, suddenly needed authorization from the very men who were stealing his empire? Furthermore, did the Dutchman seem dumb enough to supply his enemies with a narrow time frame in case they wanted to stop him?

It appears that this fabricated story originated with Meyer Lansky in his ongoing effort to protect Lucky Luciano. Luciano had no choice but to kill the Dutchman after Weinberg went missing and the Dutchman learned that Luciano, who was behind Weinberg's betrayal, had been biting chunks out of his empire for several months. But Lansky had warned Luciano that once the Dutchman was gone, Dewey would need a new target and come gunning for Luciano. 'Right now,' Lansky told Luciano, 'Schultz is your cover. If Dutch is eliminated, you're gonna stand out like a naked guy who just lost his clothes.' In an attempt to ingratiate themselves with Dewey and deflect his predictable reaction to the Dutchman's murder, which would mean the loss of his hard-earned prosecution and the media praise that would accompany a conviction, Lansky spread this story – knowing it would reach Dewey through the Woolworth Building – to make it appear as if, by hitting the Dutchman, they were saving Dewey's life. It is important to note that, although historians have been fooled by this lie, or liked the story too much to question it, Dewey did not believe a word of it.

Luciano gave the Dutchman's contract to the Jews. According to Lansky's pal Joseph 'Doc' Stacher, 'Even though Dutch Schultz became a Catholic, our Italian partners looked at us and we all knew that this was an internal Jewish matter.' Lepke, who wanted the Dutchman's union, got the job and assigned it to Charles 'The Bug' Workman and Emanuel 'Mendy' Weiss, with Seymour 'Piggy' Schechter behind the wheel of the getaway car.

The Dutchman was staying at Newark's Robert Treat Hotel while conducting his daily business out of the Palace Chop House, a bar-restaurant taken over by him and his crew. The hit team decided to ambush him there. At around 10 p.m. on 23 October 1935, the Dutchman was counting money at a back table with Abbadabba Berman, Lulu Rosenkrantz and Abe Landau. Between 10:15 and 10:30, the Dutchman headed for the loo to take a leak. While he was facing the tiled wall in front of the urinal, the restaurant's front door swung open and Charles 'The Bug' Workman barged in, told the bartender to get down, then fired at the back table with a .38 Special. Mendy Weiss whisked through the door, behind the Bug, blasting away with a twelve-gauge sawed-off shotgun. *Pump-bang, pump-bang.*

Slugs smashed into flesh, walls and mirrors. Abbadabba Berman, a genius who should have been counting his daily bonus from a casino in Monte Carlo, took six slugs over a pile of dirty money. He slid out of his chair, moaning and groaning as he hit the floor with holes in his face, chest and gut. Abe Landau was reaching for his .45 caliber when a bullet tore through his wrist; he took another slug to the neck. Lulu Rosenkrantz whipped out his .45 caliber and kicked over a table for cover; he returned fire but was hit several times.

While Berman, Landau and Rosenkrantz writhed in pain, the Bug swapped his empty .38 for a loaded .45 and headed toward the back in search of the Dutchman, who had heard the shots and knew he was trapped. Armed with only a three-inch pocketknife, his best bet was to stand still in front of the urinal and hope to get passed over. While sweeping the men's room, the Bug spotted a pissing patron. Unsure if he was one of the Dutchman's crew, the Bug squeezed off two rounds then left as fast as he had entered. One of the Bug's bullets missed the Dutchman, the other entered his back and exited through his chest, barely missing his heart.

The Bug had no idea he had just shot the Dutchman as he cleared the back room then returned to the front, certain Mendy Weiss had mopped up the dining area while he swept the back. But Weiss was gone. As the Bug bolted through the restaurant, he understood why – Rosenkrantz and Landau were near-dead but their trigger fingers were still snapping. They fired at the Bug while clumsily chasing him out the door. Rosenkrantz collapsed as Landau staggered after his prey like a zombie, with blood spurting from an artery in his neck. He chased the Bug into the street, firing as he went. The Bug reached over his shoulder and returned fire then sprinted away as Landau emptied his clip then calmly took a seat on top of a trash can as if he was a sanitation worker on a cigarette break.

Once down the street, the Bug looked around for his buddies who were nowhere in sight. Weiss had hopped into the getaway car and told Piggy to put his piggies to the pedal. Abandoned by his team, the Bug fled on foot.

Back in the restaurant, Rosenkrantz, who had been hit a dozen times, climbed to his feet and asked the bartender if he could exchange a quarter for five nickels so he could dial the police from the restaurant's payphone. (The stingy Dutchman had trained his troops well; even in this wretched state of anatomical disrepair, Rosenkrantz could not see throwing away twenty cents on a local call.) After getting change, Rosenkrantz called the police and asked them to send an ambulance before he collapsed in the phone booth. The Dutchman used his waning strength to zip up his fly, pick up his fedora from the floor, and stagger out of the men's room. He made it to a table where he plopped into a chair before his head fell straight down as though into a dinner plate.*

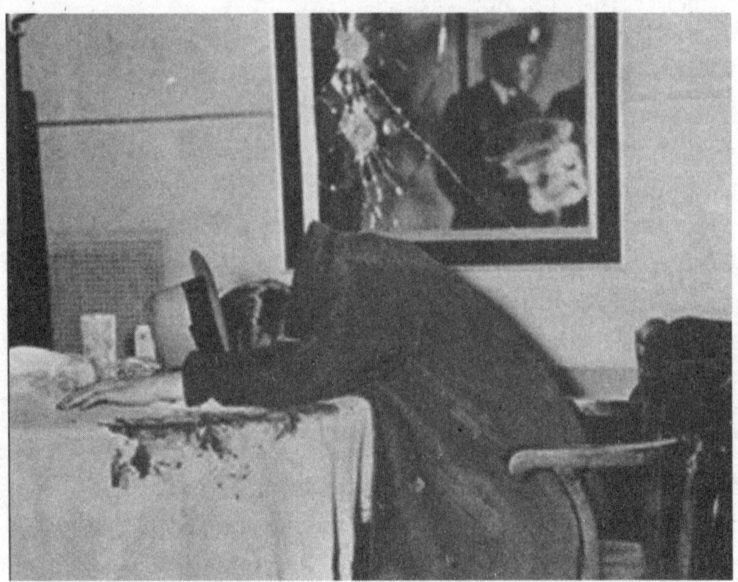

The Dutchman, face-down and clinging to life.

When the ambulance arrived, Landau was still sitting on a trash can, holding a handkerchief to his neck. The injured men were taken to Newark City Hospital. Everyone denied they knew who had shot them and feigned bewilderment that anyone would do such a thing.

* The local district attorney believed that the Bug had missed the Dutchman, and that Landau had mistakenly shot him on his way out of the men's room. This was possible but it seems more likely that the Bug got him but did not know it, since I do not believe the Dutchman would have entered the firefight armed with only a pocketknife. The Bug, moreover, was not known to lie and insisted he plugged someone in the urinal.

As for the money the gang was counting, Abbadabba's adding machine had entries for $313,711.99 and $236,295.95, indicating a profitable day for the Dutchman – also indicating that someone had made off with over a half-million dollars since I have not found any evidence that the actual money was ever recovered.

The Dutchman finally said, 'It was somebody that didn't like me, I guess.' Surgeons worked on all four men around the clock but it was difficult to undo the Bug's fine marksmanship. The least tough was the first to depart; the brainy Abbadabba Berman gave out before 3 a.m. after muttering something unintelligible. Landau followed at 6:30 a.m. and Rosenkrantz, who underwent a blood transfusion, went next.

While barely clinging to life, the Dutchman asked for a priest, sending a sigh of relief through Newark's rabbinical community. His wife, Frances, showed up with Father McInerney as the Dutchman's mother, Emma, heard the shocking news over the radio and rushed to the hospital. When asked who may have shot her son, Emma, who had taken out an insurance policy on his life, replied, 'I don't know why anybody would want to shoot him.' (Like mother, like son.)

The doctors gave the Dutchman a dose of morphine. In case any evidence fell from his lips, a police stenographer was stationed next to his bed. As the Dutchman slipped in and out of consciousness, he lapsed into a poetic delirium that rivaled Allen Ginsberg on LSD. 'Oh, oh dog biscuits and when he is happy he doesn't get snappy.' 'Get your onions up and we will throw up a truce flag.' 'Come on, open the soap duckets.' 'Talk to the sword.' 'Mother is the best bet and don't let Satan draw you too fast.' 'A boy has never wept nor dashed a thousand kim.'

As these disjointed sentences rolled off the Dutchman's quivering lips, a more measured and archaic verse arrived at the hospital's reception desk, via Western Union: 'As ye sow, so shall ye reap.' The biblical verse was signed by Madame Queenie. At 6 p.m., the 34-year-old Dutchman slipped into a coma. By 8:35, he exhaled his last breath and the bedsheet was pulled over his head. Luciano owned the policy racket in Harlem and Lepke took over the restaurant union.

Chapter 21

The Long Arm of the Law

At the time of the Dutchman's death, Harlem, New York, was home to Jews, Blacks and Italians. Since the Jews and Italians were already partners in crime, Lucky Luciano needed to bring the Blacks on board for Harlem's policy racket to run smoothly. To this end, he formed an alliance with Black gangster Bumpy Johnson.

Ellsworth Raymond 'Bumpy' Johnson was born into a poor family on 31 October 1905, in Charleston, South Carolina. One of seven children, Bumpy grew up in a small, crowded house. After Bumpy's older brother was accused of killing a white man, he fled north to avoid a tree-branch trial. Three years later, in 1919, while still in his teens, Bumpy went north, too, crashing with his sister Mabel in Harlem.

Ellsworth Raymond 'Bumpy' Johnson.

In New York, Bumpy was bullied on account of his southern accent but he always fought back and became known as a scrapper. In his late teens, he formed a gang that extorted Black store owners. As Bumpy got older and Harlem's policy bankers needed protection, he offered them his services. One night, when a thug tried to rob Alexander Pompez with a gun, Bumpy disarmed the assailant with a knife which he handled like a *Blackanese* samurai swordsman. He saved Pompez, and his heroics increased his growing reputation, which was further enhanced after a stint in Sing Sing. The 25-year-old was released from prison as the Dutchman was steamrolling through Harlem. He went to work for Madame Queenie but he disapproved of her desperate attempts to resist the Dutchman by squealing, so he quit her employ. Attuned to mafia politics, which Bumpy learned in prison where he was well liked by Italians, he called on Lucky Luciano at the Waldorf Astoria and asked for a sit-down to discuss the Dutchman. Luciano admired the young man's chutzpah and met with him. Bumpy asked Luciano if he would align with him in a war against the Dutchman. Luciano told Bumpy that he could not get involved at the moment, but he dropped a hint that he may one day inherit the Dutchman's policy racket; if he did, he promised to call on Bumpy. Bumpy understood this to mean that the Dutchman's days were numbered.

A week after the Dutchman poetically muttered his way into the afterlife, Luciano sent for Bumpy and offered him a partnership in return for handling any Black problems in Harlem. Bumpy proved to be a hard negotiator, at one point prompting a frustrated Luciano to tell him, 'I could kill you right now.' Bumpy, confident in his own value, just smiled at Luciano and told him he would never do that. Bumpy was right. They struck a deal and their working relationship evolved into a genuine friendship. (Decades later, after both men were dead, Bumpy's wife wrote a memoir in which she counted Luciano among her husband's truest friends.) Luciano's borgata became so dependent on Bumpy's smooth leadership in Harlem that when Bumpy was once hospitalized, Italians flooded the hospital to visit him, passing out hundred-dollar bills to the nurses, while telling them, 'Get him back on his feet soon.'

As Luciano was forging a new alliance with Bumpy Johnson, Thomas Dewey was searching for a new target now that the Dutchman was dead. He settled on Luciano, just as Lansky had predicted. As Dewey probed a variety of rackets under Luciano's control, one of Dewey's assistant district attorneys, while engaged in an unrelated matter, picked up on a trail of incriminating evidence that led straight to Luciano.

Eunice Roberta Hunton Carter was born on 16 July 1899 in Atlanta, Georgia. After the Atlanta race massacre of 1906, which made the lynchings in New Orleans look like a picnic, Carter's family moved to Brooklyn, New York, where they became known for their charitable

Eunice Roberta Hunton Carter.

work. Carter attended Smith College and, in 1932, became the first African-American woman to receive a law degree from Fordham University Law School, an impressive feat, but quickly outdone in 1935 when she became the first Black female assistant district attorney in New York. One day, while Carter was at work, she noticed a seemingly endless stream of prostitutes passing through a courtroom as if through a revolving door; they were all represented by the same attorney, Abe Karp. Carter 'smelled a racket' and flagged down Dewey's chief assistant, Murray Gurfein, in a courthouse corridor, telling him she had a hunch that someone powerful had Karp on retainer. 'What do you think?' she asked Gurfein, who replied, 'There's enough to show it to the boss.'

Carter and Gurfein's reasoning was as follows: if Luciano was the crime czar of New York, he might somehow be connected even to this lowly racket. They went to see Dewey, but the thought of caked-on lipstick and runny nylons did not sync with Dewey's exalted image of himself as a great crime crusader. 'I didn't give up a good law practice to chase prostitutes,' he told them. Then it dawned on Dewey; if Luciano was, by chance, involved in this racket, Dewey would appear the heroic savior of abused women while Luciano would look, quite appropriately, like a scumbag. Dewey told Carter to start digging. She compiled a list of 175 women who were arrested for prostitution but never went to jail. She then got a court order to tap several telephone lines connected to brothels; the same names kept popping up: David 'Little Davey' Betillo, James 'Jimmy Fredericks' Frederico and Tommy 'The Bull' Pennochio, all of whom were directly connected to

Luciano's borgata.* Carter returned to Dewey with plenty of evidence.

Knowing that mass round-ups are a good odds game – lock up enough people and someone will talk – Dewey planned to arrest the managers then raid multiple brothels across the city to see what would shake out. On 31 January 1936, Dewey's detectives swept up the main suspects who were already under surveillance. Aware that his own police force was infiltrated by the mob, Dewey did not share his next plan of attack until the following evening, when he and a select group of prosecutors ordered 160 policemen to form teams of two to begin raiding eighty bordellos across Brooklyn and Manhattan. Dewey told the cops to arrest everyone inside, including madams, pimps, prostitutes and johns. That evening, a hundred or so people were arrested by police and herded into the Woolworth Building. Dewey, whose offices were on the fourteenth floor, reserved the thirteenth floor to detain everyone before and after questioning, which carried on throughout the night.

At first, all of the women claimed to be housewives, art students and models, figuring they could deny the charges until they were bailed out, but once they realized that Dewey had stuck his foot in their revolving door, some got scared and opened up about attorney Abe Karp, who was found at his brother-in-law's apartment, hiding behind a piano. Try as he did, Dewey could not conceal his snobby disdain for the working women; he would greet them with a handshake then run off to scrub his hands as soon as the interview was over. This could actually be considered sensitive treatment considering that his assistants would not even interview the women without wearing rubber gloves. After one prostitute signed a statement, Dewey's secretary dropped the fountain pen into a pot of boiling water.

Dewey extracted tips that led to more arrests, including that of Dave Miller, a dirty Pennsylvania cop and part-time pimp who was thrown off the force for running a hooker house outside of Pittsburgh. Miller left for New York, where he started pimping again. When Dewey arrested Miller and threatened to imprison Miller's wife, who was also a prostitute, leaving their three children parentless, Miller buckled and agreed to turn state's evidence. He gave up Little Davey Betillo and Jimmy Frederico as the operation's mafia managers,

* Historical sources vary: Betillo is sometimes spelled Petillo, and Frederico is sometimes spelled Federico; I have chosen the spellings that appear in Thomas Dewey's indictment.

both of whom had thrown around Luciano's name in conversation. According to Miller, the mobsters made statements such as 'This has Charley Lucky's okay' and 'The boss is behind this.' Besides Miller, other 'bookers' – the name for men who managed brothels – made deals, including Pete Harris and 'Dumb Al' Weiner, who inherited his racket from his father, 'Cockeyed Louis' Weiner.

Dewey learned that Little Davey Betillo, whose rap sheet dated back to age eleven, was the visionary who first noticed that the vice industry was ripe for the taking. Betillo asked Luciano for the green light to wrangle together madams, bookers and hookers into an unofficial union. Once Betillo got the okay from Luciano, he called on Jimmy Frederico and Tommy 'The Bull' Pennochio for assistance. Equipped with their ever-handy reputations as killers, independent street pimps were driven away from their working women by way of threats and violence, while over two hundred bordellos were brought in line. The men had a central bank – or loanshark – on call for any madam or prostitute who needed quick cash to tide them over for the week. Doctors were retained to provide the ladies with weekly examinations, not out of any concern for the women, but because the transmission of sexual diseases was bad for business. Smarter mobsters were tapped as bookkeepers, and a main office was set up on Mulberry Street. Before long, Betillo's operation was grossing over twelve million dollars a year, a large chunk of which went toward police and political protection. If that failed, attorney Abe Karp was on retainer to swoop into court and bail out anyone who was stuck in a jam. This proved to be the thermal exhaust port of their Death Star, spotted by Jedi Eunice Carter.

When Luciano was tipped off to his impending arrest, he must have been shocked, never imagining Eunice Carter would unravel the leads to Abe Karp, to Dave Miller, to Little Davey Betillo and ultimately to himself. He high tailed it to Hot Springs, Arkansas, where a friend of his owned a hotel and controlled the town where it was located.

Owney 'The Killer' Madden was born in 1891 to poor Irish parents in Leeds, England. In 1903, Owney's father died and he and two siblings were sent to live with an aunt in Hell's Kitchen on Manhattan's West Side. The young man joined a gang and committed his first murder by age fourteen. By age twenty, Madden had over forty arrests on his rap sheet – fifty-seven arrests by the end of his lifetime – and he had already murdered several men. (It is worth noting that you have to kill a lot of people to be nicknamed 'The Killer' when everyone you hang around with is a killer, too.) In 1912, Madden was shot by six men inside of a dance hall. At the hospital, he refused to say who shot him. He then tracked down and killed three of the men before he was convicted of murder and sentenced to ten to twenty years in Sing Sing. He was paroled in January 1923, just in time for Prohibition. In addition to moving bootleg alcohol and opening ordinary speakeasies, Madden started the now legendary Cotton Club with a loan from Arnold Rothstein who remained his silent partner. The club, which welcomed Black patrons, drew outstanding talent such as Duke Ellington, who played there with his orchestra from 1927 to 1931, and jazz singer Cab Calloway.

Madden returned to prison in 1932. Upon his release a year later, he was sharp enough to spot Dewey's unquenchable thirst for mobsters and left for Hot Springs, Arkansas, famous for its warm mineral springs. In Hot Springs, Madden, who was already acquainted with the entertainment industry, opened a casino resort and spa, naming it Hotel Arkansas, revealing a hint of his British economy. He married the daughter of a local politician and bribed the entire three-man police force along with the mayor for about a thousand dollars a month and a steak dinner. His resort was a draw for vacationers from all over the country as well as his mob cronies, who took the baths while whispering intrigues through hot mist in the spirit of Roman senators. Until Luciano could assess the strength of Dewey's case against him, he lammed it in Hot Springs and took along his girlfriend, Gay Orlova, a professional dancer who fled revolutionary Russia.

When Dewey learned that Luciano had skipped, he declared him Public Enemy Number One. Luciano was soon arrested in Arkansas by New York detective Stephen Di Rosa, who either was tipped that Luciano was in Hot Springs or knew Madden's resort was a sanctuary for mafia fugitives. Madden called on three of the area's most prominent attorneys who sprung Luciano on a trifling $5,000 bond, put up by Hot Springs chief of detectives Dutch Akers, who must have been asked to do so by Madden. With his tight grip on the town, Madden was confident he could resolve the matter in a way that at least appeared lawful.

Upon hearing that Luciano was freed on bail, Dewey threw a tantrum. Luciano had indeed anticipated Dewey's resolve, but had underestimated his skillful management of the press, which transcended state lines; Dewey called on his favorite newspapers and attacked the governor of Arkansas, the state attorney general and the judge, calling into question their integrity. Dewey was prepared to smear the entire state if it meant getting his man and, since the only heat Madden's crooked police and politicians wanted was from fissures in the earth, it worked. The governor had the court revoke Luciano's bail. The cops who were tasked with taking Luciano into custody apologized to him and Madden, telling them their hands were tied. As Luciano sat in the clink in Hot Springs, Meyer Lansky dispatched his friend and attorney, Moses Polakoff, to assist with Luciano's defense. Polakoff helped Luciano draft a statement which Luciano recited for the press. Here is a snapshot of it with my own comments in parentheses:

'I may not be the most moral and upright man alive [an unprecedented display of honesty while still a gross understatement] but I have not, at any time, stooped to aiding prostitution [except for his own personal pleasure which he engaged in almost every night at the Waldorf]. I have never been involved in anything so messy [if we forget Sloppy Joe Masseria wrapped in a blood-stained tablecloth, Salvatore Maranzano splayed out on the floor of his office with knife wounds and bullet holes, and the most recent blood and guts splattered on the walls of the Palace Chop House].'

When the attorney general, Carl Bailey, ordered Luciano to the state capital, Little Rock, for extradition hearings, Madden's local sheriff refused to hand over Luciano, who claimed to be the victim of 'vicious politics'. With Dewey glaring at Bailey from New York, Bailey dispatched twenty Arkansas Rangers with orders to storm the jail, if necessary. They dragged Luciano to Little Rock where, according to Dewey, 'a small army of lawyers, city officials, and members of the state legislature rallied to obtain Luciano's release'. They were apparently acting at the behest of Madden, who upheld his stalwart reputation as a true gangster when he attempted to bribe the attorney general, offering him $50,000 if he would stand up to Dewey. Bailey was too afraid of the consequences and turned down the offer. He then held up a midnight train for a quarter of an hour as he had Luciano whisked from his jail cell under heavy guard and locked in a compartment for a rail ride back to New York that resembled Vladimir Lenin's sealed train ride from Zurich to Saint Petersburg – except that Lenin's ride was a triumphant return whereas Luciano was about to face a ninety-count indictment. In Manhattan, bail was set at $350,000, the highest ever for the state, quickly posted by Luciano who returned to the Waldorf as Mr Ross.

Since there was no physical evidence against Luciano and he barely oversaw the racket, he believed that Dewey's case was weak. By Dewey's own admission, the operation did not take 'more than a few minutes a day of Luciano's time. We heard his name mentioned by very few . . . who knew him or who heard him give directions.'

Luciano escorted into court by detectives.

On the morning of 13 May 1936, packed benches of curious spectators rose from their seats to honor Justice Philip McCook as he entered the courtroom. Thomas Dewey was looking chipper; his perfectly trimmed mustache offered a glimpse into his meticulous mind, which understood the smallest nuances of the law that could ensnare Luciano. After some formalities, Dewey launched into his opening statement. 'My witnesses are prostitutes, madams, heels, pimps, and ex-convicts,' he said, up front. 'We cannot get bishops, we cannot get clergymen, we cannot get bankers or businessmen to testify about gangsters, pimps, and prostitution.'

Dewey went on to explain how hookers kicked a piece of their salaries up to madams, who in turn gave a weekly cut to bookers. The bookers then delivered a piece to their mafia managers, who funneled a share to Luciano. According to Dewey, although Luciano may not have known anything about the day-to-day operations, he was just as guilty as the direct participants.

Dewey proved that over a hundred working women had been bailed out by Abe Karp. He put close to seventy witnesses on the stand, nearly forty of whom were prostitutes. Though most of the women had never seen or heard of Luciano except in the newspapers, the sheer volume of downtrodden women yoked to the world's oldest form of human bondage was designed to sway the jury against any defendant accused of exploiting them.

Throughout history, courtesans with all sorts of exotic names have been sought by kings, sultans, presidents and prime ministers: Madame du Barry, Cora Pearl, La Belle Otero, Lola Montez, Veronica Franco and Mata Hari are a few that come to mind. Dewey's courtesans did not share the same seductive names: Jenny the Factory, Sadie the Chink, Nigger Ruth, Polack Frances, Gashouse Lil, Six Bits and others who worked at dives like Hungarian Hilda's were marched onto the stand, one after another. Since most of the women, who Luciano referred to as 'beat-up broads', were admittedly addicted to heroin and testified that the ringleaders happily fed their habits, Dewey raised overtones of an unindicted drug conspiracy. Before leaving the stand, each woman thanked Dewey for getting her off drugs; the repetitious gratitude appeared choreographed.

The best direct evidence against Luciano came from Cokey Flo Brown, who was Jimmy Frederico's former girlfriend. After being arrested, Cokey Flo was locked in a cell and suffering from heroin withdrawals until she decided to help Dewey; that same moment she was cured, apparently with a fix. Frederico either trusted Flo or wanted to impress her when he brought her along to meetings with Luciano. Flo testified that at one of these meetings, which took place in a Chinese restaurant, Luciano leaned over to her and said that he was going to organize the bordellos 'just like chain grocery stores'. The emaciated ex-hooker also implicated Frederico, Betillo and Pennochio. She barely held up on the stand, asking for, and receiving, shots of brandy to keep her tuned.

Witness Nancy Presser, who by all accounts was a stunningly beautiful blonde when she arrived in New York to work as an artist's model, became a high-priced call girl before getting hooked on heroin. She testified that she was a worker on Luciano's 'assembly line', and claimed to be a personal favorite of his. She said that Luciano would send for her at the Waldorf but since he could not get it up, he would pay her to just hang out and talk. Since Presser's testimony did not hold up under cross, and she could not describe a single detail of Luciano's suite at the Waldorf, she did not seem to serve any purpose besides humiliating Luciano; the former choirboy who choked on 'Doppelgänger' must have gotten a cheap thrill out of showing the public that Mister Macho had a limp shrimp.

Most of the testimony from the male snitches was directed toward Little Davey Betillo, who would repeatedly blurt out uncontrolled responses like, 'Dirty liar.' Under cross-examination, the witnesses all admitted to getting sprung from jail in return for their testimony; most were caught lying multiple times, and some accused Dewey of bullying them.

During a recess, Luciano told reporters that he was confident in his acquittal; in truth, he was now as certain of his doom as he had once been of his vindication. In desperation, he overruled the advice of his senior counsel, George Morton Levy, and took the stand on the morning of 3 June. He could not even get past direct questioning from his own attorney without lying. When asked to state where he was born, Luciano said, 'New York City.' At least he picked an island, Manhattan, but not Sicily where he feared being returned; over the past thirty years, he had neglected to become a naturalized citizen.*

When it came time for cross, Dewey strode over to the witness box, needing only a black cape to accentuate his Count Dracula overbite. Luciano later admitted that he was terrified, saying Dewey 'had a look on his face like I was a piece of raw meat and he'd been goin' hungry for a month'.

Dewey started off with a series of seemingly innocuous questions to put Luciano at ease. He then reeled off some of Luciano's aliases, which were not a crime but would sow doubt in the jurors' minds. More doubt was sown when Dewey recited a few false occupations Luciano had claimed to have had when questioned by police in the past. Dewey finally asked Luciano if he had ever had a 'legitimate occupation'. Luciano could not at first recall any then suddenly remembered that he once owned a 'piece of a restaurant'.

---

* Later in life, author Sid Feder asked Luciano, 'Why on earth didn't you ever take out naturalization papers?' Luciano shrugged. Feder felt it was sheer laziness. I agree, in part, but I think there is more to it. When your entire life is a crime in progress, it takes gall to ask a country to naturalize you, and there is a touch of fear that this normal request can somehow backfire and result in the very thing you are attempting to avoid, deportation. Men like Frank Costello took the necessary steps to get naturalized, but Costello's comments in the winter of his life reveal the mind of a man who never thought he was doing anything wrong, just living the American dream. An author who interviewed Costello in his later years wrote, 'He considered himself a man of stature. His attitudes, even his manner, said that he felt he had maintained a life on a level far above the conventional rackets.' This slight difference in outlook may have, in some cases, decided who took the steps and who did not.

'The only legitimate business you've had in eighteen years you forgot?' asked Dewey.

Dewey then recalled a routine traffic stop in July 1926 when police pulled over Luciano and another hood as the two men were driving upstate. The cops searched the vehicle and found two handguns, a shotgun and a trunkload of ammunition. Why the arsenal? Dewey wondered aloud.

'We was hunting,' answered Luciano.

'And what had you been hunting?' asked Dewey.

'Peasants,' said Luciano.

'You mean pheasants?' asked Dewey before pointing out the absurdity of two men hunting with one shotgun, and that Luciano's arrest did not correspond with hunting season.

Dewey moved on to Luciano's infamous scar, aware that Luciano had told numerous accounts of how he had gotten it. Dewey made him rehash one version before poking holes in his story. Next, Dewey outed Luciano as a snitch. He began by asking Luciano if anything significant had happened to him in June 1923. When Luciano could not remember anything in particular, Dewey refreshed his memory, asking him if he had sold heroin to an undercover agent then broken under pressure and told the agent where he could find a whole trunkful of dope.

Luciano lowered his head, slouched in his seat, and whispered, 'Yes, I did.'

'Were you a stool pigeon?' yelled Dewey.

'I told him what I knew,' admitted Luciano, while sweating bullets.

Dewey got Luciano to admit to being a bootlegger, a heroin dealer, a liar and a snitch before he said, 'That's all', and sauntered away from the podium.

'I couldn't wait to get outa the courthouse,' Luciano later said. 'I practically ran.'

During Dewey's summation, he said to the jury, 'I am sure every one of you had not the slightest doubt there stood before you not a gambler, not a race-track man, but, stripped stark naked, the greatest gangster in America.' Luciano felt that the jurors concurred with Dewey, saying they 'looked like they all wanted to stand up and applaud'. The jury went out on 6 June, and returned with a guilty verdict for all defendants on the 7th. The judge praised the jurors for their collective intelligence then set a date for sentencing.

Chief Probation Officer Irving Halpern prepared Luciano's pre-sentencing report for the judge. Halpern deemed Luciano a 'shallow and parasitic individual who is considerably wrapped up in his own feelings . . . His social outlook is essentially childish . . . His behavior patterns are essentially instinctive and primitive . . . His ideals of life resolved themselves into money to spend, beautiful women to enjoy, silk underclothes and places to go in style.' This accurately describes the vast majority of mankind between the ages of puberty and senility, but the report provided justification for the judge to slam the gavel over Luciano's head; he hit him with thirty to fifty years in the state penitentiary. Little Davey Betillo got twenty-five to forty, while Frederico and Pennochio each got twenty-five years.

After the trial, Dewey used a state expense account to send Nancy Presser and Cokey Flo Brown on an all-expenses-paid vacation to Europe. Like spoiled kids on the Grand Tour, they complained from Paris that Daddy Dewey's allowance had run dry. Now that the case was over and Dewey had his conviction, he cut them off. The ladies felt used and, upon their return from Europe, they contacted Luciano's attorney and filed affidavits, swearing that Dewey had threatened to prosecute them if they did not cooperate; he then fed them their testimony. Polly Adler, one of 'New York's best-known and classiest' madams, confirmed that the 'girls lied because they'd been threatened by Dewey'. She added that Dewey and his attorneys 'put words into their mouths and gave them all of the information they needed to tell a convincing story'. According to Dewey, the women accused him and his team of 'coddling and threats. They swore we had kept them under the influence of liquor and rehearsed their testimony of lies.' He went on to say that their affidavits 'were filled with perjury', while only their trial testimony was truthful. One woman accused one of Dewey's assistants of pulling her around by the hair (presumably with a rubber glove on his hand). Several men who had testified and expected to get out of jail but were left to rot in prison also said they were coerced and fed a script. One witness, Joe Bendix, had written his own script; the three-time loser was looking at a fourth felony conviction that carried a life sentence when he wrote a letter to his wife that said he was going to 'think up some real clever story to tell'. He did, and Dewey bought it. A growing lot of disgruntled witnesses accused Dewey of prosecutorial misconduct, offering Luciano a chance at appeal, but the appellate court upheld his conviction.

Following his sentencing, the 38-year-old Mr Ross, Suite 39C of the Waldorf Towers, was fitted for a uniform that read: Inmate # 92168. Luciano, who had been boss of his own borgata for only five years, was shackled and sent to Clinton Dannemora. I have stayed in the Waldorf Towers and I have lived under the gun towers at Clinton, so I can speak to the contrast; it is like exiting your luxurious suite and stepping into an empty elevator shaft that drops you into the Ninth Circle of Dante's *Inferno*. Located near the Canadian border, Clinton was as far away as the New York penal system could send Luciano, a deliberate punishment to limit visits and strain his reach over the city. Despite the inconvenience, Luciano refused to step down as official boss of his borgata and attempted to maintain control by appointing Vito Genovese as his acting boss.

In search of his next target, Dewey announced, 'Genovese is an associate of Lucky Luciano. He is getting ready to take over all the rackets.' With that announcement and a pending murder case hanging over his head, Genovese was 'getting ready' all right, to board an ocean liner.

Vito Genovese was born near Naples, Italy, on 27 November 1897. In the summer of 1913, he and his family crossed the ocean in steerage and settled on Mulberry Street in Manhattan's Little Italy. When the family moved to Queens, Vito missed the big city and moved back on his own. His first arrest came in 1917 when he was pinched for carrying a gun and sentenced to sixty days in jail. In 1924, he married his first wife, Donata Ragone, who died of tuberculosis in 1931. Less than a year later, the 34-year-old Genovese fell in love with his cousin, 22-year-old Anna Petillo Vernotico. Since Anna was married to Gerard Vernotico, Genovese felt the couple should file for divorce and sent two men to expedite the proceedings. On 16 March 1932, Peter 'Petey Muggins' Mione and Michael Barrese cornered 29-year-old Gerard Vernotico and his pal, 33-year-old Antonio Lanza, on a rooftop at 124 Thompson Street. Both men were strangled to death; Vernotico was found with his arms and legs bound and a cord knotted around his neck. Twelve days later, Genovese tied another knot when he wedded Anna.

When Michael Barrese expressed concern that witnesses may have seen the murders take place, Genovese told Petey Muggins to put Barrese's concerns to rest, along with Barrese, who was never seen again.

In 1933, Genovese took Anna to Italy on a belated honeymoon. He brought with him $750,000 in cash, most of which he deposited into a Swiss bank account, while making investments in Italy with the rest; he was preparing for his escape in the event he needed to flee the States, where he returned after his European finances were in place.

The criminal case that would prompt Genovese to activate his escape plan began in Brooklyn, with the murder of Ferdinand 'The Shadow' Boccia, who ran a gambling den for Genovese. One evening in 1934, Boccia lured a wealthy mark into a high-stakes card game with Genovese and capo Mike Miranda. They took the mark for $60,000. Boccia expected a third of the take but was never paid. Meanwhile, Genovese offered the mark an opportunity to recoup his losses by printing his own money with a state-of-the-art counterfeiting machine that Genovese sold him for a hundred grand. When Boccia heard about the sale, he complained to Genovese that he was owed a cut of that, too. According to the rules of the street, Boccia was technically right but Genovese decided it was cheaper to kill him. He gave Ernie 'The Hawk' Rupolo and Billy Gallo the contract; the Hawk's extended contract was to whack Gallo after Boccia was dead.

On 19 September 1934, Boccia was shot and killed at Cristofolo Café on Metropolitan Avenue in Brooklyn. Not long after the hit, the Hawk shot Gallo, who miraculously survived and went to the police. When the Hawk was arrested, he decided to cooperate. He gave up Genovese and said that Peter LaTempa could corroborate his story with regard to the Boccia hit. LaTempa worked in a cigar store, and although he had nothing to do with the murder, he had overheard the killers as they planned it. By 1937, Genovese had at least two witnesses against him and Dewey breathing down his neck when he boarded an ocean liner for Italy. When Marco Polo returned to Venice after his twenty-four-year expedition to the East, his family failed to recognize him – until he sliced open the seams of his garments, revealing a variety of precious gems. Similarly, after Genovese started spreading around his money in Naples, everyone suddenly remembered squeezing cute little Vito's cheeks as a boy.

With Genovese gone, consigliere Frank Costello moved up to acting boss. This came as a relief to Meyer Lansky since he and Costello were cut from the same cloth, and neither of them had any love for Genovese. When the men were young, Genovese once asked Luciano and Costello why they had so many 'Hebes' in their gang. Costello, who had a Jewish wife, Jewish in-laws and plenty of Jewish pals and partners, took offense at the question and defended Lansky and Siegel, beginning a rift with Genovese that would last a lifetime. Everyone seemed happier with Costello in charge and Genovese traipsing around Mount Vesuvius – except Dewey, who needed a new target. While sitting on the fourteenth floor of the Woolworth Building, Dewey peered over the concrete jungle in search of prey. Amidst clothing racks of dresses, suits and mink coats rolling over the sidewalk in Midtown was the *schmatta* king, Lepke Buchalter.

Chapter 22

Lepke Lams It

By the time Lucky Luciano went to prison, Lepke Buchalter was overseeing 'some 250 criminal ventures simultaneously' and was believed to have extorted somewhere in the area of fifty million dollars, a generous piece of which was kicked up to Luciano's borgata, with a slice going to Tom Gagliano, via his underboss, Tommy Lucchese, and Vincent Mangano, via his underboss, Albert Anastasia. Given the magnitude of Lepke's operation, the law was hot on his heels.

Back in June 1933, Lepke was arrested with Michael 'Trigger Mike' Coppola, who was a capo in Luciano's borgata. It was a clear case of harassment and the cops tried to pin a vagrancy charge on them that did not hold up when each produced a thick wad of cash. Federal prosecutors, who had a more exact approach to criminal procedure than phony vagrancy charges, applied anti-trust laws to Lepke's monopolistic control of the fur industry. A grand jury returned two indictments against Lepke and Gurrah. They were arrested and released on bail. The case went to trial in October 1936. After they were convicted and sentenced to two years in prison, their attorneys asked Judge Martin Manton for bail, pending appeal. Thomas Dewey, who was in the process of preparing an indictment of his own, felt they were flight risks and paid the judge a visit, asking that Lepke and Gurrah be denied bail until his own charges were filed. The judge consented – then ignored Dewey's request and set bail at $10,000 each. Dewey knew that Lepke walked around with that kind of cash in his back pocket and was sure they would skip town. He was so angry with the judge that he quietly launched an investigation into him and found that he was corrupt. Judge Manton was ultimately forced to resign, convicted of accepting bribes, and sentenced to two years in prison.

As Dewey had expected, Lepke and Gurrah packed their bags and fled. They lammed it together for a brief time before they split up; New Jersey mobster Jimmy Ferraco looked after Gurrah, while Lepke put his trust in his buddy Albert Anastasia.

While on the lam, Lepke's problems were compounded when he was charged with a federal drug conspiracy. Back in January 1935, two heroin dealers, Jacob 'Yasha' Katzenberg and Jake Lvovsky, asked Lepke if he knew of an overseas contact who sold wholesale heroin. Lepke sent them to see Joe Schwartz in Mexico City who, in turn, introduced them to heroin exporters in Shanghai, China. To help smuggle the heroin into the United States, Lepke paid two corrupt customs agents to affix customs stamps to the appropriate traveling trunks when they landed in New York, making the trunks appear previously inspected.

From the start, Lepke made enemies with just about everyone involved in the ring when he demanded the lion's share of the profits from not only the wholesale smuggling operation but also the retail distribution. The conspirators reluctantly agreed since, regardless of the daring voyages they were making across the Indian Ocean, the Arabian Sea and the Suez Canal, Lepke had access to the stamps, without which the rest of the journey was for naught. From the autumn of 1935 to the start of 1937, the world's finest luxury liners, including the *Queen Mary*, *Majestic* and *Aquitania*, carried over ten million dollars' worth of heroin into the Port of New York (over 200 million dollars in today's currency). Then, one day, an anonymous woman wrote a letter to narcotics commissioner Harry Anslinger, offering inside information about Lepke's drug cartel. A few days later, the woman followed up with a telephone call to Anslinger and the two met at the Carlton Hotel where the woman told Anslinger more details about the ring. (Some suspect that Luciano put her up to it, hoping to leverage his way out of prison by giving up Lepke. By now, we know Luciano well enough to believe it.) Based on the woman's information, Anslinger built a case against Lepke and thirty other co-conspirators who were all indicted in December 1937. By then, Dewey was already looking for Lepke. He put a $25,000 dead-or-alive bounty on Lepke's head and had the police department assign twenty cops to search for him, increased to fifty after the first twenty returned each day with doughnut powder on their lips. Dewey also put Lepke's mug on 100,000 wanted posters while 'portraits and measurements of Lepke were displayed on motion picture screens throughout the country'.

Anastasia shuffled Lepke around to different safe houses in Brooklyn; Lepke once posed as the paralyzed husband of his landlady. Whenever someone knocked at the door, the disguised Lepke 'would let his arms go limp and would assume a paralytic pose in his armchair'.

The bounty on Lepke's head increased when the feds got involved. With a combined bounty of $50,000, tipsters reported sightings of Lepke across the globe. Aware he could not hide forever, Lepke arrived at a different solution to his problems. 'No witnesses . . . no indictments,' he said to an underling as he decided to murder every potential witness against him. To accomplish this, the notorious entrepreneur turned to the killing machine he had created along a business model which the press dubbed 'Murder, Incorporated'. Anastasia co-chaired this 'corporation' with Lepke, and Abe Reles was their star employee.

When Britannia ruled the seas, press gangs targeted pubs in search of idle young men to recruit into the Royal Navy. In similar fashion, aimless teens who hung out in New York's pool halls were recruited by mobsters. The Shapiro brothers – Meyer, Irving and Willie – took over the rackets in Brownsville, Brooklyn, with a small army of young toughs found in local pool halls. One such tough was Abe 'Kid Twist' Reles, a pudgy 5-foot-2-inch high-school dropout.

During Prohibition, the Shapiros were small-time bootleggers. After repeal, they oversaw bordellos, dealt drugs, ran crap games, and built up a slot machine route. 'As long as we stay in our own backyard,' said Meyer Shapiro, 'we ain't got a thing to worry about.' Meyer was right; by resisting the temptation to expand, the Shapiros avoided any major clash with the mafia. But they had overlooked a cancer within; as Kid Twist got older, he and his pal Martin 'Buggsy' Goldstein challenged the Shapiros. To beef up their ranks, they forged an alliance with another pair of young hoods from Ocean Hill, Brooklyn – Harry 'Happy' Maione, who was only happy when he was killing people, and Frank 'The Dasher' Abbandando. Maione and Abbandando were in the process of taking over their own stomping grounds when they were approached by Kid Twist; they welcomed the merger. Whereas the Shapiro brothers avoided the mafia, the young toughs happily partnered with Louis Capone (no known relation to Al Capone), who answered directly to Albert Anastasia. Capone put a claim on the young gangsters, who knocked off the Shapiros, one by one, and were eager to show off their elimination skills for the mob. Lepke, who used them most, put the entire gang of about a dozen hitmen on retainer, paying each three hundred dollars a week. When Lepke felt squeezed by Dewey, he ordered them to murder every potential witness.

The killers had warmed up even before Lepke had gone on the lam. Joe Rosen owned a trucking company that once challenged Lepke. While Lepke was bringing the truckers to heel so he could compromise Amalgamated's Sidney Hillman, Rosen resisted and was driven out of business. Needing income, Rosen opened a candy store in Brooklyn. When store traffic was slow, the former truck driver passed the time complaining about what Lepke had done to him. As Rosen's store was located on the turf of Murder, Inc., this was a dangerous pastime. His complaints got back to Lepke, who exhibited uncharacteristic patience which finally ran out when Rosen made the fatal mistake of telling a few people he might talk to Dewey. On Sunday morning, 13 September 1936, the 46-year-old family man was stacking newspapers when two men entered his store and shot him seventeen times. He lay on the floor with newspapers scattered around him, appearing like a puppy that was slaughtered while being paper-trained.

Joe Rosen gunned down inside his candy store.

Lepke ordered the next hit while he was on the lam. George 'Whitey' Rudnick was suspected of talking to Dewey. Kid Twist described the murder, which took place on 11 May 1937, as follows: 'Rudnick is laying there. Pep has an ice pick. Happy has a meat cleaver ... Pep starts with the ice pick and begins punching away at Whitey ... and Maione ... he says, "Let me hit this bastard one for luck," and he hits him with the cleaver, someplace in the head.' Rudnick was stabbed sixty-three times.

When Thomas Dewey wanted to talk with Lepke associate Max Rubin, Lepke sent Rubin to Utah, telling him to stay put until things cooled down. But Rubin found the change from Manhattan to Mormon country unbearable, and returned to New York. Lepke then tried to send Rubin to the Catskill Mountains, known as the Borscht Belt, where Jewish New Yorkers vacationed every summer. Rubin did not like the mountains, either, and returned to the city. Lepke threw a fit and now banished Rubin to New Orleans. Yet again, Rubin returned to New York, telling Lepke he missed his wife and children. Lepke finally decided that the best place to hide Rubin was in the ground. On 1 October, Rubin was walking along a Manhattan sidewalk when a man shot him in the back of his neck, giving the pain in the neck a real pain in the neck. Though the bullet passed upward through Rubin's head and exited between his eyes, he somehow lived. After a month in the hospital, he was ready for a candlelight dinner with Dewey who announced over the radio, 'The shot which struck down Max Rubin was the frightened act of a desperate criminal underworld. The racketeers have flung down their challenge. I accept that challenge.'

Anastasia continued to move Lepke around to different safe houses as they tried to keep tabs on whoever else was talking. When they found out that dressmaker Hyman Yuran was bending under Dewey's pressure, it was time for Yuran to go. On 21 August 1938, he was shot and dumped in a shallow grave. Three months later, on 10 November, Leon Sharff was murdered along with his unlucky wife who happened to be with him. Louis Cohen and Danny Fields were killed on 28 January 1939, followed by Albert 'Plug' Shuman on the 29th. On 30 March, Joseph Miller was murdered and, on 28 April, Abraham 'Whitey' Friedman was killed. Next up was Morris Diamond, who managed the Teamster Local, formerly run by William Snyder who had been killed in Garfein's restaurant. After being subpoenaed by Dewey, Diamond made a few trips to Dewey's bunker, believing his little choir calls were kept secret. Lepke found out about them and told Anastasia, who dispatched Jack 'Dandy' Parisi and Angelo 'Julie' Catalano; they murdered Diamond on 25 May.

As Dewey's pawns were being removed from the chessboard, he lamented, 'There will soon be no one left to testify when we finally catch up with Lepke.' It looked as though Dewey's concern was warranted – until Lepke's hitmen made a crucial mistake. After Lepke had taken over the Cutters Union, he placed Philip Orlovsky at its head. Since the short, pudgy, two-hundred-pound Orlovsky allowed Lepke to push him around so easily, it was no surprise when Dewey pushed Orlovsky under an interrogation lamp. When this got back to Lepke, he dispatched three assassins. Before dawn on 25 July, Martin 'Buggsy' Goldstein, Abe 'Pretty' Levine and Seymour 'Blue Jaw' Magoon stole a car and parked it across the street from where Orlovsky lived, then waited for him to leave for work. When they saw a roly-poly man leave his house, Buggsy unloaded a .32 caliber into him. The killers sped off, unaware that Buggsy had just pumped six slugs into Irving Penn, a law-abiding family man who resembled Orlovsky and lived on the same block; both men left for work each day around the same time.

The death of an innocent man led to a tide of public pressure to capture Lepke, who became Public Enemy Number One. Until now, New York's mafia bosses – three of whom benefitted from Lepke's rackets – had put up with Lepke's scorched-earth policy which littered the streets with corpses. But the murder of Irving Penn resulted in a much tighter squeeze on the rackets and tested their patience. They decided to kill Lepke but were stopped by Anastasia, who was hiding him and refused to hand him over. Once Lepke was deserted with only Anastasia guarding the front gate to his kingdom, Tommy Lucchese made a play for Lepke's unions. When Lepke heard that Lucchese was rattling around in his house, Lepke called for a sit-down. Since a sit, according to mob rules, is confined to made men of equal stature, Anastasia appeared with Lepke, as his representative.

Kid Twist drove Lepke to the sit. On their way there, Lepke said to him, 'Those bastards are more interested in their own take than they are in my hide.' At the table, Lepke and Anastasia sat across from Tommy Lucchese and capo Willie Moretti. Since Moretti answered directly to Frank Costello, who was now, in the absence of Vito Genovese, acting boss of Luciano's borgata, it was apparent that Luciano and Costello were in cahoots with Lucchese. Unlike the usual Italian sit-downs where accusations and countercharges are made by way of crafty language, the angry, plain-spoken Jew pulled no punches, accusing Lucchese and Moretti of sticky fingers. Lucchese did not deny the charge; he instead attempted to ease Lepke into the idea of letting him watch over his house until he overcame his difficulties. Lepke knew this was a power grab; nobody gives anything back in the mob (or in life, for that matter). Lepke rose from the table in a huff and yelled, 'Nobody moved in on me while I was on the outside – and nobody's gonna do it just because I'm on the lam . . . There's no argument . . . the clothing thing is mine.' With that, Lepke stormed out of the room.

Like a hawk circling an injured animal, Lucchese was not about to fly away. But he needed to get past Anastasia so he went around to the bosses, assuring them the pressure on the rackets would never let up until Lepke was dead. Costello, who was fully on board with Lucchese, had second thoughts about killing Lepke. After the Dutchman was hit, Dewey lost his prize and went after Luciano. Now that Costello was top dog, Dewey would likely come gunning for him, once Lepke was gone. Costello and Lucchese came up with an alternative plan. They visited Luciano in Clinton, where they convinced him that giving up Lepke was the key to his cell door. Luciano bought in. Their only problem was who to hand Lepke over to since Dewey and FBI director J. Edgar Hoover were both searching for Lepke. Both lawmen wanted the headlines, and neither wanted to be bested by the other. After careful consideration, Costello and Lucchese decided that Hoover was a greater threat to the mob than Dewey since Dewey could not exert any more pressure on them than he already was; if Hoover leaned on them, too, they would be stuck in a vice. Hoping to satisfy both lawmen, the final plan was to let Hoover take Lepke into custody and get the national headline, with Dewey then claiming jurisdiction and pulling Lepke over to the state for another trial.

Walter Winchell was the most famous radio host and newspaper columnist in the country when combining the two mediums. He had a daily readership of fifty million Americans and his voice was known 'from cowboys on the range to Maine lobster fishermen'. Since part of his job required him to be in the know, he hung out at New York's Stork Club, the premier nightspot where the 'most important men in the world' rubbed shoulders, including gangsters and celebrities. Whenever J. Edgar Hoover was in town, he stayed at the Waldorf Astoria and frequented the Stork Club, despite the widely known fact that mobsters hung out there, too, and the club's owner, Sherman Billingsley, was a one-time bootlegger who served time in prison. Known to patrons derisively as the 'Stork Club detective', Hoover sat at Table 50 in the VIP section, where the stiff director let his guard down while always preserving his public image by having alcoholic drinks removed from the table before posing for photographs with admirers. Walter Winchell stayed in Hoover's good graces by using his pen and microphone to defend the thin-skinned director whenever Hoover's detractors were on the attack. In return, Hoover was suspected of giving Winchell inside scoops from the Bureau, likely conveyed to him at the Stork Club where Winchell spent as much time at Hoover's table as he did Frank Costello's. (It is believed that Costello owned a piece of the Stork Club and was Sherman Billingsley's silent partner.) Using Winchell as his go-between, Costello reached out to Hoover and told him he could deliver up Lepke.*

With Hoover salivating over Lepke's imminent capture, Costello now needed to convince Lepke to turn himself in, which he did by pretending to have worked out a favorable deal in return for his surrender. To relay the terms of the deal to Lepke, Costello asked Meyer Lansky to reach out to Morris 'Moey Dimples' Wolinsky, one of the few men Lepke trusted. Since some historians have suggested that Dimples was in on the ruse, it is worth noting that Lansky did not trust Dimples with the truth, fearing he might deliberately alert Lepke, or even do so unintentionally, since Lepke was sharp and could detect a lie; it was best if Dimples believed his own words when he relayed them to Lepke.

In the summer of 1939, Moey Dimples visited Lepke in hiding and told him a 'deal is in with the feds'. Lepke was promised that if he surrendered to the FBI, Hoover would keep him away from Dewey, who could potentially strap him into the electric chair for any one of the many murders he had ordered. Lepke asked Dimples how many years he would have to serve on the federal drug rap. When Dimples told him 'twelve', Lepke, who was used to *hondeling* in the garment district, tried to shave off a third and said he might cop out to 'eight'. After Dimples left, Lepke ran the deal by Anastasia who sensed a trap and told Lepke to turn it down. For two years, Anastasia had moved Lepke around to a number of hideouts while helping him knock off a dozen witnesses; he did not want to see all that hard work end with Lepke waving a white flag. 'What's the hurry?' Anastasia said to Lepke. 'You can always walk in. But while they ain't got you, they can't hurt you.' This was sound advice but Lepke was worn down from hiding

---

* In his memoir, Walter Winchell claims an unidentified man approached him at Lindy's (Arnold Rothstein's old haunt) and told him that if Lepke 'could find someone he could trust, he'll give himself up to that person'. This story is apocryphal. Winchell must have been told by Hoover and Costello not to connect them, even though the two men sat a few tables apart at the Stork Club. They also frequented the Waldorf Astoria where they may have met, on occasion. Costello claimed that Hoover once wanted to buy him a cup of coffee at the Waldorf and Costello replied, rather humorously, 'I got to be careful of my associates. They'll accuse me of consortin' with questionable characters.' Hoover claimed that Costello once tried to start a conversation with him in the Waldorf's barbershop, to which Hoover replied, sternly, 'You stay out of my bailiwick and I'll stay out of yours.' Each of their stories seems to have been created to conceal some sort of interaction that occurred at the Waldorf; in case they were seen together, each had a cover story as to why.

and desperate to bring his troubles to a conclusion. He told Dimples to set up the surrender.

Concerned that Hoover's gung-ho agents would mow him down as he surrendered, Lepke had someone telephone Walter Winchell, telling him to announce over a radio broadcast that J. Edgar Hoover would guarantee his civil rights. Winchell was thrilled with the request since it was great for ratings. He invited Hoover to his studio, where Winchell leaned into a microphone and said, 'Attention Public Enemy Number One, Louis "Lepke" Buchalter! I am authorized by John Edgar Hoover of the Federal Bureau of Investigation to guarantee you safe delivery to the FBI if you surrender to me or to any agent for the FBI. I will repeat . . .' And Winchell did just that, twice more, before saying goodnight to America.

Once off the air, Winchell received a series of mysterious telephone calls from someone claiming to speak on Lepke's behalf. On one of the calls, the caller told Winchell to drive his wife's car to a deserted lot. Winchell, a self-admitted coward, mustered the courage to do as told – anything for a story. On Winchell's way out the door, his wife, hip to the danger he was in, yelled, 'Why do you get yourself involved with such people?'

'They get involved with me!' Winchell yelled back as he pulled away from the house. He drove through the Holland Tunnel into New Jersey, where he hung around the vacant lot for a quarter of an hour before his nerves gave out and he sped home. Next, the mysterious caller told Winchell to ask Hoover how many years Lepke should expect to serve. Winchell passed on the question to Hoover, who said, 'I'm not a lawyer, I'm just a policeman with a badge', as if the most powerful lawman in America was equal to a rookie baton-twirler.

After several weeks of waiting for Lepke to surrender, Hoover blew his top at Winchell inside the Stork Club, creating a spectacle in front of a hundred or so patrons. 'I am fed up with you and your friends! They can make a fool out of you, but you are not going to make a fool out of me and my men!'

'They are not my friends, John,' replied Winchell.

Hoover pointed a finger in Winchell's face and said, '*They are your friends!* And don't call me John! I'm beginning to think you're the champ bullshitter in town!' He finished with, 'You tell your friends that if Lepke isn't in within forty-eight hours, I will order my agents to shoot him on sight!'

Winchell made for the door. On his way out, he told Hoover's right-hand man, FBI associate director Clyde Tolson, 'You people haven't been able to find him for two years. How you gonna find him in forty-eight hours?'

The next time the mysterious caller telephoned Winchell, Winchell gave him an earful, telling him that Hoover was fed up and might yank the deal off the table. When Lepke heard, he decided it was time to surrender. He had his go-between tell Winchell who, in turn, called Hoover and said, 'John, this is the champ bullshitter. My *friends* have instructed me to tell you to be at Twenty-Eighth Street and Fifth Avenue between ten-ten and ten-twenty tonight. That's about half an hour. They told me to tell you to be alone.' Hoover said he would be there and hung up the telephone. To puff up his own image as a tough lawman, Hoover wanted to personally take Lepke into custody (with two dozen undercover agents watching his back, of course. In Hoover's Washington office, he displayed handguns taken from infamous criminals like John Dillinger. 'These pistols', wrote Hoover's longtime assistant FBI director, William Sullivan, 'were the closest Hoover ever came to a real gun since he didn't know how to use one.')

In the ten o'clock hour of 24 August 1939, Winchell drove to a drugstore where he collected a man named Jake. Winchell and Jake then drove several blocks away and parked the car close to where Hoover was waiting in a black limousine. Jake handed Winchell a mezuzah and said, 'Give this to the Lep', then hopped out of the car and disappeared into the night. Moments later, Lepke appeared, dressed in a hat and overcoat. (If I had to trust Winchell, Hoover, Costello, Luciano and Lucchese to keep me out of the electric chair, I'd have surrendered in a rubber suit with matching wellies.) Lepke climbed into the back seat of Winchell's car.

'We'll be with Mr Hoover in a minute or two,' Winchell told Lepke as he drove away from the curb. Minutes later, Winchell parked and led Lepke over to the FBI director's limousine. Winchell opened the door and said, 'Lepke, this is Mr Hoover. Mr Hoover, *this* is Lepke.'

'How do you do?' asked Hoover, as if he cared.

'Glad to meet you,' Lepke replied, as if he meant it.

After this cheery start, Hoover snapped, 'Get in the car! Where are your high and mighty friends now?'

Lepke felt double-crossed but knew he would be shot if he ran – unlike Winchell, who ran straight to a public telephone booth to break the news. He dialed the *Mirror*. 'This is Winchell,' he screamed into the receiver. 'Lepke, Public Enemy Number One, just surrendered to the FBI!' At first, the hack at the news desk did not believe Winchell, then berated him for calling with such a lousy scoop when a world war was brewing in Europe. He hung up on Winchell and two other newspapers broke the story.

On 25 August 1939, Lepke was arraigned in federal court on narcotics charges. Not long afterward, Murder, Inc. manager Mendy Weiss was captured in Kansas City, Missouri, where he was living under the false identity of a mining executive. Jacob 'Gurrah' Shapiro was already in custody. Homesick and in failing health, Gurrah had walked into a

Lepke at his arraignment.

federal detention center the year before, saying, 'I'm Jacob Shapiro. I want to give up.' He refused to snitch and accepted a fifteen-year sentence to avoid the electric chair. In 1947, he died in prison of a heart attack.

With Lepke in custody, Albert Anastasia lost a dear friend, while Frank Costello and Tommy Lucchese took out their pizza cutters and sliced up the garment center. As for Dewey, he at first swallowed his pride and congratulated Hoover, but coughed it back up and demanded that Hoover turn Lepke over to him, immediately. The director refused, causing US attorney general Frank Murphy to step in, telling Hoover that Lepke was 'guilty of eighty murders' and it did not look good to withhold him from the state.

As the feds and the state fought over Lepke, Lepke continued to eliminate potential witnesses, beginning with Irving 'Puggy' Feinstein, who was lured to Kid Twist's house where his killers employed some bizarre strangulation technique that might have won them a few admirers in an Ottoman court. Puggy was dragged to the floor where his head was pushed into his chest. While held in this position, he was tied up, 'Like a little ball . . . his knees . . . folded up against his chest.' According to Kid Twist, if Puggy moved, the rope would 'tighten up around his throat'. As Puggy inched toward death's door, a 'bloody froth bubbled' from his mouth. Kid Twist, who was worried about his carpet, was thrown into a tizzy. He ran off to get some newspapers and slid them under Puggy's lips. 'There – that's better,' he said. When Puggy stopped breathing, the men kicked his corpse. As their adrenaline wound down, one of the killers, Harry 'Pittsburgh Phil' Strauss, realized that Puggy had bitten his hand. Within seconds, he became terrified that he had contracted rabies. He darted into Kid Twist's bathroom and raided the medicine cabinet, applying a variety of ointments. After Pittsburgh Phil stopped whining about the bruise on his hand and Kid Twist stopped worrying about the stain on his carpet, the men were free to act tough again. They loaded Puggy into their car and dumped him in an empty lot where they doused him with gasoline. Because they did not douse his feet, most of his body was discovered burned to a crisp while his ankles, shoes and socks were unscathed. Anastasia was told the news and relayed it to Lepke in prison, who wasted no time ordering another hit.

Next to go was Harry 'Big Greenie' Greenberg. But before we follow Lepke's killers as they stalk Greenberg from Canada to California, let us turn back the clock a couple of years and travel to the West Coast with Benjamin 'Bugsy' Siegel, who was perfectly in place to execute Lepke's hit on Greenberg when Greenberg practically fell into Siegel's lap.

Chapter 23

Hunting for Treasure – and for Big Greenie

After Lucky Luciano became a don, Benjamin 'Bugsy' Siegel, as part of Luciano's crew, enjoyed the spoils. He moved into a suite at the Waldorf, a couple of floors below Luciano's. But money, marriage and even children did nothing to temper Siegel's wild spirit, which always seemed to be searching for something he could not find. One day, Siegel told Meyer Lansky he was relocating to Los Angeles and had already convinced his wife, Esta, and their two daughters that they would love it out west. At the time, California had its own borgata, headed by a low-key Sicilian, Ignazio 'Jack' Dragna.

Jack Dragna was born in Corleone, Sicily. He migrated to Manhattan's Little Italy at a young age but fled west when the police wanted to question him about a murder. Landing in California, he picked up with his life of crime and served a few years in San Quentin, was released, and rose to underboss in the Los Angeles borgata which operated with limited autonomy; since it was a relatively small borgata, it fell under the protection of Chicago, the same way the smaller New Jersey, New England and Philadelphia borgatas fell under the larger New York umbrella. When the boss of Los Angeles, Joe Ardizzone, disappeared, Dragna moved up and was known as a disciplinarian. Knowing that the hot-tempered Siegel, who had little respect for authority, was heading into another borgata's territory, Lansky cautioned him, saying, 'You might have a little trouble with Jack Dragna . . . I'd better tell Lucky to give him the word to cooperate.'

Lansky knew that Dragna would view Siegel's relocation as invasive and would wonder if New York was planting a flag in his backyard. How many New Yorkers would follow Siegel? And how long before they would muscle in on his turf? With a perfect understanding of mafia politics, Lansky visited Luciano in Clinton and asked him to pave the way for Siegel. Luciano sent word to Dragna that Siegel was heading out west 'for the good of his health and the health of all of us'. Luciano's message – *all of us* – would have confirmed Dragna's suspicion that Siegel was spearheading an invasion from the east. Because Dragna did not have the strength to repel the New Yorkers alone, I am absolutely certain he put it on record with the Chicago mob which would defend its client state, should the need arise.

After landing in California, the first opportunity Siegel spotted was the race wire. He inserted himself as the Trans-American wire's Los Angeles franchise manager, quickly expanding the service by bringing new bookies on board. Dragna, seeing Siegel's success, provided him with extra muscle in return for the dragon's share, which still left Siegel with a healthy $25,000 per month, his end alone.

Before Siegel left New York, Lansky had said to him, 'Take it easy with those Hollywood broads, I know you've always wanted to get laid by actresses.' Now, with plenty of money rolling in, Siegel pursued his ambition to break into Hollywood circles and called on his buddy George Raft, a movie actor who grew up on the same mean streets of New York as Lansky and Siegel. Raft invited Siegel to Hollywood parties and introduced him to actors Clark Gable, Cary Grant and Gary Cooper, as well as the most famous actresses, producers and directors. Siegel and Raft, who often went to Santa Anita Racetrack together, were an odd pair in the sense that Siegel was a gangster who secretly dreamed of being an actor while Raft was an actor who fantasized about being a gangster. 'I was crazy about a lot of these guys,' Raft once said. 'I used to copy their little mannerisms in pictures.'

Raft and Siegel were once at a bookie parlor when it was raided. The police captain cuffed Siegel and was taking him downtown when Raft yelled, 'Take me down, too.' The captain, who was trying to give Raft a break, said, 'You stay out of this, Raft.'

'But I was betting, too,' Raft insisted. Raft tried so hard to get himself arrested that we are left to wonder if he dimed the parlor to take an easy pinch and boost his fame. Raft later testified on Siegel's behalf and posed for photos with him after the court appearance as if they were on the red carpet together. The quiet Dragna saw this highly publicized arrest, and any other time Siegel made the newspapers, as a problem. Dragna was making truckloads of money with the traditional mafia rackets such as gambling and loansharking, along with labor relations that entailed settling disputes between unions and Hollywood studios; he did not need Siegel calling attention to his operations. Lansky was also concerned about Siegel's behavior and sent word to him: 'Stop thinking you're a movie star.'

Siegel brushed off the friendly warning and built himself a mansion for $150,000, a large tab at the time. He ran around behind his wife's back, dating actresses and starting an affair with the wealthy Countess Dorothy Caldwell Taylor Dentice di Frasso. Countess di Frasso, or the 'Fancy Lady' as Siegel referred to her, was the daughter of leather manufacturing mogul Bertrand LeRoy Taylor. When Taylor died, Dorothy split the family fortune with her brother and told her pilot husband to fly away. She remarried an Italian count. It was a marriage in which money craved title, and title needed money; after each got what they wanted, they were hardly seen together.

Di Frasso was impulsive, like Siegel. After seeing Gary Cooper on the big screen, she flew to Hollywood and slept with him. She then took Cooper to Rome, Italy, where she owned a sixteenth-century castle, Villa Madama, designed by Raphael. The castle, Siegel would later say, 'was bigger than Grand Central Station'. The countess also purchased a home in Hollywood where she regularly entertained Clark Gable, Fred Astaire, Marlene Dietrich and other big-screen sensations. But the thug from the Lower East Side was responsible for her biggest sensations. Di Frasso fell for Siegel after meeting him at Santa Anita Racetrack. Siegel initially viewed the millionaire countess as a mark. As it turned out, the two had a lot in common and developed a friendship that complemented their affair, rather steamy for the countess, while bearable for Siegel, given the benefits.

Just as Siegel was always gambling on something new, so was the countess, but the stakes were bigger and commensurate with her bank account. She invested in zippers but pulled out before the zipper outdid the button in 1937. She invested in shark livers knowing they were loaded with vitamin A, but sold her shares before the vitamin craze. She dumped money into soybeans but it took decades for the world to realize their variety of uses, an industry now worth billions of dollars annually. She was way ahead of her time and would have made an excellent financial advisor for Methuselah, but she always needed instant gratification and was searching for a new venture when Siegel asked her to finance a treasure hunt.

Siegel's fantastic voyage into the South Pacific began with an old drunk by the name of Billy Bowbeer, who carried a half-tattered, crudely drawn treasure map in his back pocket. While sitting at a bar, Bowbeer would spread the map out and ask other drinkers if they were interested in splitting a ninety-million-dollar fortune with him – all they had to do was underwrite a treasure hunt to Cocos Island in the Pacific Ocean. A close inspection of the map would show that it was drawn on a tablecloth; some drunk, possibly Bowbeer himself, must have sketched it out one night while in need of someone to buy him a drink, the very least you can do for a guy who is holding the key to ninety million. Who knows how many beers this map earned the stinky old fart, who must have fallen off his barstool when someone pointed him toward Siegel, who happened to be dating a checkbook named Countess di Frasso. Siegel bought into Bowbeer's story then sold it to di Frasso, who agreed to finance the trip and insisted she come along; she wanted her money's worth out of Siegel in the master cabin, a consolation prize in the event they found a bucket of piss clams.

One September morning in 1938, Siegel climbed aboard the merchant schooner *Metha Nelson* and set sail for Cocos Island, a pimple on *Mar Pacífico*'s ass, situated about two hundred miles off the coast of Costa Rica. The rest of the ship's passengers must have inspired the long-running Hollywood sitcom *Gilligan's Island*. German-born Captain Robert Hoffman was tapped as the skipper. Dr Benjamin Blank was equal to the professor (oddly enough, he was the resident doctor for the Los Angeles County Jail, where Siegel belonged). Marino Bello was actress Jean Harlow's stepfather (Siegel had a tryst with Harlow). Harry Segal was from the wealthy Segal Lock family. There was also a full crew that included maids and servants, and, of course, Billy Bowbeer, who must have been shocked that his old pub stunt won him a free cruise amidst such affluent company. It is a testament to Siegel's natural charm and persuasion that he could raise the tempo of Bowbeer's barroom pitch high enough to drag this group into Kon-Tiki territory.

Confident he would find the ninety-million-dollar treasure, Siegel hand-picked a security detail to protect the booty on their way home. He did not post an ad, like Ernest Shackleton, or solicit retired sailors living around California's naval bases; he recruited men he could trust, hoodlums from gambling dens across Hollywood, armed with snub-nosed revolvers. These men also brought dynamite; though we do not know if anyone on board was properly trained to use it, Dr Blank was trained to recognize lunatics and should have had the whole boatload committed, including himself.

Like the wealthy who climb Mount Everest with as many luxuries as their Sherpas can carry, the schooner set sail loaded with fine food and beverages, including liquor, wine and caviar. The ocean was calm, as was Siegel until he experienced gambling withdrawals. The entire trip was a gamble, but he missed day-to-day action so he found a deck of cards and started a poker game. The passengers, who expected to see a gangster leaning over the bow shooting at albatrosses, were pleasantly surprised by Siegel's warmth. 'He had authority,' said one passenger, 'but on that trip he never got out of line once.' At night, the passengers huddled on deck together or gathered in the lounge, playing music, telling jokes and talking about what they planned to do with their share of the treasure.

The schooner made a port of call in Costa Rica, where a colonel ordered his soldiers to board the vessel. After listening to dreamy *gringos* rehash the impractical story that brought them south, the colonel must have wondered if the citizens of the United States were equal to the growing threats from Nazi Germany, Fascist Italy and militaristic Japan. But just in case they were on to something, he made them sign over a third of whatever they might find.

The *Metha Nelson* cast off. The next time her crew spotted land, it was a thin strip of sand and rocks with steep cliffs, prickly grass, snakes and rats. Cocos Island was nothing like the Pacific paradise that lured the men of HMS *Bounty* away from king and country, but the group was not there for pleasure; Siegel got right down to business as he and Bowbeer led the men to the spot where they believed the treasure was hidden. They dug, drilled and dynamited. Siegel, who always did his own hits, showed the same grit as he worked harder than his shipmates. After a few days of backbreaking work under a merciless sun, the thrill began to give way to bitter frustration. When Siegel finally admitted there was nothing to be found, his warmth left him. He cursed bitterly, called it quits, and ordered the captain to set sail for Panama.

The return trip devolved into a take on the Hitchcock movie *Lifeboat*, as tension brewed with each lapping wave until everyone was at each other's throats. In Panama, Siegel abandoned ship and called home to tell his wife, Esta, to put $3,000 on Seabiscuit. He boarded the next flight to California, hoping he would be home in time to collect on his win at the track. Meanwhile, the others he had left behind were hit by a typhoon, rescued by an Italian ship, and towed into Acapulco where the countess now abandoned ship. She did not, however, abandon Siegel, who resumed his life as a mobster as if the treasure hunt never happened. He gambled, extorted and was, as always, prepared to kill when, in the autumn of 1939, Harry 'Big Greenie' Greenberg landed in his backyard.

Big Greenie Greenberg entered the United States illegally and ducked deportation with the help of Lepke Buchalter, who put him to work as a *schlammer* (Yiddish for someone who slams people over their heads, usually with a lead pipe). Big Greenie also tossed bombs through storefront windows and murdered Lepke's enemies. When Thomas Dewey started sniffing around, Lepke knew Greenie could implicate him in countless crimes so he told him to disappear. Big Greenie went to Montreal, Canada, where the goon transformed himself into an *homme de lettres*, not in the tradition of the Earl of Chesterfield, but a prolific, whiny letter writer whose intent was to elicit funds from Lepke while dropping hints that he might talk. 'I hope you guys are not forgetting me,' he once wrote. 'You better not.' He sometimes hinted that the $50,000 bounty on Lepke's head was beginning to look attractive.

Three months after Lepke surrendered to J. Edgar Hoover, his patience for Big Greenie's threats ran out. He gave the contract to Allie 'Tick-Tock' Tannenbaum, who arrived in Montreal shortly after Greenie left there for Hollywood, California. Whitey Krakower, who ran with Siegel's crew, got wind of Greenie's arrival in the Sunshine State and brought the news to Siegel, who knew Lepke had a contract on Greenie's head. Siegel touched base with Joe Adonis in New York, who sent Tick-Tock to help Siegel with the hit. Tick-Tock would drive a back-up car while Siegel would drive the getaway car, and Frankie Carbo, a part-time Murder, Inc. employee and soldier in Tommy Lucchese's borgata, would pull the trigger.*

On the night of 22 November 1939, Big Greenie ran out for a newspaper, maybe looking for updates about Lepke in the press. Upon his

---

* Before the 1930s were up, Frankie Carbo was suspected of at least five homicides. He would go on to control the sport of boxing in the United States for the better part of two decades and was known as the 'boxing commissioner of the underworld'. Giacobbe 'Jake' LaMotta, aka 'The Raging Bull', said that Carbo told him to take a dive during his bout with Billy Fox so LaMotta could, in turn, get a shot at the middleweight title, which he won two years later. Carbo also controlled heavyweight champ Charles 'Sonny' Liston when Liston was knocked out by up-and-comer Cassius Clay (later Muhammad Ali) by the infamous 'phantom punch' that may not have touched Liston's face. Even Clay, who was not in on the fix, could not believe that Liston went down for the count and would not get up.

return home, he pulled into his driveway. As he put the gear shifter into park, Frankie Carbo, who had been loitering on the sidewalk across the street from his house, moved in for the kill. Before Greenie opened his car door, Carbo fired four shots into his head at point-blank range. Greenie slumped over the wheel as Carbo calmly climbed into Siegel's car and they pulled away with Tick-Tock in tow.

Although Lepke had offed another potential witness, it was not enough to stop his federal trial from proceeding; he was convicted in December of running an international opium ring and sentenced to fourteen years in prison, two more than the twelve he was trying to trim down when Moey Dimples first brought him the deal. Lepke sucked it up; all things considered, the sentence amounted to approximately one year per corpse for his most recent murder spree. As long as he ducked Dewey, he could look forward to being with his wife one day and enjoying the piles of cash he had stashed away. This hope lasted forty-eight hours, the time it took for Dewey to get the feds to hand him over to the state. Costello and Lucchese's double-cross was complete. Dewey charged Lepke with multiple counts of extortion related to his control of the clothing industry. On 24 January 1940, Lepke's next trial began in New York's General Sessions Court. By 2 March, he was found guilty by a jury who were all, no doubt, wearing clothes taxed by Lepke. Just over a month later, he was sentenced to thirty years to life, then returned to federal custody to begin serving his first sentence, after which he would serve his state time.

Lepke wished he had taken Albert Anastasia's advice and stayed on the lam. He was doomed but undoubtedly thinking of ways he could appeal his convictions or buy a pardon. Then things got even worse. During his last trial, a short newspaper article went largely unnoticed by the public, eclipsed by reports of Lepke's courtroom battle with Dewey and the more important war in Europe. It was about three young Brooklyn hoodlums, one of whom was Abe 'Kid Twist' Reles.

Chapter 24
A Twisted Kid

On 1 January 1940, Burton Turkus became the assistant district attorney in Brooklyn. Days after taking office, he received a letter from a convict in Rikers Island:

> Dear Sir,
> I am doing a bit here. I would like to talk to the District Attorney. I know something about a murder in East New York.
> Harry Rudolph

Before the end of the month, Turkus visited Rudolph to hear what he had to say. Rudolph told Turkus, 'Those rats killed my friend Red Alpert. I saw them do it.' The rats Rudolph was referring to were Abe 'Kid Twist' Reles and his gang (since they were not yet rats, Rudolph's statement proved prophetic).

Alex 'Red' Alpert was only nineteen years old when, on 25 November 1933, Kid Twist and his pals shot and killed him. Turkus asked Rudolph why it had taken him so many years to come forward. Rudolph replied that he had been telling the cops about the murder for six years, but no one cared. He made it clear that he was not looking for a reduction in his sentence; he only wanted to see justice served.

Turkus needed more evidence to win a conviction in court, so he rounded up the gang to see if anyone would break. On 2 February, an arrest warrant was issued for Kid Twist and his companions, charging them with homicide. Twenty-five-year-old Anthony 'Dukey' Maffetore immediately flipped and told Turkus to find Abraham 'Pretty' Levine who 'knows more than me'. At twenty-three years old, Pretty Levine had already committed a half-dozen hits for Murder, Inc. but he was a tougher nut to crack than Maffetore. Levine was hauled in and holding up fairly well until Turkus realized he was a newlywed, and had left the gang for his wife, Helen. Turkus wondered, if Helen could get Levine to leave his pals, could she also get him to turn on them? Turkus asked Helen to visit him at the DA's office. Helen arrived, carrying her sixteen-month-old daughter, Barbara. Turkus then sent for Levine who, weakened by the sight of his family, opened up about a murder but refused to implicate anyone besides himself. Turkus decided to play dirty. Since Levine's confession had tumbled out in Helen's presence, Turkus charged Helen as a material witness. He politely removed baby Babs from Helen's arms and had Helen locked up. This did the trick; Levine gushed like a geyser. With Rudolph, Maffetore and Levine in Turkus's starting line-up, Kid Twist weighed his own lousy odds at trial and asked to bat clean up. 'I can tell you about fifty guys that got hit,' Reles told Turkus before demanding total immunity for every one of his murders.

Turkus worried about the public perception of him cutting a deal with a psycho-killer but he ultimately agreed to the terms and Kid Twist confessed to eleven murders by his own hand, and said that he had participated in over a dozen more. His mouth flapped for twelve straight days as Turkus blew through a string of stenographers who filled up twenty-five notebooks in shorthand. Some of his victims were buried alive; others were burned alive. Some were strangled while others were tied in such a way that they strangled themselves. Kid Twist's memory was like a running surveillance tape that recorded every last detail of every murder; names, dates, places, nothing escaped his squarish-looking head. He even told Turkus where innocent witnesses were standing when a murder occurred, and described the witnesses so well that detectives were able to find them. He identified all the members of his crew, and convinced Turkus that Lepke was the 'brains' and referred to Albert Anastasia as 'our boss'.

Turkus's boss, District Attorney William O'Dwyer, was not as excited about all this information. The reason being, unlike the squeaky-clean Turkus, O'Dwyer played ball with Frank Costello who helped O'Dwyer get elected as Brooklyn's district attorney in 1940. When O'Dwyer told Costello about Kid Twist and his twisted revelations, Costello drove up to Clinton to tell Lucky Luciano. 'Reles is singin',' said Costello. 'O'Dwyer told me he's got no way to hold it back.' Luciano contemplated the potential damage. Whenever the mafia used Murder, Inc., they went directly to Albert Anastasia, and Anastasia spoke to the assassins through his trusted manager, Louis Capone. Luciano reasoned that if they could protect Anastasia from the fallout, they would preserve the buffer between themselves and the snitches.

Lepke, however, was up the creek since he had failed to create layers of insulation between himself and Murder, Inc. Lepke dealt directly with Kid Twist and Allie 'Tick-Tock' Tannenbaum, who Kid Twist implicated in a half-dozen murders. When Tick-Tock was told, 'We've got enough to put you in the chair', he flipped and climbed into the back seat of a car with William O'Dwyer, directing him to a burial ground in Loch Sheldrake, New York, where O'Dwyer's men dug up teeth, skulls and other skeletal and clothing remains from numerous victims. With Kid Twist and Tick-Tock talking, Lepke was finished. Ben Siegel, who had murdered Big Greenie as a favor to Lepke, also had problems since Tick-Tock had helped him with the hit.

'I don't give a crap about Lep,' Luciano told Costello. 'Whatever he gets, he's got comin'. But we've got to work somethin' out to get Bugsy and Albert out of this.'

Costello knew what he needed to do; he left the visiting room and sent word to William O'Dwyer to protect Siegel and Anastasia at all costs. O'Dwyer still had the power to bury the case against Anastasia but Siegel, being in Los Angeles, was outside his jurisdiction. When Tick-Tock squealed, the Los Angeles district attorney issued a warrant for Siegel's arrest. In August 1940, detectives showed up at Siegel's house where Siegel's well-trained butler said, 'He's not home.' The detectives walked straight past the butler and said, 'We'll just take a look.' They found Siegel hiding in the attic.

'What are you doing up there, Siegel?' asked the detective who poked his head through the trap door.

'I was going to the barbershop,' answered Siegel, giving the detectives a laugh before they took him into custody.

When press photographers descended on the station house, Siegel was more concerned with his appearance than he was with the murder charge; he borrowed a comb from a cop and quickly fixed his hair.

As Siegel sat in a jail cell, O'Dwyer figured out a way to help him – and appease Costello – by refusing to transport any of his snitches across the country on the pretext that along the way, they could get killed. With no witnesses on loan from New York, Los Angeles assistant district attorney Vernon Ferguson dismissed the murder indictment against Siegel on 11 December 1940. Anastasia and Siegel were in the clear, thanks to Luciano and Costello.

As for Lepke, Turkus decided to dine on a few appetizers before cooking the main course. He put Lepke's crew of assassins on trial first, winning convictions against Frank 'The Dasher' Abbandando, Harry 'Pittsburgh Phil' Strauss, Harry 'Happy' Maione and Martin 'Buggsy' Goldstein; they were all sentenced to die in the electric chair.

On 15 September 1941, Lepke, Mendy Weiss and Louis Capone went on trial for the murder of Joe Rosen, the family man who was forced to give up his trucking company, then killed in his candy store. Before trial, Turkus offered Lepke a deal; he would reduce the murder charge to manslaughter if Lepke agreed to cooperate. Lepke refused the offer and was convicted, along with his co-defendants, in December 1941. They appeared at sentencing, aware of the penalty that awaited them. 'To consign all three to the chair took just nine minutes,' said Turkus. If the condemned men had anything to smile about, it was that Kid Twist preceded them into hell.

To keep their informants safe while testifying, the district attorney's office converted the sixth floor of a Coney Island oceanfront hotel into the 'Rat Suite', a highly guarded isolation unit protected by eighteen police officers who worked three shifts, six cops to a shift. The snitches were housed there for over a year and becoming increasingly stir-crazy when, at 6:45 a.m. on 12 November 1941, the hotel's assistant manager, Al Litzberg, heard a loud thud but thought little of it. A short while later, Kid Twist was discovered on a lower roof, six stories beneath his room, sprawled out on his back, fully dressed with his shirt open. He had crashed down in a sitting position, breaking his spine (he had one, after all) and rupturing his liver and spleen, which caused internal bleeding. Some suspected suicide, while others thought it was an escape attempt gone awry. Luciano claimed that Captain Frank Bals, who was in charge of the security detail, was in Frank Costello's pocket, and Costello had directed Bals to have his officers throw Kid Twist out the window. William O'Dwyer openly admitted that the case against Anastasia 'went out the window with Reles'.

An investigation into Reles's death concluded that it was an accident that occurred while he was trying to escape. Five cops were disciplined for negligence, but any suspicion that they murdered Reles went nowhere. Interestingly, O'Dwyer defended the cops during the departmental inquiry and subsequently, after O'Dwyer was elected mayor of New York – with Costello's help which O'Dwyer admitted to receiving – he promoted Captain Frank Bals to deputy commissioner. It is important to note that Reles was the only snitch in the Rat

Wall Street Closing RACING EXTRA ★★★★★★

BROOKLYN EAGLE

Wall Street Closing RACING EXTRA ★★★★★★

LOCAL WEATHER FORECAST: Clear and warmer tonight and tomorrow

BROOKLYN, N. Y., WEDNESDAY, NOV. 12, 1941 — 3 CENTS

RELES DIES IN HOTEL PLUNGE AS ESCAPE ATTEMPT FAILS

FLEET CRUSHING FOE ON SEAS, KING SAYS

Wire Breaks as He Slides to Freedom --Fear Held Cause

Hitler Relies On Starvation War, Says Hess

Nationwide Strike Called on Railroads

Nine From Boro Are Elected To City Council

PRO-NEW DEALER WON'T SUPPORT 'STEPS TO WAR'

Bioff and Browne Fined $40,000; Former Gets 10 Years, Latter 8

3 Feared Dead In Powder Blast

Reles's death reported as an escape attempt.

Suite who was given his own room; if indeed he was murdered, what he imagined to be a privilege afforded him on account of his prosecutorial importance was actually a setup to isolate him for the kill.

On 7 December 1941, less than a month after Kid Twist died, over three hundred Japanese aircraft attacked the US naval base at Pearl Harbor in Hawaii, pulling Murder, Inc. off the headlines and presenting the mafia with new opportunities to cash in. The war led to shortages of consumer goods, creating a boon for mobsters who were already ensconced in the meat, fish, oil and gas industries, all worth a premium on the black, white and grey markets. In cities controlled by mobsters, the public benefitted from the mob's distribution of rationed goods, as much as they had once benefitted from their distribution of illegal alcohol during Prohibition. The waterfront, also run by the mob, became far busier than ever before, with more opportunities to steal cargo and extort any businesses connected to the transportation of goods. Mobsters also stole and counterfeited ration stamps, which the government issued for scarcities like sugar and canned goods.

The SS *Normandie* was a French ocean liner that was docked in New York in 1940 when France fell to the Nazis. President Roosevelt saw no reason to return the ship to the Vichy French government, which was equal to supplying Adolf Hitler who was dancing a jig in front of the Eiffel Tower (at least on British newsreels). The US converted the *Normandie* into a troop transport ship, renaming it the USS *Lafayette* after the French war hero who helped American colonists during the War of Independence. The ship was anchored to Pier 88 along the Hudson River when, on the afternoon of 9 February 1942, flames engulfed its upper decks. The ship had been built for speed, winning an award for crossing the Atlantic in just over four days; she burned fast, too. A cloud of billowing black smoke moved over Manhattan, drawing crowds of nosy New Yorkers to the pier as emergency fire crews worked to extinguish the flames by spraying water from docks and fire boats. They filled the ship with so much water that she slid over and listed to port, her funnels coming to rest just above the water's surface. Fifteen hundred sailors and civilians escaped the burning ship. One hundred twenty-eight people were injured. Miraculously, there was only one fatality, a 38-year-old Italian-American man from Brooklyn.

USS Lafayette *on its side.*

Rumors of sabotage began to circulate after journalists wrote that fires had broken out in three or four different places at once. The US Navy conducted an official investigation and concluded that the 'fire was started by sparks from a blowtorch of a worker in the grand salon'. Although the navy never wavered from this conclusion, which was further validated by the FBI and the New York district attorney's office, rumors persisted and a skeptical public leaned toward sabotage followed by a cover-up.

The navy's top brass knew, regardless of why the *Lafayette* burned, that there was a real danger of Nazi submarines threatening America's coastline. They also knew that the Port of New York was the hub for half the country's trade, and it was controlled by the mafia. Even before the *Lafayette* rolled over, navy secretary Frank Knox discussed the port's vulnerability with President Roosevelt while Naval Intelligence secretly explored the possibility of using the mafia to help protect the eastern seaboard. The burning of the *Lafayette* transformed these discussions into action but no one in Washington knew how to contact the mafia.

Naval Intelligence officers, tasked with opening a secret channel to the mob, wandered around the docks in a clumsy effort to find out who to approach. Meyer Lansky would later recall, 'Everybody in New York was laughing at the way those naive navy agents were going around the docks. They went up to men working in the area and talked out of the corner of their mouths like they had seen in the movies.' Finally, two naval officers, Lieutenant James O'Malley and Captain Roscoe McFall, visited Frank Hogan and Murray Gurfein of the New York district attorney's office. The officers asked the career prosecutors how to contact the mafia, and if mobsters could be trusted. 'A lot of these Italian racketeers are loyal Americans,' Hogan assured them. 'I understand a lot of them don't like Mussolini.' The prosecutors said they would reach out to several defense attorneys to find out who the best mobster was to approach. Moving forward, Gurfein dealt directly with Captain McFall's underling, Lieutenant Commander Charles Radcliffe Haffenden, who openly stated, 'I'll talk to anybody, a priest, a bank manager, a gangster, the devil himself . . . This is a war. American lives are at stake.'

The defense attorneys told Gurfein to speak with Joseph 'Joe Socks' Lanza. Born in Palermo, Sicily, in 1901, Lanza led the United Seafood Workers Union and ran the Fulton Fish Market, located along the East River in Lower Manhattan. Since fish can rot quickly and the industry is reliant on fast and efficient unloading and transportation from the docks to the doors of wholesalers, the mafia easily dominated the market at its entry point. Lanza had a long arrest record that included murder, a charge that was dismissed after Lucky Luciano convinced the witnesses to recant.

In March 1942, Lanza's attorney arranged a secret meeting between Lanza and Gurfein in Manhattan's Riverside Park. Under the cover of darkness, Gurfein and Lanza sat on a park bench only steps away from Ulysses S. Grant's Tomb, modeled after the mausoleum of Halicarnassus, which was built for a Persian satrap and known as one of the Seven Wonders of the Ancient World; in Manhattan, it's where dogs piss at night. Gurfein brought Lanza up to date. Lanza agreed to help and was asked to follow up their meeting with a visit to the Astor Hotel in Midtown Manhattan where the navy rented three suites. Lanza went there that week and was introduced to a meticulously uniformed Lt Comdr Haffenden, who at first had some trouble comprehending Lanza's *New Yawk tawk* that got speedier with *cawfee*. Lanza assured Haffenden that he had come to the right man. Besides controlling a long swathe of waterfront, Lanza could tap a vast nautical network of ship captains who could report anything suspicious at sea. Haffenden gave Lanza a security badge so he could access his converted naval headquarters at the Astor, and they agreed to meet at least once a week.

Lanza quickly got to work but encountered one nagging problem: he was currently fighting a racketeering indictment, and his meetings with federal agents would look suspicious to his fellow mobsters. Anyone who held a past grudge, or was envious of Lanza's control over the fish market, need only beef that Lanza was in league with the government and he could be pulled up in a fishing net with a lobster tail sticking out of his ass. To avoid this dreaded scenario, Lanza told Haffenden that he needed to run everything by his imprisoned boss, Lucky Luciano, and the man to see was Meyer Lansky, who spoke with Luciano's tongue.

Haffenden returned to Gurfein who called Lansky's attorney, Moses Polakoff, and asked him to arrange a meeting with Lansky. In April, Polakoff, Gurfein and Lansky met at Longchamps restaurant on West 57th Street in Manhattan. After Gurfein briefed Lansky, he asked if he thought Luciano would help his country. Without hesitation, Lansky replied that he would.

'Can we trust him?' asked Gurfein, who had once worked with Dewey to paint Luciano as a lying, snitching, dope-dealing pimp.

'Sure you can,' Lansky shot back. 'I'll guarantee it. His family is all here, right in New York. They're proud to be Americans.'

Lansky asked Gurfein to transfer Luciano closer to the city so Lansky could visit him more frequently and speed up their line of communication. Gurfein agreed, as did Haffenden, who shot off a letter to the New York State commissioner of corrections, John Lyons, requesting that Luciano be transferred to Sing Sing, and informing him that the letter, once read, needed to be destroyed.

The letter was hand-delivered to Lyons by two naval messengers. When Lyons was done reading it, the messengers snatched it back and burned it in his office. (But since none of the men involved burned their tongues, you are now reading about this.) Lyons approved the transfer, saying, 'If it only saved the life of a single American soldier or a single American ship' he was happy to help. Lyons then pointed out to Haffenden that Sing Sing doubled as a hub for inmate traffic that made its way up and down the state; if the navy considered this mission secret enough to smoke up his office, he recommended that

Luciano be transferred to the less trafficked Great Meadow Prison in Comstock, New York. The navy deferred to Lyons's advice and Luciano was shackled and moved from Clinton to Comstock, having no idea why.

On 15 May, Lyons penned the following letter to Great Meadow's warden, Vernon Morhous:

> Dear Warden,
>
> This is to advise you that I have granted permission to Mr. Meyer Lansky to visit and interview Inmate Charles Luciano in your institution when accompanied by Mr. Polakoff, the inmate's attorney . . . You are authorized to waive the usual fingerprint requirements and to grant Mr. Lansky and Mr. Polakoff the opportunity of interviewing the inmate privately.

No sooner had Luciano arrived in Great Meadow than he was led into a private room and told to wait. A short while later, Lansky and Polakoff walked in and greeted him. Lansky said that Luciano 'threw his arms around me and kissed me'. Luciano then sank his teeth into a cold pastrami sandwich that Lansky had brought with him, along with a kosher spread that reminded Luciano of Dave Miller's delicatessen, where they used to eat while whispering their latest conspiracies across the table. Lansky clued in Luciano, adding that his assistance might one day help him get out of jail. Luciano could see the potential upside but was worried that if the Allies lost the war and he was deported back to Italy, Mussolini would execute him for treason. 'There's no point in getting out of jail,' said Luciano, 'if I'm going to end up with a bullet in my head.' After voicing this concern, Luciano mustered his failing courage and told Lansky to return to Great Meadow with Joe Socks Lanza so they could get started.

Lansky returned to the city, where he told Lt Comdr Haffenden, 'There'll be no German submarines in the port of New York . . . I can give you a cast iron guarantee on this, a guarantee backed by Charles Luciano.'

Two weeks after Lansky and Polakoff's first meeting with Luciano at Great Meadow, they returned with Lanza. After hugs and kisses, Luciano gave Lanza the go-ahead to use his name and let everyone know that his work with the government was sanctioned by Luciano. Lanza returned to the waterfront where he introduced undercover naval operatives to dock hands, sailors, fishing boat and cargo ship captains, as well as truck drivers. Thanks to the mob, the navy had a living, roving lighthouse along the coastline. The Port of New York, with hundreds of miles of shoreline, was secure, with troops, food, tanks, airplanes and ammunition leaving for Europe every day of the week.

Lucky Luciano and Meyer Lansky later claimed to have burned the USS *Lafayette*, which resulted in the mafia's alliance with the navy. Are we to believe them? When the great Temple of Apollo at Delphi was destroyed by fire, the Alcmaeonidae family, wishing to return to Athens from their bitter exile, won the contract to rebuild the temple and made it beautiful enough to warrant Athenian forgiveness. Does this mean the Alcmaeonidae family started the fire? The Roman general and statesman Marcus Licinius Crassus started Rome's first fire brigade. Whenever a house caught fire, Crassus raced to the scene, hoping to scoop up the burning real estate at a discount price. Some say his firemen were told to wait until Crassus closed the deal on the street, before putting out the fire. Does this mean that Crassus started the fires? The same mysterious cloud rests above the *Lafayette*.

Because the mafia capitalized on the disaster so well, we are left to wonder if they caused it. In this author's opinion, it is difficult to accept the fire as part of a master plan since no one could have guessed how it would have turned out. Burning the ship could have easily backfired; instead of turning to the mafia for help, the navy could have dispatched a marine battalion to secure the docks and drive the mafia out at bayonet point. For dramatic effect, they could have hanged a few waterfront bosses for treason, beginning with Socks Lanza. Thus, the burning of the ship may have been accidental, as the navy concluded. Thus far, we have seen how reactive the mafia is, whether responding to Prohibition or its repeal, the stock market crash and the Great Depression that followed, or a world war and the government's appeal for assistance. The mafia does not typically create the current but swims with it. For an idea of how well they swim, think of a great white shark in a pinstripe suit.

Chapter 25

Braciole and Brisket Cooked Well-Done

After the fruitless trip to Cocos Island, Ben Siegel and Countess di Frasso were walking around California with 'Sucker' painted on their backs when a group of scientists spotted the duo and lured them into the Imperial Valley desert to show off their new version of dynamite, called Atomite. The world war created a profitable weapons industry as governments sought new ways to vaporize people, and the scientists needed money to produce Atomite in bulk. To impress Siegel and di Frasso, the scientists blew off the side of a mountain. As cactus needles and dead rattlesnakes rained down around Siegel, he uncapped his ears and said, 'Oh, brother, if I'd only had some of this stuff in the old days.' Luckily for the people of Manhattan, he did not. Di Frasso was just as excited; true to form, she cut a check for $50,000 and was part owner of Atomite. She then called her husband, the count, in Rome, who in turn contacted Benito Mussolini, telling him about his wife's latest venture. Mussolini, who had stabbed schoolmates as a boy and was known to rape women as an adult, was enamored of any weapon bigger than a pocketknife or a pecker. Desperate for a weapon that might offer his unprepared nation an edge in Europe, Il Duce excitedly paid for di Frasso and her scientists to visit Italy and perform a demonstration. With Mussolini's interest piqued and the Italian treasury at his disposal, Ben could smell the Benjamins; he glued himself to di Frasso's side as they boarded a ship for Italy.

After Mussolini had seized power, he appointed his 'Iron Prefect', Cesare Mori, to purge Sicily of mafiosos whom Mussolini considered a threat to his own dictatorship. Since Mori locked up thousands of mobsters and Siegel was a well-known American gangster, di Frasso did not think it was a good idea for him to travel under his real name. Siegel chose a different first name and boarded the ship with di Frasso as the distinguished gentleman Bart Siegel.

On the outskirts of Rome, di Frasso took Siegel to her husband's ancestral estate, Villa Madama, where she played the role of Mistress

Puttana. After some frolicking in the villa, a demonstration was arranged so the heads of Italy's war department could see the same experiment di Frasso had witnessed in the American desert. Once the scientists were all set up and ready to go, they pushed the detonator. Di Frasso and Siegel braced themselves for the blast but, besides a puff of smoke, nothing happened. The only thing that blew up was Mussolini, who had paid their travel expenses to witness a fart while standing between a wealthy old tart and an imposter named Bart. Mussolini demanded his money back from di Frasso, and took over Villa Madama. While Siegel and the countess were being booted from a castle in central Italy, Vito Genovese was renovating a castle in southern Italy.

As you will recall, Vito Genovese had fled the States to avoid a murder arrest in 1937. Upon his arrival in Italy, he invested in factories, power plants and a real-estate portfolio that included a castle in Campania. On the eve of war, he obtained a letter of introduction to Fascist Party secretary Achille Starace and contributed $250,000 to help construct a party headquarters in Naples. This put Genovese in good graces with Mussolini, who awarded him the title Commendatore de Re, the equivalent of a general. Through Achille Starace, Genovese met Mussolini's son-in-law, who was also Italy's foreign minister, Count Galeazzo Ciano. It is widely believed that Genovese supplied Ciano with cocaine, which would have perked him up for those long, grueling world-domination meetings he had to attend with his Nazi counterparts. When Italy entered the war in June 1940, Genovese opened a heroin pipeline between Istanbul and Italy, via North Africa. To operate unmolested, he had to stay in favor with the Fascists, which he did through bribery and at least one murder.

Carlo Tresca was a former Italian socialist who was living in the United States where he became a 'full-fledged agitator-editor' of the newspaper *Il Martello* (The Hammer), which was highly critical of Mussolini. Whether Mussolini asked Genovese to have Tresca whacked, or Genovese took it upon himself to order a hit so as to ingratiate himself with Il Duce, is unknown. What we do know is that Genovese sent word to Anthony 'Tony Bender' Strollo in New York, telling him to drop the hammer on *The Hammer*'s editor. In January 1943, Tresca had lunch in Manhattan with author John Dos Passos then returned to his office on 5th Avenue to get some work done. Just after 8:30 p.m., Tresca, who was in his sixties and still going strong, left his office and was walking along a dark sidewalk, dressed like a spy in an old movie with black cloak and hat, when a car screeched to the curb. Carmine 'Lilo' Galante – who was sent by Tony Bender – hopped out and fired at Tresca, killing him with a bullet that entered under his right eye and settled in his brain. Galante tossed his burner to the ground and sped off in a getaway car driven by Joseph 'Joe Beck' Di Palermo.

We already know what this murder meant to Mussolini but no one has ever assessed the implications of this hit within the New York underworld. When Genovese ordered the hit on Tresca, he neglected to clear it with the borgata's official boss, Lucky Luciano, or acting boss, Frank Costello; this failure to follow the chain of command was punishable by death. Knowing the murder of Tresca would attract international headlines that would lead to police pressure on the mob, Costello would never have sanctioned the hit. The fact that Genovese and Tony Bender went through with it, without permission, and Costello failed to punish or even address their insubordination, showed Costello off as a toothless boss. And, sure enough, the resultant publicity bit Costello on the ass.

When underworld tipsters told New York City detectives that Genovese had ordered Tresca's murder to brown-nose Mussolini, District Attorney Frank Hogan figured, since Costello was Genovese's boss (at least in name), he had probable cause to tap the telephone inside Costello's seven-room penthouse apartment on Central Park West. Since Costello had no foreknowledge of Tresca's hit, the tap produced nothing in the way of solving Tresca's murder, but it did produce fruit of a juicier vine by exposing the depth of Costello's political power in New York.

On 24 August 1943, Costello received a telephone call from Magistrate Thomas Aurelio, who had just been nominated as a New York State Supreme Court justice. Aurelio said, 'Good morning, Francesco. How are you, and thanks for everything.'

'Congratulations,' said Costello. 'It went over perfect. When I tell you something is in the bag, you can rest assured.'

After a brief conversation, the call ended with Aurelio saying, 'I want to assure you of my loyalty for all you have done. It's undying.'

'I know,' replied Costello. 'I'll see you soon.'

Frank Hogan read a transcript of the telephone call, amazed that one of the biggest mob bosses in the nation was appointing judges. Unbeknownst to Hogan, Costello was also appointing prosecutors. Roy Cohn, the renowned Washington, DC, attorney, lobbyist and counselor to US presidents, would later confess that he got Irving Saypol his job as US attorney for the Southern District of New York where Saypol prosecuted infamous figures such as Alger Hiss and Julius and Ethel Rosenberg. 'I got Irving Saypol his job,' Cohn would later confess in an autumn-of-life memoir. 'Yes. Not alone . . . Not without the OK from Frank Costello.' Saypol would eventually become a judge, presumably with Costello's help.

The leaders of Tammany Hall were just as reliant on Costello. In fact, at the very same time General Douglas MacArthur was island-hopping across the Asiatic-Pacific, Costello was engaged in a district-hopping campaign to consolidate his grip over New York. The head of Tammany Hall was elected by sixteen district leaders. Whoever controlled the most district leaders elected the boss and ran the Hall, which meant appointing judges and having a large say in mayoral elections. Costello methodically seized control of ten Tammany districts, and was responsible for Michael Kennedy becoming boss of the Hall.

As Hogan tried to discern the strength of Costello's grasp over New York, he requested an audience with Kennedy, having no idea Kennedy was put in place by Costello. When Hogan asked Kennedy if he could enlighten him as to anything he may have heard about Costello around the Hall, Kennedy replied that he had no clue what Hogan was even talking about. Hogan interviewed other men from the Hall and received similar responses. After the probe went nowhere, a frustrated Hogan released the transcribed conversation between Costello and Aurelio to the press. On 29 August 1943, the *New York Times* wrote: 'GANGSTER BACKED AURELIO FOR BENCH'. Aurelio, who was otherwise squeaky clean, denied any wrongdoing. He survived the smear, got the appointment anyway, and sat on the bench for fourteen years before moving up to the appellate court.

Costello did not fare as well. Acting on sketchy information from informants, the *New York Times* connected Costello to drug trafficking. To be sure, Costello did not mind being associated with graft and gambling but drugs could cost him his powerful political allies wherein his real power lay, as did his survival on the street. Costello was a huge earner but a weak boss, as seen by the Tresca hit which went down without his permission. But no one would dare kill a boss who controlled Tammany Hall along with so many judges and prosecutors, all of whom Costello freely shared with other borgatas, keeping him extremely valuable to the Commission. Costello knew that if he ever lost that power, he was a dead man. Feeling desperate after being accused of drug dealing, Costello did the unthinkable for a mob boss – he called a press conference to clear his name. Costello met with reporters inside the office of his attorney, George Wolf. 'I detest the narcotic racket and anyone connected with it. To my mind there is no one lower than a person dealing in it,' Costello declared. 'It is low and filthy – trading on human misery. Anyone who knows me knows my opinion of narcotics and the low opinion I have of the people dealing in it or with it.'

Although Costello did not personally traffic in drugs, the statement was disingenuous. Did Costello really have a low opinion of Luciano, who was pinched for dope twice and appointed Costello acting boss? How about Genovese, a well-known drug trafficker who was, at that very moment, running a heroin triangle between North Africa, Western Europe and North America? Plenty of soldiers in Costello's borgata were dealing drugs right under his nose, and he insulted every one of them in his lame attempt to polish up his dirty image and hold onto his political allies. Costello had apparently forgotten that the true basis of his political power was grounded in the very men he had insulted; did he really believe that men like Michael Kennedy and Thomas Aurelio were enamored by his irresistible charm? It was the army of killers Costello could call on that made his offers irrefusable. Genovese took note of Costello's ill-considered press conference, while Luciano tried to use the Tresca hit as an opportunity to get out of jail.

On 1 January 1943, less than two weeks before Tresca was gunned down, Thomas Dewey was sworn in as the forty-seventh governor of New York. Luciano sent word to Governor Dewey that he would give up Tresca's assassin in return for a pardon or parole. Dewey turned down Luciano's offer. Tresca was a big fish, but as a radical socialist in a capitalist society he was also a stinky fish who had been arrested thirty-six times and, according to the *New York Times*, would 'boast that the bomb squad always called on him after an explosion'. For a governor with an eye on the White House, there was negative political value in tracking down Tresca's killer.

Like Lucky Luciano, Lepke Buchalter also took note of Thomas Dewey's new pardon power as he awaited execution on Sing Sing's death row.

Burton Turkus racked up a string of convictions that deterred the mob from ever again incorporating the business of murder. On 12 June 1941, Harry 'Pittsburgh Phil' Strauss and Martin 'Buggsy' Goldstein were moved into pre-execution cells. For lunch, they ate steak and potatoes; for their last dinner, roast chicken, French fries, salad and pie. Between meals, a terrified Goldstein broke under the weight of suspense; he threw a fit in his cell, shouting that he wanted to die immediately. By 11 p.m., the 36-year-old got his wish when he was strapped in for the ride to hell. Thirty-one-year-old Strauss swaggered in next, gazed at his audience of witnesses 'in the manner of an actor looking over a full house', then sat down and was zapped with no last words. During the executions of Goldstein and Strauss, Harry 'Happy' Maione and Frank 'The Dasher' Abbandando were housed about a hundred feet away. They moaned as the volts ran through their friends' bodies and flickered the lights throughout the prison. Their own numbers were up on 19 February 1942. Abbandando ate lamb chops and Maione had spaghetti and meatballs before both men were cooked in their own sauce.

Lepke Buchalter, Mendy Weiss and Louis Capone were up next, but Lepke's execution was more complicated than the rest. In order to execute Lepke for the murder of Joe Rosen, the state had to wrest him away from the feds, where he was returned after his state trial. The New York district attorney's office appealed to US attorney general Francis Biddle, who did not want to hand Lepke over. At the time, Governor Dewey, who had become the new face of the Republican Party, was running against incumbent Franklin Roosevelt in the upcoming presidential election. When Dewey learned of the custody battle over Lepke, he wondered aloud why Biddle, who was Roosevelt's hand-picked attorney general, was keeping Lepke's finger out of the socket. The answer was fairly obvious. Roosevelt had run as a friend of labor, and had the endorsement of Sidney Hillman, who the pre-eminent biographer of Roosevelt, James MacGregor Burns, described as 'an old friend and supporter of the president'. Hillman raised millions of dollars for Roosevelt's victorious presidential runs in 1936 and 1940, while also registering voters and getting them to the polls on time. Hillman, moreover, persuaded communists and socialists – entrenched in America's early labor movement – to stand behind Roosevelt. In return for Hillman's invaluable assistance, Roosevelt appointed him to the advisory committee to the Council of National Defense in 1940, and his War Production Board in 1942. Hillman was in charge of 'manpower supply, strike prevention and mediation', the latter two assignments being almost certainly dependent on Hillman's underworld contacts, including, first and foremost, Lepke Buchalter.

To unseat the popular Roosevelt in 1944, Dewey needed a miracle and wondered if Lepke's illicit relationship with Hillman could sully Roosevelt's reputation and allow Dewey to win the election. If Dewey could drag Lepke within sight of the electric chair, maybe Lepke would open up about Hillman in return for a reprieve. After a few subtle threats, Dewey demanded that Lepke be handed over to the state, forthwith. Biddle knew exactly what Dewey was up to and refused. Dewey's reaction to Biddle's refusal was to call on the press, as he had done when he wanted Arkansas to cough up Luciano. Republican-leaning newspapers argued that Roosevelt was 'saving Lepke' in order to protect Sidney Hillman. Americans were left to wonder why; was Roosevelt's administration somehow linked to Murder, Incorporated? If enough voters considered this to be a possibility, Dewey would have the miracle he needed.

Biddle folded under the relentless media pressure and told Dewey that he was prepared to hand Lepke over to the state, but only if Dewey was 'ready to carry out the death sentence'. In other words, promise me you will kill Lepke immediately and I'll let you have him. Dewey, never one for demands, kept up the heat in the press until Roosevelt concluded that the public's imagination was more harmful than whatever Lepke might say, which his campaign manager could quash or spin. 'Turn the son of a bitch over to New York!' Roosevelt said, heatedly.

Lepke was transferred from federal custody to Sing Sing in a bullet-proof car. Knowing exactly what Governor Dewey was after, Lepke tossed some chum into the water. 'If I would talk, a lot of big people would get hurt,' he said. 'When I say big, I mean big. The names would surprise you.' Dewey could not take the suspense and dispatched Frank Hogan and Sol Gelb, who raced to Sing Sing hoping to hear a song song. After Lepke had a conversation with Hogan and Gelb, Dewey ordered a forty-eight-hour stay of execution, enough time to digest the dirt and weigh how it might affect his presidential campaign. By morning, newspapers began to speculate about what Lepke had divulged. The *New York Daily Mirror* wrote: 'Lepke offered material to the Governor that would make him an unbeatable Presidential candidate.' The *New York Sun* reported: 'Lepke sought to escape the chair by involving a number of prominent persons in his long career of crime.' And the *New York Daily News* wrote that Lepke gave up information 'packed with political TNT'.

After holding the TNT for two days, Dewey decided to pass and denied Lepke a further stay of execution. Why had Dewey declined Lepke's most generous campaign contribution? It is of this author's opinion that Dewey realized the American electorate would not tolerate someone cozying up with murderous hoodlums as a means to higher office. As a prosecutor, making deals with killers to catch bigger fish was part of Dewey's job description, but as a governor, cutting a deal with a prolific killer to knock out a popular president was far too risky. Dewey was known to use any available means to destroy a gangster, but proved more cautious when it came to his own breed of gangsters. The sly Roosevelt, who once outfoxed Luciano and Costello at the 1932 Democratic National Convention, would have somehow turned it against Dewey. In the end, by tossing Lepke into Dewey's lap, Roosevelt had effectively brought the curtain down on Dewey's media circus.

The question remains: what did Lepke tell Hogan and Gelb? There is no official record of the conversation and both men denied that Lepke had given them any meat to chew on. Hogan said that Lepke 'knew what he was doing every minute, even though he was two days away from the electric chair . . . He knew just how far to go – and we knew pretty fast that we weren't going to get anywhere with him.' Gelb echoed Hogan when he said, 'I got the impression that we were talking to a man who was utterly desperate and frantically trying to save himself but at the same time would only tell us things we already knew.' Curiously, neither man offered a peep as to what this font of useless information entailed. Based on leaks, the most likely story is that Lepke told Hogan he had been paid $75,000 by Sidney Hillman to whack a clothing contractor who stood in Hillman's way. At the time of the murder, which Lepke ordered, Hillman had been picked up for questioning but quickly released. The rest of the details remain mysterious and the meal Lepke was offering to serve Dewey would be cooked, well-done, inside Lepke's brain.

Lepke's appeals went as high as the Supreme Court, which upheld his conviction. Roosevelt wanted him dead, Dewey now viewed him as worthless, and the mafia had already divvied up his clothing empire. On 4 March 1944, Lepke, Mendy Weiss and Louis Capone had their heads shaved to receive the electric cap. Their flesh would heat up to 200 degrees Fahrenheit, a temperature that melts eyeballs.

With only hours left to live, the men entered a pre-execution cell and were told to order the infamous last meal. Just after 11 p.m., Albert Anastasia's murder manager, the 47-year-old Louis Capone, was electrocuted without saying any last words. Three minutes later, his smoking corpse was rolled out of the room before 37-year-old Mendy Weiss 'strode rapidly into the chamber' where the smell of Capone's burned flesh was still lingering in the air. After being strapped into the chair, Weiss said he was framed then told the warden, 'Give my love to my family and everything.' The warden nodded – to the executioner, who pulled the switch.

Lepke walked in last. Whether taking over a union or dying, it was his nature to get on with it. 'His step was brisk, almost defiant,' said Burton Turkus. 'He walked across the chamber and almost threw himself into the squat seat.' Rabbi Jacob Katz recited a Jewish prayer as the 47-year-old Lepke was fastened into the chair with eight restraining belts. An electrode was stuck to his shaved leg. He rolled his eyes up to see the death cap as it was lowered into position. After the executioner got the signal from the warden, 2,200 volts surged through the flesh of Louis 'Lepke' Buchalter who jolted, straining the straps, before his body went limp.

Few examples of the Italian mafia's high-voltage relationship with Jews are more illustrative than Louis Capone's braciole ass being cooked on the same grill as Lepke's brisket ass. Burton Turkus was finally done frying mobsters, stopping just shy of Sing Sing's warden mailing him the electric bill. The same switch that transferred the current through Lepke's body had permanently transferred the bulk of the American mafia's all-time biggest racket – the garment industry – into the hands of Lucky Luciano, via Frank Costello and Tommy Lucchese. (Albert Anastasia picked off a healthy chunk, too, though he was not happy to see Lepke go.) Labor leader David Dubinsky, an associate of Sidney Hillman, would later say that Lepke's crimes were 'petty larceny' compared to the Italian leadership that took up his mantle.

Chapter 26
The War Effort

Fairly certain that an Allied victory would result in his own freedom given the contribution he was making to the war effort, Lucky Luciano hung a world map on the wall of his cell and followed every major battle. He liked the flamboyant General George Patton and became frustrated whenever the Supreme Allied Commander Europe, General Dwight Eisenhower, reined Patton in on account of negative press in the States. The correlation to Luciano's own circumstances may have escaped him; when Luciano ran his borgata like an Eisenhower – quiet, determined, diplomatic, cautious but bold – he achieved startling success. When Luciano attracted too much bad publicity, his downfall was inevitable, as was Patton's.

One day, on a prison visit, Luciano asked Tommy Lucchese and Joe Adonis to send word to Vito Genovese in Italy to whack Adolf Hitler. Lucchese and Adonis, who were not cooped up in a prison cell where men are given to delusions, talked him out of it. Colonel Claus von Stauffenberg, who had official access to Hitler's headquarters on the Eastern Front, the Wolf's Lair, could not kill Hitler with a bomb; how would Genovese take him out with a peashooter? And even if Genovese could have pulled it off, it is unlikely he would have. Genovese needed an Axis victory as much as Luciano needed an Allied victory; if the Allies won, they would drag Genovese home to face a murder rap.

As Luciano dreams up more ridiculous missions while pacing in his cell, let us briefly recap the Allied war effort, since Luciano's ultimate fate hinged upon it. In the autumn of 1942, British general Bernard Law Montgomery went *Fox* hunting in North Africa. After putting the Desert Fox, Erwin Rommel, to the chase, Allied leaders met in the French-Moroccan city of Casablanca in January 1943, where they reaffirmed their plan to attack the 'soft underbelly' of Europe by striking at Sicily.

When Lieutenant Commander Haffenden was informed that Sicily would act as a springboard onto the continent, he tapped his mafia contacts, knowing the Sicilian and American mafias maintained a long-distance relationship. Haffenden asked the American mobsters to have their Sicilian cousins assist with the Allied invasion, once it was underway. He also asked them to provide first-hand intelligence about the island's terrain; what were the coastlines like? Which beaches had harder sand that could support heavy equipment? How deep were the ports? How steep were the hillsides?

With the mafia's help, Sicilian immigrants were marched in and out of Haffenden's office, telling him anything they could remember about the lie of the land while providing old maps, postcards and photographs they had of Sicily. When Luciano heard about the upcoming invasion, he suffered his latest delusion, telling Meyer Lansky he wanted to parachute onto the island with the invasion force as a 'kind of liaison or scout'. Lansky laughed at the idea but relayed it to Haffenden, who exhibited a touch of his own nuttiness when he raised Luciano's proposal with his superiors in Washington. They rejected the idea out of hand and questioned Haffenden's judgment.

On 10 July 1943, Allied forces launched a massive airborne and amphibious assault on Sicily. German Feldmarschall Albert Kesselring called the Italian defense of the coast an 'utter failure'. What did Kesselring expect? Sicilians only fought for their families, and since they did not particularly care for Germans using their beautiful island as an air base, they barely resisted the invasion, if at all. An Allied soldier wrote, 'The Italian soldiers came down from the hills, not like members of a defeated army but in a mood of fiesta . . . filling the air with laughter and song.' One Italian division surrendered before it was even attacked. Another fired a few shots for show, then took off for France where they could drink wine and pick up Parisian women who were tired of overly serious Germans.

Once the Allies secured a foothold on the island, mafiosos who had been locked up or sent into hiding by Cesare Mori came out to greet the 160,000 soldiers who were put ashore. Well aware that Sicilian dons held local power, commanded respect and hated Fascists and Nazis alike, the Allied Military Government of Occupied Territories recruited them to help restore order in the wake of chaos; one mafia don became a mayor and an honorary colonel of the US Army.

Luciano must have been thrilled to hear that General Patton was commanding one flank of the invasion force with General Montgomery (soon to be promoted to field marshal) in charge of the other. Despite crucial mistakes, the island was secured and, by 25 July, Benito was *finito*. The king of Italy replaced Mussolini with General Pietro Badoglio, who threw Eisenhower the keys to the Italian peninsula; Allied forces need only evict the Germans. In August, Turin, Genoa and Milan were pummeled by Allied bombing, realizing Winston Churchill's vow, after Mussolini had entered the war, to expand the ruins of Italy. By September, Monty crossed the Strait of Messina, landing in Calabria, Frank Costello's birthplace, where an armistice was signed, officially knocking Italy out of the war.*

As Allied forces entered Naples in October, they found the city as poor and starving as they had found Sicily and Calabria. Food and resources were scarce, exacerbated by shoddy occupational planning on the part of the Allies. As a result, a black market sprang up. British Army officer and diarist Norman Lewis spoke of 'Neapolitan kleptomania', writing that everything was stolen, from 'telegraph poles' to 'penicillin'. It is estimated that half the ships entering the Port of Naples were robbed of their cargo. Even the papal legate was caught driving around on stolen tires. The narrow streets of Naples were turned into a winding bazaar where everything was sold, from German machine guns to light tanks. 'IF YOU DON'T SEE THE OVERSEAS ARTICLE YOU'RE LOOKING FOR,' one sign read, 'JUST ASK US AND WE'LL GET IT.' American intelligence officers needed to fill the vacuum caused by the evacuation of German forces and the sudden collapse of Fascist leadership. Spotting the need for interpreters, Vito Genovese tore off his Italian stripes and offered the US military his services as a bilingual expert. We cannot help but marvel at Genovese's adaptability. In no time at all, he went from a democratic American capitalist to an Italian Fascist, and back to an American; not since the Athenian statesman and con artist Alcibiades has anyone switched allegiances between nations so seamlessly.

---

* Shortly after the war, Sicily was granted a large degree of autonomy in order to head off a growing separatist movement that was supported by the mafia. A legislative assembly with nearly complete administrative power was established in, of all places, Palermo, handing the mafia manipulative power over a cabinet of ministers who made decisions crucial to every area of industry on the island. We are left to wonder if the city was chosen by a bunch of bumbling idiots in Rome who lacked foresight, or, to the contrary, pragmatists who were willing to mollify the only power in Sicily capable of stamping out radical movements.

The US Army appointed Colonel Charles Poletti as military governor of Italy. Back in the States, Poletti was a lawyer and politician. In late 1942, New York governor Herbert Lehman resigned, leaving Lieutenant Governor Poletti in charge for the final month of his term. In that short time, Governor Poletti, who was in Frank Costello's pocket, pardoned fifteen individuals, at least six of whom were mob-connected. His appointment in Italy was a stroke of luck for Genovese, who was given an American military uniform and appointed chief interpreter for Captain Charles Dunn. Genovese became Dunn's eyes and ears, telling him everything that was happening on the streets of Naples, even uncovering black-market gangs and extortion rings. Dunn either was unaware that Genovese was masterminding his own criminal enterprise and using the army to remove his competition, or he knew it but did not care. (Dunn might have been tipped off when Genovese, who worked around the clock, waived any pay for his services and refused reimbursement for even basic expenses.)

Using his vast underground network, Genovese provided bare essentials for Italians and rare luxuries for American officers; he gave Colonel Poletti a 1938 Packard sedan to get around in, while other officers got steak, wine, whisky, cigarettes and, according to some accounts, women. Bribed military officers helped Genovese corner the market on flour, sugar and ration stamps, which were equal to currency. Genovese acquired the stamps in bulk then allotted bundles to his crew members who peddled them on the streets. With everyone looking the other way, Genovese saw no reason to halt his drug-trafficking operation, which only needed a bit of rerouting on account of the revised military landscape.

In hindsight, some may fault the American officers for allowing Genovese's rackets to continue unhampered, but the entire Italian economy was driven by a black market and only a narrow-minded imbecile would endeavor to dismantle it and cast a conquered and starving people into an even worse state of suffering and despair. Enter 24-year-old former Pennsylvania College campus cop, Sergeant Orange Dickey. As with all odd names, Orange Dickey is one that must have made it hard to get through grammar school; it sounds like a mild sexually transmitted disease or a light rash from a tight jock strap. Answering the call of patriotism, Dickey joined the army's Criminal Investigation Division. During the Allied occupation, he was interrogating two Canadian soldiers who were caught driving trucks filled with swag. The soldiers told Dickey that they worked for Vito Genovese, whose reach went straight up to the Allied military commanders in Italy. With his interest piqued, Dickey snooped around Genovese's apartment in Naples, where he saw expensive furniture, a king's wardrobe, high-tech radio equipment that could transmit a signal for thousands of miles, and extremely hard-to-obtain travel permits that gave Genovese authority to roam around occupied Italy with the freedom of a four-star general. There were also letters from high-ranking military officers praising the one-time hitman with adjectives such as 'invaluable [and] absolutely honest' and 'trustworthy, loyal and dependable'.

This was all too much for Dickey, who got hold of an old photograph of Genovese in which he was identified as a notorious American gangster. When Dickey showed the photo to Genovese, figuring it would rattle him, Genovese replied, 'Yeah, that's me. So what?' Dickey went straight to Captain Dunn, who told him to back off and find someone else to investigate. Dunn's reply convinced Dickey he was on to something big. He ignored Dunn and traveled to Rome, where he requested a meeting with Colonel Charles Poletti, who brushed Dickey off. The former campus cop kept banging on mahogany doors with brass knockers but to no avail. Frustrated, he cabled FBI headquarters in Washington, asking if they had any interest in Vito Genovese. Dickey received a reply that Genovese had an outstanding arrest warrant for murder, and that he should be taken into custody and returned to the States to face trial.

On 27 August 1944, Sergeant Dickey tailed Genovese, who rode around in a chauffeured Fiat. Dickey finally made the arrest as Genovese was dropped off at a local mayor's office. Genovese surrendered two automatic pistols then offered Dickey $250,000 cash to let him go. 'Take the money,' Genovese told the sergeant, who earned $200 a month. 'You are set for the rest of your life. Nobody cares what you do. Why should you?' When Dickey refused, Genovese told him he was young and stupid and would one day regret having passed up this generous offer. Next, Genovese threatened to kill Dickey; when that did not work, he threatened to kill Dickey's entire family.

After realizing Dickey was not budging, Genovese directed his energies toward the murder case back home. Although a number of years had passed, the prosecution still had Ernie 'The Hawk' Rupolo as its chief witness, and Peter LaTempa was prepared to corroborate

Rupolo's testimony. LaTempa was being held in protective custody at the Raymond Street Jail in Brooklyn. On 15 January 1945, he suffered a gallbladder attack and was given pain medication mixed in water. It killed the pain – and LaTempa along with it. The city toxicologist said that LaTempa had ingested enough poison to 'kill eight horses'.

The Hawk's sole testimony was not enough to convict Genovese. Now that it was safe to go home, Genovese told Dickey, 'Kid, you are doing me the biggest favor anyone has ever done to me. You are taking me home. You are taking me back to the United States.'

On 1 June, a shackled Genovese arrived in New York. On 2 June, he was arraigned for the murder of Ferdinand 'The Shadow' Boccia, but since the case had already fallen apart, his appearance in court was a formality. When the prosecutor told Genovese that he had just missed being strapped into the electric chair, Genovese, who had swapped his military fatigues for a blue suit, white shirt and maroon necktie, just yawned. He exited prison on 11 June. Thanks to Sergeant Orange Dickey, Genovese was home from his nine-year exile.

As for Ernie 'The Hawk' Rupolo, he left prison in 1949 and lasted a lot longer than anyone expected. Fifteen years later, Rupolo's wife reported him missing. Three weeks after that, he surfaced, quite literally, when his mutilated body was fished out of Jamaica Bay in Queens after it broke loose from concrete blocks that were used to weigh him down. Ernie Rupolo and Peter LaTempa would have certainly been better off if Sergeant Dickey had accepted Genovese's bribe. We can say the same for Frank Costello, who was now headed for a reckoning with Genovese, who did not view Costello as his boss but as someone warming his seat while he was away. Those in the borgata who did not want to see Costello replaced by Genovese hoped that Luciano would be sprung from prison for his patriotic service and resume his place at the top.

Following the invasion of Normandy in June 1944, Lucky Luciano was sure of an Allied victory and became even more excited about the prospect of an early release. On 8 May 1945, the same day the Allies declared victory in Europe, Luciano's attorney, Moses Polakoff, filed a plea for executive clemency, citing his client's wartime service. By 3 January 1946, Governor Dewey commuted Luciano's sentence to time served but kicked Luciano in the ass on his way out the door by making the commutation dependent on Luciano's deportation to Italy.*

A month after Dewey commuted Luciano's sentence, the gates of Great Meadow Prison swung open and Luciano was handed over to the Immigration and Naturalization Service. 'Fuck 'em all,' said Luciano. 'I'll be back.' This was the last lie he told on American soil. By the beginning of February, Luciano was transferred to Ellis Island, where his journey had begun as a boy. From there, he was brought to Bush Terminal in Brooklyn where the SS *Laura Keene* was docked, an old freighter that would float Luciano across the Atlantic. While detained in Brooklyn, Luciano beheld Manhattan's skyline for the last time. The streets of the world's tallest city had once belonged to him. The pockmarked, scar-faced petty dope dealer who was thrown out of his parents' home had risen to dethrone the mob's old-world dons, revolutionized the American mafia, organized five borgatas, created the Commission, forged alliances with Jews and Blacks, and connected a vast web of underworld contacts across the country. The immigrant who could not vote had decided statewide elections and had come close to weighing in on the presidency.

Luciano asked his girlfriend, Gay Orlova, to accompany him to Italy. Orlova claimed to have some issues with her passport, which could have meant that she pushed it through a paper shredder. Orlova was not about to leave the wealthiest country in the world to board a rusty, barnacled transport ship en route to a beaten and beleaguered nation where nylons and cigarettes were hard to find.

At least Meyer Lansky still loved Luciano and arranged a going-away party to show it. Actually, there was a more important reason to give Luciano a grand exit that had nothing to do with love. It has never

---

* In 1950, Dewey's commutation left him open to political attacks during his gubernatorial re-election campaign. He weathered the storm that blew in again during the 1954 election, when new accusations were made that Dewey was bribed by Luciano by way of generous campaign contributions. Livid that his integrity was under fire, Dewey ordered the state commissioner of investigations, William Herlands, to conduct an official inquiry into the navy's wartime relationship with the mafia, specifically Luciano. Just as it had once been in Dewey's interest to portray Luciano as an amoral pimp, he now wanted him to look like Audie Murphy. Herlands took sworn testimony from over 150 naval officers and enlisted men who confirmed the mafia's role in secret intelligence operations. The navy asked Dewey to withhold his findings, fearing the public would not condone the military's temporary relationship with the mafia. Dewey obliged and buried the report, which only surfaced after his death. It was the Herlands report that brought to light most of what we know today.

been discussed until now, and it boiled down to power politics. Lansky, who stage-managed Luciano's entire career, knew that Frank Costello was a weak boss and that underboss Vito Genovese had a legitimate claim to the throne. Once Luciano was gone for good, Costello would lose a large degree of protection, as would Lansky, who was close with Luciano and Costello but not with Genovese. By the time Luciano was put under a deportation order, Costello was on the thinnest of ice. Besides the district attorney's wiretap on his home phone that exposed his appointment of judges, and besides his foolhardy press conference that was sneered at by the underworld, Costello had blundered into yet another mess.

On 14 June 1944, as Allied tanks were pushing through hedgerows at Saint-Lô in the region of Normandy, Costello was crawling through Manhattan traffic in a yellow cab. When he hopped out on 5th Avenue, he left behind two fat envelopes stuffed with $27,200 in cash. The money was from Dandy Phil Kastel and represented Costello's end of their casino operations. The cabbie, Ed Waters, found the envelopes on his back seat. Believing the money was counterfeit, Waters turned it over to police, an error in judgment he deeply regretted when he found out it was real. Costello should have written it off as a loss, but instead he called his attorney, George Wolf, for advice. After a brief discussion, Wolf talked Costello into visiting the police department to claim the money. The moment Costello stepped up to the police clerk, his stock plummeted on the Mafia Exchange. It is hard to believe that Costello thought the clerk would just say, 'Sure thing, here it is, Mr Costello. Have a nice night.' The clerk asked a dozen questions and before the night was up, Mayor LaGuardia was involved, vowing never to give Costello back a single dollar. At this point, Costello should have folded his cards and written off the loss; instead, he sued the city, making his situation even worse since the suit resulted in a highly publicized court battle that left everyone in the underworld shaking their heads. Costello won the suit after claiming the lost money was derived from real-estate investments. But because he owed back taxes, the money was handed over to the federal government. In the end, Costello was down an extra five hundred bucks, which he gave to the cabbie as a reward for returning the money, not to mention legal fees.

Given the long list of Costello's blunders, Lansky knew that in order to keep him in place as acting boss, Costello would have to continue 'acting' on behalf of Luciano, even after the latter was deported to Italy. To keep Luciano relevant and worthy of continued respect, Lansky worked overtime to create the legend of Lucky Luciano as the 'man who had put it all together', which was, in part, true but hyper-inflated to keep Genovese in check. In reality, Luciano was flat broke after ten long years in prison, and being shipped to Italy like grain.

To put Luciano on his feet, Lansky passed around the hat and raised $165,000 (over two million dollars in today's currency). He bought Luciano a new wardrobe, and asked him if he needed anything else. Luciano replied, 'Yeah, broads', already forgetting how he got into this mess.

'There'll be three on the ship,' Lansky assured him.

'I hope you didn't pick them,' said Luciano. '[Women] is one department in which you are not an expert.'

Luciano was pleased to hear that Lansky had sublet the task to Joe Adonis.

On the evening of 9 February 1946, a curious press pushed their way onto the pier, hoping to cover Luciano's farewell party aboard the SS *Laura Keene*, but they were turned away by mob-connected longshoremen, who formed a barrier with baling hooks at the ready. (These were the same tough guys who so recently acted as the eyes and ears of the US Navy; things were back to normal.) The next morning, the ship cast off its lines and set sail for Genoa, Italy, Detective Petrosino's first stop on his way to the grave. Luciano's final destination was his birthplace, Lercara Friddi, where the ears of John Rose had fertilized a bed of tomatoes. The poverty-stricken town welcomed Luciano who, if he chose to bird-hunt, had plenty of 'peasants' to shoot. The townsfolk did not care that Luciano was an exiled mafioso. 'Half the people I met in Sicily was in the mafia,' Luciano said, 'and by half the people, I mean half the cops, too. Because in Sicily, it goes like this: the mafia is first, then your own family, then your business, and then the mafia again.'

Luciano eventually made his way to Rome and spent a lot of time in Naples. He hopped straight into the post-war black-market trade while dreaming of his return from exile, like Napoleon on Elba. Then one day, in the early fall of 1946, Luciano received a short dispatch from Lansky that read: 'December – Hotel Nacional.' Lansky was calling Luciano to Havana, Cuba, where he had arranged to split the island's gambling industry between the mafia and the Cuban government.

While Luciano acquires a phony passport and prepares for his journey to the Caribbean, let us drop in on Ben Siegel, the adventurer who once sailed the Pacific like a pirate, as he now dreams of raising an adult playground out of the Mojave desert.

Chapter 27
King of the Desert

Back in 1930, while Ben Siegel was helping Luciano overthrow the old mafia dons in New York, the federal government contracted a company to build a dam to regulate the 'schizophrenic moods' of the Colorado River and harness its natural power with a hydroelectric plant. The project got underway at the height of the Great Depression. Hordes of unemployed men from across the country poured into the company's recruiting office in Las Vegas, Nevada, dubbed the Gateway City since it led to the more isolated construction site at Black Canyon, approximately twenty-five miles away. Because moving men and materials to the worksite was the modern equivalent of dragging stones to the pyramids, those who found work were lodged in bunkhouses at Black Canyon. With the company's recreation halls being painfully boring and dry on account of Prohibition, many of the workers piled into trucks on payday and headed straight for Las Vegas where they could blow their paychecks on whisky and women. To accommodate their vices, bordellos and gambling houses were opened at breakneck speed. When the project, known as Hoover Dam, was completed in 1936, tourists passed through Las Vegas on their way to and from the dam.

By the start of the Second World War, a number of casino-hotels were operating along Las Vegas Boulevard, known as 'the Strip'. Tourist traffic slowed during the war but reached new heights immediately thereafter. Unlike Europeans who had to rebuild their war-torn countries, Americans, in control of half the world's wealth, began living it up and tourism spiked in Las Vegas, which became its own vacation destination.

It was a hot summer's day in 1945 when Ben Siegel traveled from Los Angeles to Las Vegas to see if he could sign up new bookmaking clients for his race wire. Siegel was enamored by a number of new hotels popping up along the Strip and asked Morris 'Little Moe' Sedway, his partner in the wire, to take a ride with him in his new DeSoto station wagon. After a short drive, Siegel steered the wagon off the road and pointed through the dust cloud he had just kicked up with his tires. 'Here it is, Moe,' Siegel said to Sedway as they looked at a dilapidated motel known as Folsom's Guest Cottages, which sat on thirty acres of dry desert.

At the beginning of the war, Harold Folsom had died and his widow, Margaret, found the cottages too difficult to maintain alone. Siegel told Sedway he wanted to purchase the land, knock down the cottages and build a state-of-the-art casino-hotel. Sedway told Siegel he was nuts but slowly came around to the idea. Siegel contacted Margaret Folsom, who quitclaimed the property to him for a 'few nickels and dimes'. He then cut a deal with Billy Wilkerson, whose Nevada Projects Corporation acted as the vehicle to finance the venture by selling shares to investors. After Siegel threw in every last penny of his own money, he went to Meyer Lansky knowing Lansky's involvement would signal to the underworld that it was a sound investment. Like Sedway, Lansky was not at first sold on the idea but came around to it.

Once Lansky was on board, every mafia don in the country wanted in. After Siegel raised a million dollars, he hired architect Richard Stadelman and contacted Delbert 'Del' Webb, a real-estate developer (and co-owner of the New York Yankees). Webb's initial concern was for his own safety, given the murderous reputation of his new client. Siegel told Webb he had no need to worry, assuring him, 'We only kill each other.' To help Webb acquire the best building materials, Siegel called in favors and slowly assumed the role of general contractor. He hired the best architectural designers, master craftsmen, electricians, carpenters, plasterers, and made decisions with no regard for budget. He changed blueprints on a whim, spent $350,000 on 'matured shrubberies', and wanted each suite equipped with the best private plumbing; although the one-million-dollar estimate for sewer pipes equaled his entire original budget, he insisted on it. Each room cost $3,500 to furnish and his private suite was fit for a Saudi king. When Siegel inspected his suite, he complained about a low five-foot-eight-inch beam that would force him to bend each time he made his way across the room. Instead of designating the room as the guest suite for his Italian pals, most of whom could do jumping jacks under a five-foot-eight-inch ceiling, he told the workers, 'Never mind the cost. Get it out.' He built a state-of-the-art health club with steam rooms, a nine-hole golf course and 'stables with forty head of fine riding stock'.

Before long, Siegel had spent over four million dollars on his dream, which he named after his latest paramour, Virginia Hill.

Virginia Hill was born in Lipscomb, Alabama, on 26 August 1916. She was one of ten children. Her father, Mack, was a horse trader who abused his wife until she walked out on her large family, never to return. Hill was seventeen when she traveled to Chicago and found work as a waitress, with a second job as a stripper. She met Joe Epstein, while either taking orders for pork chops, or showing off her own chops. The older bachelor, who was an accounting genius and bookmaker for the Chicago mob, fell head over heels for her. He showered her with gifts and cash but he was still too dull for Hill, who left for Los Angeles where she rented an apartment in Hollywood. No matter how many other men Hill dated, Epstein continued to support her lavish lifestyle for decades to come. He would sometimes fly to Los Angeles just to deliver her cash then re-board the plane and fly home.

Ben Siegel first met Virginia Hill at a dinner club where she was with Joe Adonis. Hill flirted with Siegel who stole her away from Adonis, leaving a lasting scar on Adonis's fragile ego. Despite being married with children, Siegel fell madly in love with Hill and named his new Las Vegas hotel the Flamingo, which was Hill's nickname, likely on account of her slender legs. The honor did nothing for Hill, who called Siegel's project a 'stupid gambling joint that wasn't gonna draw anything but flies and losers'.*

Siegel was determined to prove Hill wrong. When Alexander the Great was trying to raise money to fund an expedition into Persia, he not only milked his aristocracy but spent every last drachma of his own, prompting his friend Perdiccas to ask, 'What have you left for yourself?' Alexander replied, 'My hopes.' Siegel exhibited a similar hope in his own dream as he nudged his investors for more money while using up his own and continuing to go over budget. He even hoped that his high-stakes gambling would cover some of the debts that piled up around him, but his consistent losses dug him into a

* Toward the end of his life, Meyer Lansky told his biographers that he came up with the idea of moving into Las Vegas and also took credit for naming the hotel by telling a fanciful story about how it came to him while pondering life as he gazed over a lake with flamingoes. When Lansky made these claims, Siegel was long dead, as was everyone else involved, and Lansky was desperately fighting for his freedom while touching up the canvas of his legend with poetic strokes. It seems by making himself the founder of Las Vegas, he hoped to endear himself to the millions of Americans who considered it their vacation paradise.

deeper hole. The race wire still buttered his bread but he drew heavily from that income, too, dumping it all into the Flamingo.

To make matters worse, casino owners on the Strip, concerned the Flamingo would draw gamblers away from their tables, began a whispering campaign, telling their patrons that Siegel was a violent gangster. Besides threatening to kill them – which only confirmed their accusations – Siegel endeavored to clean up his name. As the Flamingo neared completion, he drove over to the offices of *Las Vegas Life*, a bi-monthly magazine highlighting exactly that. He pledged to purchase the expensive back-page advertisement every month, which earned him a glowing write-up in the December issue, scheduled to coincide with the Flamingo's grand opening. The piece sought to whitewash Siegel's dangerous reputation by openly admitting it, but claiming he had transformed himself from a hoodlum into a 'polished hotel executive', calling his transformation 'Siegelian'.

For the Flamingo's opening night, Siegel wanted A-list celebrities greeting guests at the door so he reached out to Katharine Hepburn, Clark Gable, Gary Cooper, Spencer Tracy and Marlene Dietrich, who all bowed out after Hollywood studio heads warned them to stay away from the Flamingo. Siegel was insulted and complained to Hill, who told him, 'Forget those dumb bastards in Hollywood.' Hill, who rented a sprawling Spanish-colonial mansion in Beverly Hills, agreed to attend the grand opening. True to form, she practically rode into town on Cleopatra's barge with trunks of evening gowns, shoes, jewelry, pocketbooks, make-up, furs and a state-of-the-art phonograph with dozens of vinyl records. She also brought her younger brother, Charles 'Chick' Hill.

Of her many siblings, Virginia was particularly close with Chick, who was a pilot fish, content to spend his life trailing behind someone oozing money, like his sister. Virginia sometimes sent Chick to the airport to pick up money from Epstein. Chick candidly admitted to putting the envelopes on crash diets, delivering them to his sister a lot thinner, only hours later. Chick knew that Epstein would never know and trusted that if caught, his sister wouldn't care. He was right; a few bucks this way or that meant nothing to Virginia, so long as she had enough money to spend on her own luxurious lifestyle. Chick blew his cash on women; he had the same high libido as his sister, the only difference being that his ran at a deficit. To further support his lifestyle, he did odd jobs for Siegel, becoming one of the highest-paid gofers in the country.

Siegel scheduled the Flamingo's grand opening for 26 December 1946. When the big moment was only hours away, a fidgety Siegel, who looked as if he had not slept in days, performed a last-minute inspection. While picking up lint from the floor and emptying ashtrays, he came across a palm print on a wall and went looking for the nearest foreman. 'What the hell is this?' he asked. 'You think you're working in a cheap bar somewhere? This is the Flamingo – and don't forget it!' When Siegel found a cigarette butt on the floor, he threatened to find the 'dirty pig' who dropped it before stomping off in a huff.

When, at last, the doors were about to swing open, Siegel walked into the lobby where Hill was wearing a gown designed for opening night by fashion designer Howard Greer, the Gianni Versace of his day. Hill had a twinkle in her eye to match her diamonds – until she spotted Siegel wearing a sport shirt opened at the collar, no jacket or tie. 'You crummy peasant!' she yelled. 'Go back and get into a dinner jacket.' Siegel ran upstairs and returned properly dressed. He swung open the front doors but the crowd was much smaller than expected. George Raft and Jimmy Durante came, as did Xavier Cugat, who brought his orchestra, but transportation from southern California was hampered by rainy weather. Siegel's advertising flyer offered three chartered planes for the grand opening, but the bottom of the flyer read, 'The hotel portion of the Flamingo will not be open until March 1.' Since guests would have to find overnight accommodations elsewhere, and gamblers tend to play where they stay, they gambled elsewhere.

Over the next two weeks, gamblers visited the Flamingo but the books revealed a staggering loss of $300,000. I may be able to shed some light as to why. When Foxwoods Resort Casino in Connecticut opened in 1992, my crew and I sometimes drove there to celebrate after a heist. Most of the dealers were green and some had trouble tallying up the card totals at the blackjack tables. Impatient gamblers would angrily yell the tallies at the dealers. Sometimes, dealers paid out or collected chips when they should have been doing the opposite. Once, while playing blackjack late into the night at the far corner of a half-moon table, I lazily slouched down in my seat where I noticed that the dealer was slightly lifting his second card before sliding it under his first. Though I could not see exactly what the hidden card was, I could tell if it was a picture card or not; in blackjack, this is all you need to know to break the bank. Since, at the time, I would have robbed the casino's vault if I could have gotten away with it, suffice to say that a little card cheating was not beneath me, I bet big. After stacks of chips piled up in front of me, the pit boss pulled the dealer. Notwithstanding this and many other mistakes, Foxwoods was soon running on all cylinders and profiting millions.

Given my experience at Foxwoods, I am left to wonder if something similar happened at the Flamingo. Were inexperienced dealers hurting the house? Things got worse and the losses mounted when two other casino owners stopped in and must have spotted that it was amateur night; they each hit for close to a hundred grand. When Siegel spotted a croupier at the roulette wheel paying someone who did not win, he flew through the crowd and kicked the croupier onto the table, sending chips in every direction. The croupier was either working a flimflam with the player, or was inexperienced like the early dealers at Foxwoods. Whichever the case, the croupier ran off, terrified, as did the table's gamblers.

Out of touch with local custom, Siegel ordered hats removed on the casino floor. Besides offending a few baldies, most of the locals were cowboys and took great pride in their Stetsons; they took their money elsewhere. Actor George Raft, who drove his Cadillac all the way from Los Angeles to support his friend, was one of the few men who lost a bundle at the casino. After dropping $65,000 on the 26th, Raft returned the next day, hoping to win back some money. Siegel was so afraid that Raft might even up that he physically threw him off the table and told him, 'You're not playing here tonight.' Raft pleaded with Siegel to reconsider as Siegel warned the dealer not to deal to Raft. Raft left the Flamingo in disgust. He was in such a hurry to get away from Siegel that he flagged a cab to the airport, leaving his Caddy behind.

Cliff Leonard was a happy-go-lucky guy who worked in Las Vegas. He was liked by everyone in town and wanted to patronize the Flamingo despite the slanderous whispers he would have certainly heard about Siegel. The fun-loving, chubby guy had just enjoyed an evening show with his wife and kids when he spotted Siegel, and reached out a hand as he said, 'Great place, Bugsy! You've done a wonderful thing here.'

'Were you and I ever introduced?' was Siegel's un-*Siegelian* response.

Leonard was blindsided, unsure how to react.

'Do you know anybody I know?' Siegel continued, bullying the poor man in front of his family.

'No, sir,' Leonard said, sheepishly.

'Then who told you to call me Bugsy?'

Siegel threw Leonard and his family out, along with whatever cash they were yet to spend.

Next, Siegel spotted Chick Hill slipping chips into his pockets. Siegel flew into a rage and took a swing at him. The younger, nimbler Chick ducked the punch as Siegel's own momentum thrust him to the floor. He climbed to his feet, dusted off his jacket, then went upstairs to sleep it off, as if he knew he was making a complete fool of himself and should call it a night.

As if things could not get any worse, Virginia Hill poured gasoline on Siegel's fire by asking him if he was out to tarnish her good name by associating it with this major failure. During their many arguments, Hill called him a 'two-bit loser' and a 'fucking chump who . . . couldn't keep cab fare in his own pocket'. She soon hightailed it out of Las Vegas, returning to her Beverly Hills mansion where she displayed a homespun version of the same lunacy Siegel was exhibiting in the desert; she regularly accused staff of stealing and even threatened their lives.

As the casino sank deeper into debt, Siegel tried cures that were symptomatic of his gambling nature; he switched card decks and swapped dice, hoping his luck would change. But his problems were too big for a new deck or dice. In January 1947, he closed the Flamingo's doors so he could complete the hotel rooms. Billy Wilkerson used the hiatus to ask Siegel if he could cash out of his investment. Wilkerson was willing to take a loss and the fact that Siegel, while short on cash, dished out $120,000 to assume Wilkerson's shares shows that he still believed in his dream. With the doors closed, Siegel should have called on Lansky as an emergency fixer. Though I do not believe Siegel would have consigned his baby into another man's arms, Lansky was nonetheless unavailable, busy nursing his own baby in the West Indies. As Siegel takes stock of his losses, let us leave the hot desert sand for the blue-green waters of the Caribbean.

Chapter 28

The Havana Conference

During Prohibition, Meyer Lansky once traveled to Cuba to secure molasses for alcohol production. While there, he spotted the island's potential for mob-owned casinos. He struck a deal with the island's dictator, Fulgencio Batista, promising him three to five million dollars annually in return for a monopoly on Cuba's gambling industry. Batista arranged for the government to match Lansky's investments dollar for dollar, but the venture was put on hold during the Second World War. According to Lansky, 'The minute the war was over, we were back in business, opening up the casinos.' American tourists came in droves, many arriving on chartered flights that Lansky regularly scheduled from south Florida. With things underway, Lansky sent a telegram to Lucky Luciano in Italy, inviting him to a mob conference in Havana, at the Hotel Nacional de Cuba, to be held during Christmas week 1946, the same week Ben Siegel swung open the doors to the Flamingo.

Lansky invited bosses from the most powerful borgatas across the country; some were accompanied by their underbosses and consiglieres. In the case of Luciano's borgata, acting boss Frank Costello arrived with his brilliant numbers man, Dandy Phil Kastel, and two loyal musclemen, capos Willie Moretti and Anthony 'Little Augie Pisano' Carfano. Lansky also invited Vito Genovese, who came with capo Mike Miranda, a fellow Neapolitan who was more loyal to Genovese than to Costello. It appears that Lansky, aware of the tremors caused by Genovese's return from Italy, was hedging his bets. Luciano's invitation was also politically motivated; Lansky was attempting to maintain the deported don's illusion of power in the hope of counter-balancing the growing might of Genovese.

As soon as Luciano received Lansky's telegram, he purchased a phony passport and left Naples, arriving at an airport in Camaguey, Cuba, on 29 October. 'Where's Meyer?' Luciano asked an airport attendant as he stepped off the plane. Moments later, Lansky rolled across the tarmac in a Jeep. He had Luciano whisked through customs, then took him to the Grand Hotel for lunch before they headed for the Hotel Nacional. Upon Lansky's request, Cuba's interior minister, Alfredo Pequeño, granted Luciano an indefinite stay.

Luciano fell in love with Cuba and called it a 'helluva change from Dannemora', one of the prisons he had resided in only nine months earlier. After a couple of weeks of living in the Hotel Nacional, Luciano

Hotel Nacional, Cuba.

moved into the upscale neighborhood of Miramar where wealthy Americans mixed with upper-class Cubans. He rented a mansion a few blocks away from Cuban president Ramón Grau San Martín, who was also on Lansky's payroll. (In 1946, Batista was splitting his time between New York and Florida; he regained power on the island in 1952.) Luciano was seen hobnobbing with Cuban politicians like Senator Eduardo Suárez Rivas, who was a suspected drug trafficker. He was also seen all over Havana with Cuban beauties, and was living it up until Vito Genovese arrived like a cloud of radiation. Genovese, who had not seen Luciano since 1937, paid him a visit at his Miramar home. After they greeted one another, Genovese told Luciano that he wanted to replace Costello as boss, and asked Luciano to authorize the transfer of power. 'You'll have all the dough you can ever need,'

Genovese told him. 'I give you my personal word on that. You won't have to worry about what's goin' on. You won't have to think up ideas on how to get back to New York – which is gonna be tough. And you'll still be the boss . . . It's like you'll be the head, but I'll be runnin' things on the spot.'

Luciano did not take kindly to Genovese's attempt at a polite coup and shouted his disapproval, which only revealed his impotence since the old Luciano would have silently nodded along then arranged for Genovese to visit the shipwrecks at the bottom of Havana Harbor.

Back at the Hotel Nacional, Lansky secured the top floors from 22 to 26 December, when only his guests were allowed entry. As the first meeting commenced, Albert Anastasia stood up and declared that Lucky Luciano was still the undisputed boss of Luciano's borgata. This declaration was so out of place for the meeting yet relevant to the earlier conversation Luciano had had with Genovese that it seems Luciano (and perhaps Costello, who was exceptionally close with Anastasia) had put Anastasia up to it. The message, no doubt directed at Genovese, was to let him know that Anastasia would oppose any move against the status quo.

Next, Lansky asked everyone to kick up a tribute to Luciano who, in turn, handed all the money back to Lansky as his buy-in for the Havana venture. It was a crafty way to honor Luciano as a man worthy of offerings while getting others to cover his investment.

As the week wore on, one discussion turned to Ben Siegel and his grand opening in Las Vegas. Many historians contend that Siegel's fate was decided in Cuba when the bosses, who were invested in the Flamingo through Lansky, decided to whack Siegel on account of the Flamingo's losses. The theory does not hold up under the slightest scrutiny. The Flamingo opened the very same week these men were in Cuba. Do you murder a man because his start-up is not an overwhelming success in one lousy week? Siegel would die for other reasons which we will discuss in due time.

Chicago mobsters Rocco and Joe Fischetti traveled to the conference with Frank Sinatra, who was booked to perform at the Hotel Nacional for Christmas. The Fischetti brothers once lived in New York before relocating to Chicago, where they fell in with their cousin, Al Capone (whose death from natural causes roughly coincided with this trip to Havana). Joe, nicknamed 'Stingy' for his tight pockets, once said, 'I'm the only one in the family who hasn't killed anybody.' Sinatra, who had become famous in 1943, stepped off a Pan Am flight in Havana carrying a suitcase and bookended by Rocco and Joe; the suitcase was reported to contain two million dollars (over 27 million in today's currency) which represented the Chicago mob's investment in Cuba.*

In Havana, Sinatra spent a lot of time with Luciano. Sinatra's paternal grandfather was from Lercara Friddi, the same place Luciano was born, and his grandparents were married in the same church where Luciano was baptized; it is quite possible that their ancestors knew each other. Luciano was also seen with Manhattan socialite Beverly Paterno, though he did not know that Paterno was an incurable gossip who wanted everyone to know she was holding a gangster's gun. She hired a public relations firm to run stories in the *Havana Post*, calling attention to herself and Luciano, who may have thought a few mentions in a local newspaper were harmless, until a Scripps-Howard columnist, Robert Ruark, read an article and wondered what Luciano was doing in Cuba. When Ruark found out that Luciano was buddying around with Sinatra, he wrote a piece for the American press, headlined: 'Ruark Is Puzzled as to Why Sinatra Chooses to Associate with Hoodlums.' Ruark's snarky piece was aimed more at Sinatra's questionable character than Luciano's mysterious presence in Havana. He portrayed Sinatra as a hypocrite who had 'millions of kids' fooled, while he hung out with mobsters, including Luciano, a 'panderer and permanent deportee from the United States'. Sinatra took offense at

* Early on in Sinatra's career, the singer was stuck in an entertainment contract with bandleader Tommy Dorsey, who released him in return for 43.33 percent of his earnings for the next ten years. When Sinatra started earning big money, he complained to a reporter 'that he believes it is wrong for anybody to own a piece of him and collect on it when that owner is doing nothing'. Dorsey was unmoved by Sinatra's complaints – until Sinatra visited Willie Moretti, who agreed to help him break free of the contract; Moretti supposedly made Dorsey 'an offer he couldn't refuse'. Once out of the contract, Sinatra told the press, 'I now own myself', a statement Moretti and the rest of the mob may not have agreed with.

Even those who refute this story still concede that Moretti kept Sinatra – both of whom lived in New Jersey before the latter moved to California – working at his own nightclubs while Sinatra was on his way up. Sinatra later admitted that 'Moretti made some band dates for me when I first got started', and Sinatra's daughter Tina said her dad knew Moretti 'all his life'. Sinatra returned the favor by helping Moretti and other mobsters when asked – unlike baseball legend Joe DiMaggio, who owed them nothing. DiMaggio attended a meeting where he was asked to lend his name and prestige to their Cuban endeavor, but declined; Joltin' Joe reportedly ran out of the room when Albert Anastasia entered. The wholesome ballplayer opted to become the face of a coffee machine over a killing machine.

Ruark's article, stating, 'Any report that I fraternized with goons and racketeers is a vicious lie. I was brought up to shake a man's hand when I am introduced to him without first investigating his past.' After Sinatra sang his way out of it, Luciano was left alone under the spotlight.*

US Narcotics Bureau commissioner Harry Anslinger (who Luciano referred to as Harry Asslicker) was blindsided by the news that Luciano was vacationing in Cuba. Anslinger was sure Luciano was there to traffic in drugs and further imagined the entire conference to be about a narcotics pipeline between Cuba and Miami, overlooking the mob's gambling agenda. Anslinger's hunch was correct to the extent that drug trafficking was indeed discussed at the conference but only to debate if its sale in the States should be banned by the rules of Cosa Nostra. Costello argued that it was a dirty business that did not have the support of the American people, unlike drinking and gambling, and any association with it would cost him his valuable judges and politicians. After a lengthy debate, the consensus ruled against a universal prohibition and concluded that each boss would have the sole authority to decide for his own borgata. Even though Anslinger had no solid evidence to back up his assumptions, he portrayed Luciano as the new cartel leader of Cuba, then asked President Truman to pressure the Cuban government to deport him. The US State Department contacted the Cuban president who held an emergency session with his cabinet. They discussed international law, and must have weighed the consequences of selling out Luciano while Lansky was throwing money around the island like *arroz y frijoles*. The Cuban government ultimately told the State Department that Luciano was there lawfully and they would not deport him.

A confused Truman ordered the US ambassador to Cuba, R. Henry Norweb, back to Washington so Norweb could explain to him what in hell was going on. After conferring with Norweb and Anslinger, Truman viewed Luciano as a nuclear warhead, tolerable in Europe but too close to home in the Caribbean. He ordered the State Department to stop the flow of medicinal drugs to the island, a diplomatic response in line with Luciano's alleged drug trafficking. Anslinger, along with his colleague Colonel Garland Williams of the Treasury Department's

* A week after Ruark's story was printed, FBI director J. Edgar Hoover opened a file on Sinatra, more so for his own intelligence than to pursue any criminal prosecution. The file would fatten over the years.

Narcotics Division, drew public attention to the feud by telling journalists that a 'large shipment of European heroin – $250,000 worth' turned up in the United States about the same time Luciano was gallivanting around Cuba. There was absolutely no connection between the shipment and Luciano but it sounded a public alarm.

Luciano complained, 'I'm taking bum raps. Now they got me handling junk. It's just one headache on top of a headache. If I can't be left alone, what am I gonna do?' He could have stayed in Italy and not purchased a phony passport, for starters. Instead, he dug in as more money found its way into Cuban pockets, gaining him additional allies. Secret police chief Benito Herrera said, 'There is no evidence that he is mixed up in any illicit business in Cuba.' Interior minister Alfredo Pequeño's response was just as defensive, albeit more measured, as he tried to balance international relations with mafia diplomacy. 'He is a dangerous character and a perjurer, to be sure,' said Pequeño, 'but his papers are in perfect order.' Public health minister Dr José Andreu refuted claims from Washington that the island's illegal narcotic supply had increased since Luciano's arrival.

With a chorus of defenders supporting him, Luciano felt safe – until the US embargo put a strain on Cuba's health sector that reverberated across the economy. Luciano advised the Cuban government to counter the embargo by cutting off sugar exports to the States. The hot sun must have been melting Luciano's brain since the Cubans were not about to withhold their most profitable export and ruin their relationship with a superpower over a washed-up mob boss. A worn-down President Ramón Grau San Martín reluctantly caved and signed off on Luciano's deportation order. For the second time in his life, Luciano was deemed an undesirable alien (can everyone be wrong?).

On 23 February 1947, Luciano's Caribbean holiday ended abruptly. He was having lunch in a Havana restaurant when police surrounded his table and took him into custody. They shuffled him across the Bay of Havana under an armed guard and tossed him into the Tiscornia immigration camp. Knowing the gig was up, Luciano asked to be sent to South America, but President Truman did not want him anywhere within the boundaries of the Monroe Doctrine; Luciano's request was denied. On 12 April, Luciano was put aboard a Turkish freighter, the SS *Bakir*. As the ship crept out to sea, politicians and mobsters must have danced the cucaracha now that *Don Caliente* was gone.

*

Harry Anslinger later said that Meyer Lansky had dimed Lucky Luciano, escorting him to and from Cuba for his own purpose. Though this assertion is not implausible, it is improbable. Lansky was averse to publicity and would never have broadcast Luciano's presence on the island, which invited negative press, accusations of drug trafficking and attention from Washington. It is more likely that Lansky brought Luciano to Cuba with intent to check Genovese, as noted, and may have reluctantly taken part in his removal once the mafia's group interests were at stake. When Anslinger wrote the book in which his claim appeared, it was 1971. By then, Luciano was dead and Lansky was buckling under the full weight of the Justice Department. Anslinger's claim, if believed, could have turned mobsters against Lansky and placed him in a vise, which would have thrilled Anslinger. In the end, nobody was more responsible for Luciano's deportation than the man himself. Knowing that publicity had hurt him in New York and placed a target on his head, he should have lain low and avoided the limelight in Cuba.

Chapter 29

The Desert King Dethroned

At the same time Lucky Luciano was awaiting deportation in a Cuban detention center, Ben Siegel and Virginia Hill were secretly married in Mexico, adding bigamy to Siegel's long catalog of crimes. After a brief honeymoon, Siegel flew back to Las Vegas where the Flamingo's price tag had surpassed six million dollars. Pressure from investors may have driven him to unfurl the second set of 'grand opening' banners prematurely, since many of the guest rooms were still unfinished. On 1 March 1947, Siegel reopened the Flamingo as the Fabulous Flamingo, hoping to change his luck with an adjective.

Although Siegel proved as good at business as Bill Gates would be on a hit, he realized that the expensive press campaign to tidy up his name brought more negative attention to it. When *Las Vegas Life* proposed a new article about the great Ben Siegel who had unclenched his fists to become a hotel host, Siegel declined. And yet, he made no effort to improve his reckless behavior. One day, he ran up to a guy who was lounging by the pool and kicked the chair out from under him while ordering him to return to work. The unfortunate man could not return to work because he was a guest! Siegel mistook him for an employee because he was poolside in a sport jacket instead of swim trunks.

When Siegel saw a little girl vomiting in the lobby, he yelled at her for ruining his carpet; she ran off, crying. One afternoon, hotel guests were invited to a poolside barbecue and were told to 'bring the kiddies'. Abe and Doris Schiller showed up with their three children. When Siegel heard that Abe had once referred to him as 'that gangster up the road', Siegel added a little adult entertainment for the kiddies. He ran up to Abe and pistol-whipped him as the family man crawled around the edge of the pool in swim trunks, trying to get away. When Siegel heard that a clerk at the El Rancho was telling people to stay away from the Flamingo because it was run by gangsters, Siegel went there and pistol-whipped the clerk. He also turned on his own men. One night, during a heated argument on the gaming floor, Siegel planted the tip of his shoe in the crack of Little Moe Sedway's ass. He then threw him out and threatened to kill him if he ever returned. Aside from being publicly humiliated, Sedway took the threat to his life seriously and began reporting Siegel's erratic behavior to the bosses in New York and Chicago, who were heavily invested in the hotel's success.

The casino was still running at a loss when Siegel increased the payout ratio for the slot machines, opened a sumptuous buffet table, added a bingo room, and advertised a weekly raffle for a new automobile. On the afternoon of the first raffle, the casino was packed. When floor manager Hank Greenspun told a worker to announce that the drawing would be held momentarily, Siegel rushed at Greenspun who stepped aside and belted Siegel who crashed to the floor and rolled down a short flight of steps. With the Flamingo's biggest crowd to date looking on, Siegel embarrassingly climbed to his feet and told Greenspun that he only wanted to delay the drawing for a few minutes since a large crowd was still waiting to get in. Greenspun calmly explained to Siegel that the people inside would get angry if the drawing did not go off on time, and the Flamingo would get an even worse name than it already had. The weekly raffles helped but could not stem the tide as casino losses mounted and the Flamingo's checks bounced. When Countess di Frasso heard about Siegel's problems, she offered him $50,000. Siegel thanked her but refused the money. When a gangster turns down free money, it is time to retire or die; Siegel was six weeks away from both.

Virginia Hill returned to Las Vegas like a Roman unable to resist a gladiatorial day at the Colosseum. As if Hill could not allow Siegel to out-menace her in public, she too began to pick fights inside the hotel. When Hill was convinced that a young hat-check girl had her eye on Siegel, Hill seized the girl by the hair and pummeled her with her free hand. As Hill was being torn away from her victim, she scratched the girl's face to shreds. The poor girl was rushed to a nearby hospital. Besides scratches and bruises, the petite woman's vertebrae had been dislocated by Hill, who was in the habit of roughing up gangsters and neglected to dial down her strength. The injured girl filed a lawsuit against the hotel. After the fight, Hill went upstairs to Siegel's suite where she swallowed a vial of sleeping pills. She was rushed to the hospital where her stomach was pumped. After coming around, Hill said to Siegel, 'Ben, why don't you sell this crummy joint before you fall apart.' They were both falling apart, but instead of removing themselves from the scene and appointing a starchy suit to oversee the Flamingo, the Nevada desert's Bonnie and Clyde continued to wreak havoc while wondering why guests were always fleeing.

One day, Siegel walked into his suite where Hill was reading *Time* magazine. When he asked her why she was reading that 'crummy magazine', Hill spat back that she would read whatever she wanted. Siegel slapped the magazine out of her hands. When Hill bent over to pick it up, he kicked her. Hill took off her shoe and dug the spiked heel into Siegel's forehead, then ran out the door and returned home to Beverly Hills, where she lifted herself out of depression by purchasing a ten-thousand-dollar bracelet and a new Cadillac convertible. Her lavish spending, coupled with her sporadic appearances in Las Vegas, led to rumors that she and Siegel were stealing from the casino and its investors. Even though Hill's extravagant lifestyle was bankrolled by Joe Epstein, not Siegel, Siegel's enemies, like Little Moe Sedway and Hank Greenspun, knew that the mere optics of their stormy relationship, along with Hill's shopping sprees, offered plenty of fodder for gossip which they spread like wildfire.

In the second week of June, Siegel demanded that the bookmakers who used his Trans-American wire appear at the Flamingo for a business conference he was obviously unfit to chair. When the bookies arrived at the hotel, Siegel told them he was doubling their monthly service fee. The bookies erupted in a collective protest, shouting their grievances across the conference table; they knew Siegel was squeezing them to cover his staggering losses at the Flamingo. Siegel knew they were right but he would not budge.

On 13 June, the bookies left the Flamingo, grumbling. Although we have no record of what they did next, we need only imagine ourselves as one of them. They must have gotten on the horn, filing complaints with Jack Dragna, who sublet the wire service to Siegel, and Rocco Fischetti, who controlled the wire from its Chicago headquarters. Until now, Dragna had been looking after a neighbor's dog and had been very careful not to tug at the leash. Dragna ignored rumors that the dog stole a few bones and humped a few bitches, but once the wire was threatened, he had no choice but to convince the dog's owner – originally Lucky Luciano, now Frank Costello – that the dog was dangerous and needed to be put down.

Three years earlier, in June 1944, Dragna and Fischetti had sat with Costello to discuss Siegel's recurring disciplinary problems. Costello went to bat for Siegel and put their beef to rest. But a lot had changed since then. After Vito Genovese's return from Italy, Costello found himself hanging on to power by the hair on his ass. If Costello again stood up to Dragna and Fischetti, by refusing to sell out Siegel and sign off on the contract they were asking for, they could hold it against him and pose a threat to his power. Here's how: Costello and his partner, Frank Erickson, were New York's premier bookmakers with hundreds, if not thousands, of bookies under them. It would not be hard for Fischetti to disrupt their wire service and derail Costello's massive business, literally overnight. This could result in a bookie mutiny, similar to the one underway in Las Vegas. Genovese would no doubt capitalize on their discontent and use it to make a move inside the borgata. Moreover, Chicago had a seat on the Commission – which had grown to also include bosses from Detroit, Philadelphia, Tampa and New Orleans. In order to displace Costello, Genovese would need Commission approval; if Fischetti was unhappy with Costello for any reason, he could shift his support to Genovese, who would, no doubt, return the favor by handing over Siegel. Given the above, Costello's hands were tied.

As we move on to the sit-down where Siegel's fate was ultimately decided, we must first dispel the error that so many books, movies and documentaries have made in misattributing Siegel's death to his and Hill's thieving from the Flamingo. To start with, Siegel was a degenerate gambler who, according to Hill, 'couldn't keep cab fare in his own pocket'. He certainly wasn't stashing millions in Switzerland, as some have contended. There is more, and it has to do with the Chicago mafia's prized bookie, Joe Epstein, who ran a multimillion-dollar layoff parlor for smaller bookies across the country. Everyone knew how much Epstein loved Hill. If, at a sit-down with Costello, Fischetti accused Siegel and Hill of stealing, Costello would have spotted an opening to save Siegel's life by simply saying, 'Fine, let's dispose of them both!' Costello's unspoken message to Fischetti would have been as follows: go explain to your top earner why his little *bubbeleh* has to die, go piss off your most valuable asset and cross your fingers that he does not hold a grudge, sit on his hands or kill himself. Fischetti would have been checkmated, and forced to withdraw his beef against Siegel. Such are the clever ways that sit-downs are brought to a draw without bloodshed. Since Fischetti would have anticipated this defense from Costello, he would have undoubtedly confined his beef to Siegel's extortion of the wire's bookmakers while almost certainly mentioning Siegel's erratic behavior – Siegel alone – that was threatening everyone's investment in the Flamingo, including that of Costello.

As the final sands of Siegel's life were slipping through the hourglass, Hill was sent on a European vacation by none other than Epstein, who must have been tipped off by Fischetti and told to get his princess out of Dodge. Some suspect that Hill also knew of the fate that awaited Siegel but I am certain Epstein would have hidden it from her, if only to protect her. Besides, Hill was too much of an emotional rollercoaster for anyone to entrust with foreknowledge of a murder; she was up and down on pills and capable of warning Siegel.

To put one more fallacy to rest that also falls apart under scrutiny, Lucky Luciano later claimed that rainy weather on the Flamingo's opening night moved Meyer Lansky to pull him aside in Cuba and tell him, 'Charlie, with that kind of weather, only a miracle can save the Flamingo.' Are we to believe that Lansky, the mafia's Albert Einstein, was not intelligent enough to know that weather changes like . . . the weather? And yet, on opening night, as if rain clouds are fixed in the sky for eternity, Siegel was supposedly sentenced to death by his childhood friend. Luciano's assertion is ridiculous. Luciano did, however, admit that the job was assigned to Fischetti and Dragna, which was true, but claimed to have ordered the contract which was more so *permitted* by Costello as opposed to *ordered*. Why did Luciano lie? By the time Siegel was sentenced to death, Luciano was weak (and Costello was vulnerable), and it is better to claim credit for a hit on one of your own men than admit you had no power to stop it.

Before Costello told Fischetti and Dragna, 'Do what you have to do', Lansky seems to have been given a final opportunity to talk some sense into Siegel. In mid-June, Lansky arrived at the Flamingo. He did not register a room in his own name, and remained inside his suite for most of his stay, with the exception of trips to Siegel's suite where the two were overheard arguing loudly. Lansky was most likely telling Siegel to stop bullying the bookies and to allow someone else to run the hotel in his stead. Siegel did not accept Lansky's advice and was seen by witnesses walking around more agitated than usual. After Lansky left town, Siegel flew to California, where he stayed at Hill's Beverly Hills mansion at 810 Linden Drive.

On 16 June, Hill boarded a flight for Paris after a brief stop in Chicago to pick up spending cash from Epstein and maybe give him a spin on her carousel. By the 20th, Hill was six thousand miles away from Siegel, who enjoyed a fish dinner at a Santa Monica restaurant with Allen Smiley, Chick Hill and Jerri Mason, a lady friend of Chick's. At dinner, Siegel was relaxed, showing no signs of that unease so visible at the Flamingo only days before. While conversing, he expressed no fears or concerns for his life. Before leaving the restaurant, an employee gave Siegel a newspaper to take home. Siegel was not in the news, nor was he directed to read any particular article; it was just a friendly gesture. The dinner party retired to Hill's mansion, magnificently decorated with a grand piano, large oil paintings, antique torchieres and bronze statues, the usual fixtures of a cultured woman though a bit pretentious for an Alabamian brawler who recently hospitalized a hat-check girl and twisted her spiked heel into her lover's forehead.

When Siegel entered the house, he smelled carnations. He asked Chick if he smelled them, too, but Chick did not. After searching the house for a bouquet, Chick asked Jerri Mason if she smelled carnations. When Jerri said she did not, Chick recalled the old lore that people sometimes smell flowers before they die. Jerri dismissed it as superstition since neither of them had ever known anyone who whiffed a petal before passing. As Chick and Jerri readied for bed upstairs, Siegel and Smiley sat on the couch downstairs. Siegel was only a few feet inside the living-room window with the *Los Angeles Times* spread out across his lap and just enough lamp-light in the room to read it. Between his underworld enemies and the prying eyes of lawmen, it is hard to believe that Siegel did not draw the curtains when darkness fell.

Just after 10:30 p.m., a car pulled to the curb in front of the house next door. A man got out and crept up the neighbor's driveway. He rested a .30-30 carbine on a lattice fence, took aim and pulled the trigger. The first shot blasted through Hill's living-room window, breaking the bridge of Siegel's nose and blowing one of his baby blue eyes into the dining room, fifteen feet away. Smiley dove off the couch and crawled into the large fireplace for cover. The assassin squeezed off eight more rounds, splattering pieces of Siegel's face against the living-room walls. With Siegel's blood and brains all over the newspaper, it can be said that the *Los Angeles Times* got the story first.

Siegel dead in Virginia Hill's home.

Chick Hill, who thought he heard firecrackers, ran downstairs to find Siegel a bloody mess. Smiley, still hiding inside the fireplace, told Chick to kill the lights. Chick did, then told Jerri to call the cops while he ran off to open his sister's safe and hide her jewelry elsewhere. (Any notion that Virginia Hill had even the slightest inkling of what awaited Siegel should be dashed at this point; she'd never have left her brother in the firing line, and would have hidden her gold and diamonds beforetime.)

Within twenty minutes of the murder, while Hill's couch cushions were still soaking up Siegel's blood, Little Moe Sedway, Gus Greenbaum and Maurice 'Moe' Rosen sauntered into the Flamingo and informed the staff that Siegel was dead and they were now in charge. The men showed no sign of the shock that froze the faces of the staff as they digested the tragic news.

A newspaper photograph of the 41-year-old Siegel leaning back on the couch with an eye shot out made its way around the world. He looked like one of my uncles when they'd doze off between meals at family gatherings, except that my uncles were covered not in blood, but spaghetti sauce. Captain William White and Lieutenant P.R.

Smith were the first ranking officers on the scene. Cops who scoured the area found nine shell casings in the driveway next door and questioned neighbors who all said they saw nothing. Journalists speculated about events surrounding Siegel's death, printing outlandish stories, one being that Virginia Hill, who had gone off to Europe, went there to beg or blow Luciano so he would spare her lover. Another story said that Siegel abandoned the sinking Flamingo to search for Hill in California, like the smitten Antony who deserted the battle of Actium to pursue Cleopatra. Yet another story said that gunmen stalked Hill in Europe and were supposed to knock her off at the same time as Siegel, but missed.

Upon hearing the news of Siegel's death, Hill contacted her brother Chick, asking him about her jewels; she was relieved to learn that he had thrown them down the laundry chute. Once Hill knew her treasure was safe, the loss of lesser things, like Siegel, began to rise in importance. Hill would have certainly figured out that Epstein sent her to Paris to be out of harm's way, so she called Epstein repeatedly but was told he was unavailable. Epstein was too smart to take her calls, knowing the line could be tapped. A veiled conversation of riddles was impossible with the plain-spoken Hill. She then called Joe Adonis who also avoided her calls, likely for the same reason. Adonis had been having a grand ole time listening to reports about Siegel's self-destruction, and had pestered Costello to put an end to it. (Recall that Hill dumped Adonis's tight ass for the big spender.) Sad, anxious and alone, Hill swallowed a bottle of sleeping pills; her life was saved by a French physician.

The hit on Ben Siegel was a tactical masterpiece on the part of Jack Dragna and Rocco Fischetti, who first rendered Frank Costello helpless, then allowed Meyer Lansky a final plea which they knew, based on Siegel's stubbornness, would never work. Joe Epstein quietly removed Virginia Hill from the scene by offering the spendthrift a shopping spree in Paris. And Little Moe Sedway was on standby, ready to take over the Flamingo within minutes of Siegel's death. As Siegel was zipped into a body bag, Dragna had the wire to himself, and reclaimed his home turf from the swashbuckling media magnet. No more Bugsy mugging it up for the cameras in Hollywood and riding around Las Vegas like the Electric Horseman.

Ben Siegel was buried in a five-thousand-dollar silver and bronze casket lined with silk. Sadly, he had alienated a lot of friends toward the end of his life and the turnout was slightly better than that of a pauper's funeral. As an example of how Americans react to acts of violence, the morning after Siegel was killed, Virginia Hill's mansion was incorporated into a star-studded tour of Hollywood homes. Tour guides pointed out where 'Bugsy Siegel' was whacked. He was finally among the stars – and the mob was in complete control of the city he had, in a sense, founded.

As the mafia continued to strengthen its hold on the American economy throughout the second half of the 1940s, gambling and loansharking would still form the backbone of its wealth, while the money derived from such, along with threats, bribery and murder, was the war machine that allowed it to expand into every nook and crevice of American industry. Most mobsters remained in the shadows, using front men to run their companies or protect their interests, while a few, like Frank Costello, wanted to use his vast wealth to become part of American high society, having failed to learn one of the key takeaways from Siegel's death and Luciano's demise – that exposure, for any mobster, is the prelude to problems.

Part Five

CHALLENGES FROM WITHIN AND WITHOUT

Chapter 30
The Mob's Television Debut

Frank Costello and his wife, Lauretta, known as 'Bobbie', mingled with Manhattan's Upper East Side crowd and spent weekends on Sands Point, Long Island, where they had a home near the Hearst, Harriman and Guggenheim estates. When visiting the West Coast, Costello golfed with Jack Warner of Warner Brothers Studios, or George Wood, vice president of William Morris talent agency. Unlike Ben Siegel, who wooed the wives of Hollywood moguls while engendering the hatred of their husbands, Costello charmed the husbands and had no interest in their wives. Like a man in complete control of an identity crisis, Costello masterfully balanced his East Harlem ghetto upbringing with his Upper East Side lifestyle. He lost his balance, however, when he gave in to the idea of being psychoanalyzed, the latest trend among his more fashionable friends.

In 1947, Costello leaned back on the Freudian couch of a well-known Park Avenue psychiatrist, Dr Richard Hoffmann. Costello regularly visited Hoffmann until 1949 when a newspaper reported that Costello was seen in the office of a shrink. When Dr Hoffmann was confronted by journalists, he told them he had simply advised Costello to 'mingle with a better class of people'. Upon hearing Hoffmann's remark, Costello indignantly replied that he had 'introduced Hoffmann to a better class of people than Hoffmann had introduced him to'. Regardless of who could boast of classier friends, the damage was done and the mob was hysterically laughing at Costello while questioning his mental fitness. But the exposé did nothing to diminish Costello's stature in polite society, and as long as his political allies did not abandon him, Costello was still valuable to the mob. But things got worse.

The same year Costello was outed as Hoffmann's patient, he made the list of the Salvation Army's biggest donors and was asked to vice-chair a fundraiser. As a mafia boss, Costello should have declined the honor, but his continuing desire for social recognition deluded him into accepting. His next mistake was to hold the event at the

Copacabana, a nightclub he was suspected of secretly co-owning. His third mistake was to comingle his two different worlds by inviting over a hundred businessmen, politicians, justices of the Supreme Court – and mobsters. Two detectives, posing as guests, snuck into the event and were surprised to see this variety of characters in one room, and even more surprised to see Costello fawning over Vito Genovese, who was seated at the head of a table with Costello at his side. Mobsters saw this, too, and wondered if Costello thought he could avoid kissing Genovese's ring by kissing his ass.

When reporters got wind of Costello's event, they tried to ignite a scandal. Politicians and judges who attended the event feigned ignorance of Costello's underworld reputation, while the Salvation Army's executive board issued a public apology and pledged to return the $10,000 Costello had raised. Only one board member, a woman who had bigger balls than all the men, courageously defended Costello, saying, 'We hope we'll meet a Frank Costello on every corner. We need the money, and that is the prime object, not where it comes from.' Costello resigned his position as vice chairman but the press would not let up. By October 1949, *Time* magazine put Costello's face on the cover; in November, *Newsweek* put one of his slot machines on its cover. As the press began calling him the 'prime minister of the underworld', Genovese began viewing him as the prime rib of the underworld, a cooked man he was about to sink his teeth into. Genovese was sharpening his steak knife when his plans were put on hold by an ambitious junior senator from Tennessee.

In 1950, Senator Estes Kefauver attended two conferences in Washington, DC. The first was the American Conference of Mayors, where serious concerns over the growing problems of organized crime were discussed. The second was the Conference of United States Attorneys, where federal prosecutors downplayed the very same concerns, denying the existence of a national syndicate that required attention. Senator Kefauver reconciled these two contrasting views by concluding that federal prosecutors, who worked for the US Department of Justice, were parroting FBI director J. Edgar Hoover's well-known stance on the subject. Even before the lynchings in New Orleans, which Mayor Shakspeare and the national press billed as a blow to the 'mafia', there was overwhelming evidence of the mob's existence. Was Lucky Luciano a persecuted Italian businessman? And why would Naval Intelligence ask him to secure the waterfront if he wasn't a mob boss? Yet Hoover, whose agents were able to uncover 2,700 members of the Communist Party in America, resulting in over five hundred arrests, could not identify a single member of the mafia.

While Hoover's G-men were grabbing headlines by unloading Tommy guns into notorious bank robbers, and poking under rocks in search of microfilm in the garden of Whittaker Chambers, Frank Costello was turning his sitting room into the city's foremost Democratic club while Meyer Lansky was taking over a small nation off the coast of Florida. Did Hoover not see any of this? To explain why Hoover ignored the mafia, some historians suspect that the mob had photographs of him dressed in drag, while others believe they had compromising photos of him with his alleged boyfriend and second-in-command, Clyde Tolson, and had threatened to release them to the press if Hoover did not leave them alone. To this day, no evidence to support these suspicions has ever surfaced, just gossip from a variety of sources. Others have accused Hoover of being on the take and getting horse-racing tips from Costello, who once commented to attorney William Hundley, 'Hoover will never know how many races I had to fix for those lousy ten-dollar bets.' According to Herman Klurfeld, who ghostwrote columns for Walter Winchell, Winchell regularly relayed horse-racing tips from Costello to Hoover. Hoover did indeed frequent the finest racetracks across the country and made a show of betting at the two-dollar window to deflect criticism that he was a high-roller. 'Hoover did make a few bets at the two-dollar window,' wrote assistant FBI director William Sullivan, in a revealing memoir, 'but that was just for show. He had agents assigned to accompany him to the track place his real bets at the hundred-dollar window.'

Although I do not doubt that Costello fixed races for Hoover, it is hard to imagine the patriotic director selling out his country for a hundred-dollar bet. Hoover's reasons to deny the existence of the mafia seem to be more complex than horse racing and drag queening. Let us start with Hoover's general outlook. Throughout his career, he was primarily concerned with 'groups advocating the overthrow or replacement of the government of the United States, by illegal methods', as he wrote in a memo to field agents in 1936. Unlike subversive groups that Hoover targeted, the mafia posed no threat to American institutions. To survive and prosper, the mafia needs a capitalist system along with a democratically elected and stable, yet greedy and incompetent, government; in all of this, they have never been disappointed in the

United States. Hoover knew that the mafia worked the system, never against it, unlike a few thousand Marxists or even a dozen pacifists chanting anti-war slogans, all of whom concerned Hoover much more than mobsters who never caused a single political stir, and even helped protect the home front during the Second World War. In fact, it could be argued that the mob was beneficial to national security by providing a pressure valve for public tension: alcohol when the country was dry, gambling when it was illegal, and cash loans to small businesses when banks clamped down after the stock market crash. Even Lucky Luciano's chain of bordellos was the perfect ointment for the hard-up.

Another reason Hoover may have ignored the mob was his obsession with statistics. The FBI had a high conviction rate that Hoover liked to flaunt before the Congressional Budget Committee; his statistics would have plummeted once his agents started arresting mobsters who were known to bribe judges and juries alike, and walk out of courtrooms acquitted. Hoover preferred quick and easy convictions that made national headlines. According to William Sullivan, Hoover 'didn't want to tackle organized crime. He preferred his agents to spend their time on quick, easy cases – he wanted results, predictable results which produced the statistics Hoover thrived on.' Sullivan went on to say that organized crime is 'complicated; the Mafia runs legitimate businesses as front for their illegal operations. Mafioso are rich and can afford the best lawyers, while we have to use government lawyers, some of whom are excellent, some of whom aren't worth a damn. And the Mafia is powerful, so powerful that entire police forces or even a mayor's office can be under Mafia control. That's why Hoover was afraid to let us tackle it. He was afraid that we'd show up poorly.' (Note that Sullivan, by the end of his career, had challenged Hoover over a number of issues and was forced into retirement. He was no fan of Hoover and his memoir makes this point abundantly clear. Sullivan's overall tone toward Hoover, and the damaging revelations included in his book, has convinced this author that had there been a more nefarious reason for Hoover's willful and glaring ignorance of organized crime, Sullivan would have, at the very least, alluded to it.)

In addition to Hoover's concerns, pointed out by Sullivan, in the 1950s an FBI agent's starting annual salary was $5,500, a paltry sum for men like Frank Costello, who carried that around in his back pocket and whose forte was bribing public officials. While mired in organized crime cases, Hoover's agents could become susceptible to bribes that, if exposed, would tarnish the Bureau's lily-white image. Perhaps most importantly, Hoover knew that a relentless pursuit of the mafia would cut a trail straight to Washington, DC. Until now, the furthest Hoover had ventured into the mob's dark underworld was when he snagged Lepke Buchalter. And what happened then? Lepke's web of criminal associates nearly reached President Roosevelt, via Sidney Hillman. And what about Roosevelt's successor, President Harry Truman? Truman was a product of Kansas City's mafia-controlled Pendergast Machine, which was as corrupt as Tammany Hall. Who else in Washington owed the mob a favor? Who else was on their payroll? Hoover did not care to know, and felt it was safer to plug John Dillinger full of holes and fry the Rosenbergs at 8 p.m. just as Americans were settling onto their couches to hear the trusted voice of Edward R. Murrow.

As Senator Kefauver left the Washington conferences in 1950, he was certain Hoover and the feds were either mistaken or covering their eyes. To prove that a national syndicate did indeed exist, Kefauver formed a bi-partisan congressional committee with a mandate to investigate organized crime in cities across the country. The senator later told journalist Jack Anderson that Hoover did his darnedest to stop him from forming the committee, and Kefauver's assistant counsel, Joseph Nellis, said that after the committee was formed, 'we tried to enlist the FBI's help . . . but got none. Hoover was polite to the senators – he had to be, because they controlled his purse strings. But he gave us nothing.'

The committee still had congressional subpoena power, and President Truman signed an executive order allowing Kefauver access to tax records of the accused. Another weapon in the committee's arsenal was the nation's newest medium for influencing public opinion, the television set. Instead of holding hearings in Washington, the senators took to the road, targeting corrupt cities across the country, and the hearings aired on all three major television networks. Nearly everyone in America tuned in; families gathered around televisions in their living rooms, pedestrians stopped to watch televisions on display in storefront windows, 'housewives did their ironing and mending in front of their TV sets', while wealthier women threw 'Kefauver parties'. In a single year, from May 1950 to May 1951, the committee traveled over fifty thousand miles inside the United States (while the self-appointed crime-buster slyly avoided his home state of Tennessee).

Many of the mobsters who were subpoenaed to testify before the committee failed to show, claiming illnesses such as heart attacks, nervous breakdowns, laryngitis and a host of other sudden ailments that became known as *Kefauveritis*. Of those who did show, most invoked their Fifth Amendment right to remain silent, which, until now, had never been used so often. Frustrated with the amendment's overuse – which was tailor-made for *omertà* – one senator told a mobster, 'Why don't you have a little sign painted and hold it up and save your voice?' When corny sarcasm like this gave television viewers a laugh, the senators began to ham it up for the cameras. Mobsters proved just as comical. When Paul 'The Waiter' Ricca was asked about his many aliases, he replied, 'Any place I go I mention any name that comes to mind . . . just a habit.'

When Joseph Fusco was questioned about sending cases of liquor to police chiefs and other public officials for Christmas, he told the senator, 'If you were in Chicago maybe I would send you a case, too.'

'Maybe I would return it to you,' said the senator.

'I don't know,' answered Fusco. 'I have never got any back.'

Ben Siegel's former protégé Mickey Cohen and another hood, Joe Sica, had been dispatched by the mob to work over Russell Brophy, who headed up a competing wire service in Chicago. When the Kefauver Committee asked Cohen about the incident, Cohen freely admitted that he and Sica had assaulted Brophy since the case had been resolved in court. When the committee asked Cohen why the court fined him one hundred dollars while Sica was fined two hundred, Cohen answered, 'I must have hit him less.'

When capo Willie Moretti was asked how he got involved in one particular company, Moretti replied, 'Fortunately God helped me.' Moretti went on to explain that an executive 'went horseback riding, fell off the horse, got kicked in the head . . . and died', which led to Moretti taking his place in the company. If, in fact, a horseshoe, and not a man's shoe, ended the executive's life, then we are still left with Moretti's cuckoo assumption that God had dispatched a horse to help him take over a company. As if this wasn't crazy enough, enter Virginia Hill, who was subpoenaed to testify about the many hoodlums she had once hung around with. Reporters swarmed Hill as she alighted from her taxi in a mink stole. 'Get your fucking cameras out of my face,' she yelled, in true *Hillian* style. She pushed through the press corps while swinging her purse at them. 'Get out of my fucking way!'

When questioned, Hill was evasive, saying, 'I never knew anything about their business . . . why would they tell me?'

A top aide to Kefauver, Ernie Mittler, told of an exchange that occurred between Hill and Senator Charles Tobey during an early-morning closed-door session routinely used to sift through potentially sensitive material that could not be viewed on live television. Behind closed doors, Senator Tobey asked Hill why Joe Epstein kept a river of cash flowing into her purse for decades. Hill replied, 'You really want to know?'

'Yes,' replied Tobey. 'I want to know why.'

'Then I'll tell you why. Because I'm the best cocksucker in town.'

Hill was also the best reality TV star in America and I am amazed, given the ratings during her performance in front of the cameras, it took Hollywood another fifty years to 'invent' reality television. Before leaving in a cab, Hill kicked one reporter in his shin and socked another in the jaw, telling the whole bunch, 'I hope the atom bomb falls on every one of you.'*

For the first time since he had been deported to Italy, Lucky Luciano felt lucky as he was beyond the reach of the Kefauver Committee. But his pal Meyer Lansky was forced to appear on 11 October 1950. Lansky showed up without an attorney, telling the committee, 'I don't think it is necessary.' He answered basic questions about his many relationships with suspected mobsters but invoked the Fifth Amendment whenever he sensed a trap. Upon instructions from the committee, he returned the following day with attorney Moses Polakoff, who got into a heated exchange with Senator Tobey after Tobey asked Polakoff why he had once represented Luciano. 'How did you become counsel for

* After Ben Siegel's death, Hill settled down in Europe with an Austrian ski instructor, Hans Hauser. Sometime after the Kefauver hearings, she broke with Hauser and was left with a fifteen-year-old son in a foreign country, a situation that would tax the wits of a sane woman. Hauser did not support Hill (ski instructors are known for hooking wealthy women, not supporting sponges) and Epstein's gravy train had finally derailed. Hill drank heavily and popped pills while trying to get her old mob boyfriends to send her money. Her badgering them has led to endless speculation that they hunted her down because she knew too much and was threatening to use it against them if they did not comply. There is no evidence to support this theory and Hill had already proven she could be trusted, at the Kefauver hearings. Sadly, Hill was no longer desirable to anyone and that may have contributed to a deepening depression. She survived several suicide attempts until she swallowed a bottle of pills, walked out into the cold, and was found face-down in the snowy Alps of Austria, as tragic an end as Siegel's.

Luciano in Italy, safe from Kefauver.

such a dirty rat as that?' asked Tobey. 'Aren't there some ethics in the legal profession?'

Polakoff, a decorated First World War veteran and former chief of the Southern District of New York's Criminal Division, shot back, 'Minorities and undesirables and persons with bad reputations are more entitled to the protection of the law than are the so-called honorable people. I don't have to apologize to you.'

'I look upon you in amazement,' answered Tobey.

Polakoff told Tobey that he looked upon him with greater amazement before Kefauver interjected and said, 'Mr Lansky is the witness.'

The inquiry into Lansky's gambling empire revealed, among other things, that he controlled a number of casinos in Broward County, Florida. Lansky's start in Broward County began with an introduction to Julian 'Potatoes' Kaufman, who once dominated the Chicago potato market. Kaufman was later drawn to the world of gambling and opened a casino in Florida called The Plantation. Since New York mobsters vacationed in Florida, Vincent 'Jimmy Blue Eyes' Alo, a capo in Luciano's borgata, put a claim on Kaufman then brought in his pal Meyer Lansky, who slowly took over the casino while also opening the Beach Club and the Colonial Inn.*

* Back in January 1930, Meyer Lansky's first wife, Anne, gave birth to a son, Bernard 'Buddy' Lansky, who had cerebral palsy. Anne believed that Meyer's criminal lifestyle had brought a curse down on their house and their ill child was the result of God's anger. Shaken up over his son's illness and his wife's accusation, Lansky drove to Boston and spent a dark week staring down at the Charles River from a hotel window. Suddenly, there was a knock at the door; it was Vincent 'Jimmy Blue Eyes' Alo. Alo, the son of a humble and hard-working Calabrian tailor, did not try to bring Lansky back to New York or offer up some frail human advice; he just wanted to sit with him, an ear in case he felt like talking, a waiter in case he wanted something to eat, a friend in case he needed a sympathetic pat on the back. Lansky would later say of that trying time, 'I lost a wife and gained a friend.'

Lansky bribed Broward County sheriff Walter Clark, who acted as Lansky's personal armored courier service by deputizing the mobsters who drove Lansky's cash from the casinos to the bank every night. Clark was not the only policeman exposed as a willing associate of the mob; sheriffs from across the country were called before the committee to answer questions about their curious behavior. Some were asked to explain how they accumulated wealth and assets worthy of an investment broker as opposed to an underpaid cop with a tin badge. One sheriff claimed to have found an old box stuffed with cash in his attic which sustained his opulent lifestyle for decades. Chicago police captain Bill Drury was suspected of being on the mob's payroll. After being called by the committee, Drury was shot-gunned to death while parking his car in his home garage, all but confirming the committee's suspicions.

When Frank Costello was called, he should have gone into hiding or checked himself into a faraway hospital with *Kefauveritis*. Costello instead consulted with Vito Genovese, who told him to go in front of the committee; this should have been Costello's cue to do the exact opposite. When revolutionary Ireland's Éamon de Valera and Michael Collins were vying for control of the Irish Republican Army, de Valera told Collins it was okay to go to England on a diplomatic mission to negotiate a peace settlement, knowing that however good or bad the outcome, de Valera would disparage the deal and label Collins a traitor to his country. When Collins returned, de Valera did just that and had Collins whacked. Genovese used the same strategy when he advised Costello to go before the committee, but did not go himself; it was a double-cross.

After all the heat that stemmed from his mug adorning popular magazine covers, Costello did not want to appear on television so his attorney, George Wolf, complained to the TV directors, who came up with the idea of only showing Costello's hands on camera. The directors must have been deceitfully convincing since Wolf agreed, even though it is difficult to imagine any single part of the human anatomy with a voice over it not coming across as ghoulish. Wolf talked Costello into it, both men apparently forgetting that Italians talk with their hands. If, for example, you were to focus exclusively on my grandmother's hands while she explained something as trivial as how to make homemade ravioli, you would be hard-pressed to distinguish her hand motions from the isolated hand movements of Benito Mussolini gesticulating from a balcony at a Fascist rally; you might even think that Mussolini is explaining the ravioli recipe and my grandmother is roiling up a crowd.

The final piece of this cheap theatre was Costello's mousy voice – the result of a medical procedure, years earlier, that damaged his vocal cords – which would be broadcast over his hands. This made-for-TV drama took place in March 1951. As the television directors must have expected, Costello's hands did not disappoint. Depending on the question, his hands reacted in kind. Sometimes, Costello's fingers were jittery; at other times they tapped on the table. He would rub his sweaty palms together, roll up paper into tiny balls, point, squeeze, or play with his eyeglasses. 'When he attempted to control his hand movements,' wrote one of Costello's early biographers, 'the fingers would tear at each other.' Viewers across America ate it up as cigarette companies offered Costello advertising money if he would fiddle with a pack on national television.*

Adonis watching Costello's hands on television.

* Charles Addams was a Manhattan cartoonist during Frank Costello's time, known for creating dark characters. One such character was a disembodied hand that lived in a box. It snapped its fingers, used Morse code, wrote, or represented letters of the alphabet. The character first appeared in print in a 1954 book written by Addams titled *Homebodies*, and made its television debut in 1964 when it became known in the popular series *The Addams Family*. Given the number of viewers who watched the hearings, I am surprised no one has ever asked what seems to be an obvious question: did Addams get the idea from Costello?

Whoever Costello may have once been, he now came across as a weak-kneed shell of a man. Although he did not squeal on anyone, Kefauver may have summed up his performance best when saying Costello 'exposed himself as a whiner and something of a crybaby'. Joe Adonis, who watched the hearings on television, is reported to have yelled at the screen, 'What a sucker!' Costello eventually invoked the Fifth Amendment but it was too late; the damage had already been done. He emerged from the hearings with two targets on his back, one placed there by law enforcement, and the other by Genovese. Now that Costello was red-hot, politicians ran away from him, rendering him far less valuable to the mob. Genovese owed Kefauver a thank-you letter, as did Albert Anastasia who took advantage of the distraction caused by the hearings to seize power in his own borgata.

Vincent Mangano had been the don of his own borgata since the creation of New York's five families. Whenever the Mangano household needed an exterminator, Mangano gave the contract to Albert Anastasia who often used Murder, Inc. In the spring of 1951, Mangano expressed concerns to a fellow mob boss about Anastasia's unbridled ambition, but Mangano failed to act fast enough. On 19 April, Mangano vanished without a trace. His brother, Phil, was then found in a Brooklyn marsh, lying face-down with three bullet holes in the back of his head. With both Manganos dead, Anastasia took over the borgata. He was summoned before the Commission where he did not admit to killing the Manganos, but said that Vincent was planning to kill him which was a thinly veiled confession. Frank Costello, who sat on the Commission and needed Anastasia's protection as a defense against Genovese, confirmed that Mangano was looking to clip Anastasia. With Costello's help at the table, the Commission was persuaded to allow Anastasia to carry on as boss, the inference being that he had acted in self-defense. There was, however, a slight miscalculation on the part of Costello. Anastasia's coup proved to be the perfect trial run for Genovese, who was planning the same move against Costello. By persuading the Commission to approve Anastasia's takeover, Costello inadvertently became the instrument of his own demise.

In September 1951, after listening to testimony from over eight hundred witnesses, Senator Kefauver packed up his traveling circus and went home, where his children referred to him as 'that man on television'. He complemented his road show with a book titled *Crime in America*, in which he called men like Frank Costello and Meyer Lansky the 'new aristocrats of the criminal world . . . cleaning their fingernails, polishing up their language, and apeing the manners and sartorial trappings of captains of industry'. Kefauver also pointed out that corrupt politicians had '*sunk to a new low*'.

Kefauver received countless letters and telegrams from around the country, many prodding him to run for president. On 12 March 1951, he made the cover of *Time* magazine, which described him as presidential, and he came close to snagging the Democratic presidential nomination in 1952, earning him a second *Time* magazine cover. Costello, who had also made the cover of *Time*, was not faring so well. Before we see how Genovese issued his loud vote of no confidence to the prime minister of the underworld, let us skip back in time to nineteenth-century Bavaria, where we will find a precise analogy for Genovese's next step in isolating Costello.

Chapter 31
The Waddler and the Whiner

King Ludwig II of Bavaria, known to history as the 'Mad King', exhibited questionable behavior but may not have been all that mad – until, that is, his prime minister, Johan von Lutz, felt threatened by the king and decided to get rid of him. Since Ludwig was a constitutional monarch, Lutz gave the constitution a quick read and learned that the king could be removed if deemed mentally unfit to serve. Lutz began spreading rumors about the king's erratic behavior and spending habits, then visited the royal family which was quickly going bankrupt as Ludwig burned through their fortune. Lutz assured them that once the king was removed from the throne, not only would his constant spending stop but the government would square away the family's debts.

The family signed on and Lutz ordered Dr Bernhard von Gudden to interview the king's servants, many of whom Lutz had bribed. After the interviews, the doctor concluded that there was no need to examine the king. Without being asked a single question, Ludwig was diagnosed with an incurable mental illness and taken into custody. The next day, he was found dead, and is believed to have been murdered. Almost certainly without knowing it, Vito Genovese tore a page from Lutz's playbook when he sought to remove Willie Moretti, which returns us to our story.

As we already know, Willie Moretti was a capo in Lucky Luciano's borgata. He grew up in East Harlem with Frank Costello, who served as the best man at Moretti's wedding. Moretti was, in turn, Costello's right-hand man and his most vocal defender besides Albert Anastasia, which rendered them both – Anastasia and Moretti – obstacles in Genovese's path to power as he sought to replace Costello.

Moretti did not snitch at the Kefauver hearings but some of his exchanges, like God collaborating with a horse on his behalf, sounded screwy. Moretti may have been having some fun while trying to entertain everyone, but just as Lutz used Ludwig's questionable behavior to impugn his sanity, Genovese used Moretti's jesting before the committee to question his mental health. And just as Lutz needed to convince the royal family that Ludwig was better off gone, Genovese needed to convince the Luciano family that Moretti needed to go. Knowing how fond everyone was of Moretti, Genovese positioned his argument as a 'mercy killing', while invoking the larger idea of protecting La Cosa Nostra. 'If tomorrow I go wrong,' Genovese said to his crew, 'I would want to be hit so as not to bring harm to this thing of ours.' Even Costello, who knew exactly what Genovese was up to, could not refute this argument without appearing more concerned about Moretti than he was for the borgata. Costello took a shot at saving Moretti – and himself – by sending him out west for a 'vacation'. While Moretti was away, Genovese continued to push the idea that Moretti was *pazzo*. By the time Moretti returned home, Genovese had sealed his fate.*

On 4 October 1951, John 'Johnny Roberts' Robilotto scheduled a lunch meeting with Moretti to discuss business. They met at an eatery called Joe's Elbow Room on the New Jersey side of the Hudson River, across from Manhattan. Moretti parked his white Cadillac convertible, entered the restaurant, and sat at a table where Johnny Roberts introduced him to three other men; unbeknownst to Moretti, he had just greeted his killers. Waitress Dorothy Novack said hello to the men and heard them joking in Italian as she made her way to the kitchen. After Novack disappeared into the back, one of the men grabbed Moretti's necktie from behind and pulled him against the back of his chair. Another stood up and fired a bullet into Moretti's chest, then three more into his head and face before all four men left the restaurant. When Novack and chef Joe Amento mustered the courage to poke their heads out from the back, they saw Moretti lying on the tiled floor with blood pooling around him.

Although every historian has laid Moretti's death at the feet of Genovese, there may be more to the story. Frank Costello, who left for Hot Springs, Arkansas, after the hit, must have been forced by Genovese's brilliant scheming to sanction the contract on Moretti, since

* Moretti may have been experiencing a slight degree of mental illness caused by neurosyphilis, the same disease that ravaged the brain of Al Capone. But Capone was fishing in his own swimming pool and still permitted to die naturally. Moretti, who may have shown milder symptoms that were open to interpretation, was afforded no such sympathy. Although a couple of spark plugs may have been blown out in Moretti's brain, the fact that Genovese feared him, in and of itself, is a strong argument in favor of Moretti's sanity.

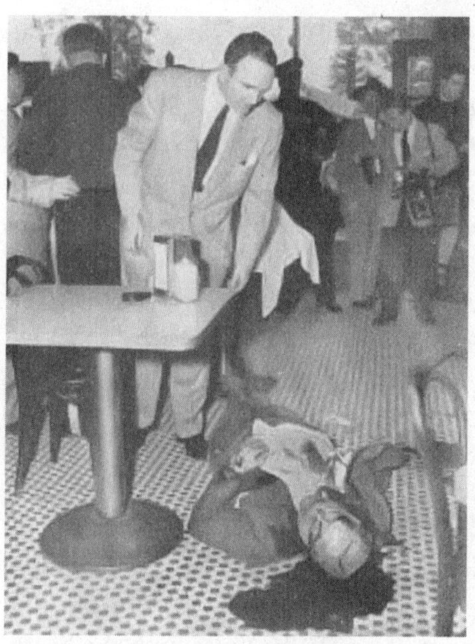

Moretti dead, a victim of power politics.

Costello was still Moretti's official boss. Moreover, Johnny Roberts, who carried out the hit, was part of Anastasia's borgata, and Anastasia would never have sent Roberts for Genovese, only for Costello. Anastasia, who lived in New Jersey, may have been given a chunk of Moretti's Jersey assets in return for his participation. Whatever the case may be, Costello should have moved on Genovese without delay, but he was distracted by legal problems that continued to haunt him ever since his shameful appearance in front of the Kefauver Committee.

Costello had gone nearly four decades without seeing the inside of a prison cell. That incredible run came to a sudden end in August 1952, when he was sentenced to eighteen months in prison for contempt of Congress, after he had finally zipped his mouth shut at the Kefauver hearings. He was handcuffed and sent to Lewisburg Penitentiary in Pennsylvania. (Handcuffs were never so apropos, considering the part his hands played in getting him into this mess.) He was released in 1953, but his problems were not over. In April 1954, Costello was found guilty of tax evasion and sentenced to five years. While in prison, he made a name for himself among the Italian inmate population as a chronic complainer. His attorneys eventually won him bail pending appeal, and he was released. When Genovese heard Costello was a wuss in jail, he began to ask how he had miraculously made bail, the inference being that Costello had talked his way out of the slammer. Costello was ironically spared from being mislabeled a snitch by an appellate court when he lost his appeal and was returned to Atlanta Penitentiary. While Costello was away, Genovese had easily slid into power by simply picking up the reins of a riderless horse. Luciano and Costello did not appoint him boss, the capos did not vote him in, and the Commission did not officially approve him, but Genovese had built up enough strength inside the borgata to destroy any opposition. In the event of a protest, Genovese could rely on tough work crews headed by Mike Miranda, who controlled much of the East Side, 'Trigger Mike' Coppola, who was strong in Harlem, and Anthony 'Tony Bender' Strollo, who controlled Greenwich Village on behalf of Genovese.

Upon Costello's next release from prison, the 65-year-old whiner, who had never shot a spitball at anyone, had no stomach for a civil war. His legal battles, which were far from over, had zapped him of his waning strength. Since he was already a multimillionaire, he decided to step down and let Genovese inherit all the headaches. He sent word to Genovese that he would like to retire and would ask the Commission to authorize a peaceful transition as long as he could take the rackets that personally belonged to him. The last part of this deal was a problem for Genovese; technically, every racket belongs to the borgata. Was Costello trying to leave the banquet with the buffet table? Genovese beefed to the other bosses, arguing that Costello must throw everything into a pot so they could divvy it up. Genovese was not a sharing man but he needed the Commission's approval and was buying it with Costello's money. However, since the other bosses did not want anyone stripping them or their children on their way out the door, and they were already partners with Costello in many of his larger rackets, they were in favor of Costello taking what was his, forcing Genovese to move on to his alternative plan; he told Tony Bender to ice Costello. Bender farmed out the hit to Tommaso 'Tommy Ryan' Eboli, who passed the contract on to his most promising protégé, Vincent 'Chin' Gigante.

On 2 May 1957, Costello relaxed in a Turkish bath located in the Biltmore Hotel on Madison Avenue. After a shower, he cabbed it over to Chandler's restaurant in the theatre district for a meeting with capo Tony Bender, who was with soldier Vincent 'Vinnie Bruno' Mauro, a known heroin trafficker. Costello's edict against drugs would have bothered Bruno, but he held an even deeper grudge against Costello that started at the Gold Key Club on West 56th Street, a place where mobsters mixed with celebrities. One night, while Tony Bender, Vinnie Bruno and Gerardo 'Jerry' Catena were drinking at the club, a celebrity entertainer, Billy Daniels, got into a loud tiff with his wife and smacked the shit out of her in front of everyone. Bruno picked up the singer and flung him out of a second-story window. Daniels was hospitalized but lived. Bruno's pals saw nothing wrong with what he had done, but because Daniels was part African-American and his wife was very white and very blonde, New York's high society accused Bruno of racism. Since Costello and his wife hung out with these same socialites, Costello told Bruno to apologize to Daniels. Bruno refused, pointing out to Costello that Daniels had always brought white women into the club, including his wife, and was always welcome; if Bruno was a racist, he would have thrown Daniels out of a window a dozen times already. Bruno also pointed out that Bumpy Johnson dated plenty of white women, including the milky-white editor of *Vanity Fair*, Helen Lawrenson, and they adored Bumpy. Bruno assured Costello it had nothing to do with race and refused to apologize to a public wife-beater. Costello's virtuous stance may have scored him a few points on 5th Avenue, but the borgata saw him as a weakling, bending to peer pressure. This marked yet another incident that played straight into the hands of Genovese, who easily recruited Bruno into the plot.

Bender and Bruno wrapped up their meeting with Costello. Before parting ways, Bruno accepted Costello's invitation to L'Aiglon, a French restaurant where he and his wife were having dinner that evening with John and Cindy Miller, Phil Kennedy and Generoso Pope Jr.*

During dinner, Bruno telephoned the restaurant and spoke with John Miller, telling him to relay his apologies to everyone for missing dinner; he said he would catch up with them later for cake and coffee. Bruno also failed to show for dessert, and again called to apologize. After Miller told him they were going for a nightcap at Monsignore, Bruno asked Miller to call him when Costello left there. The clueless columnist agreed, unaware he was fielding phone calls for a hit team.

While the dinner party headed over to Monsignore, two black sedans parked on the street in front of Costello's apartment building on Central Park West. One car was in front of a telephone booth,

* Costello's dinner guests offer us another glimpse into his casual mingling of social circles, as seen at his Salvation Army fundraising event. Generoso Pope Jr was the grandson of peasant Italians who traveled to America in steerage. He graduated from Massachusetts Institute of Technology while still in his teens and worked for the CIA's Psychological Warfare Unit. He purchased what would become the *National Enquirer* in 1952 with the help of a loan from Costello, who became godfather to his son. John Miller was a columnist for the *Enquirer*, and Phil Kennedy owned a modeling agency.

the other across the street. At 10:40 p.m., Costello said goodnight to everyone, telling them he had to run home to take a phone call from his Washington-based attorney, Edward Bennett Williams (who would one day own the National Football League's Washington Redskins, now the Washington Commanders). The rest stayed behind except for Phil Kennedy, who left with Costello, figuring they would share a taxi for part of their way home. After Costello and Kennedy left Monsignore, Miller dialed Bruno to tell him. Bruno thanked Miller for the update then called the public phone booth near Costello's apartment building. The driver of the car nearest the phone picked up the call from Bruno. When he hung up the phone, he flashed his lights at the other car, signaling Costello's imminent arrival.

While Costello and Kennedy's cab maneuvered through Manhattan's light traffic, Vincent 'Chin' Gigante paced up and down the block, waiting for Costello to arrive. When the cab rolled up in front of Costello's apartment building, Costello said goodnight to Kennedy, climbed out of the cab and walked toward the glass entrance. It was 10:55 p.m. when Gigante entered the lobby, just before Costello. As Costello walked in, Gigante raised a .32 caliber revolver to Costello's face and said, 'This is for you, Frank!' He fired a single shot then brushed past the doorman, Norval Keith, and got into a getaway car which sped away. Gigante's melodramatic line, which served no purpose unless he was on a movie set with Martin Scorsese, allowed Costello a split second to flinch away from the gun barrel. The bullet entered behind Costello's right ear, cut a path beneath his skin, and exited at the back of his neck before hitting a marble wall and bouncing across the floor.

Phil Kennedy heard the gunshot and pushed open the passenger door of the cab, which was stopped at a traffic light. As he raced back to Costello's building, he saw the getaway car speed through a red light. Kennedy entered the lobby, where he found Costello sitting on a bench, pressing a bloody handkerchief against the hole in his head; his double-breasted brown suit was speckled with blood. Costello was calm, like an elderly man taking a time-out after being touched by a dizzy spell. He told Kennedy he was okay and expressed no fear or concern for his life. His decade-long whining streak had finally come to an end; it took a bullet to knock a little courage into him. He asked Kennedy to call his wife and tell her he was fine. Kennedy first hailed a cab and accompanied Costello to Roosevelt Hospital, only a few

Costello injured but alive.

minutes away. After gleaning bits of the conversation inside the car, the cabbie dropped them off and sped away without asking for his fare.

Chin Gigante botched the hit. Had he kept his mouth shut, Costello would have almost certainly been dead. Why, moreover, didn't Gigante unload his gun? Who fires a single shot besides a duelist or a colonial soldier with a musket? Genovese must have been asking this same question as he braced himself for possible legal repercussions, the threat of a civil war, or a death sentence from the Commission. Even if Costello was inclined to forgive Genovese for the attempted hit, Genovese could not predict the reaction of Costello's many loyalists and therefore had no choice but to prepare for war. He told Tony Bender to mobilize the troops as he barricaded himself inside his New Jersey mansion with armed guards surveilling the perimeter. Genovese then carried out a test of loyalty by summoning all the capos to see who would or would not show. The attendance record was perfect save for Anthony 'Little Augie Pisano' Carfano. Carfano's absence would eventually cost him his life, but, for the moment, Genovese had his own life to worry about. He sent word to the Commission that the majority of capos were behind him and laid out a case for his actions, charging Costello with anything that might stick, beginning with greediness which was subjective depending on who you talked to. Genovese, moreover, said that Costello had neglected his crew (meaning Genovese's crew), never mentioning that many in his crew were heroin traffickers, a business Costello wanted to stay away from. Genovese also charged Costello with snitching to get out of jail which was untrue, and attempting to kill Genovese first, which may have been true; Costello would have been totally out to lunch if he did not, at least, consider it. Genovese exercised his usurped authority by breaking Costello down to a soldier and putting him on the shelf, which meant he was off limits to anyone in the borgata; sympathizers would be considered enemies of the new regime and treated as such.

Chin Gigante went into hiding as sixty detectives pounded the pavement looking for a man 'between thirty and thirty-five years old, six feet tall, heavy thighs, potbelly, wears a size 50 suit, and waddles while he walks'. Journalists referred to Costello's shooter as 'The Waddler' and 'The Fat Man'. Since Chin's bungled hit has led journalists and historians to mistakenly conclude that this was his first rodeo, I will presently set the record straight. As it is not enough to simply tell you that I was close with Chin's family and visited his house for many years, even sleeping there on weekends, and that I know from first-hand sources that this was not his first contract, let us look at it in terms of mafia logic. An amateur would *never* have been sent to whack a boss, nor would anyone entrust such a big hit to a lone gunman – unless Chin had proven himself capable in the past, which he had. Chin's criminal record began at age sixteen, and he had been arrested seven times before the age of twenty-five; although none of the charges were for murder, he was already known for work. The reason he was trusted to get the job done alone was because he was so good at it. He was also cocky, a detriment that balloons with success, and he probably blew the hit thinking he could get fancy and deliver a cinematic line.

Chin was now in hot water since Genovese was not the forgiving type as can be seen by the corpses of Gerardo Vernotico, Ferdinand Boccia, Peter LaTempa, Willie Moretti and many more; let us include the vent in Costello's head as the most recent example of his thoughts on amnesty. Because of Chin's error, instead of mopping up a little mess, Genovese was now in open conflict with Costello, who had deep pockets and could dispatch hitmen not only from New York, but from New Orleans, Chicago, California, Las Vegas or any other place where his far-flung business partners would rather keep things as they were. Chin hid out in an upstate cabin while Genovese, Tommy Ryan, Jerry Catena and Tony Bender tried to fix things on the street.

After being treated for a superficial head wound, detectives questioned Costello, asking him who might have wanted him dead. 'I haven't an enemy in the world,' said Costello, echoing his mentor, Arnold Rothstein, when the latter had been shot decades earlier. While Costello's head was being bandaged, a detective illegally searched his coat pockets and found $3,200 in cash along with a curious slip of paper that read:

> Gross casino wins as of 4/26/57, $651,284
> Casino wins less markers, $435,695
> Slot wins $62,844
> Markers $153,745
> Mike $150 per week
> Jake $100 per week
> L. – $30,000; H. – $9,000

Hoping to stir up some talk on the street, detectives made the paper public. Besides the possibility of Mike and Jake demanding a raise after seeing the larger figures, Costello had bigger problems. Aaron Kohn, head of the New Orleans Crime Commission, had been watching Costello and Dandy Phil Kastel in relation to their illegal gambling activity in New Orleans, and knew they also had something to do with the Tropicana Hotel and Casino in Las Vegas. When Kohn saw the figures in the newspaper, he matched them to the monthly earnings at the Tropicana, then called the Manhattan district attorney, giving Costello another problem that he needed like another hole in his head. Costello was subpoenaed to a grand jury. This time, he took the Fifth from the get-go and refused to elaborate on the paper in his pocket. His attorney pleaded with him to talk and avoid a contempt charge, but Costello kept his mouth shut. He was sentenced to Rikers Island for a month and served fifteen days.

When the paper came to light, Genovese put up a stink, telling everyone that Costello should not have been walking around with incriminating evidence in his coat pocket. Costello's response was, if he had not been shot by Genovese's hitman, no one would have seen it. Between the bullet, the publicity, the note, the subpoena and the quick stint in Rikers, Costello was exhausted. He arranged to meet with Genovese at the home of Abner 'Longie' Zwillman, Willie Moretti's old partner in crime and still a close friend of Costello, which rendered his house a safe space (while making Zwillman an instant enemy of Genovese). Costello made it clear to Genovese that he would not seek revenge for the attempted hit and only wished to walk away from The Life with what he had initially asked for. This time, Genovese agreed. After five decades of faithful service to the mob, Costello got his full retirement package at the cheap cost of one night in the hospital, a splitting headache and a discarded handkerchief. Considering how these things usually turn out, he did pretty well. As did Chin Gigante, who emerged from hiding with a warrant for his arrest but a guarantee that Costello would throw the case in court. He self-surrendered accompanied by his attorney, Maurice Edelbaum.

For the upcoming trial, Chin's biggest problem would be doorman Norval Keith, who had identified Chin from a photo spread and would serve as a witness for the prosecution. When Chin appeared in court fifty pounds lighter than when he had shot Costello, journalists speculated that he had gone on a crash diet while in hiding so he would look thinner in court and avoid being identified by Keith. This stupidity has been repeated by historians for sixty years. The truth is that Chin whittled down from nerves as he awaited news of his fate. Blowing a hit is punishable by death. And if Costello or the Commission demanded justice in the form of blood, Chin could have been killed by Genovese as a sacrificial offering to put the ordeal to rest. Every time a car pulled up outside his cabin hideaway, Chin did not know if it was someone to greet him or kill him.

A more recent biographer added a new twist to this erroneous weight loss theory. Instead of repeating the old fallacy that Chin had *lost weight after* the shooting to avoid being identified at trial, he said that Chin intentionally *gained weight before* the ambush so no one would recognize him at the scene. These writers have no idea what they are talking about. You go on a heist or a hit the way you look, period! No one ever thinks they are going to get caught. At most, you hide your face with a bandana or a ski mask. To think that Chin, who did not even bother to cover or disguise his face at all, spent the entire month *after* the shooting on WeightWatchers while hooked up to a JCPenney Fat Jiggling Machine, or sat at a kitchen table *before* the shooting shoveling pounds of pasta into his trap, is so absurd that I cannot even believe I am addressing it.

At trial, Chin's attorney, Maurice Edelbaum, asked Costello if he knew who shot him. Costello said that he did not. Phil Kennedy was also asked if he saw Chin and said that he didn't, either, which was the truth. When doorman Norval Keith was questioned by Edelbaum, Keith admitted to having poor eyesight but insisted that Chin was the shooter, exhibiting even poorer judgment. In his trial summation, Edelbaum painted Keith as a drunk who was as blind as a bat. The jury was out just over six hours before returning a verdict of not guilty. Chin's support group of about forty friends and relatives burst into a 'wild applause' as his mother, who wore her fingers out praying the rosary throughout the trial, yelled, 'It was the beads!' His father wept.

The Commission approved Genovese's takeover with a majority vote, the exception being Albert Anastasia who held out despite Costello's request to accept it. (Recall that Anastasia had declared at the 1946 Havana conference that he would never allow anyone to displace Luciano and Costello; he was bound by his own words.) Genovese took Anastasia's disapproval as a threat; would Anastasia make a move on Genovese and attempt to reinstall Costello? With this possibility in mind, Genovese began to call into question Anastasia's faculties, as he had once done with Willie Moretti. Like an archivist poring over the records of Anastasia's reign, Genovese looked for an error in judgment he could magnify. Short of that, he would make one up.

In March 1952, about a year into Anastasia's rule, he was watching television in his New Jersey mansion when a newsflash about the notorious bank robber Willie Sutton aired. Sutton had escaped from prison and was traveling on a Brooklyn subway when a 23-year-old clothing salesman and wannabe sleuth, Arnold Schuster, spotted him. Schuster followed the fugitive up from the subway and through the streets. When Sutton entered a garage, Schuster ran off and alerted police officers Donald Shea and Joseph McClellan who, in turn, told Detective Louis Weiner, who arrested Sutton and returned him to prison. The media billed Schuster as a hero. Schuster proudly accepted news interviews, one of which was supposedly seen by Anastasia who was reported to have slammed his fist on the arm of his chair while shouting at the television, 'I hate squealers! Hit him!'

Since this image of Anastasia's outburst has come down to us through Joe Valachi, a soldier in Genovese's borgata, we must wonder if he was fed the story by Genovese, who was floating rumors about Anastasia. No one is said to have witnessed the episode and there is no evidence that Anastasia personally knew Sutton, but Schuster was, in fact, murdered. It was very odd for Anastasia to risk his soldiers and avenge a criminal he was unacquainted with, regardless of how angry he was over a news segment. It so happens that one of Anastasia's soldiers, Freddie 'Angel of Death' Tenuto, had served time with Sutton and even escaped from a county jail with him back in 1947. It is possible that Tenuto either asked Anastasia for permission to whack

Schuster as a favor to his buddy, or did it on his own. When the gun Tenuto had used to shoot out both of Schuster's eyes – a penalty for spotting Sutton – was traced back to Tenuto, Tenuto was killed by Anastasia, either for his carelessness if Anastasia okayed the hit, or for his insubordination if he did not.

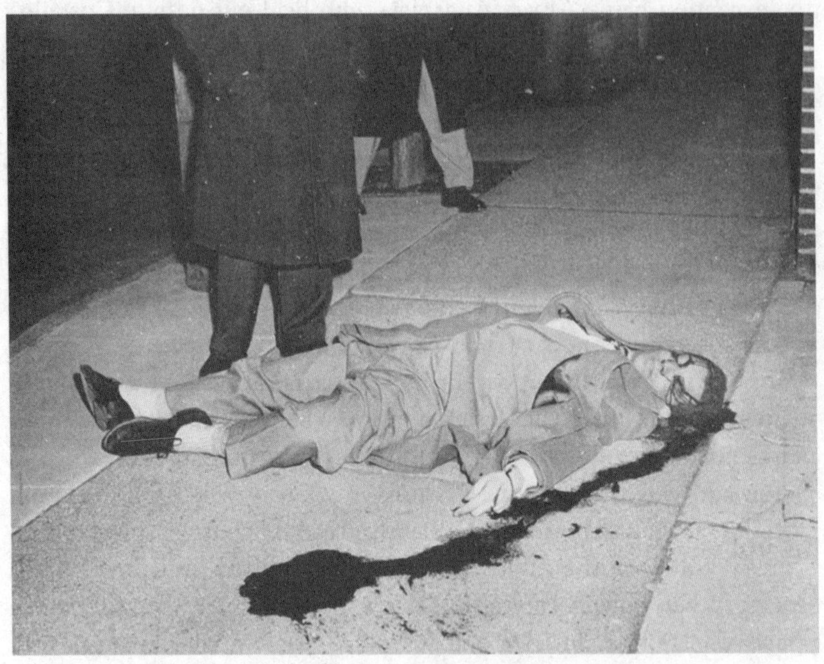

Arnold Schuster dead with both eyes shot out.

To get to the truth, we must first deal with Genovese's portrayal of Anastasia as a hothead who could not control himself; one mobster, who knew Anastasia intimately, said 'he was anything but that'. Next, we are confronted with a time lapse. Schuster was murdered in March 1952; it was not until May 1957, right after Frank Costello was shot, that rumors of Anastasia's recklessness began to circulate. Why didn't anyone care about Anastasia's armchair fit and the death of citizen Schuster for five years? Because Genovese did not need to kill Anastasia until now. Since the image of Anastasia screaming at a television set has been too dramatic for historians to discard, they have seared it into mafia history, never questioning the source of the story which has Genovese's fingerprints all over it.

Aside from painting Anastasia as a lunatic fit for a straitjacket,

Genovese, needing powerful allies, reminded Tommy Lucchese of Anastasia's past loyalty to Lepke Buchalter. By hiding Lepke, Anastasia had extended the heat on the New York mafia. Anastasia had also defended Lepke at a sit-down and warned Lepke against accepting the shady deal the mob had cooked up with J. Edgar Hoover. In light of Lucchese's prior differences with Anastasia, he was fully behind Genovese. With Lucchese's help, Genovese recruited Joe Profaci, who had his own borgata since the creation of the five families. In 1921, Profaci had traveled to the United States with his dear friend Vincent Mangano, who Anastasia had murdered, contributing to Profaci's willingness to join the plot, if only to avenge his *paisan*. Profaci also had a stronghold in Red Hook, Brooklyn, where Anastasia controlled much of the waterfront. Genovese and Lucchese told Profaci that once Anastasia was gone, his men could move into territory that was currently in dispute. Profaci would even supply the hit team, all of whom happened to be from Red Hook, and would benefit from the changes to the area. To seal Anastasia's fate, Genovese exploited a bone of contention brewing in Cuba where we will return to in the next chapter.

Chapter 32
It Is Written

After Meyer Lansky's Havana conference in late 1946, the Kefauver hearings interrupted the mob's plan to colonize Cuba. By March 1952, Kefauver had disbanded his committee and Cuban president Carlos Prío Socarrás was ousted by Fulgencio Batista in a bloodless coup. Batista's resumption of power in Cuba proved exceedingly beneficial to the mafia as well as to America's legitimate industry, which invested close to a billion dollars on the island over the next seven years. In that time, business executives, politicians and lobbyists frequented Havana, including Dana Smith, a California lawyer who, in the spring of 1952, stopped into a casino to try his luck. After Smith lost his ass, he accused the casino of cheating. Upon his return to the States, he complained to his personal friend, Senator Richard Nixon, who contacted the US State Department, telling them that Smith had been swindled and he expected some form of redress. The State Department called the US embassy in Havana, and Batista was told about the sore loser. Batista promised to clean up the casinos, and hired his old pal Meyer Lansky as his official gambling advisor. In a word, a Cuban usurper, in order to pacify an

Lansky and Batista enjoying an evening together.

American Dick, called on the mafia's gambling czar, who let his buddies know they were back in action.

Lansky left for Cuba along with some of his most experienced casino employees. In Havana, he opened a dealer and croupier school so locals could learn the trade and benefit from the expected economic boom. Inside the casinos, Lansky insisted that gamblers be treated honestly and installed hawk-eyed surveillance teams to spot card-counters, dice-swappers and other cheaters. He banned hookers from the casinos, in part to promote a classier atmosphere, but he also knew that *cubanos* were furious that *cubanas* were being exploited by *gringos*. To be sure, there were still hookers and sex shows in Havana, but not in Lansky's casinos.

On a personal front, Lansky loosened up a bit when he took on a beautiful, 29-year-old Latina mistress, something a middle-aged Jewish man should never do without consulting a cardiologist. Keeping a mistress was highly uncharacteristic of Lansky, though he did maintain his usual discretion.*

Lansky and his pals began to build and renovate casinos. The largest shareholder besides Lansky was Florida don Santo Trafficante Jr. Trafficante had inherited his borgata from his father, a Sicilian immigrant who arrived in America in 1904. The elder Trafficante, who encouraged Junior to quit school as a boy so he could learn the family business, made a fortune during Prohibition, smuggling liquor from Havana to Tampa. Because Cuba was so close to his Florida turf, Trafficante Sr claimed the island as part of his domain. After Prohibition was repealed, Senior used the same pipeline for drug trafficking. (Oddly, the word trafficker is translated as *trafficante* in Italian.) Trafficante Sr also monopolized Tampa's Bolita business, which was similar to today's Powerball lottery. (*Bolita* means 'little ball' in Spanish.) Bolita is believed to have grossed the Trafficantes fifteen to twenty million dollars annually, a staggering sum disclosed at the Kefauver hearings by Charlie Wall, who ended up dead with his throat slashed as recompense for divulging this and a few other indiscretions.

---

* Toward the end of the war, Lansky's wife, Anne, who still blamed him for Buddy's illness, suffered a nervous breakdown and was confined to a mental institution. By February 1947, Lansky had divorced Anne and, in December 1948, he married his manicurist, Thelma Scheer Schwartz, aka Teddy. In June 1949, they honeymooned in Italy where Lansky met up with Lucky Luciano.

Trafficante Sr never spent a single day in jail and few photos of him exist. During his final years, he showed a rare concern for succession planning when he stepped down and acted as his son's consigliere so that the young man could become accustomed to real power while still having a mentor to rely on for advice. In 1954, Senior died of cancer, and the 39-year-old Santo Trafficante Jr became the official boss of the borgata. Thin and studious-looking with horn-rimmed glasses, the new don looked as though he should be walking across the Princeton campus discussing physics with J. Robert Oppenheimer. Since Cuba was considered an extension of Trafficante's Florida turf, Lansky offered him a large share of the casinos in Havana. Though some have claimed their relationship was contentious, they got on rather well. Both men hardly drank and never gambled, both were avid readers, both were low-key, and both appeared harmless but were extremely dangerous; they were too smart to ruin a great thing by not getting along with one another.

In 1955, the Cuban government passed Hotel Law 2074, granting generous tax exemptions to hotels which, as a result, sprung up like tents at a campsite. By the spring of 1956, Lansky started construction on the Riviera Hotel and Casino, a 21-floor, 352-room waterfront resort. He easily found investors for the fourteen-million-dollar price tag, nearly half of which was covered by Cuban banks, via development incentives created by Batista. Although Lansky held the controlling interest, he was listed as the hotel's kitchen director. He and his mafia investors also had a stake in the Tropicana, the Sevilla Biltmore and the Havana Hilton. Using their labor-racketeering experience acquired in the States, they arranged for some of the Hilton's 24-million-dollar cost to come from the pension fund of the Cuban Cooks and Bartenders Union.

Meyer Lansky welcomed publicity at the Riviera, which opened on 10 December 1957. Just over a month later, the *Steve Allen Show* broadcast a television special about America's new offshore resort. The show reached millions of American viewers who watched Allen stroll through the Riviera while making wisecracks about the underworld. We do not know if Lansky arranged for the production, but there is nothing to suggest that he opposed it. With the president of Cuba in his pocket, and US senators frequenting his hotels, he must have felt an unusual sense of security.

One senator who visited Havana was John F. Kennedy of

Massachusetts. Kennedy's traveling companion and 'fellow philanderer' was Florida senator George Smathers, who was tucked snugly into Trafficante's pocket ever since Smathers was a congressman. Smathers introduced Kennedy to Trafficante, who arranged for three high-priced call girls to service the young senator. What we are told happened next, as related by Trafficante's longtime attorney, Frank Ragano, is open to question, though it certainly falls within the scope of what we know today about Kennedy's reckless trysts with the opposite sex. While Trafficante and a pal looked on through a secret two-way mirror, Kennedy had sex with all three women. It is hard to believe that filming this romp did not occur to Trafficante; what better way to place an up-and-coming senator in your pocket? Then again, if we are to assume the story is true, it was not as easy to film on short notice before the age of iPhone cameras. Although Smathers never denied or confirmed this particular story, he did say that Kennedy 'liked groups' when it came to women and talked about a hidey-hole he and Kennedy had at Washington, DC's Carroll Arms Hotel, where more than one woman would often meet with Kennedy at once.

Besides Santo Trafficante, Meyer Lansky shared the casinos in Havana with other bosses across the country – except Albert Anastasia, who was only given part of a racetrack. When Anastasia complained, Lansky offered him a thin sliver of the Havana Hilton. It was unlike Lansky, who controlled the share-out, to nickel and dime Anastasia, especially since Anastasia was *compadres* with Lansky's pal Frank Costello. Lansky's sudden and uncharacteristic stinginess did not make sense to me, and I was surprised to learn that no historian has asked the obvious question: what was behind it? Or, more accurately, who? It did not take me long to figure it out.

Anastasia once griped to Costello, 'Vito is bad-mouthing me. He's claiming I'm muscling in on the Cuba business.' Though this statement is all we have to connect Vito Genovese to Anastasia in relation to Cuba, it is enough to shed light on the entire affair. It becomes apparent that Lansky was hamstrung by Genovese, who did not want him to make a deal with Anastasia, since Genovese was at odds with Anastasia. Once denied his rightful share, Anastasia's legitimate complaints were blown up and turned against him by Genovese, who spread rumors that Anastasia was a greedy buffoon who was never satisfied. Ahh, now we see why the plodding Genovese had cultivated an image of

Anastasia screaming at a television set. Can anyone make a crazy man happy? How can a lunatic who killed good citizen Schuster be trusted to stroll around happy Havana?

To understand why Lansky played along with Genovese's squeeze play on Anastasia, entirely inconsistent with Lansky's generous reputation, it is necessary to understand Lansky's role in organized crime. Italian mobsters treated Lansky with the same respect as a don because he was the right-hand man of Lucky Luciano and chief counselor to Frank Costello. But he was not, as many historians contend, a godfather, nor was he a Jewish godfather since the Jews did not have the same regimental structure as the Italians. Lansky was part of Luciano's borgata (as was Ben Siegel, the reason why Lansky asked Luciano to send word to Jack Dragna when Siegel traveled to California, also the reason why Costello had to sign off on Siegel's death). When Genovese displaced Costello, Lansky could not say, 'Oh well, I'm done with this borgata. I'm going to hop over to the Bonanno family, or maybe I'll go with Tommy Lucchese since he's much nicer to me than Vito ever was.' Unfortunately, the mafia does not work this way. Made members are stuck in the same borgata for life – till death do us part – and associates like Lansky must be officially 'released', and only a fool would let go of Lansky.

When Genovese took over the borgata, he put Lansky with capo Vincent 'Jimmy Blue Eyes' Alo, which was perfect since Lansky and Alo were the best of friends. Mob stoolie Vincent Teresa said that Alo 'protects Lansky from any mob guy who thinks he can shake Lansky down. Anyone in the mob who had any ideas about muscling Lansky would have Jimmy Blue Eyes on his back in a second.' But Genovese was Alo's boss, so when Genovese told Lansky to play hardball with Anastasia, with intentions to portray Anastasia's expected reaction as greedy, Lansky had no choice but to comply.

In the event Anastasia complained to Trafficante, who had just as much juice in Cuba as Lansky, this was also rendered a dead end by Genovese. Trafficante had a seat on the Commission but he was not about to race up north every time the Commission sat for a vote, so he sent his ballot in with Lucchese, meaning however Lucchese voted, so did Trafficante. Genovese easily recruited Lucchese into his plot against Anastasia for reasons noted in the last chapter, and since Trafficante was allied with Lucchese, he was also against Anastasia.

By the autumn of 1957, Genovese had built up a strong enough coalition to move on Anastasia, who was, according to Joe Bonanno, attempting to rally support against Genovese, forcing Genovese to expedite his plot. Since Anastasia was a don, the conspirators needed someone inside his own borgata to take his place. Lucchese suggested a short, quiet, unassuming Sicilian-born Brooklynite named Carlo Gambino. Gambino's rise in Anastasia's borgata was due to Anastasia's own mistakes. Anyone familiar with Martin Luther's revolt against the church in 1517 knows that Pope Leo X blew through the Vatican's coffers until he was pressed for cash and began selling cardinal hats, giving Luther a solid argument for a revolt. Likewise, when Anastasia gambled over his head and was pressed for cash, he started selling Cosa Nostra buttons, or memberships, for $40,000 apiece, which cheapened the honor for everyone else who had earned it.

When the scheme was exposed by none other than Genovese, Anastasia dumped the blame on his underboss, Frank 'Cheech' Scalise. But everyone knew that Anastasia's involvement was certain since he would have otherwise been wondering why men who had not made their bones were taking oaths at his initiation ceremonies. (My best guess is that Anastasia gave Cheech the nod to work the scheme, then pinned it on him to cover his tracks after Genovese exposed it.) On 17 June 1957, the 63-year-old Scalise was gunned down on Arthur Avenue in the Bronx; two hitmen shot him in the head and neck as he picked fruit and vegetables at an outdoor market. Aware that Anastasia had killed Vincent Mangano and his brother Phil, Cheech Scalise's brother, Joe, went into hiding while vowing to avenge his brother's death. Anastasia sent word to Joe that Cheech's death was strictly business and if he was willing to forgive and forget, it was safe to come out of hiding. Joe returned home – and was hacked to death by a hit team led by Vincent 'Jimmy Jerome' Squillante (who was also suspected of shooting Cheech). Anastasia's back-to-back betrayals of the Scalise brothers did not sit well with the rest of the borgata and gave Genovese and Lucchese a good reason to tell Anastasia's newly appointed underboss, Carlo Gambino, that Anastasia would eventually cross him, too. Gambino signed on; his role in the coup was simple – sit back and wait until Anastasia was dead then step into his shoes.

In mid-October 1957, Trafficante traveled from Florida to New Jersey under an assumed name. From Newark airport, Trafficante cabbed it over to Manhattan, where he checked into the Warwick Hotel under another fugazi name. That week, Trafficante and several mob associates involved in Cuban endeavors met with Anastasia at his private tenth-floor suite in the Warwick. Top of the agenda was the Havana Hilton. Trafficante told Anastasia they needed two million dollars to grease Batista. Anastasia agreed to contribute his share, happy to get a larger slice of the pie.

On 24 October 1957, Trafficante had dinner with Anastasia. The next morning, the Warwick's doorman saw Trafficante leave in a hurry. Around the same time, Anastasia left his mansion overlooking the bluffs in Fort Lee, New Jersey, where he lived with his wife and children. He crossed the George Washington Bridge and made his way to the Park Sheraton Hotel, where he entered the hotel's barbershop and was greeted by several barbers with fawning respect. Barber Joe Bocchino used a towel to smack hair off chair number four so Anastasia could sit. It was just after 10 a.m. when Anastasia reclined in the chair and Bocchino draped a hot towel over his face to open his pores for a shave. Moments later, two men with bandanas covering their faces shuffled into the barbershop and told the shop's owner, Arthur Grasso, 'Keep your mouth shut if you don't want your head blown off.' They drew two handguns, a .32 and a .38, then shoved Bocchino aside and opened fire on Anastasia who rolled out of his chair and attacked the

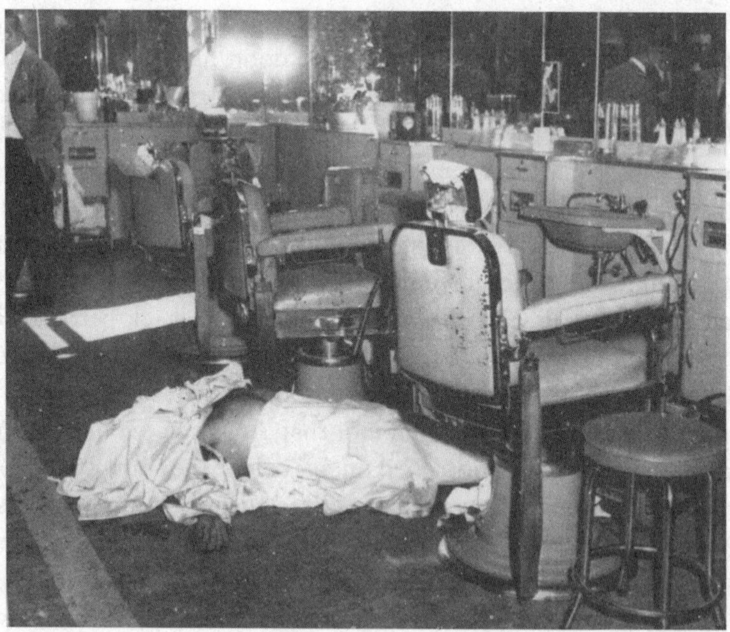

Anastasia dead in a barber shop.

mirror. (The Greek tragedians might have told us that Anastasia was attacking his own reflection for he alone was responsible for the life he had led and how it was ending.) Ten shots were fired; glass shattered as scissors, combs and bottles of hair tonic crashed to the floor. Anastasia was hit in the lungs, kidney, hip, spleen, hands and head; one bullet settled in his brain. With Anastasia lying on the floor, the hitmen calmly walked out the door and discarded their weapons nearby. Four barbers, three customers and two shoeshine boys witnessed the shooting but were luckily unscathed.

At 10:12 a.m., the New York Police Department's switchboard fielded an emergency call from the Park Sheraton Hotel. Detectives arrived at the barbershop to find the barbers dramatically wailing over the body. They questioned the witnesses, who could describe the scene in vivid detail but could not identify the hitmen whose faces were covered with bandanas. Lansky immediately came under suspicion as a conspirator, as did Trafficante given the timing of his meeting with Anastasia, as well as his hasty departure on the morning of the hit. Since Trafficante did not fly back to Tampa but flew straight to Havana, we must wonder if he had a suitcase full of Anastasia's buy-in cash and the final meeting was to strip Anastasia of his share of the two million before they killed him. As planned, Gambino took control of the borgata, and Genovese no longer had any opposition on the Commission.

A dapper Genovese, finally in control of Luciano's borgata.

In the 1962 film *Lawrence of Arabia*, there is a dramatic scene in which Lawrence and his band of Arab warriors cross a swathe of the Arabian desert amidst a blinding sandstorm. Toward the end of this seemingly endless journey, the men notice a riderless camel in their midst; they have lost a rider named Gasim. Lawrence is determined to ride back into the hot sands of hell to rescue Gasim but the Arabs attempt to dissuade him, one man telling him, 'Gasim's time is come [Lawrence]. It is written.' Lawrence boldly responds, 'Nothing is written.' He fades into the desert in search of Gasim and eventually returns with him. Before drinking a jug of water, the exhausted and dehydrated Lawrence, proud that he has proven the power of human will over fatalistic folklore, repeats to the Arabs, 'Nothing is written.'

Not long afterward, the tribes that Lawrence has worked so hard to unite become entangled in a dispute that threatens to divide them. One tribesman has murdered a man from another tribe that is, in response, demanding revenge. To prevent what can easily result in a never-ending blood feud, Lawrence, a neutral Englishman, decides to execute the offender. With gun in hand, Lawrence approaches the murderer whose head is bowed low as he awaits justice. As the murderer slowly raises his face, Lawrence sees it is Gasim. A thousand emotions tear at Lawrence's countenance before he angrily unloads his pistol into Gasim, as though shooting at destiny itself which has proven him wrong. After watching Lawrence's emotional collapse, one Arab said to another, 'It was written then. Better to have left him.'

At the tender age of nineteen, Albert Anastasia was convicted of murder and sentenced to die in the electric chair. He spent a grueling eighteen months on death row while his attorneys worked on his appeal and his brothers murdered the four primary witnesses against him. When he was finally granted a new trial, the case was dismissed for lack of evidence. Anastasia had escaped one chair only to die in another; the wise Arabs would have likely said, 'It was written then.'

Chapter 33

Disorderly Retreats

On the afternoon of 13 November 1957, just three weeks after Albert Anastasia's bad hair day, 44-year-old Sergeant Edgar Croswell of the New York State Police noticed a parking lot full of fancy fin-tailed automobiles at the Parkway Motel in the town of Vestal, New York. Some of the vehicle identification plates were from other parts of the country, so Croswell went inside the motel to inquire about the unusual guests. At the front desk, Helen Schroeder, who owned the motel along with her husband, Warren, told Croswell that most of their guest rooms were booked by Mr Joseph Barbara. Croswell knew exactly who that was.

Joseph Barbara was born in Castellammare del Golfo in 1905. At age sixteen, he immigrated to the United States along with his family and became a citizen in 1927, the same year he became a made member of the mob. By 1957, Barbara lived in a sprawling hilltop estate in Apalachin, New York, a hamlet adjacent to Vestal, and he owned a bottling company in the nearby village of Endicott. Now and then, Barbara hosted soda conferences at his estate for his corporate pals in the bottling industry, who either did not know or overlooked his long rap sheet which included over a dozen arrests, two for homicide, both of which he beat. Sergeant Croswell did, in fact, know about Barbara's criminal record and had been up his ass for a long time, often watching him with binoculars or photographing his estate. 'I was always annoyed by them, and their sleek cars, and fancy clothes, and flashy diamonds,' Croswell said of mobsters in general. 'Sneering at the police, as if we didn't exist or blundered around not knowing what we were doing.'

The day after Sgt Croswell visited the motel, he asked fellow state trooper Vincent Visisko to take a ride with him up to the Barbara estate so they could have a look around. The troopers found the same cars from the motel, now parked up and down Barbara's long driveway. Certain he was witnessing some sort of mafia gathering, Croswell recruited a dozen other troopers from nearby state police barracks, along with two agents from the Treasury Department's Alcohol and Tobacco unit. Although the lawmen had no probable cause to interfere with a private gathering, they threw up a net around the roads leading in and out of Barbara's estate.

Aside from a large main house and three guest cottages, Barbara had a massive outdoor grill where twenty boxes of steak were sizzled and served to his three hundred-plus guests, who also ate enough fish to deplete the Adriatic Sea. When a fish truck salesman, Bartolo Guccia, was summoned to drop off another round of porgies and mackerel, he obliged and spotted the roadblock. As Guccia passed the cops, he waved with a smile then told his generous customers that the place was surrounded.

Croswell and company knew it was time to move and raided the property. Many of Barbara's guests stayed put inside the main house, knowing they had done nothing wrong, while others darted into the surrounding woods. Numbers vary depending on the source but it is safe to say that around sixty men were caught and detained. Between them, they had over $300,000 in cash, fifty or so had criminal records, and quite a few had been arrested for murder with over a dozen dismissed homicide cases in all.

Under questioning, the men all told the same story of how they were visiting Barbara because he was recovering from a heart attack. Why such a thoughtful deed would drive them sprinting into the woods at the mere sight of police they failed to explain. Despite their suspicious backgrounds, they owned trucking companies, garment factories, restaurants, funeral homes, landfills and other businesses essential to the US economy. One guest in particular was a former city councilman and delegate to the New York State Constitutional Convention. He claimed to know Vice President Richard Nixon and New York governor Averell Harriman, which seemed true, and said that his car had mechanical trouble causing him to pull into Barbara's driveway seeking assistance, which seemed false.

The mafia conference held on Barbara's estate was widely covered by the press and became known to the public as the Apalachin meeting. The big surf and turf was prompted by Papa Smurf, Vito Genovese, after he killed Willie Moretti and Albert Anastasia while also deposing Lucky Luciano and Frank Costello. The bosses wanted to calm the seismic shifts in the underworld, while lesser topics on the agenda included the approval of Carlo Gambino as Anastasia's replacement, how to split up the Havana casinos, and how the new Narcotics Control Act of 1956 would impact their stance on drug trafficking. They also needed to figure out what to do with the recent initiates who had purchased their buttons from Cheech Scalise and Albert Anastasia.

For several decades, most historians have made it sound as if a backwoods cop had stumbled onto a mafia picnic, though a few have accurately pointed out Croswell's long-held obsession with Barbara and his deep hatred of mafiosos. Some historians suspect that an underworld informant dropped a dime on the gathering. Meyer Lansky's pal Doc Stacher said the tipster was Lansky. This is not outside the realm of possibility given Lansky's loathing for Genovese, compounded by the difficult position Genovese had placed him in with Anastasia. Lansky fueled suspicions when he declined to attend the conference, later claiming he had lost his voice on account of the flu.

Other suspects who have not yet been considered as possible snitches are the men who bought their buttons; their memberships, perhaps even their lives, were on the line and nothing moves men more than fear. Any one of them could have made an anonymous telephone call to derail the conference and stall an inquiry into their bogus buttons.

For a change, Lucky Luciano is not on our list of potential snitches but he proudly claimed credit for subsequently setting up Genovese and sending him to prison for the rest of his life. After Frank Costello had been demoted to a soldier, Luciano no longer had any pull in the borgata and was bitter about it. He did what he always did in a tight spot: he squealed. 'I decided the best and easiest way to get Genovese out of everybody's hair without knockin' him off', said Luciano, 'was to let the U.S. government do the job.' Luciano went on to explain that he, Costello, Lansky and Gambino paid a convicted drug dealer, Nelson 'The Melon' Cantellops, $100,000 to testify against Genovese, Chin Gigante and thirteen other mobsters they wanted to get rid of. We should question Luciano's claim since Gambino is blatantly out of place in this clique. Did Luciano include Gambino in his confession to drive a wedge between Gambino and Genovese who were, at the moment, a bit too palsy-walsy for everyone's comfort? Why, moreover, would Luciano out Lansky and Costello as his fellow snitches when they were supposed to be his best friends?

Luciano was, at the time, seething with anger, not only toward Genovese for slapping the plastic crown off his head, but also toward Lansky and Costello for paying him lip service for years which stuffed his ego but not his wallet. It is possible that Luciano lied to get everyone at each other's throats; it is otherwise hard to reconcile why he would further taint his own legacy by admitting, yet again, that he ratted.

In July 1958, the US attorney for the Southern District of New York, Paul Williams, indicted Genovese and company for drug trafficking. Before any boss goes to prison for a long time, he typically makes an example of one or two guys in the event anyone is eyeing the vacant throne, a precautionary measure Costello failed to take – and was rudely reminded of it inside the lobby of his apartment building. Since every borgata has, at all times, a few contracts on the backlog, the boss need only pluck one off the shelf.

On 26 February 1959, a body began to stiffen in the basement of a West Orange, New Jersey, mansion. Abner 'Longie' Zwillman was found hanging from a rafter with a wire around his neck. Zwillman was once partners with Willie Moretti and still had business interests with Frank Costello, with whom he remained close after Costello was shelved. His death was ruled a suicide even though he had been beaten like a piñata. Lansky later said, 'Genovese was behind that killing. He just ordered his killers to make it look like Zwillman had taken his own life.' They did a lousy job but Genovese owned the local Jersey police and the medical examiner.

On 3 April 1959, after twelve hours of deliberation, the jury returned guilty verdicts for Genovese and his co-defendants. Like Thomas Dewey, who ran for governor after prosecuting Luciano, Paul Williams immediately announced his candidacy for the governor of New York, which led to a failed run. Before sentencing, several defendants insisted on their innocence and asked to take polygraph tests to prove it, even saying they would submit to truth serum, apparently forgetting what else might fall from their lips, leading to even more trouble than they were in.

Genovese surrendered himself in May, beginning a fifteen-year stint. Once confined to a cell, it was time for Genovese to make his second example of someone, ensuring that no one would ever underestimate his reach. Anthony 'Little Augie Pisano' Carfano had failed to come in when Genovese called in the borgata's capos after the attempted hit on Costello. Like Zwillman, Carfano further aggravated Genovese by remaining chummy with Costello after the latter was broken and shelved. Genovese was never in a rush to kill Carfano, knowing he could get him anytime. When Genovese was sent away for fifteen years, the time had come. Genovese dispatched a hit team who repeatedly spotted Carfano with Tony Bender and held their fire, afraid they might accidentally kill Bender, too, who was still useful to Genovese. When Genovese heard about Bender's unwitting interference, he reassigned the contract to him.

On 25 September 1959, Carfano shared an early drink with Costello at the Waldorf Astoria, then left to pick up his date, Janice Drake, a former Miss New Jersey. Carfano and Drake began the evening at the Copacabana, where they washed down a few drinks before bumping into Tony Bender who pretended it was a chance encounter. Bender invited them to dinner at Marino's Italian restaurant. This should have alerted Carfano that something was amiss since Bender was too cheap to take anyone to dinner. At the restaurant, Bender received a telephone call and asked Carfano if he could pick up two men at LaGuardia airport in Queens. Carfano obliged and left with Drake. The two were later found slumped in the front seats of Carfano's car with bullet holes in their heads. The car was close to the airport where jet engines would have muffled the shots.

As Vito Genovese sat in Atlanta Penitentiary wondering if another felon had put the Melon up to tellin', Lansky and Trafficante learned that their biggest problem in Cuba was never Anastasia but a man who would never sit for a shave. Fidel Castro was once held in Batista's jails but released during a national amnesty for political prisoners. The freed revolutionary left for Mexico where he boarded an old yacht, appropriately named *Granma*, with eighty-two of his followers. In December 1956, they landed on Cuba's southwestern tip and took to the mountains to begin a guerilla war against Batista's wobbly regime.

Throughout 1957, Lansky could see the water filling up in the hull of Batista's ship. He and Trafficante attempted to hedge their bets by opening a back channel to Castro. They sent guns and other supplies to his rebel army, something the CIA was also doing at the same time, and for the same reason. Batista must have also sensed his impending doom since he began demanding more money from the mob. Lansky attributed Batista's incessant demands to greed, failing to recognize that he was cashing in his chips as he prepared to walk away from the table.

When Castro organized a nationwide strike that closed the casinos, Lansky decided it was high time to enlist the support of the US government. Together with attorney Joseph Varon, Lansky met with the FBI in Florida where he openly admitted that his decision to speak with the agents was self-serving – he wanted to preserve his island paradise – but he also saw himself as a patriot concerned with national security. During the conversation, the self-educated Lansky accurately predicted exactly what would happen to Cuba over the coming decade and offered ways to avert the disaster. Unfortunately, his warnings went unheeded by the agents who, unbeknownst to Lansky, saw the meeting as nothing more than an opportunity to gather intelligence about the mafia's illicit relationship with the Cuban government.

Back in Havana, Batista isolated himself inside the presidential palace while his world fell apart around him. In the autumn of 1958, bombs were heard in the distance as chips flew across tables, roulette wheels spun, and the band played on above the faint sound of explosions. The gamblers were in a state of denial as Castro marched toward Havana. By midnight of New Year's Eve, as party-goers kissed and toasted the new year, Batista announced to his inner circle that he was leaving the island for good. He added that the vice president was accompanying him into exile and the senior Supreme Court justice would be left in charge of the country. To highlight Batista's negligent statecraft, especially in the area of law, he could not recall the justice's name.

Batista's parting sentiments to the Cuban people were just as unsettling, leaving us to wonder if he had a poor understanding of his own downfall or a great sense of humor; he warned the Cuban people 'not to become victims of tumultuous passions'. Batista's military planes were warming up on the tarmac as he left the palace and abandoned his flag, his people and his mafia cronies. With a luxurious retirement in mind, he took off with planeloads of cash from bribes, graft, skim and other *gangsterismo* rackets. He also had Swiss bank accounts which held, according to some estimates, over three hundred million dollars. A list of his valuables included Napoleon's telescope, used by the exiled emperor to gaze out to sea from Saint Helena, a curious keepsake for another dictator going into exile.

Shortly after midnight, a loud explosion rocked the Tropicana. Blood was splattered everywhere as casino guests panicked and scrambled in all directions, screaming in at least two languages. The arm of a young woman, Magaly Martínez, was severed at the shoulder. As if there was any hope of salvaging this mess through public relations, the Tropicana pledged to pick up Martínez's medical bills, fit her with a nice new arm, and pay for the seventeen-year-old's college education. It did not occur to anyone at the time that Martínez was the bomber.

At around 1:30 a.m., Lansky was sitting in the bar of his Riviera Hotel when one of his underlings ran over to him and whispered in his ear, telling him that Batista was in the clouds. Lansky took the news calmly then swung into action, telling his personal chauffeur and bodyguard, Armando Jaime Casielles, 'We got a lot of work to do . . . we have to make the most of what's left of the evening.' Lansky ordered every last cent removed from the hotel premises and brought over to Joseph 'Hoboken Joe' Stassi's house. Lansky then told Casielles, 'We need to make the rounds to all the casinos and secure the money.' With Lansky in his passenger seat, Casielles raced through Havana streets with the driving skills of Fernando Alonso. Their first stop was the Sans Souci, where Lansky told Trafficante that the chain across the Golden Horn had snapped; their empire was about to be sacked by looters and revolutionaries. Trafficante was stunned by the news. Lansky told him, 'Make the rounds at all your casinos. Get the money. All of it . . . Take it to Stassi's house for safekeeping . . . close the casinos – and fast. Because at dawn the crowds will take to the streets and nothing and nobody will be able to stop them.'

In the mafia's version of Paul Revere's ride, Lansky and Casielles sped into the night, warning other gangsters at other casinos. As the Cuban people cautiously considered if Batista's departure was just a rumor, most remained safely indoors and 'an atmosphere of eerie calm pervaded the city'. Once the people were convinced Batista was gone, they poured into the streets to

Trafficante in the Sans Souci, Havana, Cuba.

celebrate and loot. Within hours, the casinos looked like a Category 5 hurricane had torn through them. Luckily, Castro's race to Havana from the Sierra Maestra mountains turned into a six-hundred-mile vaudeville show, as the impresario stopped along the way to gloat about his victory. His delayed entry into the city allowed the mobsters time to shuttle their wives and children to safety and gather all the cash at Hoboken Joe's house. With stacks of money spread around the living-room floor, Lansky and Trafficante discussed their next move.

When Castro finally arrived in Havana, his ragtag army claimed the Hilton Hotel as its headquarters. They saw the casinos as a symbol of American debauchery and threatened to close them, while vowing to 'run all these fascist mobsters . . . out of Cuba'. Trafficante did not believe Castro would do that, telling an associate, 'You think he's going to close up a hundred million dollars' worth of business that we got? We generate over ten thousand people working. He's going to put all these Cubans out of work? He'll never do it.' He did it. But with no sound economic plan of his own, Castro experienced a temporary change of heart and decided to give the mobsters back their casinos. But who in the world was coming to Cuba as Castro's regime executed over five hundred Batista loyalists? Not the most festive atmosphere. With hardly anyone visiting the casinos, the mobsters had no profits to report and Castro became infuriated, convinced they were scamming him. The revolutionaries arrested the mobsters and took over the counting rooms. Lansky escaped the country in the nick of time, but Trafficante and Hoboken Joe were unwilling to fold their cards just yet, unsure if the *barbudos* would last. They were repeatedly questioned or scooped up and thrown into a detention center, then released and rearrested, never knowing which ordeal would end in front of a firing squad. 'They used to come and get me at nighttime,' Trafficante

Castro with his comrade Che Guevara.

later said, 'take me out to the woods, trying to [get me] to tell where I had my money . . . until finally I went into hiding.'

Hoboken Joe eventually slipped off the island and Trafficante was found and jailed. He told his attorney, Frank Ragano, 'They're going to execute me. I'm on the damn list.' At the last minute, Trafficante bribed Fidel Castro's brother Raúl with one of his hidden piles of cash and, in October 1959, he left Cuba for good.

In 1776, Adam Smith's *Wealth of Nations*, the blueprint for modern economic prosperity, was published within a month of Edward Gibbon's *History of the Decline and Fall of the Roman Empire*. At the very same time Gibbon was pondering civilization's long and painful decline, Smith was envisioning its rise. Although these two ageless works are entirely unconnected, their close publication dates are strikingly symbolic of humanity's historic resilience. And as man is a model of his race, Trafficante presents us with an individual example of humankind's irrepressible spirit, as he followed up his decline in Cuba with a bold economic plan that would earn him and his borgata untold millions.

Following Castro's seizure of power, the new dictator failed to deliver on his promise to allow free elections and began persecuting dissidents, driving over 200,000 Cuban refugees into Miami, Florida. Soon, Miami's Little Havana was as densely populated with Cubans as Cuba's big Havana. Upon Trafficante's return to Florida, he realized that this large exiled community, suffering from the stunning blow of persecution and the dizzying bends of relocation, could use assistance from a mob boss who spoke fluent Spanish, had a massive network of connections, and could provide them with cash loans, opportunities, and help them get jobs. Trafficante moved his headquarters from Tampa to Miami, placing himself smack in the middle of Florida's next economic boom. And since Florida was already Trafficante's exclusive turf, he did not have to share Little Havana with a dozen other mob bosses from around the country.

As for Lansky, the Cuban debacle proved to be his biggest loss ever. He put it in gambling terms, saying, 'I crapped out.' Seeking the polar opposite of machete politics, Lansky looked toward mannerly London where, if you happen to get screwed, it is done with a polite smile and the utmost etiquette, leaving one to wonder on the way out the door if a simple 'thank you' will suffice. In 1960, after the Brits legalized gambling in London, the mob began to ship slot machines there (under the guise of farm equipment since the Johnson Act prohibited the shipment of gambling machines). Lansky tried his luck in London's gambling clubs, but the Brits were quickly on to him and sent him packing (presumably with a smile).

Back in the States, the 'wizard of illicit money management' set up numbered Swiss bank accounts to help his mob cronies hide some of the money he had helped them steal. 'First,' said Justice Department attorney Ronald Goldfarb, 'the money would be laundered through the Bank of World Commerce and the Atlas Bank in the Bahamas, and then sent to the International Credit Bank in Switzerland. The mob had representatives on the boards of directors.' This may have been Lansky's final favor to the mafia since his better days were behind him, as were Lucky Luciano's, who continued to pine for America from his Italian exile.

Epilogue: LCN in the DNA

After Charles 'Lucky' Luciano was officially dethroned by Vito Genovese, Genovese sent him a meager monthly allowance in Italy, most of which Luciano blew on women. At age sixty-two, Luciano fell in love with a 23-year-old Italian beauty, Adriana Rizzo, who reduced the underworld's Augustus Caesar to 'my Sharlie'. Adriana wore him out in bed, and about a month after she moved into his apartment, he had a heart attack and began visiting a doctor. Since Luciano's health problems were partly caused by stress over a lack of money, he entertained an offer to make a movie about his life. When word of the movie deal reached Genovese, the imprisoned don was against it and became especially angered when he found out that the screenplay included scenes of Frank Costello and Albert Anastasia being shot. Genovese dispatched his acting boss, 'Tommy Ryan' Eboli, to Italy to have a word with Luciano.

On 17 January 1962, Tommy Ryan dropped in on Luciano in Naples and told him to get hold of the movie script and hand it over, pronto, or suffer the consequences. For Luciano's ailing heart, this ultimatum was like pouring a bucket of salt down his throat as Adriana gave him a lap dance. Luciano immediately reached out to writer-producer Martin Gosch, who was in Spain, and told him to deliver the script, without delay. Since the US Narcotics Bureau had previously told Italian authorities that Luciano was involved in an international drug ring, the carabinieri were regularly listening in on Luciano's telephone calls. When they overheard him ask Gosch for a 'script', they believed it was a veiled reference to drugs, as 'script' is a common term for pharmaceutical prescriptions. They barged into Luciano's apartment and tossed it, searching for drugs, but found none so they took him in for questioning. With Tommy Ryan threatening his life and the carabinieri threatening his freedom, Luciano's blood pressure skyrocketed and he began having angina attacks that sent him crashing to the floor.

Since Gosch was on his way to Naples with the movie script, Luciano invited the carabinieri to accompany him to the airport so they could see the script for themselves. The carabinieri took him up on his offer and secured a warrant to search Gosch's property. Officer Cesare Resta drove Luciano to the airport where they awaited Gosch's flight. Shortly after the plane landed, Gosch entered the terminal and gifted Luciano a bottle of brandy and a box of chocolates. Gosch noticed that Luciano looked as if he had 'aged twenty-five years' since they had last met, only two months earlier. Luciano introduced Gosch to Officer Resta then whispered to Gosch, 'I fucked myself, Marty, they're gonna kill me.'

'Who's going to kill you?' asked Gosch.

'All of 'em,' said Luciano, knowing Genovese would enlist the support of the Commission. 'First, they'll kill me, then they'll kill you . . . I oughta know . . . I'm as good as dead. And maybe you, too.'

Gosch told Luciano that the movie script was in his suitcase which they would retrieve momentarily at the baggage claim. They then exited the terminal with Resta in tow, but along their walk Luciano suddenly squeezed the box of chocolates as he collapsed to the floor; he was having a massive heart attack. Gosch kneeled down beside him and tried to help as Resta, instead of performing the medical assistance he was trained to administer, reached a hand into Gosch's pocket and felt around for his baggage-claim ticket. 'For God's sake, never mind the damned suitcase,' Gosch yelled at Resta. 'Get a doctor, you idiot.'

Resta snapped out of it and told Gosch that Luciano had heart pills in his pocket. Gosch rifled through Luciano's pockets and found nitroglycerin. He shoved a half-dozen pills under Luciano's tongue but it was too late; Luciano's labored breaths came to an end with his eyes wide open. The American mafia's founding father, who had ducked a thousand deaths on the streets of New York, was arguably done in by his fear of Genovese at the relatively young age of sixty-four.

Since Officer Resta needed a medical official to sign off on Luciano's death before he could have the corpse transported to the morgue, Luciano lay on the pavement for several hours until the airport physician, apparently on Italian time, finally arrived. Tommy Ryan, who was still in town, was thrilled with the news; the movie deal was dead, as was Luciano. Mission accomplished.

Back in the States, Frank Costello received news of Luciano's death the way a man receives news that a brother who he has not seen in many years has died; it is a sad occasion but time and space had already tempered the blow. After a bullet ricocheted off Costello's

Luciano dead at the airport in Naples.

noggin and he had worked out his differences with Genovese, he settled into a comfortable retirement. He held large stakes in numerous companies, owned real estate on Wall Street and oil wells in Texas, suffering none of the usual financial woes attendant with old age in America. By 1972, Costello was sought out by the publishing industry who wanted to record his life story for posterity. 'I told him that he was a legitimate figure in American history, and I meant it,' said author Peter Maas. 'There isn't a level of society that his career didn't touch.' Maas successfully appealed to Costello's decades-long yearning to be recognized as a genuine model of the American dream and agreed to sit for a series of interviews that would contribute to a book about his life. The former prime minister of the underworld was scheduled to meet with Maas at Costello's regal estate at Sands Point, New York, when Maas received a telephone call. 'He's gone,' said the caller. The 82-year-old ex-don had passed on from complications of heart disease, leaving us to forever wonder what secrets he might have revealed (or what tales he'd have told to disguise the truth, and further confuse us).

Just as Costello had lived in style, he went out in style; he was buried at Saint Michael's Cemetery, inside a marble mausoleum with Ionian columns. A year after his death, someone affixed a bomb to the doors of his crypt. Authorities said, and historians have continued to repeat, that the explosion was an act of vandalism committed by Carlo Tresca's killer and future Bonanno family boss, Carmine 'Lilo' Galante, as a show of disrespect to Costello. Here, again, we see history written and repeated by people who have no idea what they are talking about. I knew one of the men involved in the incident and he told me that the price of gold had spiked during that time. He and his crew were pretty sure that Costello, who had no children or grandchildren, was buried with some of his jewelry, and figured, at the very least, his skeletal hand would be adorned with one of his many solid-gold wristwatches and pinky rings. The crew was after the gold! I had no reason to distrust my friend's story, though it was, in fact, easy enough to confirm by simply checking the price of gold, which was $35 an ounce in 1971 and had jumped to $180 an ounce by 1974 when the doors to Costello's mausoleum were blown up.

Of the few and limited preliminary conversations Maas had with Costello, Maas was able to say that, 'He certainly didn't hold in awe some of the mafia leaders of the past who are revered by everybody else in the organization, yet he spoke with great regard about Meyer Lansky.'

In his later years, Lansky continued to reap profits from his wide-ranging investments while beset by a series of legal battles. The government believed he was worth over three hundred million dollars (over two billion in today's money), and was not about to let him rest, unmolested. Lansky tried to leave the country. After several nations turned him away, he applied for Israeli citizenship, invoking Israel's Law of Return which allows Jews to relocate to Israel. Unfortunately for Lansky, Prime Minister Golda Meir did not want to aggravate the United States by welcoming a wanted mobster, nor did she see him as equal to the forty-two US Phantom fighter jets she needed for Israeli defense forces; she denied Lansky entry and took the jets.

With nowhere to run, Lansky retired to south Florida while continuing to fight subpoenas, endure drawn-out legal trials – and read books! He was a loyal member of the Book-of-the-Month Club, and often visited the Miami Beach Public Library, where a librarian remembered him as 'mild mannered' and 'very pleasant'. Under a lazy

Florida sun, where most retirees bake while playing endless rounds of golf, Lansky also spent his days with some of his old pals, a mix of retired Jewish and Italian gangsters who had a lot to reminisce about. The Italian-American mafia had experienced an incredible era of expansion spearheaded, in part, by Jewish gangsters. The Dutchman consolidated the underworld gambling industry in Harlem, a racket the heirs to Luciano's crime family would monopolize for the remainder of the twentieth century. (In 1986, Anthony 'Fat Tony' Salerno, a native of Harlem who controlled the racket Luciano had once wrested from the Dutchman's corpse, topped the list of the nation's wealthiest mobsters, compiled by *Fortune* magazine, which estimated the mob's annual revenues at fifty billion dollars.) Lepke Buchalter's skillful infiltration of numerous labor unions and the garment center's trucking industry would pay the mob huge dividends beyond the twentieth century. (According to the *New York Times*, by 1989, mobsters in the garment industry 'controlled at least a dozen trucking concerns . . . The cartel's dominance was so entrenched that violence was all but unnecessary.' In 1999, one mobster said the district 'could not run without us. Every truck that went in and out of the area, every . . . rack of clothing moved only with our approval.') And for decades to come, mobsters from all over the country would reap untold millions from the seeds Siegel had sown in the dry desert sands of Las Vegas. (Frank Costello and Meyer Lansky went on to become silent partners in the Sands Hotel and Casino which opened in 1952 and closed in 1996, and the Tropicana which opened in 1957; after numerous renovations, it is still in operation, as is the Flamingo.) By the close of the twentieth century, the mafia was still in control of the waterfront across New York and New Jersey, and members of Luciano's crime family were overseeing two billion dollars in annual sales moving through Manhattan's Fulton Fish Market alone, once controlled by Joe 'Socks' Lanza.

Meyer Lansky lived until 1983, dying of natural causes at age eighty, but it is here that he will exit our story along with most of the American mafia's Jews. Plenty of Italian-Americans also participated in a mass exodus from The Life, beginning in the 1960s. Where did they go and why did they leave?

To cue up the answer to this question, let us turn to Dorset, England, in 1653, where a boy named Thomas Pitt was born. Thomas's dad was a clergyman but the boy had more exciting ambitions. In 1674, 21-year-old Thomas traveled to India and went to work with the East India Company in search of his fortune. He was soon trading on his own, in stark defiance of the company's 'legal' monopoly on trade, prompting the company to shut Thomas down by calling for 'justice'. Thomas was prosecuted and fined, neither of which did anything to temper his ambitious nature.

In 1702, an Indian merchant asked Thomas if he was interested in buying a 410-carat uncut diamond. Thomas purchased the stone for the staggering sum of £20,400, then sent it to England with his oldest son, Robert, who hid it in his shoe. The purchase of this stone earned Thomas his legendary nickname, 'Diamond Pitt'. (In my time, we'd have also nicknamed his son 'Robbie the Shoe'.) Diamond Pitt sold the stone to a French regent, Philippe II, Duke of Orléans, for £135,000, and used the money to buy land and consolidate formerly purchased properties. Of Diamond Pitt's children, his daughter became the Countess of Stanhope, one son became the Earl of Londonderry, and Robbie the Shoe entered parliament and gave birth to William Pitt the Elder, the namesake for Pittsburgh, Pennsylvania. Pittsburgh Pitt gave birth to the famous prime minister Pitt the Younger, whose leadership helped defeat the Little Corsican, Napoleon Bonaparte. The fortune behind this illustrious family, whose lives are inextricably tied to the history of England and America, sprung from a giant diamond, which, according to legend, was smuggled out of the Kollur Mine, near the Krishna River, by a slave who concealed it in a leg wound suffered while escaping the siege of Golconda. The slave approached a British sea captain and offered to split the profit received from the sale of the diamond in return for safe passage off the Indian coast. But the captain reasoned that it was cheaper to kill the slave and provided him instead with direct passage to Svarga. The captain then sold the blood diamond to Jamchand, our Indian merchant, who fenced it to Diamond Pitt, who, in turn, used it to elevate his descendants.

In a similar cleansing of money, many of the mobsters who were dedicated to the mafia throughout the first half of the twentieth century would use their vast ill-gotten wealth for the social and economic advancement of their law-abiding children and grandchildren. As institutional discrimination receded in America and immigrants felt less isolated, new opportunities in the overworld became available to their descendants, and the children of countless mobsters pursued different paths to success. But not everyone was prepared to forsake a centuries-old way of life that coursed through their bloodstream. For many Italian-Americans, La Cosa Nostra was still part of their DNA and they would proudly pass on the gene by raising their sons and grandsons in The Life. Moreover, there was never a shortage of new recruits. And so, our story continues as the mafia's Golden Age, ushered in by Lucky Luciano, is about to end under America's golden boy who threatened the mob with extinction.

Robert F. Kennedy billed himself as the 'one man in America who was above and beyond a price'. He would launch a relentless crusade against the mafia and awaken a slumbering FBI, placing dons across the country in his crosshairs – until the crosshairs were turned on his older brother, the president of the United States.

Acknowledgments

My last book about the mafia, *Mob Rules: What the Mafia Can Teach the Legitimate Businessman*, was an international bestseller translated into twenty languages. Because of the book's global appeal, I was invited by the German media conglomerate Axel Springer to speak at their annual retreat for editors being held at the Hotel Villa Athena in Agrigento, Sicily. The first evening, I met an older gentleman who introduced himself as George. We struck up an enjoyable conversation that centered around our mutual love of history, and, at some point, George said to me, 'I would like to publish your next book.' This softly spoken man, who conversed with me as if we had known each other forever, was Lord Weidenfeld, one of the most talented and influential book publishers of the twentieth century. But his long, illustrious career had a tragic start. Days after the Nazis entered Austria, George's father was arrested by Brown Shirt auxiliaries. He was eventually released, but George's grandmothers were not as lucky; both were gassed to death in the Holocaust. Nineteen-year-old George fled Vienna for London where the Brits welcomed him and hired him at the British Broadcasting Corporation as a radio monitor. After the war, George and Nigel Nicolson started their own publishing firm, Weidenfeld & Nicolson, and, for decades to come, George was well known for matching ideas with authors, exactly what he was doing with me as we conversed on that fateful day.

The following afternoon, George and I met for lunch along with his charming wife, Annabelle. George suggested that I write a history of the mafia. Annabelle – who was educated in a convent boarding school where she became an avid reader – helped us flesh out the idea, and her brilliant input cannot be overstated.

As I traveled home from Sicily, I assessed the size and scope of the project and wondered if I was getting myself in over my head; a proper history of the mafia would take many years to research and write, and the mafia's genesis, in and of itself, seemed an unsolvable riddle.

The commitment was daunting so I put it aside and pursued other endeavors until my dear friend and *goombah*, Bruce Ramer, and his lovely wife, Madeline, were attending an event in Germany where they happened upon George and Annabelle. Bruce ducked out of the event to call me from Germany and tell me that George was asking about me and the status of the book. I saw this chance occurrence as a reinforcement of the first fateful encounter in Sicily and began to write a history that would chain me to my desk for the next seven years of my life, eventually completing what George and Annabelle had known I was capable of as we sat overlooking the ruins of Agrigento.

Throughout his long career, George had published authors such as Truman Capote, Henry Miller, Gore Vidal and Norman Mailer, while personally pitching ideas to legendary historians such as Eric Hobsbawm, Richard Pipes, Michael Grant, Arnold Toynbee, Lady Elizabeth Longford and Lady Antonia Fraser. George also published the memoirs of de Gaulle, Tito, Pope John Paul II, Lyndon Johnson, Moshe Dayan and life-altering books such as *The Double Helix* by James Watson. As I understand it, I was the last author George had personally commissioned before sadly passing on in 2016. I am forever grateful to him for giving me this opportunity and for placing a self-taught ex-convict in the company of the literary titans mentioned above.

In addition to George, I thank Annabelle, Bruce and Madeline, Danny Passman, Reggie Glosson and Alan Samson, formerly of Weidenfeld & Nicolson, who patiently stuck with me over the years. I am also grateful to Jenny Lord, who took over for Alan and breathed fresh air into the project. When I informed Jenny that I had an enormous 550,000-word book on my hands, she advised me to trim it down and carve it up into three volumes while she worked to approve the publication of a trilogy. I cannot thank her enough for her unwavering support. For their enthusiasm and resolve to bring The Borgata Trilogy to the US market, I'm also thankful to Claiborne Hancock and Jessica Case of Pegasus Books.

Lastly, I thank Jo Roberts-Miller and Lorraine Jerram for the meticulous proofread, and Gabriella, who tirelessly typed my handwritten draft into a Word doc – I still write longhand, the same way I taught myself in a prison cell. She also acted as my sounding board, listening to me read my final manuscript aloud and calling out for clarity whenever something might not make perfect sense to a reader.

SOURCE NOTES

Preface

xi 'almost all of . . .': William Shirer, *The Rise and Fall of the Third Reich: A History of Nazi Germany* (New York: MJF Books, 1990), xi.

xv 'There are men . . .': Marc Bloch, *The Historian's Craft: Reflections on the Nature and Uses of History and the Techniques and Methods of the Men Who Write It*, trans. Peter Putnam (New York: Alfred A. Knopf, 1971), 26.

xv 'sat musing amidst . . .': Edward Gibbon, *Memoirs of My Life*, ed. George A. Bonnard (London: Nelson, 1966), 136.

Introduction

2 'We just shoot . . .': Gene Mustain and Jerry Capeci, *Murder Machine: A True Story of Murder, Madness and the Mafia* (New York: Dutton, 1992), 227.

3 'Your electricity get . . .': *ibid*, 228.

3 'Go get some . . .': *ibid*, 229.

Chapter 1

7 'Death to the French': Michele Amari, *The History of the War of the Sicilian Vespers*, edited and with an introduction and notes by the Earl of Ellesmere. Volume 1 (London: Richard Bentley, 1850), 183.

8 'In the world . . .': Bill Bonanno, *Bound by Honor: A Mafioso's Story* (New York: St Martin's Press, 1999), xvi.

9 'The Sicilian thinks . . .': Gaspare Nicotri, *Rivoluzioni e Rivolte in Sicilia: Studio di Psicologia Sociale* (Palermo: Alberto Reber, 1906), 52–53.

10 'What can the . . .': George Orwell, from 'England Your England', in *A Collection of Essays* (New York: Harvest Book/Harcourt, 1981), 254.

10 'the most ancient . . .': Jean-Jacques Rousseau, *The Social Contract and Discourse on the Origin of Inequality*, ed. Lester G. Crocker (New York: Washington Square Press/Pocket Books, 1973), 8.

10 'has always been . . .': Jean François-Marie Arouet de Voltaire, *The Age of Louis XIV*, trans. Martyn P. Pollack (London: J.M. Dent & Sons Ltd, 1969), 121.

12 'We must cultivate . . .': Jean François-Marie Arouet de Voltaire, *Candide and Philosophical Letters*, trans. Richard Aldington and Ernest Dilworth (New York: The Modern Library, 1992), 103.

Chapter 2

13 'Republic's granary': Cato, quoted in M.I. Finley, Denis Mack Smith and Christopher Duggan, *A History of Sicily* (New York: Elisabeth Sifton Books/Viking, 1987), 33.

14 'act of fealty': Marc Bloch, *Feudal Society*, trans. L.A. Manyon (London: Routledge & Kegan Paul Ltd, 1962), 146.

14 'sacrifice my life . . .': Jean Baptiste Colbert, *Lettres, Instructions et Memoires*, ed. Pierre Clement. Volume 2 (Paris: Imprimerie Impériale, 1863), xxx.

14 'If I betray . . .': Selwyn Raab, *Five Families: The Rise, Decline, and Resurgence of America's Most Powerful Mafia Empires* (New York: Thomas Dunne Books, 2005), 6.

15 'written agreement corresponding . . .': Bloch, *op. cit.*, 224.

15 'This family comes . . .': Raab, *op. cit.*, 7.

15 'had told me . . .': Rosalie Bonanno, with Beverly Donofrio, *Mafia Marriage: My Story* (New York: William Morrow & Co., 1990), 64.

15 '*amis charnels*': Bloch, *op. cit.*, 124.

15 'The general assumption . . .': Bloch, *ibid.*

15 'the act of association . . .': Bloch, *ibid*, 131.

16 'thy friends shall . . .': Colbert, *op. cit.*, 450.

16 'whole kindred . . .': Bloch, *op. cit.*, 126.

16 'No matter what . . .': Raab, *op. cit.*, 7.

16 'notorious association . . .': Georg Wilhelm Friedrich Hegel, *The Philosophy of History*, trans. J. Sibree, revised edition (London: The Colonial Press, 1900), 401.

16 'give the lord . . .': Norman F. Cantor, *The Civilization of the Middle Ages: A Completely Revised and Expanded Edition of Medieval History: The Life and Death of a Civilization* (New York: HarperCollins, 1993), 201.

17 'bond established on . . .': Hegel, *op. cit.*, 370.

17 'physical violence until . . .': Henner Hess, *Mafia and Mafiosi: Origin, Power and Myth*, trans. Ewald Osers (London: C. Hurst & Co., 1998), 45.

18 'All the heads . . .': E.J. Hobsbawm, *Primitive Rebels: Studies in Archaic Forms of Social Movement in the 19th and 20th Centuries* (New York: W.W. Norton & Co., 1965), 37.

18 'not from the middle . . .': Hess, *op. cit.*, 48.

19 'Mafia godfathers are . . .': Roberto Olla, *Godfathers: Lives and Crimes of the Mafia Mobsters* (Richmond, Surrey, UK: Alma Books, 2007), 28.

Chapter 3

21 'To suppose that Italy . . .': Stuart J. Woolf, *A History of Italy, 1700–1860: The Social Constraints of Political Change* (London: Methuen, 1979), 343.

22 'a shimmering canvas . . .': Alfredo Niceforo, *Italia Barbara Contemporanea* (Palermo: Sandron, 1898), 9–10.

22 'It has taken 100 . . .': J. Philip di Franco, *The Italian Americans (The Peoples of North America)* (New York: Chelsea House, 1988), 31.
23 'Centuries are required . . .': Gustave Le Bon, *The Crowd: A Study of the Popular Mind* (New York: The Macmillan Co., 1896), 79.
25 'violence can be . . .': Leopoldo Franchetti and Sidney Sonnino, quoted in Nelson Moe, 'The Emergence of the Southern Question in Villari, Franchetti, and Sonnino', in *Italy's Southern Question: Orientalism in One Country*, ed. Jane Schneider (Oxford and New York: Berg, 1998), 66.
27 'world of semi-feudalism . . .': Christopher Duggan, *Fascism and the Mafia* (New Haven and London: Yale University Press, 1989), 20.
27 'not possible to . . .': Franco Molfese, *Storia del Brigantaggio dopo l'Unità*, 66, quoted in Nelson Moe, *The View from Vesuvius: Italian Culture and the Southern Question* (Berkeley, CA: University of California Press, 2006), 182.
28 'special handshakes, secret . . .': Paul Johnson, *The Birth of the Modern: World Society 1815–1830* (New York: HarperCollins, 1991), 666.
28 'an initiation ceremony . . .': *The New Encyclopaedia Britannica, Micropaedia: Ready Reference, 15th Edition.* Vol. 2 (Chicago, IL: Encyclopaedia Britannica, Inc., 1995), 851.
28 'keep the secrets . . .': Thomas Frost, *The Secret Societies of the European Revolution, 1776–1876*. Vol. I (London: Tinsley Brothers, 1876), 216.
28 'I consent, if . . .': *ibid.*
28 'well-organised body . . .': *ibid*, 213.
28 'protection rackets, smuggling . . .': Johnson, *op. cit.*, 667.
29 'I was conducted . . .': Joseph Mazzini, *Life and Writings of Joseph Mazzini: Volume I: Autobiographical and Political. A New Edition* (London: Smith, Elder & Co., 1890), 15.
29 'They called us . . .': Testimony of Joe Valachi, 1 October 1963. Organized Crime and Illicit Traffic in Narcotics: Hearings before the Permanent Subcommittee on Investigations of the Committee on Government Operations, United States Senate, 85th Congress, 1st Session. Part 1 (Washington, DC: United States Government Printing Office, 1963), 181–183.
29 'I devoted all . . .': from Cavour's speech before parliament, 27 March 1861, as quoted in *Italica: The Quarterly Bulletin of the American Association of Teachers of Italian* (Vol. 38, No. 3, September 1961), 178.
29 'were enrolled with . . .': Frost, *op. cit.*, Vol. II, 4.
33 'Belief in the . . .': *Encyclopaedia Britannica, Expo Edition.* Vol. 14 (Chicago, IL: Encyclopaedia Britannica, Inc., 1970), 631.
34 'the curious absence . . .': John Julius Norwich, *Sicily: An Island at the Crossroads of History* (New York: Random House, 2015), xiii.
34 'Sicily's Islamic past': *ibid*, xiv.
34 'They are seldom . . .': *ibid*, xiii.
34 'I was not . . .': Rosalie Bonanno, with Beverly Donofrio, *Mafia Marriage:*

My Story (New York: William Morrow & Co., 1990), 35.

34 'Ro and I . . .': Bill Bonanno, *Bound by Honor: A Mafioso's Story* (New York: St Martin's Press, 1999), 21.

34 'restrain the Moors . . .': Hugh Thomas, *The Spanish Civil War* (New York: Harper & Row, 1961), 247*n*.

35 'Omerta would tend . . .': Cesare Mori, *The Last Struggle with the Mafia*, trans. Orlo Williams (London: Black House Publishing, 2016), 40.

36 'The first thing . . .': Dorothy Sayers, *Gaudy Night* (New York: HarperTorch, 2006), 363.

Chapter 4

39 'country gentlemen': 'Captured by Brigands: An Englishman Carried Off by Italian Robbers, Details of a Bold Act', *New York Times* (2 December 1876), 2.

43 'Why don't you . . .': John Dickie, *Cosa Nostra: A History of the Sicilian Mafia* (London: Hodder & Stoughton, 2004), 139.

45 'I believe that . . .': *ibid*, 135.

Chapter 5

51 'Don't waste my . . .': John Dickie, *Cosa Nostra: A History of the Sicilian Mafia* (London: Hodder & Stoughton, 2004), 117.

53 'Bolognese justice': *ibid*, 146.

54 'Victory for the . . .': from London *Daily Express*, 7 July 1904, quoted in John Dickie, *Blood Brotherhoods: A History of Italy's Three Mafias* (New York: Public Affairs, 2014), 180.

Chapter 6

58 'The country needed . . .': Joseph Bonanno and Sergio Lalli, *A Man of Honor: The Autobiography of Joseph Bonanno* (New York: Simon & Schuster, 1983), 289.

58 'Italians were considered . . .': 'Alo Quietly Built Empire in Gambling', *Miami Herald* (8 April 2001), 2L.

59 'The way to . . .': cartoon caption, *The Mascot* (7 September 1889), 8.

61 'body of a . . .': Herbert Asbury, *The French Quarter: An Informal History of the New Orleans Underworld* (New York: Thunder's Mouth Press, 2003), 96.

61 'notorious Sicilian murderers . . .': from *New Orleans True Delta*, 19 March 1869, quoted in Michael L. Kurtz, 'Organized Crime in Louisiana History: Myth and Reality', *Louisiana History: The Journal of the Louisiana Historical Association* (Vol. 24, No. 4, Autumn 1983), 363.

63 'model of American . . .': Richard Gambino, *Vendetta: The True Story of the Largest Lynching in U.S. History* (Toronto: Guernica, 2000), 35.

64 'deliberate and bloody . . .': from *New Orleans Daily States*, quoted in Jerre Mangione and Ben Morreale, *La Storia: Five Centuries of the Italian Immigrant Experience* (New York: Harper Perennial, 1993), 203.

65 'We can't get . . .': 'Italians in New York', *New York Daily Tribune* (2 June 1895), 26.

65 'the Italian immigrant . . .': from Edmondo Mayor des Planches, *Attraverso gli Stati Uniti per l'Emigrazione Italiana*, 137, 321, quoted in Ernesto R. Milani, 'Peonage at Sunnyside and the Reaction of the Italian Government', *The Arkansas Historical Quarterly* (Vol. 50, No. 1, Spring 1991), 36.

66 'get them off': Gambino, *op. cit.*, 47.

Chapter 7

68 'The mafia doesn't . . .': James D. Horan, *The Pinkertons: The Detective Dynasty That Made History* (New York: Crown Publishers, 1969), 420.

68 'untimely death': 'Colonel Thos. N. Boylan', *Times-Picayune* (25 March 1894), 14.

69 'Oh Billy, Billy!': 'Assassinated: Superintendent of Police David C. Hennessy Victim of the Vendetta', *Times-Picayune* (16 October 1890), 1.

69 'four ugly, gaping . . .': *ibid.*

69 'The dagos shot . . .': Humbert S. Nelli, *The Business of Crime: Italians and Syndicate Crime in the United States* (Chicago, IL: University of Chicago Press, 1981), 49.

70 'take care of': Tom Smith, *The Crescent City Lynchings: The Murder of Chief Hennessy, the New Orleans 'Mafia' Trials, and the Parish Prison Mob* (Guilford, CT: The Lyons Press, 2007), xxvi.

70 'neat roll of . . .': *ibid.*

70 'prevent any Italians . . .': 'Narrowing Down. The Police Appear to Be Getting Closer and Closer to the Facts', *Times-Picayune* (19 October 1890), 8.

70 'God be merciful': 'Hennessy Dead', *New Orleans Times-Democrat* (17 October 1890), 1.

70 'victim of Sicilian . . .': 'To Hunt the Assassins', *New York Times* (19 October 1890), 1.

71 'We must teach . . .': *ibid.*

71 'scour the whole . . .': 'Assassinated: Superintendent of Police David C. Hennessy Victim of the Vendetta', *Times-Picayune* (16 October 1890), 1.

71 'oath-bound assassins': 'In Special Session', *Times-Picayune* (19 October 1890), 3.

71 'The little jail . . .': 'Hennessy Dead', *New Orleans Times-Democrat* (17 October 1890), 1.

71 'The disposition to assassinate . . .': from the *Baltimore News*, quoted in Horan, *op. cit.*, 421.

71 'murderous society': '"The Mafia" in New Orleans', *Harper's Weekly* (Vol. 34, No. 1768, 8 November 1890), 874.

71 'Who killa de . . .': John Kendall, 'Who Killa de Chief?', *Louisiana Historical Quarterly* (Vol. 22, 1939), 492.

72 'hothead': from *The Mascot*, quoted in Smith, *op. cit.*, 101.

72 'Stiletto societies . . .': 'To the Italian Population of New Orleans', *Times-Picayune* (23 October 1890), 4.
72 'We were shocked . . .': 'Narrowing Down. The Police Appear to Be Getting Closer and Closer to the Facts', *Times-Picayune* (19 October 1890), 8.
73 'Mafia Society': *ibid.*
73 'peculiar whistle': E. Benjamin Andrews, *The History of the Last Quarter-Century in the United States 1870–1895*. Vol. 2 (New York: Charles Scribner's Sons, 1897), 177.
74 'looked suspicious': Richard Gambino, *Vendetta: The True Story of the Largest Lynching in U.S. History* (Toronto: Guernica, 2000), 14.
75 'I'm glad he's . . .': Smith, *op. cit.*, 81.
75 'no intention of . . .': 'Narrowing Down. The Police Appear to Be Getting Closer and Closer to the Facts', *Times-Picayune* (19 October 1890), 8.
76 'I will do everything . . .': Horan, *op. cit.*, 422.
78 'vendetta society': *The Annual Register: A Review of Public Events at Home and Abroad for the Year 1890, New Series* (London: Longmans, Green and Co., 1891), 424.
78 'mafia society': 'The Hennessy Case', *Times-Picayune* (17 March 1891), 2.
78 'mute amazement': from *New Orleans Daily Item*, 14 March 1891, quoted in Gary Krist, *Empire of Sin: A Story of Sex, Jazz, Murder, and the Battle for Modern New Orleans* (New York: Broadway Books, 2014), 43.

Chapter 8

80 'ALL GOOD CITIZENS . . .': 'Mass Meeting', *New Orleans Times-Democrat* (14 March 1891), 1.
80 'a movement to correct . . .': *The American Law Review*, published bi-monthly, eds. S.D. Thompson and Leonard A. Jones. Vol. 25 (St Louis, MO: Review Pub. Co., 1891), 427.
80 'Mafia Society': 'Avenged. D.C. Hennessy's Murderers Killed by the Enraged Populace', *New Orleans Times-Democrat* (15 March 1891), 2.
80 'When courts fail . . .': *ibid.*
80 'I want to . . .': *ibid.*
81 'at the mercy . . .': *ibid.*
81 'Shall the execrable . . .': 'The New Orleans Tragedy', *The Deseret Weekly: Pioneer Publication of the Rocky Mountain Region*. Vol. 42, December 1890 to June 1891 (Salt Lake City, UT: The Deseret News Co., 1891), 400.
81 'lack of discipline': Tom Smith, *The Crescent City Lynchings: The Murder of Chief Hennessy, the New Orleans 'Mafia' Trials, and the Parish Prison Mob* (Guilford, CT: The Lyons Press, 2007), 219.
81 'To the Parish . . .': 'Avenged. D.C. Hennessy's Murderers Killed by the Enraged Populace', *New Orleans Times-Democrat* (15 March 1891), 2.

81 'There are always . . .': *ibid.*
82 'execution squad': Richard Gambino, *Vendetta: The True Story of the Largest Lynching in U.S. History* (Toronto: Guernica, 2000), 80.
82 'Telephone poles, lamp . . .': from *New Orleans Picayune*, 15 March 1891, quoted in James D. Horan, *The Pinkertons: The Detective Dynasty That Made History* (New York: Crown Publishers, 1969), 438.
83 'We want the . . .': Thomas Reppetto, *American Mafia: A History of Its Rise to Power* (New York: MJF Books, 2004), 15.
83 'not to shoot . . .': Smith, *op. cit.*, 223.
84 'Death to the dagos': Maria Laurino, *The Italian Americans: A History* (New York: W.W. Norton & Co., 2015), 36.
84 'God bless you!': 'Avenged. D.C. Hennessy's Murderers Killed by the Enraged Populace', *New Orleans Times-Democrat* (15 March 1891), 6.
84 'Chief Hennessy Avenged . . .': 'Chief Hennessy Avenged', *New York Times* (15 March 1891), 1.
84 'No reasonable, intelligent . . .': 'The New Orleans Outbreak', *Frank Leslie's Illustrated Newspaper* (28 March 1891), 127.
84 'Personally I think . . .': letter from Theodore Roosevelt to Anna Roosevelt, 21 March 1891. Theodore Roosevelt Center, Dickinson State University.
84 'No, sir, I . . .': 'A Doomed Man', *St. Louis Post-Dispatch* (17 March 1891), 1.
85 'After the first . . .': 'New Orleans' War on the Mafia', *The Illustrated American* (Vol. 6, No. 59, 4 April 1891), 322.
85 'reptiles': *ibid.*
85 'Italy's indignation . . .': 'The Dead Buried', *New Orleans Times-Democrat*, (16 March 1891), 2.
85 'Where is Charles . . .': 'Avenged. D.C. Hennessy's Murderers Killed by the Enraged Populace', *New Orleans Times-Democrat* (15 March 1891), 6.
86 'were often marked . . .': Brent Staples, 'How Italians Became White', *New York Times* (12 October 2019).
87 'The reign of . . .': Smith, *op. cit.*, 278.

Chapter 9

88 'the Dago': Selwyn Raab, *Five Families: The Rise, Decline, and Resurgence of America's Most Powerful Mafia Empires* (New York: Thomas Dunne Books, 2005), 19.
88 'Italian expert': John Oller, *Rogues' Gallery: The Birth of Modern Policing and Organized Crime in Gilded Age New York* (New York: Dutton/Penguin, 2021), 337.
89 'were virtually without . . .': from London *Times* article, quoted in Thomas Monroe Pitkin and Francesco Cordasco, *The Black Hand: A Chapter in Ethnic Crime* (Totowa, NJ: Littlefield, Adams & Co., 1977), 31.

92 'Man is a wolf . . .': from Titus Maccius Plautus, *Asinaria*, quoted in *Collected Works of Erasmus: Adages Ii1 to Iv100*, trans. Margaret Mann Phillips (Toronto: University of Toronto, 1982), 115.
93 'most pretentious mercantile . . .': 'Rich Italian Gone; Once Mafia Leader', *New York Times* (5 December 1908), 1.
94 'as thoroughly Italian . . .': Ernest Harvier, 'A Walk in Harlem Brings Surprises', *New York Times* (2 January 1921), 18.
95 'Chesty George': 'Mighty Shake-Up Stirs the Police', *New York Times* (7 November 1908), 1.
95 '*I know the man* . . .': Mike Dash, *The First Family: Terror, Extortion, Revenge, Murder, and the Birth of the American Mafia* (New York: Ballantine Books, 2010), 30.
95 'Send for the . . .': Arrigo Petacco, *Joe Petrosino*, trans. Charles Lam Markmann (New York: Macmillan Publishing Co., 1974), 3.
95 'That is . . .': William J. Flynn, *The Barrel Mystery* (New York: The James A. McCann Co., 1919), 13.
95 'My father was killed . . .': from *Evening Journal*, 22 April 1903, quoted in Dash, *op. cit.*, 146.
97 'teacup': 'Italian Murdered', *Wilkes-Barre Semi-Weekly Record* (24 October 1905), 2.
98 'DiPrimo was smarter . . .': Petacco, *op. cit.*, 14.
98 'gave Lupo a severe . . .': 'Ruined by Lupo, the Mafia Leader', *New York Times* (17 March 1909), 1.
99 'The Italians pay . . .': from *New York Journal*, quoted in Pitkin and Cordasco, *op. cit.*, 114–115.
99 'little band of zealots': A.R. Parkhurst Jr, 'Police Activity against the Black Hand', *Sun* (2 October 1914), 3.
100 'brilliant work performed . . .': Petacco, *op. cit.*, 107.
100 'Joe, you may be . . .': 'Detective Petrosino Black Hand Victim', *New York Tribune* (14 March 1909), 3.
100 'Don't go to Italy . . .': 'Petrosino Buried with High Honors', *New York Times* (13 April 1909), 2.

Chapter 10

102 'The police department . . .': Stephan Talty, *The Black Hand: The Epic War between a Brilliant Detective and the Deadliest Secret Society in American History* (Boston, MA: Houghton Mifflin Harcourt, 2017), 24.
102 'constant danger of assassination': Frank Marshall White, 'A Man Who Was Unafraid. The Courage of "Joe" Petrosino, the New York Detective, Which Led Him through Many Perils to Violent Death', *Harper's Weekly* (Vol. 53, No. 2727, 27 March 1909), 8.
103 'in search of . . .': Mike Dash, *The First Family: Terror, Extortion, Revenge, Murder, and the Birth of the American Mafia* (New York: Ballantine Books, 2010), 238.
104 'Lieutenant Joseph Petrosino': from *New York Herald*, 20 February

1909, quoted in Arrigo Petacco, *Joe Petrosino*, trans. Charles Lam Markmann (New York: Macmillan Publishing Co., 1974), 123.
104 'My trip is secret': Petacco, *ibid*, 132.
105 'rehabilitated': *ibid*, 139.
106 'There goes Petrosino . . .': Dash, *op. cit.*, 244.
107 'Vito Cascia Ferro . . .': Petacco, *op. cit.*, 145.
107 'It was successful': Dash, *op. cit.*, 256–257.
107 'PETROSINO SHOT': Western Union telegram, 13 March 1909.
108 'Well, boss': 'Thousands Pray at Petrosino's Bier', *New York Times* (11 April 1909), 3.

Chapter 11

111 'Abe the Just': 'A.E. Rothstein Dies; Labor Mediator, 81', *New York Times* (21 November 1939), 26.
111 'Who cares about . . .': Leo Katcher, *The Big Bankroll: The Life and Times of Arnold Rothstein* (New York: Harper & Brothers, 1959), 20.
112 'King of Gamblers': 'Arnold Rothstein, Gambler Prince, Shot in Mystery', *New York Daily News* (5 November 1928), 4.
112 'was heavily interested . . .': 'No Tammany War on Racing Reform', *New York Times* (4 February 1908), 3.
113 'Rothstein's a good . . .': Katcher, *op. cit.*, 52.
113 'different from us': *ibid*.
113 'Tell the Jew . . .': *ibid*, 61.
115 'that Jew': David Pietrusza, *Rothstein: The Life, Times, and Murder of the Criminal Genius Who Fixed the 1919 World Series* (New York: Carroll & Graf Publishers, 2003), 125.

Chapter 12

116 'Americans spent more . . .': *Prohibition*, three-part documentary directed by Ken Burns and Lynn Novick, written by Geoffrey C. Ward, Sarah Botstein, Ken Burns and Lynn Novick. Florentine Films/The Prohibition Film Project, Inc., PBS, 2011.
116 'wild scramble': 'John Barleycorn Takes Final Count in Nation', *Boston Daily Globe* (17 January 1920), 8.
117 'larcenous schemes': Emanuel Perlmutter, 'Master Criminal. The Big Bankroll', *New York Times* (26 July 1959), 80.
117 'The Series could be . . .': Edwin P. Hoyt, *A Gentleman of Broadway: The Story of Damon Runyon* (Boston, MA: Little, Brown & Co., 1964), 158.
117 'I don't want . . .': Leo Katcher, *The Big Bankroll: The Life and Times of Arnold Rothstein* (New York: Harper & Brothers, 1959), 146.
117 'You might be . . .': *ibid*.
120 'He picked me . . .': Dennis Eisenberg, Uri Dan and Eli Landau, *Meyer Lansky: Mogul of the Mob* (New York: Paddington Press Ltd, 1979), 81.

Chapter 13

121 'I loved school': Paul Sann interview, quoted in Robert Lacey, *Little Man: Meyer Lansky and the Gangster Life* (Boston, MA: Little, Brown & Co., 1991), 22.
121 'winners are those . . .': Dennis Eisenberg, Uri Dan and Eli Landau, *Meyer Lansky: Mogul of the Mob* (New York: Paddington Press Ltd, 1979), 37.
122 'promised that nobody . . .': *ibid*, 52.
122 'Go fuck yourself': *ibid*.
123 'I patted him . . .': Martin A. Gosch and Richard Hammer, *The Last Testament of Lucky Luciano* (Boston, MA: Little, Brown & Co., 1975), 24.
123 'For some reason . . .': Eisenberg, Dan and Landau, *op. cit.*, 53.
123 'became stained with . . .': *ibid*, 49.
123 'washed up on . . .': *ibid*.
123 'agreed to combine . . .': *ibid*, 54.
123 'That extra buck . . .': Gosch and Hammer, *op. cit.*, 12.
123 'A dollar was . . .': *ibid*.
124 'Why did you . . .': *ibid*, 17.
124 'If you needed . . .': *ibid*.
124 'My only mistake . . .': Eisenberg, Dan and Landau, *op. cit.*, 61.
124 'What I'd promised . . .': Gosch and Hammer, *op. cit.*, 19.
124 'I changed my . . .': *ibid*.
124 'You are not . . .': *ibid*, 20.
125 'They were more . . .': Eisenberg, Dan and Landau, *op. cit.*, 143.

Chapter 14

127 'Artichoke King': 'Artichoke King in Cell', *New York Daily News* (16 January 1930), 2.
128 'into an army . . .': Andrew Sinclair, *Prohibition: The Era of Excess* (Norwalk, CT: The Easton Press, 1986), 226.
129 'The old mafia . . .': Dennis Eisenberg, Uri Dan and Eli Landau, *Meyer Lansky: Mogul of the Mob* (New York: Paddington Press Ltd, 1979), 120.
129 'I'm a federal . . .': Sid Feder and Joachim Joesten, *The Luciano Story* (New York: Da Capo Press, 1994), 58.
129 'I must've been . . .': Martin A. Gosch and Richard Hammer, *The Last Testament of Lucky Luciano* (Boston, MA: Little, Brown & Co., 1975), 53.
130 'something conservative and . . .': *ibid*, 57.
130 'Within twenty-four . . .': *ibid*.
130 'I have a business . . .': *ibid*, 59.
130 'I understand you . . .': *ibid*, 46.
130 'Why the hell . . .': *ibid*.
130 'disgusted': *ibid*, 46–47.

130 'Come into my . . .': *ibid*, 47.
131 'short, fat [and] . . .': *ibid*, 64.
133 'I'm going over . . .': Carolyn Rothstein and Donald Henderson Clarke, *Now I'll Tell* (New York: Vanguard Press, 1934), 250.
133 'game was rigged': Leo Katcher, *The Big Bankroll: The Life and Times of Arnold Rothstein* (New York: Harper & Brothers, 1959), 321.
133 'Call me a . . .': *ibid*, 4.
133 'Who shot you?': *ibid*, 5.
133 'I'm a hackie . . .': *ibid.*
134 'What happened to . . .': 'Tell How Rothstein Shielded Assassin', *New York Times* (3 December 1929), 1.
134 'I'm not talking . . .': from *New York World Telegram*, 5 November 1928, quoted in Robert Lacey, *Little Man: Meyer Lansky and the Gangster Life* (Boston, MA: Little, Brown & Co., 1991), 60.

Chapter 15

137 'It's a tough . . .': George Murray, *The Madhouse on Madison Street* (Chicago, IL: Follett Pub. Co., 1965), 3.

Chapter 16

140 'Reina was a . . .': Martin A. Gosch and Richard Hammer, *The Last Testament of Lucky Luciano* (Boston, MA: Little, Brown & Co., 1975), 126.
140 'When he done . . .': *ibid*, 127.
140 'fatter, uglier, and . . .': *ibid.*
142 'with a machine gun . . .': Joseph Bonanno and Sergio Lalli, *A Man of Honor: The Autobiography of Joseph Bonanno* (New York: Simon & Schuster, 1983), 104–105.
142 'some kind of big . . .': Peter Maas, *The Valachi Papers* (New York: Perennial, 2003), 71.
142 'eyes gouged out . . .': Gosch and Hammer, *op. cit.*, 113.
142 'They'll find you . . .': *ibid.*
144 'The cops. They were . . .': Sid Feder and Joachim Joesten, *The Luciano Story* (New York: Da Capo Press, 1994), 71.
145 'Scarpato fixes the . . .': Burton B. Turkus and Sid Feder, *Murder, Inc.: The Story of 'The Syndicate'* (New York: Da Capo Press, 1992), 85.
145 'for an hour . . .': Feder and Joesten, *op. cit.*, 77.
146 'As soon as . . .': *ibid*, 78.

Chapter 17

147 'Once you accept . . .': Dennis Eisenberg, Uri Dan and Eli Landau, *Meyer Lansky: Mogul of the Mob* (New York: Paddington Press Ltd, 1979), 121.
147 'thronelike chair': Martin A. Gosch and Richard Hammer, *The Last Testament of Lucky Luciano* (Boston, MA: Little, Brown & Co., 1975), 133.

148 'All right . . . Sit . . .': Joseph Bonanno and Sergio Lalli, *A Man of Honor: The Autobiography of Joseph Bonanno* (New York: Simon & Schuster, 1983), 126.
148 'What's past is . . .': *ibid.*
148 'nerve to pat . . .': Eisenberg, Dan and Landau, *op. cit.*, 137.
148 'He told us . . .': *ibid*, 136.
149 'Lepkeleh': Meyer Berger, 'Lepke: The Shy Boss of Murder Inc. Awaits Death in the Electric Chair', *Life* magazine (28 February 1944), 87.
149 'soft-voiced, soft-eyed . . .': *ibid*, 86.

Chapter 18

153 'Maranzano loved perfection . . .': Joseph Bonanno and Sergio Lalli, *A Man of Honor: The Autobiography of Joseph Bonanno* (New York: Simon & Schuster, 1983), 75.
154 'calmly rode the . . .': Martin A. Gosch and Richard Hammer, *The Last Testament of Lucky Luciano* (Boston, MA: Little, Brown & Co., 1975), 143.
155 'runs everything in . . .': Stanley Frank, 'The Rap Gangsters Fear Most', *Saturday Evening Post* (9 August 1958), 64.
155 'hero': Bonanno and Lalli, *op. cit.*, 70.
155 'honored and privileged . . .': *ibid.*
155 'misfit': *ibid*, 137.
155 'didn't live in Sicily . . .': *ibid.*
156 'Luciano had given . . .': *ibid*, 139.
156 'I have no . . .': *ibid*, 141.
157 'the little Jew whine': George Murray, *The Legacy of Al Capone: Portraits and Annals of Chicago's Public Enemies* (New York: G.P. Putnam's Sons, 1975), 120.
158 'I may have . . .': Hank Messick, *Lansky* (New York: Berkley Medallion, 1971), 23.
158 'Did I ever . . .': Gosch and Hammer, *op. cit.*, 51.
158 'You should have . . .': *ibid*, 138.

Chapter 19

163 'We was both . . .': Martin A. Gosch and Richard Hammer, *The Last Testament of Lucky Luciano* (Boston, MA: Little, Brown & Co., 1975), 166.
164 'When the detectives . . .': 'Slot Machine Profit $20,000,000 a Year, Court Inquiry Finds', *New York Times*, Late City Edition (2 May 1931), 1.
164 'The people seem . . .': 'Huey Long Abandons Crusade on Gambling', *Stephens County Sun* (31 May 1935), 6.
164 'raked in more . . .': Paul H. Jeffers, *The Napoleon of New York: Mayor Fiorello La Guardia* (New York: John Wiley & Sons, 2002), 194.
164 'God, don't let . . .': T. Harry Williams, *Huey Long* (New York: Alfred A. Knopf, 1970), 876.

164 'It will take . . .': Philip C. Jessup, *Elihu Root. Volume II: 1905–1937* (New York: Dodd, Mead & Co., 1938), 476.
165 'It is a truth . . .': Jane Austen, *Pride and Prejudice* (London: Gresham, 1898), 1.
166 'Let Tom get . . .': Thomas E. Dewey, *Twenty Against the Underworld*, ed. Rodney Campbell (Garden City, NY: Doubleday & Co., 1974), 57.
166 'the glamor of . . .': *ibid*, 62.
166 'young and inexperienced . . .': *ibid*, 75.
166 'This is the . . .': Thomas E. Dewey to Joseph Finnegan, 9 April 1931, quoted in Richard Norton Smith, *Thomas E. Dewey and His Times: The First Full-Scale Biography of the Maker of the Modern Republican Party* (New York: Simon & Schuster, 1982), 117.
168 'runaway': 'Dodge's Statements to "Runaway" Jury in 1935', *New York Times* (21 February 1939), 11.
168 'We have labored . . .': Dewey, *op. cit.*, 149.
168 'spies in adjacent buildings': *ibid*, 157.
168 'telescope and see . . .': Smith, *op. cit.*, 157.
169 'untappable telephone cable': Dewey, *op. cit.*, 157.
169 'one large room under . . .': *ibid*.
169 'Any man who . . .': from Dewey's radio speech, 30 July 1935, *ibid*, 18, 20.
169 'could tell with . . .': *ibid*, 173.

Chapter 20

170 'I don't take . . .': T.J. English, *The Westies: Inside the Hell's Kitchen Irish Mob* (New York: G.P. Putnam's Sons, 1990), 41.
171 'baby killer': 'Nab Coll as Baby Killer; Gang, Cops in Gun Fight', *New York Daily News* (5 October 1931), 1.
172 'I'll pay good . . .': Paul Sann, *Kill the Dutchman!: The Story of Dutch Schultz* (New York: Da Capo Press, 1991), 138.
172 'Keep cool now . . .': *ibid*, 154.
174 'You do what . . .': J. Richard Davis, 'Things I Couldn't Tell till Now', *Collier's Weekly*, part two of a six-part series (29 July 1939), 38.
175 'the racket he . . .': Sann, *op. cit.*, 176.
175 'frame colored policemen': Mayme Johnson and Karen E. Quinones Miller, *Harlem Godfather: The Rap on My Husband, Ellsworth 'Bumpy' Johnson* (Philadelphia, PA: Oshun Pub. Co., 2008), 75.
176 'You'd better do . . .': Thomas E. Dewey, *Twenty Against the Underworld*, ed. Rodney Campbell (Garden City, NY: Doubleday & Co., 1974), 288.
176 'dressed like a pig': Martin A. Gosch and Richard Hammer, *The Last Testament of Lucky Luciano* (Boston, MA: Little, Brown & Co., 1975), 176.
177 'I am a rich . . .': Meyer Berger, 'Schultz Offered to Pay $100,000 Tax; Defense Is Closed', *New York Times* (26 April 1935), 1.
177 'I offered $100,000 . . .': *ibid*.

178 'as casually as . . .': Davis, *op. cit.*, part one of a six-part series (22 July 1939), 9.
178 '[Dutch Schultz] won't be . . .': Gerald Duncan, 'Schultz Defies LaGuardia Ban', *New York Daily News* (3 August 1935), 2.
178 'guilty of some . . .': John Leyden, *Scenes of Infancy: Descriptive of Teviotdale* (Edinburgh: James Ballantyne for T.N. Longman, and O. Rees, 1803), 176.
178 'loaded with great . . .': Walter Scott, *The Poetical Works of Sir Walter Scott. With Memoir and Critical Dissertation. Volume III. Containing Rokeby, and the Lord of the Isles, with the Original Notes of the Author.* Unabridged (London and New York: Cassell, Petter & Galpin, 1870), 176.
179 'Weinberg was taken . . .': Dewey, *op. cit.*, 118.
179 'Dewey's gotta go!': Rich Cohen, *Tough Jews: Fathers, Sons, and Gangster Dreams* (New York: Vintage Books, 1999), 165.
180 'Right now . . .': Gosch and Hammer, *op. cit.*, 187.
180 'Even though Dutch . . .': Dennis Eisenberg, Uri Dan and Eli Landau, *Meyer Lansky: Mogul of the Mob* (New York: Paddington Press Ltd, 1979), 162.
182 'It was somebody . . .': Sann, *op. cit.*, 39.
183 'I don't know . . .': *ibid*, 53.
183 'Oh, oh dog . . .': 'Transcript of Death Bed Statements Made by Schultz', *New York Times* (26 October 1935), 6.
183 'As ye sow . . .': Sann, *op. cit.*, 56.

Chapter 21

185 'I could kill . . .': Mayme Johnson and Karen E. Quinones Miller, *Harlem Godfather: The Rap on My Husband, Ellsworth 'Bumpy' Johnson* (Philadelphia, PA: Oshun Pub. Co., 2008), 101.
185 'Get him back . . .': *ibid.*
186 'smelled a racket': Thomas E. Dewey, *Twenty Against the Underworld*, ed. Rodney Campbell (Garden City, NY: Doubleday & Co., 1974), 187.
186 'What do you think?': Sid Feder and Joachim Joesten, *The Luciano Story* (New York: Da Capo Press, 1994), 36.
186 'There's enough to . . .': *ibid.*
186 'I didn't give . . .': Richard Norton Smith, *Thomas E. Dewey and His Times: The First Full-Scale Biography of the Maker of the Modern Republican Party* (New York: Simon & Schuster, 1982), 176.
187 'This has Charley . . .': Martin A. Gosch and Richard Hammer, *The Last Testament of Lucky Luciano* (Boston, MA: Little, Brown & Co., 1975), 189.
187 'The boss is . . .': Ovid Demaris, *The Lucky Luciano Story: The Mafioso and the Violent 30's* (New York: Tower, 1969), 74.
190 'I may not . . .': Gosch and Hammer, *op. cit.*, 196.
190 'vicious politics': 'Luciano Indicted in Vice Ring Quiz', Washington *Evening Star* (3 April 1936).

190 'a small army . . .': Dewey, *op. cit.*, 205.
190 'more than a few . . .': *ibid*, 203.
191 'My witnesses are . . .': George Wolf, with Joseph DiMona, *Frank Costello: Prime Minister of the Underworld* (New York: William Morrow & Co. 1974), 117.
191 'We cannot get . . .': Dewey, *op. cit.*, 256.
191 'beat-up broads': Gosch and Hammer, *op. cit.*, 206.
192 'just like chain . . .': '"Cokey Flo" Links Luciano in Proposal for "Vice Chain"', *Rochester Democrat and Chronicle* (23 May 1936), 2.
192 'assembly line': Gosch and Hammer, *op. cit.*, 209.
192 'Dirty liar': Smith, *op. cit.*, 196.
192 'New York City': Russ Symontowne, 'Luciano Cringes on Stand, Admits "Record" under Fire', *New York Daily News* (4 June 1936), 7.
193 'Why on earth . . .': Feder and Joesten, *op. cit.*, 321.
193 'He considered himself . . .': Denny Walsh, 'The Secret Story of Frank Costello That Was Almost Written', *New York Times* (27 February 1973), 39.
193 'had a look . . .': Gosch and Hammer, *op. cit.*, 215.
193 'legitimate occupation': *ibid*, 216.
193 'piece of a restaurant': 'Luciano Is Forced to Admit Crimes', *New York Times* (4 June 1936), 10.
193 'The only legitimate . . .': *ibid*.
193 'We was hunting': Russ Symontowne, 'Luciano Cringes on Stand, Admits "Record" under Fire', *New York Daily News* (4 June 1936), 6.
194 'Yes, I did': Dewey, *op. cit.*, 242.
194 'Were you a . . .': *ibid*.
194 'I told him . . .': *ibid*.
194 'That's all': Smith, *op. cit.*, 202.
194 'I couldn't wait . . .': Gosch and Hammer, *op. cit.*, 219.
194 'I am sure every . . .': Dewey, *op. cit.*, 260–261.
194 'looked like they . . .': Gosch and Hammer, *op. cit.*, 221.
194 'shallow and parasitic . . .': 'Luciano Is Called Shallow Parasite', *New York Times* (19 June 1936), 22.
195 'New York's best-known . . .': Paul H. Jeffers, *The Napoleon of New York: Mayor Fiorello La Guardia* (New York: John Wiley & Sons, 2002), 142.
195 'girls lied because . . .': Jerre Mangione and Ben Morreale, *La Storia: Five Centuries of the Italian Immigrant Experience* (New York: Harper Perennial, 1993), 255.
195 'put words into . . .': *ibid*.
195 'coddling and threats . . .': Dewey, *op. cit.*, 267.
195 'were filled with perjury': *ibid*, 268.
195 'think up some . . .': *ibid*, 211.
196 'Genovese is an . . .': Leonard Katz, *Uncle Frank: The Biography of Frank Costello* (London: Star Book/W.H. Allen, 1975), 96.
197 'Hebes': Gosch and Hammer, *op. cit.*, 39.

Chapter 22

199 'some 250 criminal . . .': Meyer Berger, 'Lepke: The Shy Boss of Murder Inc. Awaits Death in the Electric Chair', *Life* magazine (28 February 1944), 86.
200 'portraits and measurements . . .': Thomas E. Dewey, *Twenty Against the Underworld*, ed. Rodney Campbell (Garden City, NY: Doubleday & Co., 1974), 475.
200 'would let his . . .': Berger, *op. cit.*, 92.
201 'No witnesses . . . no indictments': *ibid*, 90.
201 'Murder, Incorporated': 'Harry Feeney, Police Reporter, Coined Murder Inc. Label', *Brooklyn Daily Eagle* (20 September 1950), 15.
201 'As long as . . .': Burton B. Turkus and Sid Feder, *Murder, Inc.: The Story of 'The Syndicate'* (New York: Da Capo Press, 1992), 108.
202 'Rudnick is laying . . .': *ibid*, 231.
202 'Pep starts with . . .': *ibid*, 232.
203 'The shot which . . .': Dewey, *op. cit.*, 304.
203 'There will soon . . .': Harry J. Anslinger and Will Oursler, *The Murderers: The Story of the Narcotics Gangs* (New York: Farrar, Straus & Cudahy, 1961), 50.
204 'Those bastards are . . .': Turkus and Feder, *op. cit.*, 357.
204 'Nobody moved in . . .': *ibid*, 351.
205 'from cowboys on . . .': Walter Winchell, *Winchell Exclusive: 'Things That Happened to Me – and Me to Them'* (Englewood Cliffs, NJ: Prentice Hall, 1975), iv.
205 'most important men . . .': Curt Gentry, *J. Edgar Hoover: The Man and the Secrets* (New York: Plume, 1992), 218.
205 'Stork Club detective': Westbrook Pegler, 'Fair Enough', *Washington Post* (1 March 1940), 13.
206 'could find someone . . .': Winchell, *op. cit.*, 135.
206 'I got to be . . .': Leonard Katz, *Uncle Frank: The Biography of Frank Costello* (London: Star Book/W.H. Allen, 1975), 256.
206 'You stay out . . .': Gentry, *op. cit.*, 329.
206 'deal is in . . .': Turkus and Feder, *op. cit.*, 358.
206 'twelve': Paul R. Kavieff, *The Life and Times of Lepke Buchalter: America's Most Ruthless Labor Racketeer* (Fort Lee, NJ: Barricade Books, 2006), 128.
206 'eight': *ibid.*
206 'What's the hurry?': Turkus and Feder, *op. cit.*, 359.
207 'Attention Public Enemy . . .': Winchell, *op. cit.*, 136.
207 'Why do you . . .': *ibid*, 137.
207 'I'm not a lawyer . . .': *ibid*, 138.
207 'I am fed up . . .': *ibid*, 139–140.
208 'You people haven't . . .': *ibid*, 140.
208 'John, this is . . .': *ibid*, 142.

208 'These pistols . . .': William C. Sullivan and Bill Brown, *The Bureau: My Thirty Years in Hoover's FBI* (New York: W.W. Norton & Co., 1979), 101.
208 'Give this to . . .': Winchell, *op. cit.*, 143.
208 'We'll be with . . .': *ibid*, 144.
208 'Lepke, this is . . .': *ibid*, 145.
209 'This is Winchell': *ibid.*
209 'I'm Jacob Shapiro . . .': 'Jacob (Gurrah) Shapiro Gives Up Here after Eluding World-Wide Hunt for a Year', *New York Times*, Late City Edition (15 April 1938), 1.
210 'guilty of eighty murders': Gentry, *op. cit.*, 221.
210 'Like a little . . .': Turkus and Feder, *op. cit.*, 308.
210 'tighten up around . . .': *ibid*, 309.
210 'bloody froth bubbled': *ibid.*
210 'There – that's better': *ibid.*

Chapter 23

211 'You might have . . .': Hank Messick, *Lansky* (New York: Berkley Medallion, 1971), 92.
211 'for the good . . .': Dennis Eisenberg, Uri Dan and Eli Landau, *Meyer Lansky: Mogul of the Mob* (New York: Paddington Press Ltd, 1979), 176.
212 'Take it easy . . .': *ibid*, 175.
212 'I was crazy . . .': Dean Jennings, *We Only Kill Each Other: The True Story of Mobster Bugsy Siegel, the Man Who Invented Las Vegas* (New York: Pocket Books, 1992), 20.
212 'Take me down, too': *ibid*, 142.
212 'Stop thinking you're . . .': Eisenberg, Dan and Landau, *op. cit.*, 177.
213 'was bigger than . . .': Jennings, *op. cit.*, 40.
215 'He had authority . . .': *ibid*, 56.
216 'I hope you . . .': Rich Cohen, *Tough Jews: Fathers, Sons, and Gangster Dreams* (New York: Vintage Books, 1999), 196.
216 'boxing commissioner of . . .': Jack Roth, 'Carbo Ends Trial with Guilty Plea', *New York Times* (31 October 1959), 1.

Chapter 24

218 'Dear Sir, I . . .': Burton B. Turkus and Sid Feder, *Murder, Inc.: The Story of 'The Syndicate'* (New York: Da Capo Press, 1992), 30.
218 'Those rats killed . . .': *ibid*, 31.
218 'knows more than me': *ibid*, 37.
219 'I can tell you . . .': *ibid*, 64.
219 'brains': 'Lepke Is Indicted in Coast Slaying', *New York Times* (21 August 1940), 40.
219 'our boss': Al Binder and Jack Turcott, 'Reles Puts Finger on 2 Ex-Pals', *New York Daily News* (17 September 1940), 4.

219 'Reles is singin'': Martin A. Gosch and Richard Hammer, *The Last Testament of Lucky Luciano* (Boston, MA: Little, Brown & Co., 1975), 248.
220 'We've got enough . . .': Turkus and Feder, *op. cit.*, 156.
220 'I don't give . . .': Gosch and Hammer, *op. cit.*, 248.
220 'He's not home': Dean Jennings, *We Only Kill Each Other: The True Story of Mobster Bugsy Siegel, the Man Who Invented Las Vegas* (New York: Pocket Books, 1992), 100.
220 'What are you . . .': *ibid.*
221 'To consign all three . . .': Turkus and Feder, *op. cit.*, 406.
221 'Rat Suite': Rich Cohen, *Tough Jews: Fathers, Sons, and Gangster Dreams* (New York: Vintage Books, 1999), 216.
221 'went out the . . .': 'Inquiry Discredits O'Dwyer for Calling Reles Important', *New York Times* (22 December 1951), 1.
223 'fire was started . . .': '12-Hour Fight Vain', *New York Times* (10 February 1942), 7.
223 'Everybody in New York . . .': Dennis Eisenberg, Uri Dan and Eli Landau, *Meyer Lansky: Mogul of the Mob* (New York: Paddington Press Ltd, 1979), 183–184.
224 'A lot of these . . .': Sid Feder and Joachim Joesten, *The Luciano Story* (New York: Da Capo Press, 1994), 182.
224 'I'll talk to . . .': Eisenberg, Dan and Landau, *op. cit.*, 181.
225 'Can we trust him?': *ibid.*
225 'If it only . . .': *ibid*, 191.
226 'Dear Warden, This . . .': Statement of Vernon A. Morhous. University of Rochester, Thomas E. Dewey Papers, Series 13, Box 13, 2.
226 'threw his arms . . .': Eisenberg, Dan and Landau, *op. cit.*, 191.
226 'There's no point . . .': *ibid*, 192.
226 'There'll be no . . .': *ibid*, 193.

Chapter 25

228 'Oh, brother, if . . .': Dean Jennings, *We Only Kill Each Other: The True Story of Mobster Bugsy Siegel, the Man Who Invented Las Vegas* (New York: Pocket Books, 1992), 74.
229 'full-fledged agitator-editor': Nunzio Pernicone, *Carlo Tresca: Portrait of a Rebel* (Oakland, CA: AK Press, 2010), 15.
230 'Good morning, Francesco . . .': 'Gangster Backed Aurelio for Bench, Prosecutor Avers', *New York Times* (29 August 1943), 31.
231 'I got Irving . . .': Sidney Zion, *The Autobiography of Roy Cohn* (Secaucus, NJ: Lyle Stuart, Inc., 1988), 60.
231 'GANGSTER BACKED AURELIO . . .': 'Gangster Backed Aurelio for Bench, Prosecutor Avers', *New York Times* (29 August 1943), 1.
232 'I detest the narcotic . . .': 'Costello Denies Underworld Links', *New York Times* (21 December 1946), 20.
232 'boast that the bomb . . .': 'The Death of Carlo Tresca', *New York Times* (13 January 1943), 22.

233 'in the manner of . . .': 'Pittsburgh Phil Struts to Chair but Buggsy Dies with Eyes Shut', *Brooklyn Daily Eagle* (13 June 1941), 4.
233 'an old friend . . .': James MacGregor Burns, *Roosevelt: The Soldier of Freedom*. Vol. 2 (New York: Harcourt Brace Jovanovich, 1970), 51.
234 'manpower supply, strike . . .': *ibid*, 55.
234 'saving Lepke': 'Roosevelt Saving Lepke, Says Dewey', *New York Times* (21 November 1943), 1.
234 'ready to carry . . .': 'State Bars Pledge to Execute Lepke', *New York Times* (1 December 1943), 23.
234 'Turn the son . . .': Curt Gentry, *J. Edgar Hoover: The Man and the Secrets* (New York: Plume, 1992), 221.
234 'If I would . . .': Burton B. Turkus and Sid Feder, *Murder, Inc.: The Story of 'The Syndicate'* (New York: Da Capo Press, 1992), 416.
235 'Lepke offered material . . .': from *New York Daily Mirror*, quoted in Turkus and Feder, *ibid*, 421.
235 'Lepke sought to . . .': from *New York Sun*, quoted in Turkus and Feder, *ibid*, 495.
235 'packed with political TNT': Gilbert Millstein, 'Lepke and 2 Pals Die in Chair; Mobster Chief Calm, Last to Go', *New York Daily News* (5 March 1944), 3.
235 'knew what he . . .': Paul Sann, *Kill the Dutchman!: The Story of Dutch Schultz* (New York: Da Capo Press, 1991), 285.
235 'I got the impression . . .': *ibid*, 286.
236 'strode rapidly into . . .': Gilbert Millstein, 'Lepke and 2 Pals Die in Chair; Mobster Chief Calm, Last to Go', *New York Daily News* (5 March 1944), 3.
236 'Give my love . . .': *ibid*.
236 'His step was . . .': Turkus and Feder, *op. cit.*, 415.
236 'petty larceny': David Dubinsky and A.H. Raskin, *David Dubinsky: A Life with Labor* (New York: Simon & Schuster, 1977), 151.

Chapter 26

237 'soft underbelly': Winston S. Churchill, *Churchill by Himself*, ed. Richard M. Langworth (London: Ebury Press, 2008), 43.
238 'kind of liaison . . .': Dennis Eisenberg, Uri Dan and Eli Landau, *Meyer Lansky: Mogul of the Mob* (New York: Paddington Press Ltd, 1979), 208.
238 'utter failure': Albert Kesselring, *The Memoirs of Field-Marshal Kesselring*, trans. Lynton Hudson (London: William Kimber, 1953), 163.
238 'The Italian soldiers . . .': Farley Mowat, *And No Birds Sang* (Boston, MA: An Atlantic Monthly Press Book/Little, Brown & Co., 1979), 143.
239 'Neapolitan kleptomania': Norman Lewis, *Naples '44: A World War II Diary of Occupied Italy* (New York: Carroll & Graf, 2005), 79.
239 'telegraph poles': *ibid*.
239 'IF YOU DON'T . . .': *ibid*, 123.

241 'invaluable [and] absolutely . . .': Ed Reid, *Mafia* (New York: Random House, 1952), 211.
241 'trustworthy, loyal and . . .': *ibid*, 212.
241 'Yeah, that's me . . .': Peter Maas, *The Valachi Papers* (New York: Perennial, 2003), 176.
241 'Take the money': *ibid*, 177.
242 'kill eight horses': 'Int [sic] Gang Forced Death of Key Witness in Jail', *Brooklyn Daily Eagle* (9 February 1945), 1.
242 'Kid, you are doing . . .': Testimony of Orange C. Dickey, 2 July 1958. Investigation of Improper Activities in the Labor or Management Field: Hearings before the Select Committee on Improper Activities in the Labor Management Field, 85th Congress, 2d Session. Part 32 (Washington, DC: United States Government Printing Office, 1958), 12383.
243 'Fuck 'em all': Martin A. Gosch and Richard Hammer, *The Last Testament of Lucky Luciano* (Boston, MA: Little, Brown & Co., 1975), 278.
245 'man who had . . .': *ibid*, 194.
245 'Yeah, broads': Hank Messick, *Lansky* (New York: Berkley Medallion, 1971), 127.
245 '[Women] is one . . .': Eisenberg, Dan and Landau, *op. cit.*, 224.
245 'Half the people . . .': Gosch and Hammer, *op. cit.*, 301.
246 'December – Hotel Nacional': *ibid*, 304.

Chapter 27

247 'schizophrenic moods': Michael Hiltzik, *Colossus: Hoover Dam and the Making of the American Century* (New York: Free Press, 2010), 3.
248 'Here it is, Moe': Dean Jennings, *We Only Kill Each Other: The True Story of Mobster Bugsy Siegel, the Man Who Invented Las Vegas* (New York: Pocket Books, 1992), 149.
248 'few nickels and dimes': *ibid*.
248 'We only kill . . .': *ibid*, 4.
248 'matured shrubberies': Herman Milton Greenspun, 'Flamingo', *Las Vegas Life* magazine (17 December 1946), 14.
248 'Never mind the . . .': Jennings, *op. cit.*, 152.
248 'stables with forty . . .': Herman Milton Greenspun, 'Flamingo', *Las Vegas Life* magazine (17 December 1946), 14.
249 'stupid gambling joint . . .': Andy Edmonds, *Bugsy's Baby: The Secret Life of Mob Queen Virginia Hill* (New York: Birch Lane Press, 1993), 129.
249 'What have you . . .': Peter Green, *Alexander of Macedon, 356–323 B.C.: A Historical Biography* (Berkeley, CA: University of California Press, 1992), 155–156.
250 'polished hotel executive': Herman Milton Greenspun, 'Flamingo', *Las Vegas Life* magazine (17 December 1946), 14.
250 'Siegelian': *ibid*.
250 'Forget those dumb . . .': Jennings, *op. cit.*, 160.
251 'What the hell . . .': *ibid*, 155.

251 'dirty pig': *ibid.*
251 'You crummy peasant!': *ibid*, 161.
251 'The hotel portion . . .': full-page ad, *The Hollywood Reporter* (23 December 1946).
252 'You're not playing . . .': Jennings, *op. cit.*, 163.
252 'Great place, Bugsy! . . .': *ibid*, 166.
253 'two-bit loser': Edmonds, *op. cit.*, 138.
253 'fucking chump who . . .': *ibid.*

Chapter 28

254 'The minute the . . .': Dennis Eisenberg, Uri Dan and Eli Landau, *Meyer Lansky: Mogul of the Mob* (New York: Paddington Press Ltd, 1979), 228.
254 'Where's Meyer?': T.J. English, *Havana Nocturne: How the Mob Owned Cuba . . . and Then Lost It to the Revolution* (New York: MJF Books, 2008), 4.
255 'helluva change from . . .': Martin A. Gosch and Richard Hammer, *The Last Testament of Lucky Luciano* (Boston, MA: Little, Brown & Co., 1975), 307.
255 'You'll have all . . .': *ibid*, 310.
256 'I'm the only . . .': Anthony Summers and Robbyn Swan, *Sinatra: The Life* (New York: Alfred A. Knopf, 2005), 130.
257 'that he believes . . .': 'Sinatra Sued in Foreclosure', *Tampa Bay Times* (25 August 1943), 11.
257 'I now own myself': 'Sinatra Pays Up; Now Out of Hock', *Camden Morning Post* (27 August 1943), 18.
257 'Moretti made some . . .': Summers and Swan, *op. cit.*, 50.
257 'all his life': Tina Sinatra and Jeff Coplon, *My Father's Daughter: A Memoir* (New York: Simon & Schuster, 2000), 73.
258 'Ruark Is Puzzled . . .': Robert C. Ruark, 'Ruark Is Puzzled as to Why Sinatra Chooses to Associate with Hoodlums', *Albuquerque Tribune* (20 February 1947), 8.
258 'millions of kids': *ibid.*
258 'panderer and permanent . . .': *ibid.*
258 'Any report that . . .': 'Voice Denies Luciano Link', *New York Daily News* (23 February 1947), 50.
259 'large shipment of . . .': 'U.S. Ends Narcotic Sales to Cuba While Luciano Is Resident There', *New York Times* (22 February 1947), 27.
259 'I'm taking bum raps . . .': Sid Feder and Joachim Joesten, *The Luciano Story* (New York: Da Capo Press, 1994), 245.
259 'There is no . . .': *ibid*, 242.
259 'He is a dangerous . . .': *ibid.*

Chapter 29

261 'bring the kiddies': Steve Fischer, *When the Mob Ran Vegas: Stories of Money, Mayhem and Murder* (New York: MJF Books, 2007), 18.

261 'that gangster up . . .': *ibid.*
263 'Ben, why don't . . .': Dean Jennings, *We Only Kill Each Other: The True Story of Mobster Bugsy Siegel, the Man Who Invented Las Vegas* (New York: Pocket Books, 1992), 184.
263 'crummy magazine': *ibid*, 172.
264 'coudn't keep cab fare . . .': Andy Edmonds, *Bugsy's Baby: The Secret Life of Mob Queen Virginia Hill* (New York: Birch Lane Press, 1993), 138.
265 'Charlie, with that . . .': Martin A. Gosch and Richard Hammer, *The Last Testament of Lucky Luciano* (Boston, MA: Little, Brown & Co., 1975), 318.
265 'Do what you . . .': Bill Bonanno and Gary B. Abromovitz, *The Last Testament of Bill Bonanno: The Final Secrets of a Life in the Mafia* (New York: Harper, 2011), 122.

Chapter 30
273 'mingle with a . . .': Leonard Katz, *Uncle Frank: The Biography of Frank Costello* (London: Star Book/W.H. Allen, 1975), 158.
273 'introduced Hoffmann to . . .': *ibid.*
274 'We hope we'll . . .': 'Need MORE Costellos, Mme. Chairman Replies', *New York Daily News* (29 January 1949), 4.
274 'prime minister of . . .': Harold Lavine, 'Kingpin Costello, Gamblers' Gambler', *Newsweek* (21 November 1949), 27.
275 'Hoover will never . . .': Anthony Summers, *Official and Confidential: the Secret Life of J. Edgar Hoover* (New York: G.P. Putnam's Sons, 1993), 239.
275 'Hoover did make . . .': William C. Sullivan and Bill Brown, *The Bureau: My Thirty Years in Hoover's FBI* (New York: W.W. Norton & Co., 1979), 87.
275 'groups advocating the . . .': Hearings and Final Report of the Select Committee to Study Governmental Operations with Respect to Intelligence Activities of the United States Senate, 94th Congress, 1st Session, 1975–1976, Book 3 (Washington, DC: United States Government Printing Office, 1976), 396.
276 'didn't want to . . .': Sullivan and Brown, *op. cit.*, 117.
276 'complicated; the Mafia . . .': *ibid*, 118.
277 'we tried to . . .': Summers, *op. cit.*, 229.
277 'housewives did their . . .': Estes Kefauver, *Crime in America*, ed. Sidney Shalett (London: Victor Gollancz Ltd, 1951), 218.
277 'Kefauver parties': Henry McLemore, 'Kefauver Parties', *Tampa Times* (29 March 1951), 6.
278 *'Kefauveritis'*: *ibid*, 12.
278 'Why don't you . . .': Testimony of Harry Russell, 22 September 1950. Proceedings against Harry Russell for Contempt of the Senate: Special Committee to Investigate Organized Crime in Interstate Commerce.

Report No. 2580, 81st Congress, 2d Session (Washington, DC: United States Government Printing Office, 23 September 1950), 21.

278 'Any place I go . . .': Testimony of Paul Ricca, 9 September 1950. Investigation of Organized Crime in Interstate Commerce: Hearings before the Special Committee to Investigate Organized Crime in Interstate Commerce, United States Senate, 81st Congress, 2d Session. Part 5, Illinois (Washington, DC: United States Government Printing Office, 1951), 1.

278 'If you were in . . .': Testimony of Joseph Fusco, 17 October 1950, *ibid*, 604.

278 'I must have . . .': Testimony of Mickey Cohen, 17 November 1950. Investigation of Organized Crime in Interstate Commerce: Hearings before the Special Committee to Investigate Organized Crime in Interstate Commerce, United States Senate, 81st Congress, 2d Session. Part 10, Nevada – California (Washington, DC: United States Government Printing Office, 1951), 201.

278 'Fortunately God helped me': Testimony of Willie Moretti, 13 December 1950. Investigation of Organized Crime in Interstate Commerce: Hearings before the Special Committee to Investigate Organized Crime in Interstate Commerce, United States Senate, 81st Congress, 2d Session. Part 7, New York – New Jersey (Washington, DC: United States Government Printing Office, 1951), 353.

278 'Get your fucking . . .': Andy Edmonds, *Bugsy's Baby: The Secret Life of Mob Queen Virginia Hill* (New York: Birch Lane Press, 1993), 182.

278 'Get out of my . . .': *ibid*.

279 'I never knew . . .': Testimony of Virginia Hill Hauser, 15 March 1951. Investigation of Organized Crime in Interstate Commerce: Hearings before the Special Committee to Investigate Organized Crime in Interstate Commerce, United States Senate, 82nd Congress, 1st Session. Part 7, New York – New Jersey (Washington, DC: United States Government Printing Office, 1951), 1165.

279 'You really want . . .': Harold Conrad, *Dear Muffo: 35 Years in the Fast Lane* (New York: Stein & Day, 1982), 237.

279 'I hope the atom . . .': 'Virginia Swats Newspaper Gal', *Atlanta Constitution* (16 March 1951), 1.

279 'I don't think it . . .': Testimony of Meyer Lansky, 11 October 1950. Investigation of Organized Crime in Interstate Commerce: Hearings before the Special Committee to Investigate Organized Crime in Interstate Commerce, United States Senate, 81st Congress, 2d Session. Part 7, New York – New Jersey (Washington, DC: United States Government Printing Office, 1951), 150.

279 'How did you . . .': Senator Tobey, 12 October 1950, *ibid*, 157.

280 'Minorities and undesirables . . .': Moses Polakoff, 12 October 1950, *ibid*, 158.

280 'I lost a wife . . .': Hank Messick, *Lansky* (New York: Berkley Medallion, 1971), 46.

282 'When he attempted . . .': Katz, *op. cit.*, 165.
283 'exposed himself as . . .': Kefauver, *op. cit.*, 230.
283 'What a sucker!': 'The U.S. Gets a Close Look at Crime', *Life* magazine (26 March 1951), 33.
283 'that man on television': Kefauver, *op. cit.*, 16.
284 'new aristocrats of . . .': *ibid*, 23.
284 '*sunk to a new low*': *ibid*, 25.

Chapter 31

286 'mercy killing': Peter Maas, *The Valachi Papers* (New York: Perennial, 003), 197.
286 'If tomorrow I . . .': *ibid*, 195.
286 'vacation': Leonard Katz, *Uncle Frank: The Biography of Frank Costello* (London: Star Book/W.H. Allen, 1975), 134.
290 'This is for you, Frank!': Edward Kirkman and Henry Lee, 'Ex-Boxer Hunted as No. 1 Costello Suspect', *New York Daily News* (18 July 1957), 3.
292 'between thirty and thirty-five . . .': Larry McShane, *Chin: The Life and Crimes of Mafia Boss Vincent Gigante* (New York: Pinnacle Books, 2016), 33.
292 'The Waddler': Edward Kirkman and Henry Lee, 'Ex-Boxer Hunted as No. 1 Costello Suspect', *New York Daily News* (18 July 1957), 3.
292 'The Fat Man': Loren Craft, 'Gigante Is Indicted in Costello Gunning', *New York Daily News* (23 August 1957), 8.
292 'I haven't an enemy . . .': Henry Price, 'Costello Assassination Plot Misfires', *Buffalo Evening News* (3 May 1957), 1.
293 'Gross casino wins': 'Costello Jailed, Silent on Winnings', *Buffalo Evening News* (8 May 1957), 3.
294 'wild applause': Norma Abrams and Henry Lee, 'The Chin's Not Guilty of Creasing Costello', *New York Daily News* (28 May 1958), 2.
295 'It was the beads!': *ibid*.
295 'I hate squealers! . . .': Jack Roth, 'F.B.I. Giving Hogan Valachi Details', *New York Times* (8 August 1963), 17.
296 'he was anything . . .': Bill Bonanno, *Bound by Honor: A Mafioso's Story* (New York: St Martin's Press, 1999), 15.

Chapter 32

301 'fellow philanderer': Peter Collier and David Horowitz, *The Kennedys: An American Drama* (New York: Summit Books, 1984), 197.
301 'liked groups': *ibid*, Collier and Horowitz interview with George Smathers.
301 'Vito is bad-mouthing . . .': George Wolf, with Joseph DiMona, *Frank Costello: Prime Minister of the Underworld* (New York: William Morrow & Co., 1974), 248.
302 'protects Lansky from . . .': Vincent Teresa and Thomas C. Renner, *My*

Life in the Mafia (New York: Doubleday & Co., 1973), 217.
304 'Keep your mouth . . .': Meyer Berger, 'Anastasia Slain in a Hotel Here; Led Murder Inc.', *New York Times* (26 October 1957), 12.
305 'Gasim's time is . . .': *Lawrence of Arabia*, screenplay by Robert Bolt, Horizon Pictures/Columbia Pictures, 1962, 71.
305 'Nothing is written': *ibid*, 77.
306 'It was written . . .': *ibid*, 99.

Chapter 33

307 'I was always . . .': from 'Final Victory of Apalachin Sleuth', *New York Daily Mirror*, 17 January 1960, quoted in Gil Reavill, *Mafia Summit: J. Edgar Hoover, the Kennedy Brothers, and the Meeting That Unmasked the Mob* (New York: Thomas Dunne Books/St Martin's Press, 2013), 27.
309 'I decided the best . . .': Martin A. Gosch and Richard Hammer, *The Last Testament of Lucky Luciano* (Boston, MA: Little, Brown & Co., 1975), 402.
310 'Genovese was behind . . .': Dennis Eisenberg, Uri Dan and Eli Landau, *Meyer Lansky: Mogul of the Mob* (New York: Paddington Press Ltd, 1979), 247.
312 'not to become . . .': Robert E. Quirk, *Fidel Castro* (New York: W.W. Norton & Co., 1995), 207–208.
313 'We got a lot . . .': T.J. English, *Havana Nocturne: How the Mob Owned Cuba . . . and Then Lost It to the Revolution* (New York: MJF Books, 2008), 300.
313 'We need to make . . .': *ibid*, 301.
313 'Make the rounds . . .': *ibid*.
313 'an atmosphere of . . .': Quirk, *op. cit.*, 209.
314 'run all these fascist . . .': William Scott Malone, 'The Secret Life of Jack Ruby', *New Times* (23 January 1978), 48.
314 'You think he's . . .': *ibid*.
314 'They used to come . . .': Testimony of Santo Trafficante, 28 September 1978. Investigation of the Assassination of President John F. Kennedy: Hearings before the Select Committee on Assassinations of the U.S. House of Representatives, 95th Congress, 2d Session. Vol. 5 (Washington, DC: United States Government Printing Office, 1979), 353.
315 'They're going to . . .': Frank Ragano and Selwyn Raab, *Mob Lawyer* (New York: Charles Scribner's Sons, 1994), 56.
315 'I crapped out': Robert Lacey, *Little Man: Meyer Lansky and the Gangster Life* (Boston, MA: Little, Brown & Co., 1991), 258.
316 'wizard of illicit . . .': Cartha D. DeLoach, *Hoover's FBI: The Inside Story by Hoover's Trusted Lieutenant* (Washington, DC: Regnery Publishing, 1995), 301.
316 'First, the money . . .': Ronald Goldfarb, *Perfect Villains, Imperfect Heroes: Robert F. Kennedy's War Against Organized Crime* (New York: Random House, 1995), 131.

Epilogue

318 'aged twenty-five years': Martin A. Gosch and Richard Hammer, *The Last Testament of Lucky Luciano* (Boston, MA: Little, Brown & Co., 1975), 446.

318 'I fucked myself . . .': *ibid.*

318 'All of 'em': *ibid*, vii.

318 'For God's sake . . .': *ibid*, 447.

319 'I told him . . .': Denny Walsh, 'The Secret Story of Frank Costello That Was Almost Written', *New York Times* (27 February 1973), 39.

319 'He's gone': *ibid.*

320 'He certainly didn't . . .': *ibid.*

320 'mild mannered': Robert Lacey, *Little Man: Meyer Lansky and the Gangster Life* (Boston, MA: Little, Brown & Co., 1991), 3.

321 'controlled at least . . .': Ralph Blumenthal, 'When the Mob Delivered the Goods', *New York Times* magazine (26 July 1992), 31.

321 'could not run . . .': Bill Bonanno, *Bound by Honor: A Mafioso's Story* (New York: St Martin's Press, 1999), 122.

323 'one man in America . . .': Robert F. Kennedy, *The Enemy Within* (New York: Harper & Brothers, 1960), 55.

BIBLIOGRAPHY

Books

Alexander, Shana. *The Pizza Connection: Lawyers, Money, Drugs, Mafia*. New York: Weidenfeld & Nicolson, 1988.

Allen, Oliver E. *The Tiger: The Rise and Fall of Tammany Hall*. Reading, MA: Addison-Wesley Pub. Co., 1993.

Amari, Michele. *History of the War of the Sicilian Vespers*. Edited by the Earl of Ellesmere. Three Volumes. London: Richard Bentley, 1850.

The American Law Review. Edited by S.D. Thompson and Leonard A. Jones. Volume 25. St Louis, MO: Review Pub. Co., 1891.

Andrews, E. Benjamin. *The History of the Last Quarter-Century in the United States 1870–1895*. Volume II. New York: Charles Scribner's Sons, 1897.

The Annual Register: A Review of Public Events at Home and Abroad for the Year 1890, New Series. London: Longmans, Green and Co., 1891.

Anslinger, Harry J., and Will Oursler. *The Murderers: The Story of the Narcotics Gangs*. New York: Farrar, Straus & Cudahy, 1961.

Arlacchi, Pino. *Mafia Business: The Mafia Ethic and the Spirit of Capitalism*. Translated by Martin Ryle. London: Verso, 1987.

_____. *Men of Dishonor: Inside the Sicilian Mafia: An Account of Antonino Calderone*. Translated from the Italian by Marc Romano. New York: William Morrow & Co., 1993.

Arons, Ron. *The Jews of Sing Sing: Gotham Gangsters and Gonuvim*. Fort Lee, NJ: Barricade Books, 2008.

Asbury, Herbert. *The French Quarter: An Informal History of the New Orleans Underworld*. New York: Thunder's Mouth Press, 2003.

_____. *The Gangs of Chicago: An Informal History of the Chicago Underworld*. New York: Thunder's Mouth Press, 1986.

_____. *The Gangs of New York: An Informal History of the Underworld*. New York: Thunder's Mouth Press, 2001.

Austen, Jane. *Pride and Prejudice*. London: Gresham, 1898.

Balsamo, William, and John Balsamo. *Young Capone: The Untold Story of Scarface in New York, 1899–1925*. New York: MJF Books, 2011.

Baron, Salo W., Arcadius Kahan and others. *Economic History of the Jews*. Edited by Nachum Gross. New York: Schocken Books, 1976.

Barzini, Luigi. *From Caesar to the Mafia: Sketches of Italian Life*. New York: The Library Press, 1971.

_____. *The Italians: A Full-Length Portrait Featuring Their Manners and Morals*. New York: Atheneum, 1985.

Benjamin, Sandra. *Sicily: Three Thousand Years of Human History*. Hanover, NH: Steerforth Press, 2006.

Bergreen, Laurence. *Capone: The Man and the Era*. New York: Simon & Schuster, 1994.

Bloch, Marc. *Feudal Society*. Translated by L.A. Manyon. London: Routledge & Kegan Paul Ltd, 1962.

_____. *The Historian's Craft: Reflections on the Nature and Uses of History and the Techniques and Methods of the Men Who Write It*. Translated by Peter Putnam. New York: Alfred A. Knopf, 1971.

Blumenthal, Karen. *Bootleg: Murder, Moonshine, and the Lawless Years of Prohibition*. New York: Roaring Brook Press, 2011.

Blumenthal, Ralph. *Last Days of the Sicilians: At War with the Mafia: The Assault on the Pizza Connection*. New York: Times Books, 1988.

Bolzoni, Attilio. *White Shotgun: The Sicilian Mafia in Their Own Words*. Translated by Shaun Whiteside. London: Pan Books, 2014.

Bonanno, Bill. *Bound by Honor: A Mafioso's Story*. New York: St Martin's Press, 1999.

Bonanno, Bill, and Gary B. Abromovitz. *The Last Testament of Bill Bonanno: The Final Secrets of a Life in the Mafia*. New York: Harper, 2011.

Bonanno, Joseph, and Sergio Lalli. *A Man of Honor: The Autobiography of Joseph Bonanno*. New York: Simon & Schuster, 1983.

Bonanno, Rosalie, with Beverly Donofrio. *Mafia Marriage: My Story*. New York: William Morrow & Co., 1990.

Buccellato, James A. *Early Organized Crime in Detroit: Vice,*

Corruption and the Rise of the Mafia. Charleston, SC: The History Press, 2015.

Burckhardt, Jacob. *The Civilization of the Renaissance in Italy*. Authorized Translation from the Fifteenth Edition by S.G.C. Middlemore. New York: Albert & Charles Boni, 1935.

Burns, James MacGregor. *Roosevelt: The Soldier of Freedom*. Volume 2. New York: Harcourt Brace Jovanovich, 1970.

Cannato, Vincent J. *American Passage: The History of Ellis Island*. New York: Harper Perennial, 2010.

Cantor, Norman F. *The Civilization of the Middle Ages: A Completely Revised and Expanded Edition of Medieval History: The Life and Death of a Civilization*. New York: HarperCollins, 1993.

Capozzola, Richard A. *Five Centuries of Italian American History*. Altamonte Springs, FL: Five Centuries Books, 2003.

Carpozi, George Jr. *Bugsy: The Godfather of Las Vegas*. New York: Pinnacle Books, 1973.

Carter, Lauren. *The Most Evil Mobsters in History*. New York: Barnes & Noble, 2004.

Castles, Stephen, and Mark J. Miller. *The Age of Migration: International Population Movements in the Modern World*. New York: The Guilford Press, 1993.

Cellini, Benvenuto. *My Life*. Translated with an Introduction and Notes by Julia Conway Bondanella and Peter Bondanella. Oxford: Oxford University Press, 2009.

Chepesiuk, Ron. *Gangsters of Harlem: The Gritty Underworld of New York's Most Famous Neighborhood*. Fort Lee, NJ: Barricade Books, 2007.

Chicago Days: 150 Defining Moments in the Life of a Great City. By the staff of the *Chicago Tribune*. Edited by Stevenson Swanson. Wheaton, IL: Cantigny First Division Foundation, 1997.

Churchill, Winston S. *Churchill by Himself*. Edited by Richard M. Langworth. London: Ebury Press, 2008.

Cimino, Al, Jo Durden Smith and M.A. Frasca. *The Mafia: The Complete Story*. London: Arcturus, 2019.

Clark, Martin. *Modern Italy 1871–1982*. London: Longman, 1990.

Cohen, Rich. *Tough Jews: Fathers, Sons, and Gangster Dreams*. New York: Vintage Books, 1999.

Colbert, Jean-Baptiste de. *Lettres, Instructions et Memoires*. Edited by Pierre Clement. Volume 2. Paris: Imprimerie Impériale, 1863.

Collected Works of Erasmus: Adages Ii1 to Iv100, trans. Margaret Mann Phillips. Toronto: University of Toronto Press, 1982.

Collier, Richard. *Duce!: A Biography of Benito Mussolini*. New York: Viking Press, 1971.

Collingwood, R.G. *The Idea of History*. Revised Edition with Lectures 1926–1928. Edited and with an Introduction by Jan Van Der Dussen. Oxford: Oxford University Press, 1994.

Collins, Max Allan, and A. Brad Schwartz. *Scarface and the Untouchable: Al Capone, Eliot Ness, and the Battle for Chicago*. New York: William Morrow, 2018.

Conrad, Harold. *Dear Muffo: 35 Years in the Fast Lane*. New York: Stein & Day, 1982.

Corrina, Joe. *Mobsters: A Who's Who of America's Most Notorious Criminals*. North Dighton, MA: JG Press, 2003.

Cowell, F.R. *Cicero and the Roman Republic*. Harmondsworth, Middlesex, UK: Penguin Books, 1956.

Dainotto, Roberto M. *The Mafia: A Cultural History*. London: Reaktion Books, 2018.

Dash, Mike. *The First Family: Terror, Extortion, Revenge, Murder, and the Birth of the American Mafia*. New York: Ballantine Books, 2010.

Davies, Norman. *Europe: A History*. Oxford: Oxford University Press, 1996.

Deitche, Scott M. *Cigar City Mafia: A Complete History of the Tampa Underworld*. Fort Lee, NJ: Barricade Books, 2004.

_____. *The Silent Don: The Criminal Underworld of Santo Trafficante*. Fort Lee, NJ: Barricade Books, 2007.

DeLoach, Cartha D. *Hoover's FBI: The Inside Story by Hoover's Trusted Lieutenant*. Washington, DC: Regnery Pub., 1995.

Demaris, Ovid. *The Boardwalk Jungle: How Greed, Corruption, and the Mafia Turned Atlantic City Into . . .* New York: Bantam Books, 1986.

_____. *Captive City*. New York: Lyle Stuart, Inc., 1969.

_____. *The Director: An Oral Biography of J. Edgar Hoover*. New York: Harper's Magazine Press, 1975.

_____. *The Lucky Luciano Story: The Mafioso and the Violent 30's*. New York: Tower Pub., 1969.

D'Epiro, Peter, and Mary Desmond Pinkowish. *Sprezzatura: 50*

Ways Italian Genius Shaped the World. New York: Anchor Books, 2001.

The Depression Years. As reported by the *New York Times*. Edited by Arleen Keylin. New York: Arno Press, 1976.

The Deseret Weekly: Pioneer Publication of the Rocky Mountain Region. Volume 42, December 1890 to June 1891. Salt Lake City, UT: The Deseret News Co., 1891.

DeStefano, Anthony M. *Gangland New York: The Places and Faces of Mob History*. Guilford, CT: The Lyons Press, 2015.

_____. *Top Hoodlum: Frank Costello, Prime Minister of the Mafia*. New York: Citadel Press, 2018.

Dewey, Thomas E. *Twenty Against the Underworld*. Edited by Rodney Campbell. Garden City, NY: Doubleday & Co., 1974.

Dickie, John. *Blood Brotherhoods: A History of Italy's Three Mafias*. New York: Public Affairs, 2014.

_____. *Cosa Nostra: A History of the Sicilian Mafia*. London: Hodder & Stoughton, 2004.

_____. *Darkest Italy: The Nation and Stereotypes of the Mezzogiorno, 1860–1900*. New York: Palgrave Macmillan/St Martin's Press, 1999.

_____. *Mafia Brotherhoods: Camorra, Mafia, 'Ndrangheta: The Rise of the Honoured Societies*. London: Sceptre, 2012.

Di Franco, J. Philip. *The Italian Americans*. New York: Chelsea House Pub., 1988.

Dolci, Danilo. *Report from Palermo*. Translated from the Italian by P.D. Cummins. New York: Hillman/MacFadden, 1961.

Dorigo, Joe. *Mafia: A Chilling Illustrated History of the Underworld*. Secaucus, NJ: Chartwell Books, 1992.

Dubinsky, David, and A.H. Raskin. *David Dubinsky: A Life with Labor*. New York: Simon & Schuster, 1977.

Duggan, Christopher. *Fascism and the Mafia*. New Haven, CT: Yale University Press, 1989.

_____. *The Force of Destiny: A History of Italy Since 1796*. Boston, MA: Houghton Mifflin Co., 2008.

Edmonds, Andy. *Bugsy's Baby: The Secret Life of Mob Queen Virginia Hill*. New York: Birch Lane Press, 1993.

Eisenberg, Dennis, Uri Dan and Eli Landau. *Meyer Lansky: Mogul of the Mob*. New York: Paddington Press Ltd, 1979.

Ellis, Edward Robb. *The Epic of New York: A Narrative History from 1524 to the Present*. New York: Coward-McCann, 1966.

Encyclopaedia Britannica. Expo Edition. Volume 14. Chicago, IL: Encyclopaedia Britannica, Inc., 1970.

English, T.J. *Havana Nocturne: How the Mob Owned Cuba . . . and Then Lost It to the Revolution*. New York: MJF Books, 2008.

_____. *The Westies: Inside the Hell's Kitchen Irish Mob*. New York: G.P. Putnam's Sons, 1990.

Fahey, Kathleen, and Greg Nickles. *The Italians: We Came to North America Series*. New York: Crabtree Pub. Co., 2001.

Feder, Sid, and Joachim Joesten. *The Luciano Story*. New York: Da Capo Press, 1994.

Ferguson, Wallace K. *Europe in Transition, 1300–1520*. Boston, MA: Houghton Mifflin Co., 1962.

Ferrara, Eric. *Manhattan Mafia Guide: Hits, Homes and Headquarters*. Charleston, SC: The History Press, 2011.

Finan, Christopher M. *Alfred E. Smith: The Happy Warrior*. New York: Hill & Wang, 2002.

Finkelstein, Monte S. *Separatism, the Allies, and the Mafia: The Struggle for Sicilian Independence, 1943–1948*. Bethlehem, PA: Lehigh University Press, 1998.

Finley, M.I., Denis Mack Smith and Christopher Duggan. *A History of Sicily*. New York: Viking, 1987.

Fischer, Steve. *When the Mob Ran Vegas: Stories of Money, Mayhem and Murder*. New York: MJF Books, 2007.

Flynn, William J. *The Barrel Mystery*. New York: The James A. McCann Co., 1919.

Forgacs, David. *Italy's Margins: Social Exclusion and Nation Formation Since 1861*. Cambridge Social and Cultural Histories. Cambridge, UK: Cambridge University Press, 2016.

Fox, Stephen. *Blood and Power: Organized Crime in Twentieth-Century America*. New York: William Morrow & Co., 1989.

Frasca, Dom. *King of Crime: The Story of Vito Genovese, Mafia Czar*. New York: Crown, 1959.

Fried, Albert. *The Rise and Fall of the Jewish Gangster in America*. New York: Holt, Rinehart & Winston, 1980.

Frost, Thomas. *The Secret Societies of the European Revolution, 1776–1876. In Two Volumes*. London: Tinsley Brothers, 1876.

Gage, Nicholas. *The Mafia Is Not an Equal Opportunity Employer*. New York: McGraw-Hill, 1971.

Gambino, Richard. *Blood of My Blood: The Dilemma of the Italian-Americans*. New York: Anchor Press/Doubleday, 1975.

_____. *Vendetta: The True Story of the Largest Lynching in U.S. History*. Toronto: Guernica, 2000.

Garvey, Joan B., and Mary Lou Widmer. *Beautiful Crescent: A History of New Orleans*. New Orleans, LA: Garmer Press, Inc., 1991.

Gentry, Curt. *J. Edgar Hoover: The Man and the Secrets*. New York: Plume, 1992.

Getty, J. Paul. *As I See It: The Autobiography of J. Paul Getty*. Los Angeles, CA: Getty Pub., 2003.

Gibbon, Edward. *Memoirs of My Life*. Edited from the Manuscripts by George A. Bonnard. London: Nelson, 1966.

Gilmour, David. *The Pursuit of Italy: A History of a Land, Its Regions, and Their People*. New York: Farrar, Straus & Giroux, 2011.

Goldfarb, Ronald. *Perfect Villains, Imperfect Heroes: Robert F. Kennedy's War Against Organized Crime*. New York: Random House, 1995.

Gosch, Martin A., and Richard Hammer. *The Last Testament of Lucky Luciano*. Boston, MA: Little, Brown & Co., 1975.

Green, Peter. *Alexander of Macedon, 356–323 B.C.: A Historical Biography*. Berkeley, CA: University of California Press, 1992.

Hack, Richard. *Puppetmaster: The Secret Life of J. Edgar Hoover*. Beverly Hills, CA: New Millennium Press, 2004.

Hammer, Richard. *Playboy's Illustrated History of Organized Crime*. Chicago, IL: Playboy Press, 1975.

Hanson, Neil. *Monk Eastman: The Gangster Who Became a War Hero*. New York: Alfred A. Knopf, 2010.

Hegel, Georg Wilhelm Friedrich. *The Philosophy of History*. Translated by J. Sibree. Revised Edition. London: The Colonial Press, 1900.

Hess, Henner. *Mafia and Mafiosi: Origin, Power and Myth*. Translated by Ewald Osers. London: C. Hurst & Co., 1998.

Hibbert, Christopher. *Garibaldi and His Enemies: The Clash of Arms and Personalities in the Making of Italy*. Boston, MA: Little, Brown & Co., 1966.

Hiltzik, Michael. *Colossus: Hoover Dam and the Making of the American Century*. New York: Free Press, 2010.

Hobsbawm, Eric. *Bandits*. London: Abacus, 2003.

_____. *Primitive Rebels: Studies in Archaic Forms of Social Movement in the 19th and 20th Centuries*. New York: W.W. Norton & Co., 1965.

Hoffer, Eric. *The True Believer: Thoughts on the Nature of Mass Movements*. New York: Perennial Library, 2002.

Hofmann, Paul. *That Fine Italian Hand*. New York: Owl Books/ Henry Holt, 1991.

Horan, James D. *The Pinkertons: The Detective Dynasty that Made History*. New York: Crown Publishers, 1969.

Hortis, C. Alexander. *The Mob and the City: The Hidden History of How the Mafia Captured New York*. New York: Prometheus Books, 2014.

Hourani, Albert. *A History of the Arab Peoples*. Cambridge, MA: The Belknap Press of Harvard University Press, 2002.

Hoyt, Edwin P. *A Gentleman of Broadway: The Story of Damon Runyon*. Boston, MA: Little, Brown & Co., 1964.

Immigration and Crime: Race, Ethnicity, and Violence. Edited by Ramiro Martinez Jr and Abel Valenzuela Jr. New York: New York University Press, 2006.

Isbouts, Jean-Pierre. *Secret Societies: True Tales of Covert Cults and Organizations and Their Leaders*. Washington, DC: National Geographic, 2017.

Italy's Southern Question: Orientalism in One Country. Edited by Jane Schneider. Oxford and New York: Berg, 1998.

Jacobs, David H. *The Mafia's Greatest Hits*. New York: Citadel Press, 2006.

Jeffers, H. Paul. *The Napoleon of New York: Mayor Fiorello La Guardia*. New York: John Wiley & Sons, 2002.

Jennings, Dean. *We Only Kill Each Other: The True Story of Mobster Bugsy Siegel, the Man Who Invented Las Vegas*. New York: Pocket Books, 1992.

Jessup, Philip C. *Elihu Root, Volume II: 1905–1937*. New York: Dodd, Mead & Co., 1938.

Johnson, Mayme, and Karen E. Quinones Miller. *Harlem Godfather: The Rap on My Husband, Ellsworth 'Bumpy' Johnson*. Philadelphia, PA: Oshun Pub. Co., 2008.

Johnson, Nelson. *Boardwalk Empire: The Birth, High Times, and Corruption of Atlantic City*. Medford, NJ: Medford Press/Plexus Pub., 2002.

Johnson, Paul. *The Birth of the Modern: World Society 1815–1830*. New York: HarperCollins, 1991.

Kahn, E.J., Jr. *The Voice: The Story of an American Phenomenon*. New York: Harper & Brothers, 1947.

Katcher, Leo. *The Big Bankroll: The Life and Times of Arnold Rothstein*. New York: Harper & Brothers, 1959.

Katz, Leonard. *Uncle Frank: The Biography of Frank Costello*. London: Star Book/W.H. Allen, 1975.

Kavieff, Paul R. *The Life and Times of Lepke Buchalter: America's Most Ruthless Labor Racketeer*. Fort Lee, NJ: Barricade Books, 2006.

Kefauver, Estes. *Crime in America*. Edited and with an Introduction by Sidney Shalett. London: Victor Gollancz Ltd, 1951.

Kelley, Kitty. *His Way: The Unauthorized Biography of Frank Sinatra*. Toronto: Bantam Books, 1986.

Kennedy, Robert F. *The Enemy Within*. New York: Harper & Brothers, 1960.

Kephart, William M., and William W. Zellner. *Extraordinary Groups: An Examination of Unconventional Life-Styles*. Fourth Edition. New York: St Martin's Press, 1991.

Kesselring, Albert. *The Memoirs of Field-Marshal Kesselring*. Translated by Lynton Hudson. London: William Kimber, 1953.

Kessler, Ronald. *The Bureau: The Secret History of the FBI*. New York: St Martin's Press, 2002.

Kobler, John. *Capone: The Life and World of Al Capone*. New York: G.P. Putnam's Sons, 1971.

Krist, Gary. *Empire of Sin: A Story of Sex, Jazz, Murder, and the Battle for Modern New Orleans*. New York: Broadway Books, 2014.

Kwitny, Jonathan. *Vicious Circles: The Mafia in the Marketplace*. New York: W.W. Norton & Co., 1979.

Lacey, Robert. *Little Man: Meyer Lansky and the Gangster Life*. Boston, MA: Little, Brown & Co., 1991.

Lansky, Sandra, and William Stadiem. *Daughter of the King: Growing Up in Gangland*. New York: Weinstein Books, 2014.

Lawrence, T.E. *Seven Pillars of Wisdom: A Triumph*. New York: Doubleday & Co., 1938.

Le Bon, Gustave. *The Crowd: A Study of the Popular Mind*. New York: The Macmillan Co., 1896.

_____. *The Psychology of Peoples: Its Influence on Their Evolution*. New York: The Macmillan Co., 1898.

_____. *The Psychology of Revolution*. Translated by Bernard Miall. London: T. Fisher Unwin, 1913.

Lee, Alexander. *The Ugly Renaissance: Sex, Greed, Violence and Depravity in an Age of Beauty*. New York: Doubleday, 2013.

Lewis, Norman. *The Honoured Society: The Sicilian Mafia Observed*. London: Eland, 1984.

_____. *Naples '44: A World War II Diary of Occupied Italy*. New York: Carroll & Graf, 2005.

Leyden, John. *Scenes of Infancy: Descriptive of Teviotdale*. Edinburgh: James Ballantyne for T.N. Longman, and O. Rees, 1803.

Lieberman, Paul. *Gangster Squad: Covert Cops, the Mob, and the Battle for Los Angeles*. New York: Thomas Dunne Books, 2012.

Lombroso, Cesare. *Criminal Man*. Translated and with a new Introduction by Mary Gibson and Nicole Hahn Rafter. Durham, NC: Duke University Press, 2009.

Longrigg, Clare. *Boss of Bosses: A Journey into the Heart of the Sicilian Mafia*. New York: Thomas Dunne Books, 2008.

Loon, Hendrik van. *The Story of Mankind*. New York: Cardinal Edition, 1952.

Lunde, Paul. *Organized Crime: An Inside Guide to the World's Most Successful Industry*. New York: DK Pub., 2004.

Maas, Peter. *The Valachi Papers*. New York: Perennial, 2003.

Mack Smith, Denis. *Mazzini*. New Haven, CT: Yale University Press, 1994.

_____. *Mussolini: A Biography*. New York: Vintage Books, 1983.

Mafia: Profiles of the Most Notorious Kingpins of Organized Crime. By the editors of Time-Life Books. Alexandria, VA: Time-Life Books, 1993.

Mafia, U.S.A. Edited by Nicholas Gage. Chicago, IL: Playboy Press, 1972.

The Making of Italy 1796–1870. Edited by Denis Mack Smith. New York: Harper Torchbooks, 1968.

Mammoth Book of the Mafia: First-Hand Accounts of Life Inside the Mob. Edited by Nigel Cawthorne and Colin Cawthorne. Philadelphia, PA: Running Press, 2009.

Manchester, William. *A World Lit Only by Fire: The Medieval Mind and the Renaissance: Portrait of an Age*. New York: Back Bay Books/Little, Brown & Co., 1993.

Mangione, Jerre, and Ben Morreale. *La Storia: Five Centuries of the Italian Immigrant Experience*. New York: Harper Perennial, 1993.

Mannion, James. *The Everything Mafia Book: True-Life Accounts of Legendary Figures, Infamous Crime Families, and Chilling Events*. Avon, MA: Adams Media Corp., 2003.

Maran, A.G.D. *Mafia: Inside the Dark Heart: The Rise and Fall of the Sicilian Mafia*. New York: Thomas Dunne Books/St Martin's Press, 2010.

Mazzini, Giuseppe. *The Duties of Man*. London: Chapman & Hall, 1862.

_____. *Life and Writings of Joseph Mazzini: Volume One: Autobiographical and Political. A New Edition*. London: Smith, Elder & Co., 1890.

McConaughy, John. *From Cain to Capone: Racketeering Down the Ages*. New York: Brentano's, Inc., 1931.

McGirr, Lisa. *The War on Alcohol: Prohibition and the Rise of the American State*. New York: W.W. Norton & Co., 2016.

McShane, Larry. *Chin: The Life and Crimes of Mafia Boss Vincent Gigante*. New York: Pinnacle Books, 2016.

Mee, Charles L., Jr. *The Ohio Gang: The World of Warren G. Harding*. New York: M. Evans & Co., 1981.

Messick, Hank. *John Edgar Hoover: A Critical Examination of the Director and of the Continuing Alliance Between Crime, Business, and Politics*. New York: David McKay Co., 1972.

_____. *Lansky*. New York: Berkley Medallion, 1971.

_____. *The Silent Syndicate*. New York: The Macmillan Co., 1967.

Messick, Hank, and Joseph L. Nellis. *The Private Lives of Public Enemies*. New York: Peter H. Weyden, 1975.

Mob: Stories of Death and Betrayal from Organized Crime. Edited by Clint Willis. New York: Thunder's Mouth Press, 2001.

Modern Italy: A Topical History Since 1861. Edited by Edward R. Tannenbaum and Emiliana P. Noether. New York: New York University Press, 1974.

Moe, Nelson. *The View from Vesuvius: Italian Culture and the Southern Question*. Berkeley, CA: University of California Press, 2006.

Molfese, Franco. *Storia del Brigantaggio dopo l'Unità*. Milan: Feltrinelli, 1964.

Monaco, Richard, and Lionel Bascom. *Rubouts: Mob Murders in America*. New York: Avon Books, 1991.

Mori, Cesare. *The Last Struggle with the Mafia*. Translated by Orlo Williams. London: Black House Pub., 2016.

Morreale, Ben, and Robert Carola. *Italian Americans: The Immigrant Experience*. Beaux Arts Editions, 2000.

Morris, Lloyd. *Incredible New York: High Life and Low Life of the Last Hundred Years*. New York: Random House, 1951.

Mowat, Farley. *And No Birds Sang*. Boston, MA: An Atlantic Monthly Press Book/Little, Brown & Co., 1979.

Murray, George. *The Legacy of Al Capone: Portraits and Annals of Chicago's Public Enemies*. New York: G.P. Putnam's Sons, 1975.

_____. *The Madhouse on Madison Street*. Chicago, IL: Follett Pub. Co., 1965.

Mussolini, Vittorio. *Mussolini: The Tragic Women in His Life*. Translated from the Italian, and with an Introduction, by Graham Snell. London: New English Library, 1975.

Mustain, Gene, and Jerry Capeci. *Murder Machine: A True Story of Murder, Madness and the Mafia*. New York: Dutton, 1992.

Nash, Jay Robert. *Jay Robert Nash's Crime Chronology: A Worldwide Record, 1900–1983*. New York: Facts on File Pub., 1984.

Nation, Carry A. *The Use and Need of the Life of Carry A. Nation, Written by Herself*. Revised Edition. Topeka, KS: F.M. Steves & Sons, 1909.

Nelli, Humbert S. *The Business of Crime: Italians and Syndicate Crime in the United States*. Chicago, IL: University of Chicago Press, 1981.

Ness, Eliot, and Oscar Fraley. *The Untouchables*. New York: Julian Messner, Inc., 1957.

The New Encyclopaedia Britannica, Micropaedia: Ready Reference, 15th Edition. Volume 2. Chicago, IL: Encyclopaedia Britannica, Inc., 1995.

Newark, Tim. *Lucky Luciano: The Real and the Fake Gangster*. New York: Thomas Dunne Books, 2010.

_____. *Mafia Allies: The True Story of America's Secret Alliance with the Mob in World War II*. St Paul, MN: Zenith Press, 2007.

News of the Nation: A Newspaper History of the United States. A Special Bicentennial Edition. Edited by Robert M. Hoffman. New York: Prentice Hall, 1975.

Niceforo, Alfredo. *Italia Barbara Contemporanea*. Palermo: Sandron, 1898.

Nicotri, Gaspare. *Rivoluzioni e Revolte in Sicilia: Studio di Psicologia Sociale*. Palermo: Alberto Reber, 1906.

Noel, Roden. *Life of Lord Byron*. London: Walter Scott, 1890.

Norwich, John Julius. *Sicily: An Island at the Crossroads*. New York: Random House, 2015.

Ogden, Christopher. *Legacy: A Biography of Moses and Walter Annenberg*. Boston, MA: Little, Brown & Co., 1999.

Okrent, Daniel. *Last Call: The Rise and Fall of Prohibition*. New York: Scribner, 2010.

Olla, Roberto. *Godfathers: Lives and Crimes of the Mafia Mobsters*. Richmond, Surrey, UK: Alma Books, 2007.

Oller, John. *Rogues' Gallery: The Birth of Modern Policing and Organized Crime in Gilded Age New York*. New York: Dutton/Penguin, 2021.

Orwell, George. *A Collection of Essays*. New York: Harvest Book/Harcourt, 1981.

Patai, Raphael. *The Arab Mind*. Revised Edition. New York: Charles Scribner's Sons, 1983.

Pernicone, Nunzio. *Carlo Tresca: Portrait of a Rebel*. Oakland, CA: AK Press, 2010.

Petacco, Arrigo. *Joe Petrosino*. Translated by Charles Lam Markmann. New York: Macmillan Pub. Co., 1974.

Pietrusza, David. *Rothstein: The Life, Times, and Murder of the Criminal Genius Who Fixed the 1919 World Series*. New York: Carroll & Graf Pub., 2003.

Pitkin, Thomas Monroe, and Francesco Cordasco, *The Black Hand: A Chapter in Ethnic Crime*. Totowa, NJ: Littlefield, Adams & Co., 1977.

Planches, Edmondo Mayor des. *Attraverso gli Stati Uniti per l'Emigrazione Italiana*. Turin, Italy: Unione Tipografico-Editrice Torinese, 1913.

Pope, Paul David. *The Deeds of My Fathers: How My Grandfather and Father Built New York and Created the Tabloid World of Today*. Lanham, MD: Philip Turner Books/Rowman & Littlefield Pub., 2010.

Porch, Douglas. *The Path to Victory: The Mediterranean Theater in World War II*. New York: Farrar, Straus & Giroux, 2004.

Powell, Hickman. *Lucky Luciano: The Man Who Organized Crime in America*. New York: Barricade Books, 2000.

Powers, Richard Gid. *Secrecy and Power: The Life of J. Edgar Hoover*. New York: The Free Press, 1987.

Pulera, Dominic J. *Green, White, Red: The Italian-American Success Story*. San Marino, CA: L'Italo-Americano, 2009.

Quennell, Peter. *Byron in Italy*. New York: Viking Press, 1941.

Quirk, Robert E. *Fidel Castro*. New York: W.W. Norton & Co., 1995.

Raab, Selwyn. *Five Families: The Rise, Decline, and Resurgence of America's Most Powerful Mafia Empires*. New York: Thomas Dunne Books, 2005.

Ragano, Frank, and Selwyn Raab. *Mob Lawyer*. New York: Charles Scribner's Sons, 1994.

Readings in the Classical Historians. Selected and introduced by Michael Grant. New York: Charles Scribner's Sons, 1992.

Reavill, Gil. *Mafia Summit: J. Edgar Hoover, the Kennedy Brothers, and the Meeting That Unmasked the Mob*. New York: Thomas Dunne Books/St Martin's Press, 2013.

Reeves, Pamela. *Ellis Island: Gateway to the American Dream*. New York: Crescent Books, 1991.

Reid, Ed. *Mafia*. New York: Random House, 1952.

Reppetto, Thomas. *American Mafia: A History of Its Rise to Power*. New York: MJF Books, 2004.

Reski, Petra. *The Honored Society: A Portrait of Italy's Most Powerful Mafia*. Translated by Shaun Whiteside. New York: Nation Books, 2013.

Richards, David A.J. *Italian American: The Racializing of an Ethnic Identity*. New York: New York University Press, 1999.

Ridley, Jasper. *The Freemasons: A History of the World's Most Powerful Secret Society*. New York: Arcade Pub., 2011.

_____. *Garibaldi*. New York: The Viking Press, 1976.

_____. *Mussolini: A Biography*. New York: St Martin's Press, 1997.

Riordan, William L. *Plunkitt of Tammany Hall: A Series of Very Plain Talks on Very Practical Politics*. New York: Signet Classic, 1995.

Rizzo, Michael F. *Gangsters and Organized Crime in Buffalo: History, Hits and Headquarters*. Charleston, SC: The History Press, 2013.

Robb, Peter. *M: The Man Who Became Caravaggio*. New York: A John Macrae Book/Henry Holt & Co., 2000.

_____. *Midnight in Sicily: On Art, Food, History, Travel and La Cosa Nostra*. New York: Picador, 2007.

Rothstein, Carolyn, and Donald Henderson Clarke. *Now I'll Tell*. New York: Vanguard Press, 1934.

Rousseau, Jean-Jacques. *On the Social Contract*. Translated by G.D.H. Cole. Mineola, NY: Dover Pub., 2003.

_____. *The Social Contract and Discourse on the Origin of Inequality*. Edited and with an Introduction by Lester G. Crocker. New York: Washington Square Press/Pocket Books, 1973.

Russell, Francis. *The Shadow of Blooming Grove: Warren G. Harding in His Times*. New York: McGraw-Hill, 1968.

Salerno, Ralph, and John S. Tompkins. *The Crime Confederation: The Untold Story of America's Most Successful Industry – the Strategies and Techniques of the Cosa Nostra and Allied Operations in Organized Crime*. New York: Doubleday & Co., 1969.

Samenow, Stanton E. *Inside the Criminal Mind*. New York: Times Books, 1984.

Sann, Paul. *Kill the Dutchman!: The Story of Dutch Schultz*. New York: Da Capo Press, 1991.

Sayers, Dorothy L. *Gaudy Night*. London: Victor Gollancz Ltd, 1958.

Schoenberg, Robert J. *Mr. Capone: The Real – and Complete – Story of Al Capone*. New York: William Morrow & Co., 1992.

Schurman, Anna Van. *Secret Societies and the French Revolution*. New York: John Lane Co., 1911.

Scott, Walter. *The Poetical Works of Sir Walter Scott. With Memoir and Critical Dissertation. Volume III. Containing Rokeby, and the Lord of the Isles, with the Original Notes of the Author.* Unabridged. London and New York: Cassell, Petter & Galpin, 1870.

Sereni, Emilio. *History of the Italian Agricultural Landscape*. Translated by R. Burr Litchfield. Princeton, NJ: Princeton University Press, 1997.

Shirer, William L. *The Rise and Fall of the Third Reich: A History of Nazi Germany*. New York: MJF Books, 1990.

Siciliano, Vincent. *Unless They Kill Me First*. New York: Hawthorn Books, Inc., 1970.

Sifakis, Carl. *The Mafia Encyclopedia: From Accardo to Zwillman*. Third Edition. New York: Checkmark Books, 2005.

Sinatra, Tina, and Jeff Coplon. *My Father's Daughter: A Memoir*. New York: Simon & Schuster, 2000.

Sinclair, Andrew. *Prohibition: The Era of Excess*. Norwalk, CT: The Easton Press, 1986.

Smith, Jo Durden. *A Complete History of the Mafia*. New York: Metro Books, 2007.

Smith, Richard Norton. *Thomas E. Dewey and His Times: The First Full-Scale Biography of the Maker of the Modern Republican Party*. New York: Simon & Schuster, 1982.

Smith, Tom. *The Crescent City Lynchings: The Murder of Chief Hennessy, the New Orleans 'Mafia' Trials, and the Parish Prison Mob*. Guilford, CT: The Lyons Press, 2007.

Stephenson, Carl. *Medieval Feudalism*. Ithaca, NY: Cornell University Press, 1948.

Sterling, Claire. *Octopus: The Long Reach of the International Sicilian Mafia*. New York: W.W. Norton & Co., 1990.

Stevens, Joseph E. *Hoover Dam: An American Adventure*. Norman, OK: University of Oklahoma Press, 1988.

Stille, Alexander. *Excellent Cadavers: The Mafia and the Death of the First Italian Republic*. New York: Pantheon Books, 1995.

Stoddard, John L. *John L. Stoddard's Lectures. Volume 14: Sicily, Genoa, A Drive through the Engadine*. Chicago, IL: Geo. L. Shuman & Co., 1925.

Stonehouse, Frederick. *Great Lakes Crime: Murder, Mayhem, Booze and Broads*. Gwinn, MI: Avery Color Studios, 2004.

Sullivan, William C., and Bill Brown. *The Bureau: My Thirty Years in Hoover's FBI*. New York: W.W. Norton & Co., 1979.

Summers, Anthony. *Official and Confidential: The Secret Life of J. Edgar Hoover*. New York: G.P. Putnam's Sons, 1993.

Summers, Anthony, and Robbyn Swan. *Sinatra: The Life*. New York: Alfred A. Knopf, 2005.

Tales of Gaslight New York. Compiled by Frank Oppel. Secaucus, NJ: Castle, 1985.

Talese, Gay. *Honor Thy Father*. New York: World Pub., 1971.

_____. *Unto the Sons*. New York: Alfred A. Knopf, 1992.

Talty, Stephan. *The Black Hand: The Epic War Between a Brilliant Detective and the Deadliest Secret Society in American History*. Boston, MA: Houghton Mifflin Harcourt, 2017.

Taraborrelli, J. Randy. *Sinatra: Behind the Legend*. Secaucus, NJ: Carol Pub. Group, 1997.

Tereba, Tere. *Mickey Cohen: The Life and Crimes of L.A.'s Notorious Mobster*. Toronto: ECW Press, 2012.

Teresa, Vincent, and Thomas C. Renner. *My Life in the Mafia*. New York: Doubleday & Co., 1973.

Thomas, Hugh. *The Spanish Civil War*. New York: Harper & Row, 1961.

Toynbee, Arnold J. *Greek Historical Thought: From Homer to the Age of Heraclius*. Introduction and Translation by Arnold J. Toynbee. New York: A Mentor Book/The New American Library, 1952.

Tully, Andrew. *Treasury Agent: The Inside Story*. New York: Simon & Schuster, 1958.

Tuohy, John William. *Joe Petrosino's War on the Mafia: The Mob Files Series*. Lexington, KY: 2017.

Turkus, Burton B., and Sid Feder. *Murder, Inc.: The Story of 'The Syndicate'*. New York: Da Capo Press, 1992.

United States Treasury Department Bureau of Narcotics. *Mafia: The Government's Secret File on Organized Crime*. New York: Collins, 2007.

Voltaire, Jean François-Marie Arouet de. *The Age of Louis XIV*. Translated by Martyn P. Pollack. London: J.M. Dent & Sons Ltd, 1969.

_____. *Candide and Philosophical Letters*. Translations by Richard Aldington and Ernest Dilworth. New York: The Modern Library, 1992.

Waller, George. *Saratoga: Saga of an Impious Era*. New York: Bonanza Books, 1966.

Wells, H.G. *The Outline of History: Being a Plain History of Life and Mankind*. Revised and brought up to the end of the Second World War by Raymond Postgate. Two Volumes. Garden City, NY: Garden City Books, 1949.

What Life Was Like in the Age of Chivalry: Medieval Europe, AD 800–1500. By the editors of Time-Life Books. Alexandria, VA: Time-Life Books, 1997.

Wheatcroft, Andrew. *Infidels: A History of the Conflict Between Christendom and Islam*. New York: Random House Trade Paperbacks, 2005.

_____. *The Ottomans*. London: Viking, 1993.

Willebrandt, Mabel Walker. *Inside of Prohibition*. Indianapolis, IN: Bobbs-Merrill, 1929.

Williams, T. Harry. *Huey Long*. New York: Alfred A. Knopf, 1970.

Winchell, Walter. *Winchell Exclusive: 'Things That Happened to Me – and Me to Them'*. Englewood Cliffs, NJ: Prentice Hall, 1975.

Witmer, David, and Catherine Rios. *Murder in the Garment District: The Grip of Organized Crime and the Decline of Labor in the United States*. New York: The New Press, 2020.

Wolf, George, with Joseph DiMona. *Frank Costello: Prime Minister of the Underworld*. New York: William Morrow & Co., 1974.

Woolf, Stuart J. *A History of Italy, 1700–1860: The Social Constraints of Political Change*. London: Methuen, 1979.

Wop!: A Documentary History of Anti-Italian Discrimination in the United States. Edited and with an Introduction by Salvatore J. LaGumina. San Francisco, CA: Straight Arrow Books, 1973.

Yablonsky, Lewis. *George Raft*. Lincoln, NE: iUniverse.com, Inc., 2001.

Zacks, Richard. *Island of Vice: Theodore Roosevelt's Doomed Quest to Clean Up Sin-Loving New York*. New York: Doubleday, 2012.

Zion, Sidney. *The Autobiography of Roy Cohn*. Secaucus, NJ: Lyle Stuart, Inc., 1988.

_____. *Loyalty and Betrayal: The Story of the American Mob*. San Francisco, CA: Collins Publishers San Francisco, 1994.

Additional Sources

Print

Applegate, Joseph H. 'The Crimson Trail of the Unholy Three Brothers of Brownsville.' *Brooklyn Times-Union*, 16 May 1937.

'Body of Informer, Tied to Concrete, Pulled from Bay.' *New York Times*, 25 August 1964.

Botein, Barbara. 'The Hennessy Case: An Episode in Anti-Italian Nativism.' *Louisiana History: The Journal of the Louisiana Historical Association*, Vol. 20, No. 3, Summer 1979.

'Crime Probers Get Picture of Wide-Open Gaming in Saratoga by State Police Who Did Not Act.' *Daily Home News*, 16 March 1951.

Davis, J. Richard. 'Things I Couldn't Tell till Now.' *Collier's Weekly*, 22 & 29 July 1939.

Denison, Lindsay. 'The Black Hand.' *Everybody's Magazine*, Vol. 19, No. 3, September 1907.

Jäger, Daniela G. 'The Worst "White Lynching" in American History: Elites vs. Italians in New Orleans, 1891.' *AAA: Arbeiten aus Anglistik und Amerikanistik*, Vol. 27, No. 2, 2002.

'Life for Workman as Schultz Killer. Gangster Sentenced after He Ends Trial by Changing Plea to No Defense.' *New York Times*, 11 June 1941.

'Link to Lepke Sought in Jersey Slaying.' *Brooklyn Daily Eagle*, 12 December 1939.

'Murder Ring Members Die in Sing Sing.' *New York Daily Press*, 20 February 1942.

'The President's Habeus Corpus Proclamation and the Act of Congress on the Subject.' *New York Herald*, 18 September 1863.

'Reles Described as Vicious Thug.' *New York Times*, 24 March 1940.

Santoro, Marco. 'Introduction. The Mafia and the Sociological Imagination.' *Sociologica*, No. 2, May–August 2011.

Schneider, Jane, and Peter Schneider. 'Mafia, Antimafia, and the Question of Sicilian Culture.' *Politics & Society*, Vol. 22, No. 2, June 1994.

'Strauss, Goldstein Get Chair Tonight.' *Brooklyn Eagle*, 12 June 1941.

Online

Cockayne, James. 'Corruption for Decades: That Time When the Mafia Almost Fixed the Democratic National Convention.' *Salon*, 26 July 2016. https://www.salon.com/2016/07/26/corruption_for_decades_that_time_when_the_mafia_almost_fixed_the_democratic_national_convention_partner/

Herlands, William B. *The Herlands Commission Investigation Report*, University of Rochester Department of Rare Books and Special Collections, Thomas E. Dewey Papers, 17 September 1954. https://lib.rochester.edu/IN/RBSCP/ATTACHMENTS/Series-13-17-2-Herlands-report.pdf

Letter from Theodore Roosevelt to Anna Roosevelt, 21 March 1891. Theodore Roosevelt Center, Dickinson State University. https://www.theodorerooseveltcenter.org/Research/Digital-Library/Record?libID=0280928

Milner, Catherine. 'Red-Blooded Caravaggio Killed Love Rival in Bungled Castration Attempt.' UK *Telegraph*, 2 June 2002. https://www.telegraph.co.uk/news/worldnews/europe/italy/1396127/Red-blooded-Caravaggio-killed-love-rival-in-bungled-castration-attempt.html#:~:text='Red%2D-blooded%20Caravaggio%20killed%20love%20rival%20in%20bungled%20castration%20attempt',-By%20Catherine%20Milner&text=One%20of%20the%20greatest%20murder,botched%20attempt%20to%20castrate%20him.

Sandbrook, Dominic. 'Il Duce and His Women by Roberto Olla.' London *Sunday Times*, 6 November 2011. https://www.thetimes.co.uk/article/il-duce-and-his-women-by-roberto-olla-zqsx8tpknnc

Staples, Brent. 'How Italians Became White.' *New York Times*, 12 October 2019. https://www.nytimes.com/interactive/2019/10/12/opinion/columbus-day-italian-american-racism.html?searchResultPosition=1

The Steve Allen Show, from the Havana Riviera Hotel, NBC Television Network, 19 January 1958. https://youtube.com/watch?v=epvLDIOVpFY

Watkinson, William. 'Mussolini Was a "Violent Rapist and Sex Addict Who Imagined All of His Lovers as Prostitutes".' *International Business Times*, 25 February 2017. https://www.ibtimes.co.uk/mussolini-was-violent-rapist-sex-addict-who-imagined-all-his-lovers-prostitutes-1608537

PICTURE CREDITS

Page 30) *The Duties of Man*; Library of Congress
Page 33) Palermo church © Salvatore Ciambra
Page 35) *I Mafiusi la Vicaria*; courtesy Pitre Museum, Palermo
Page 41) Picking lemons in a grove near Palermo; Library of Congress
Page 42) Emanuele Notarbartolo being murdered in his train compartment; *L'Unita* © Foto Archivio Storico de l'Unità
Page 49) Ignazio Florio and family; unknown author
Page 57) Italian family lands on Ellis Island © Lewis W. Hines, New York Public Library Digital Collections
Page 59) Italians Lynched in the South © Leland Hawes Collection, MS-2010-05, University of Southern Florida Special Collections Library
Page 60) Cartoon of Italian immigrants; published in *The Mascot*, a New Orleans, Louisiana, newspaper, on 7 September, 1889
Page 62) New Orleans Police Chief David Hennessy; courtesy of the Tulane University, Louisiana Collection
Page 69) Chief Hennessy returns fire; published in *The Mascot*, 18 October, 1890
Page 73) Pietro Monasterio's shanty; *The Illustrated American*, 8 November, 1890, Volume IV, Number 38, page 342, courtesy of HathiTrust
Page 81) Lynch mob meets at the Clay statue; illustration by Thure de Thulstrup, in *Harper's Weekly*, 28 March, 1891
Page 83) Battering down the door of Parish Prison; courtesy of E. Benjamin Andrew, *History of the United States*, Volume V. Charles Scribner's Sons, New York. 1912
Page 84) Sicilian prisoners dead in the yard; *The Illustrated American*, 4 April, 1891
Page 89) Young Joseph Petrosino; Wikimedia Commons
Page 90) Barrel Murder; *New York Evening World* (Night Edition), front page, 14 April, 1903; Library of Congress
Page 92) Barrel Murder suspects; *New York Evening World* (Night

Edition), front page, 16 April, 1903, Library of Congress
Page 93) Ignazio 'Lupo the Wolf' Saietta; National Archives, Atlanta Penitentiary
Page 94) Giuseppe Morello; Wikimedia Commons
Page 96) Petto the Ox; Library of Congress © New York World-Telegram & Sun Newspaper Photograph Collection
Page 99) Vito Cascia Ferro; United States Department of Treasury
Page 102) An older Joseph Petrosino; Library of Congress © New York World-Telegram & Sun Newspaper Photograph Collection
Page 105) Cartoon of Italy happily sending its criminals and mafiosos to America; S.D. Ehrhart, published by Keppler & Schwarzmann in *Puck* magazine, 2 June, 1909; Library of Congress
Page 108) Petrosino's funeral wagon; Wikimedia Commons
Page 111) Mulberry Street; Detroit Publishing Co., Library of Congress
Page 112) Arnold Rothstein; *Chicago Daily News* Archive, Staff Photographer, 1 November, 1919
Page 121) Meyer Lansky; New York Police Department, Wikimedia Commons
Page 122) Charles Luciano; New York Police Department, Wikimedia Commons
Page 125) Frank Costello; Library of Congress © New York World-Telegram & Sun Newspaper Photograph Collection
Page 127) Giuseppe Masseria; New York Police Department, Wikimedia Commons
Page 140) Albert Anastasia; NYC Municipal Archives
Page 146) Masseria dead; *New York Daily News*
Page 153) New York Central Building; Irma and Paul Milstein Division of United States History, Local History and Genealogy, The New York Public Library Digital Collections
Page 154) Maranzano dead; FBI photo
Page 166) Thomas Dewey; Greystone Studio, NY, Library of Congress Prints & Photographs Division
Page 169) Woolworth Building; Library of Congress Prints & Photographs Division
Page 172) Vincent 'Mad Dog' Coll; Library of Congress © New York World-Telegram & Sun Newspaper Photograph Collection
Page 176) Dutch Schultz wanted poster; Library of Congress © New York World-Telegram & Sun Newspaper Photograph Collection

Page 182) The Dutchman shot; *New York Daily News*
Page 184) Ellsworth Raymond 'Bumpy' Johnson; National Archives, Leavenworth Penitentiary
Page 186) Eunice Roberta Hunton Carter, Wikimedia Commons
Page 191) Luciano escorted into court by detectives; Library of Congress © New York World-Telegram & Sun Newspaper Photograph Collection
Page 202) Crime scene photograph of body of Joseph Rosen in candy store; Burton B. Turkus Papers, Lloyd Sealy Library Special Collections, John Jay College of Criminal Justice (CUNY)
Page 209) Lepke arraigned; Library of Congress © New York World-Telegram & Sun Newspaper Photograph Collection
Page 222) Abe Reles; *Brooklyn Eagle*, 12 November, 1941, Brooklyn Public Library
Page 223) USS Lafayette On Its Side; U.S. Navy Photograph, National Archives and Records Administration
Page 255) Hotel Nacional, Cuba; Wikimedia Commons
Page 267) Siegel dead in Hill's home; Library of Congress © New York World-Telegram & Sun Newspaper Photograph Collection
Page 280) Luciano in Italy; Public Domain
Page 282) Adonis Watching Costello on TV; Michael Rougier/The LIFE Picture Collection/Shutterstock
Page 287) Willie Moretti dead; *New York Daily News*
Page 291) Costello injured; *New York Daily News*
Page 296) Arnold Schuster dead; *New York Daily News*
Page 298) Lansky with Batista; Wikimedia Commons
Page 304) Anastasia dead; *New York Daily News*
Page 305) Vito Genovese; Library of Congress © New York World-Telegram & Sun Newspaper Photograph Collection
Page 313) Trafficante in Sans Souci, Havana, Cuba; Library of Congress © New York World-Telegram & Sun Newspaper Photograph Collection
Page 314) Castro with Che Guevara; Museo Che Guevara, Havana, Cuba, Wikimedia Commons
Page 319) Luciano dead in Italy; Public Domain

INDEX